THE BLACK SHIP

OTHER TITLES IN THE
HEART OF OAK SEA CLASSICS SERIES INCLUDE:

Doctor Dogbody's Leg by James Norman Hall

Peter Simple by Frederick Marryat

·

DUDLEY POPE

The Black Ship

HEART OF OAK SEA CLASSICS

Dean King, Series Editor

Foreword by

Dean King

Introduction by

Christopher McKee

AN OWL BOOK

HENRY HOLT AND COMPANY   NEW YORK

Henry Holt and Company, Inc.
Publishers since 1866
115 West 18th Street
New York, New York 10011

Henry Holt® is a registered
trademark of Henry Holt and Company, Inc.

Library of Congress Cataloging-in-Publication Data
Pope, Dudley.
The black ship / Dudley Pope ; foreword by Dean King ;
introduction by Christopher McKee. — 1st Holt ed.
p.   cm. — (Heart of oak sea classics series)
"Owl Books."
ISBN 0-8050-5566-5 (pbk.: alk. paper)
1. Great Britain—History, Naval—18th century.   2. British—West
Indies—History—18th century.   3. West Indies, British—History,
Naval.   4. Pigot, Hugh, 1769–1797.   5. Hermione Mutiny, 1797.
I. Title.   II. Series.
DA87.7.P6   1998
359.1'334—dc21   97-41890

First published in 1963 by Weidenfeld and Nicolson.

First Owl Books Edition 1998

Designed by Kate Nichols

Cartography by Jeffrey L. Ward.

Printed in the United States of America
All first editions are printed on acid-free paper. ∞

1   3   5   7   9   10   8   6   4   2

HEART OF OAK

Come cheer up, my lads, 'tis to glory we steer,
To add something new to this wonderful Year:
To honour we call you, not press you like slaves,
For who are so free as the sons of the waves?

CHORUS:
Heart of Oak are our ships,
Heart of Oak are our men,
We always are ready,
Steady, boys, steady,
We'll fight and we'll conquer again and again.

We ne'er see our foes but we wish them to stay;
they never see us but they wish us away:
If they run, why we follow, and run them on shore,
for if they won't fight us, we cannot do more.

Heart of Oak, etc.

They swear they'll invade us, these terrible foes,
They'll frighten our women, and children, and beaux;
But should their flat-bottoms in darkness get o'er,
Still Britons they'll find to receive them on shore.

Heart of Oak, etc.

We'll still make them run and we'll still make them sweat,
In spite of the Devil, and Brussels Gazette:
Then cheer up, my lads, with one voice let us sing
Our soldiers, our sailors, our statesman, and King.

Heart of Oak, etc.

—DAVID GARRICK

Source: C. H. Firth, *Naval Songs and Ballads*. Publications of the Navy Records Society, vol. XXXIII (London, 1908), p. 220.

CONTENTS

FOREWORD

I

T WAS while reading a footnote to chapter twenty-two of Christopher McKee's outstanding book *A Gentlemanly and Honorable Profession: The Creation of the U.S. Naval Officer Corps, 1794–1815* that I decided I must read Dudley Pope's *The Black Ship*. In citing Pope's book about the horrific mutiny on board HMS *Hermione* in 1797, McKee called it "a classic to which no summary here can do justice" (p. 554).

Just as with *American Heritage* editor Richard Snow's statement that *Master and Commander*, Patrick O'Brian's first Aubrey-Maturin novel, was "the best historical novel I'd ever read," *(New York Times Book Review*, January 6, 1991), I sensed that McKee's unequivocal praise really had teeth. Professionals of such integrity don't issue hype. I was right. He was right.

One of the things I most like about *The Black Ship*—the true story of the mutiny of HMS *Hermione*, which was then handed over to the Spanish by the mutineers, and her subsequent recapture from the Spanish at Puerto Cabello (on the Spanish Main) by Captain Edward Hamilton's HMS *Surprise*—is that while the events narrated were of profound importance for the Royal Navy and other navies around the world, they are gritty and emotional stories without pomp and circumstance. This is not Nelson at Trafalgar, a story of glory and tragedy on a mythic scale. Relatively little known, these events do not reach us today with the chill of a gilded statue but, even after two centuries, hot, like the human blood that was shed on the deck of the *Hermione.*

The Black Ship is not a tidy story. It is often eerie, provocative, discomfiting. It contains two main events, with two separate casts of characters. It is both a story of human tragedy—placing one group of men, the perpetrators of a heinous mutiny, beyond earthly redemption—and a story of human courage—elevating another group of men, the captain and crew of HMS *Surprise,* to heroes. The tragedy of the one event amplified the glory of the other. But while the Royal Navy found a measure of redemption in the retaking of the *Hermione,* there was no solace for the mutineers, who were hunted and hanged whenever possible. However, the majority simply disappeared, anonymous seamen melding into the naval or merchant crews of other nations. Thus, there is no neat ending here, but the many loose ends with which accurate history often leaves us.

The two main events related in this book present one of the Royal Navy's lowest and one of its highest moments. Each incident, the story of which was undoubtedly told and retold by seamen in ports everywhere, had an impact that belied its relatively small scale and remote location, affecting in both instances the very fabric of the Royal Navy.

Pope's account is a thorough, often necessarily painful, and yet very readable study of one of the defining events of men at sea during the Napoleonic wars. The mutiny of the *Hermione* demonstrated all too clearly one possible result of a breakdown in the delicate relationship between officers and seamen. It loomed as a black gale in the back of every officers' mind. From thenceforth there existed what McKee called in his book "the *Hermione* phobia," the fear of what could happen if a crew was pushed too far by a despotic captain.

In enlightening us about this seminal set of events, Pope not only opens our eyes to the reality of conditions at sea, but he imbues us with another piece of the common body of knowledge possessed by almost every sailor during the Napoleonic wars. As readers, we take that knowledge with us each time we open a book on the subject. We better understand the seaman's mentality. For that reason, *The Black Ship* is a most valuable addition to Heart of Oak Sea Classics.

For bringing *The Black Ship* to my attention and for accepting an invitation to edit and introduce the book for Heart of Oak Sea Classics, my thanks go to Professor Christopher McKee, who along with Professor John B. Hattendorf is a scholarly advisor to the series. To that, I add my compliments and admiration for a job well done.

—Dean King

INTRODUCTION

WHEN BRITISH NAVAL HISTORIAN and novelist Dudley Pope died at St. Martin in the French West Indies on April 25, 1997, obituaries in *The Daily Telegraph, The Guardian, The Independent,* and *The Times* told the story of a notably self-directed life.

Born at Stubb's Corner, Kent, on December 29, 1925, Dudley Bernard Egerton Pope (to give his full name) attended Ashford Grammar School in his home county, then—in 1941—lied about his true age, which was really sixteen, so that he could join the Merchant Navy and Britain's war. A year later, in October 1942, he experienced that war in a most immediate way, one that heavily influenced the later course of his life, when the ship in which he was serving, M.V. *Silverwillow,* was torpedoed near Madeira. Pope and the other survivors spent several days adrift in lifeboats before they were rescued—days that must have been exceedingly painful for Pope, because he had sustained spinal and other injuries that sent him to hospital for a long period of surgery and recuperation.

The worst part for Pope was that, once he was finally released, he found himself, much to his dislike and despite vigorous attempts to get back into action, permanently sidelined from further direct participation in the war. Frustrated, in 1943 Pope tried his hand at journalism and by 1944 he was naval correspondent for London's

Evening News, a post that he continued to hold until 1957 when he was promoted to deputy foreign editor.

While Dudley Pope earned his keep through journalism another career was incubating. The long months of surgery and convalescence had given him ample enforced opportunity for reading, and it was from this reading that Pope's lifelong interest in naval history took fire. His first books focused on the recent past, events of the Second World War: *Flag 4* (1954), the story of Coastal Forces operations in the Mediterranean; *The Battle of the River Plate* (1956), called *Graf Spee: The Life and Death of a Raider* in its American edition; and *73 North* (1958), a narrative of the 1942 Battle of the Barents Sea. Then he made a radical turn deeper into the past with the November 1959 publication of *England Expects,* his much-admired recounting and analysis of Nelson's victory at the Battle of Trafalgar, which appeared in the United States a year later under the title *Decision at Trafalgar.*

In the same month that Pope published *England Expects* he resigned his position with *The Evening News,* abandoning the job security of journalism for the riskier life of a full-time author of books. Pope was already an enthusiastic and experienced yachtsman. When he could not be out sailing boats, he lived on them at Hoo in Kent and Shoreham-by-Sea in Sussex and commuted to his work in London. Free at last to live where it suited him to write, Pope moved to Porto San Stefano in Italy where he resided for four years. Then in search of a still-warmer climate that would be even kinder to his old wartime injuries, and accompanied by his wife, Kay, and their infant daughter, Pope sailed his twenty-one-ton cutter, *Golden Dragon,* across the Atlantic in 1965 to the West Indies, where he would live for the remainder of his life. Here were waters that he came to know intimately as he sailed across their surface or dived into them in pursuit of another passion: the collecting of seashells.

But always he was researching and writing, for Dudley Pope was nothing if not a workaholic. First it was more history: *At Twelve Mr. Byng Was Shot* (1962), the story of the events leading up to the scapegoat execution of Admiral John Byng in 1757; *The Black Ship* (1963); and *The Great Gamble* (1972), about Nelson's controversial 1801 attack on the Danish fleet at Copenhagen. Then a new writing interest appeared when, encouraged by C. S. Forester and drawing on his vast and detailed knowledge of the navy of Nelson and his contemporaries, Pope tried his hand at the historical novel, creating a character, Nicholas Ramage, R.N., whose adventures he narrated in a series of eighteen books.

In spite of the success of the Ramage stories, Pope never abandoned his first love: fine naval history. *The Devil Himself: The Mutiny of 1800,* published in 1987, was his last major historical work. Already by 1985 Pope's old wartime injuries were causing him serious health problems. He was compelled to abandon his floating West Indian home, the thirty-seven-ton ketch *Ramage,* and move ashore. His health continued to deteriorate—Pope was by this time using a wheelchair—and finally the old spinal injuries played their cruelest card, memory loss, which compelled him to abandon all writing in 1989.

Oddly perhaps, the obituaries that noted Pope's death and recorded his life made scant reference to what is, arguably, his finest historical writing, *The Black Ship.* Only the anonymous writer in *The Daily Telegraph* referred to *The Black Ship* in any detail, calling it "a chilling account"—surely the words of a person who had read its pages with that same fascination with which one watches the approach of a large and possibly deadly snake. The terrible power of this work comes most of all from the compelling stories that it tells: the story of mutiny, on the night of September 21, and the morning of September 22, 1797, by a portion of the crew of the British frigate *Hermione,* in which the mutineers, pushed to the breaking point by the sadism of Captain Hugh Pigot, R.N., hacked to death with cutlasses and tomahawks, and/or threw overboard to drown, the captain and most of the ship's officers; the tale of the British navy's relentless efforts to track down and condignly punish the mutineers; and the account of Captain Edward Hamilton's recapture of *Hermione,* which the fleeing mutineers had handed over to the Spanish authorities in South America.

But good stories are not enough. A fine story can always be badly told. Other qualities that make *The Black Ship* a masterwork of historical narration are Pope's keen skills as a writer and his knowledge of—and visceral appreciation for—life and war at sea in the years of the French Revolution and the Napoleonic wars; his inspired and original research in the archives of Britain and Spain; and his personal knowledge and love of the waters in which these bloody and tragic events took place, a familiarity that adds so much to the immediacy and vividness of Pope's narrative.

The Black Ship charted two courses subsequent historians have followed to the enrichment of our understanding of the naval world that existed as the eighteenth century became the nineteenth. Although Pope was not the first historian to use court-martial records, *The Black Ship* highlighted the importance of these verbatim trial transcripts as sources conveying the immediacy of events through their sharply remembered detail and recording of words, be they dramatic or routine, as they were actually spoken. Just as important, Pope's exploration of ships' logs to determine the quantitative dimensions of flogging as it was practiced by Captain Pigot alerted historians who followed in *The Black Ship*'s wake to the possibility of exploiting log books to delineate the true story of corporal punishment at sea and to discover variations in punishment practices and philosophies among different naval commanders.

Reviewers at the time of *The Black Ship*'s publication were unanimously positive in their assessment of Pope's achievement but seemed perplexed how to evaluate a volume of naval history that was not a tale of ship-to-ship battle at sea. The sole serious criticism offered (and it is a caveat with which I agree) came from an anonymous, but clearly very knowledgeable, reviewer in *The Times Literary Supplement* of November 21, 1963, who engaged the book on its own terms and regretted that Pope "has not always treated his sources with more critical caution and thoroughness." The critic cited

> Mr. Pope's uncritical acceptance of Midshipman Casey's account of his treatment by Pigot and of the details of the mutiny. It was written by Casey forty-two years later in a document designed to present himself in the most favourable light and therefore its allegedly verbatim accounts of conversations and phrases must be taken with due caution. Moreover Mr. Pope omits completely the very relevant account of Casey's previous career and relationship with Pigot, which the document contains. Casey admits to having been court martialled on his previous ship for quarrelling with his captain on the quarter deck: the identical crime for which Pigot

had him flogged. Moreover Pigot was a member of this court martial, which sentenced Casey to lose his acting rank of Lieutenant, and yet had, according to Casey, especially asked for him to be transferred to the *Hermione.*

Armed with this information, the reader watches for Midshipman Casey's appearances in *The Black Ship,* alert for psychological ambiguities of the Pigot-Casey interaction that Dudley Pope failed to exploit.

As any truly good book does, *The Black Ship* stirred up questions. To some of those questions later historians have proposed answers different from the ones Dudley Pope offered. Pope attributed the *Hermione* mutiny more to the capricious, inconsistent, and sadistic character of Hugh Pigot's punishments than to their frequency or harshness. However, when one compares Pigot's punishment record in the *Success* (Appendix C) with the punishment records of eight captains of the pre–1815 U.S. Navy, which I tabulated in my *A Gentlemanly and Honorable Profession: The Creation of the U.S. Naval Officer Corps, 1794–1815* (Annapolis: Naval Institute Press, 1991, pages 242–247, 480–481), one discovers that Pigot punished far more frequently (but not more harshly) than any of the eight Americans, none of whom was reluctant when it came to inflicting the lash to correct the perceived misdeeds of sailors.

Also open to serious challenge, I think, is Pope's assertion in chapter 5, "The Red Baize Bag," that floggings of as few as 24 or 36 lashes—let alone those that exceeded 100 lashes—were often the de facto equivalents of death sentences. In *A Gentlemanly and Honorable Profession* (pages 253–254), I looked at the post-flogging fates of 37 sailors in the U.S. Navy of 1794–1815 who were sentenced by courts-martial to receive punishments of 100 or more lashes, and I could find no definite evidence that a single one of the 37 died as a result of the flogging. It is all but impossible to imagine a man receiving 150, 200, or 300 lashes with a cat-of-nine-tails and surviving to continue life as a naval sailor. But the record shows that sailors did, and the historians' jury must remain out with respect to Pope's claim of the fatal nature of punishment under the lash.

If a good definition of a classic is a work that one can see or hear or read many times and still derive some new experience on each encounter, Dudley Pope's *The Black Ship* is definitely a classic. The role of the introducer of such a book is rather like that of an usher in the theater: to see the reader comfortably seated, then get out of the way as quickly and as unobtrusively as possible. The real show begins when the reader reaches the first page of the classic's text, and the usher–introducer is no part of the cast. My task is to persuade you to turn the page and let Pope tell the story of dark and violent deeds on board the *Hermione* and their pitiless retribution.

—Christopher McKee

THE BLACK SHIP

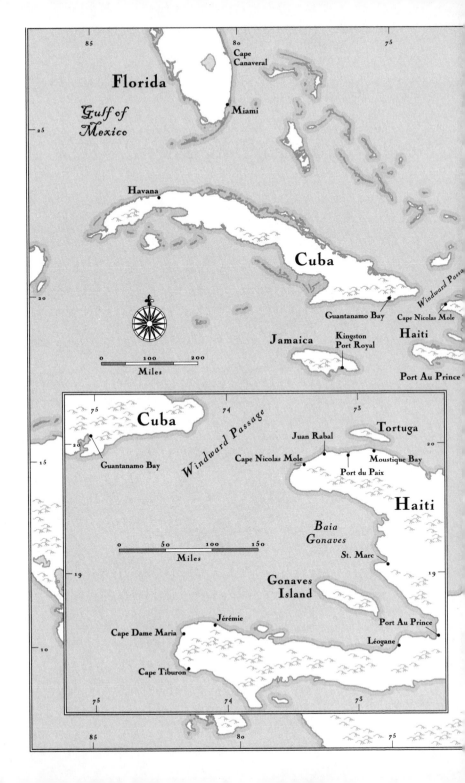

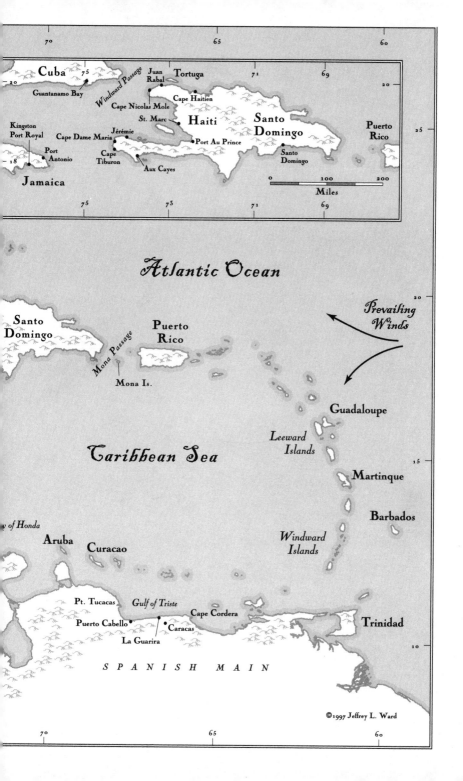

For the Mate of *Tokay,*

who only rarely

mutinies

"The Evidence saw a great quantity of blood in the Cabin window and at the afterhatch leading from the Gun Room. He heard repeated groans and screeches from the officers . . .

"There was only one woman on board, the Boatswain's wife . . .

"The HERMIONE *is painted black with white mouldings."*

*Deposition of John Mason,
former carpenter's mate in
His Majesty's frigate*
HERMIONE

AUTHOR'S NOTE

THIS BOOK is the first detailed story of the bloodiest mutiny that ever occurred in a ship of the Royal Navy, and it is written entirely from contemporary official and private documents. The facts are relatively simple: Captain Hugh Pigot, at the age of twenty-seven, commanded the frigate *Hermione* in the West Indies. He was possibly the cruellest captain in the service, and we can now say with certainty that eventually he drove his men too far. There is no question of the men being led or inspired by revolutionaries: constant flogging with the cat-o'-nine-tails and sheer terror of a man whom they had seen kill their shipmates in the name of smartness drove a section of the crew to a point where the law of the jungle, kill or be killed, overcame ingrained discipline.

At that point the men mutinied, murdering Pigot and nine other officers in a most brutal manner: ironically, in destroying a tyrant they established a worse tyranny. They then sailed to the Spanish Main and handed the ship over to the enemy. Naïvely, they thought they had found liberty: instead they found themselves despised by the Spaniards and ruthlessly hunted down by the Royal Navy, so that over the next ten years more than a score of them were hanged from the foreyardarms of the King's ships.

First I must explain why I came to write this book. Sometime in

1950 I was checking a fact in James's *Naval History of Great Britain,* published in 1822, when I saw a brief reference—less than 700 words—to the mutiny in H.M.S. *Hermione* in 1797. The well-respected James, in explaining why the mutiny occurred, wrote: "This most tyrannical conduct on the part of Captain Pigot, operating upon a very motley, and, from a succession of similar acts of oppression, ill-disposed ship's company, produced discontent, which kept increasing until the next evening, when it fatally burst forth . . ."

He added that if he could describe Pigot's humanity or kind behaviour it would heighten the guilt of his murderers, "but a regard to truth compels us to state, that Captain Hugh Pigot bore a character very opposite to a mild one; in short, he has been described to us by those who knew him well, as one of the most cruel and oppressive captains belonging to the Royal Navy."

I had earlier seen many brief and passing references to the *Hermione* mutiny: indeed, I had read that particular passage more than once; but this time the phrase describing Pigot's "tyrannical conduct . . . operating on a very motley, and, from a succession of similar acts of oppression, ill-disposed ship's company . . ." stuck in my mind.

Although engaged on other research but becoming ever more intrigued, I began to investigate further the *Hermione* story. There was little published; apart from James, there was a highly inaccurate article in the *Cornhill Magazine,* 1899; and a selection in *The Sailors' Rebellion,* pp. 285–303, by J. G. Bullocke (London, 1938), drawn from published sources. Much later a short but accurate article appeared in *The Mariner's Mirror'*s May 1955 issue. Slowly I accumulated material and the story became more extraordinary. Always I came back to the question: if Pigot was cruel—and James, for instance, who knew many of his contemporary captains, had no doubt about it—why did the crew stand Pigot's tyranny for so long and then suddenly mutiny? Why one day and not another?

Finally, three years ago, my publishers became as interested in the *Hermione* mutiny as my wife and I, so we started full-scale research. Carefully we built up the picture of the daily life of the 170-odd men crammed into the tiny *Hermione,* came to know the habits and idiosyncrasies of many of the individuals, and accumulated fact after damning fact which bore out the words written by William James nearly one and a half centuries earlier.

From a large number of documents in Britain and Spain we have been able to reconstruct the mutiny almost minute by minute, and always using the men's own words. Every single quoted or reported word of dialogue in the book is taken directly from original sources, except for occasional sail orders, which are of course those used at that period. Apart from that, there is a source for every word or phrase in quotation marks.

After we had re-created all the extraordinary events leading up to the mutiny, the mutiny itself, and the ship's arrival in a Spanish port, we then went to Spain to search among the Spanish archives and discover what the *Hermione* did under the red and gold flag of Carlos IV. At this point the story became almost ludicrous.

We came eventually to the extraordinary epilogue: how the Spaniards' problems were neatly solved by a small British warship, the *Surprise*.

The result of all this research is a book derived almost entirely from hitherto unpublished material which tells a story considerably stranger than fiction, and which is also, incidentally, a series of studies—of the life on board a British frigate in the West Indies during the long war against Revolutionary France; of the men of more than a dozen nations—ranging from Portugal to America, and Italy to Prussia, who formed the crew; of the personality, upbringing, background and behaviour of Hugh Pigot; of the way in which a mutiny actually occurs.

This book, then, is a study of many men and one ship; and of the qualities of leadership, courage and fear. The facts always to be borne in mind are that the *Hermione* mutiny was the worst in the Navy's history; that Pigot was one of the cruellest, if not the most cruel, of the Navy's captains; and that the conditions described in the *Success* and the *Hermione* were by no means common. The behaviour of the officers and men in the twenty-seven British battleships as they sailed down to give battle off Cape Trafalgar, as described in my book (published in Britain as *England Expects* and in the USA as *Decision at Trafalgar*) gives a better idea of the more usual living conditions in the King's ships.

Having shared at this remote date their hopes and fears, and sought out their activities and motives, we feel we know many of the *Hermione's* officers and men, both loyalist and mutineer, and Captain Pigot is no mystery: he had a personality and background which is all too familiar today. The ordinary reader as well as the experienced psychiatrist will recognize the type; many will be unfortunate enough to number a similiar sort of man among their acquaintances.

It is accepted that such things as microfilming and tape-recording are among the necessary everyday tools of people engaged today in detailed historical research among original and unpublished documents. The assistance of a highly-experienced psychiatrist is less usual. However, since I, for instance, was concerned mainly with discovering the secrets of the personality of Pigot, the most modern methods of finding out about them had to be used if the research was to be effective—in the same way that recent scientific developments have helped the archaeologist in his task of dating the earth's history.

No one does anything without a reason or motive. It was comparatively easy to find out *what* Pigot did, said and wrote; but it was more important to know *why*. Some of his actions were governed by orders from his superiors; but most—those which caused the mutiny—resulted from defects in his character. It was in elucidating and evaluating those defects that an experienced psychiatrist was of help—if only to confirm, in several cases, my own analysis which, of necessity, was only instinctive.

A word on sources: to avoid scattering footnotes on relevant material of a more specialized nature, and detailed source references, throughout the book, they have all been included in the Notes and Bibliography section, beginning on page 351 and listed chapter by chapter.

The research has been arduous, inevitably; and it would never have been completed but for my wife's unflagging encouragement and assistance, whether helping me to triple check a fact or dig our car out of snow drifts on the Pyrenean passes while returning from research in Madrid; transcribing a mass of microfilmed papers, translating Spanish documents, or typing the MS.

Many people have helped us, but particularly I must thank Brigadier-General Sir Robert Pigot, Bt., a direct descendant of Captain Hugh Pigot, for material concerning his family; Admiral Julio F. Guillen Tato, head of the Museo Naval, Ministerio de Marina, Madrid, and his son, for their welcome and assistance while we were working on the Spanish naval archives; and Mr. David Crossley, of the British Embassy in Madrid.

Lieutenant-Colonel Harold Wyllie, OBE, has once again proved to be more than a friend. In addition to his two paintings—the view from the *Hermione*'s maintop and the scene on the *Surprise*'s quarter-deck, which were executed specially for the book*—he has always been ready to answer the most complicated questions about sea life at the time of the *Hermione*—a subject on which he is one of the world's experts. Viscount Bridport, Commodore W. R. Rowbotham, and Rear-Admiral A. H. Taylor, CB, OBE, DL, JP, have likewise helped over similar queries.

When re-creating and analysing the personality of Hugh Pigot from documentary evidence of the letters he wrote, the statements he made, his actions and his family background, I was very fortunate in being able to discuss it in detail with Dr. John Randall. I am deeply indebted to him, although of course the responsibility for the assessment of Pigot's character and opinions expressed is entirely mine.

The staff of the Public Record Office, London, and particularly Messrs. E. K. Timings and R. Anslow, gave unfailing and patient help. (Unpublished Crown Copyright material in the Public Record Office has been reproduced by permission of the Controller of H.M. Stationery Office); and the staff of the Admiralty Library, London, particularly Commodore Peter Kemp, the Head of Historical Section, and Mr. Young, were of great assistance. Our friend Mrs. Anthea Barker made good use of her knowledge of the Public Record Office and unearthed some extra material at a time when we were a thousand miles from London, and we are most grateful to her, as we are to another old friend, Mr. Henry Bailey, who kindly read the proofs.

Mrs. Gloria Smyth put her fluent knowledge of Spanish at our disposal and worked on the translation of dozens of Spanish documents which age had faded and, with my wife, bore with fortitude the numerous local electricity failures which frequently plunged the microfilm projector into darkness and myself into a fury.

To our other friends who have helped with encouragement, com-

*Not reproduced in the Heart of Oak Sea Classics edition.

ments and suggestions, and to my patient publishers in Britain and America, my wife and I extend our thanks.

D.P.
Porto Santo Stefano,
(Grosseto),
Italy, 1963

I

Mr. Jesup's Petition

—ww—

A CAPTAIN of one of His Majesty's frigates in the long war against Revolutionary and Napoleonic France was forced to lead a solitary existence: although surrounded night and day by scores of men, he lived the life of a recluse. Because of the rigid bulkhead of discipline and tradition he was isolated from his own officers, entertaining them occasionally at his table but otherwise remaining socially aloof. He seldom saw his fellow captains since there were so few frigates and so many tasks that they were usually at sea during his infrequent stays in port. On the remoter stations like the West Indies the frigates were either escorting convoys or acting as lone wolves, hunting enemy merchantmen and warships, and at the same time keeping the seas cleared of the French and Spanish privateers lurking in the sheltered bays and lagoons.

In addition to this unnatural and enforced solitude the captain bore the sole responsibility for the fighting efficiency, safety and welfare of upwards of seven-score men, and for the ship herself. Combined with the knowledge that one error of judgment or navigation by himself or his officers could wreck his ship and possibly his career, it imposed a great strain on every type of captain, except perhaps the rare man who was a born leader or the less unusual person who knew he had so much influence and patronage in high places that only a massive blunder could affect his future in the service.

In the West Indies the solitary captain and his ship were further burdened with the ever present triple threat of virulent disease, which could decimate a crew overnight; dangerous and unpredictable currents which could, and not infrequently did, sweep a ship off her course in the darkness and fling her on to a shoal of uncharted rocks; and uncertain sub-tropical weather—for the Caribbean is the birthplace of the hurricane and the playground of the notorious white squall which, suddenly appearing out of a clear sky, would send the topmen racing aloft to reef or furl before its invisible strength tore the canvas of the sails out of the bolt-ropes.

Occasionally all these responsibilities put too great a load on the moral fibres which kept a captain's sense of proportion and temper under control so that, nearing breaking point, they became distorted and slowly warped the man's personality. This rarely affected his efficiency as a fighting machine; but since he wielded almost absolute power over his ship's company—a power backed by the Articles of War, and behind which was the whole weight and approval of the State—it could and often did have a powerful effect on the life and happiness of the men serving under him, particularly on the justice and the punishement he meted out to them.

It must be emphasized, because it says much for the natural resilience of the human spirit, and the rough and ready training which an officer received in the Royal Navy from the time he first joined as a young boy, that only rarely did a captain become so warped that he became an irresponsible tyrant; and this book is a study of one particular case, the worst in the whole history of the Royal Navy.

The commander-in-chief of "His Majesty's ships and vessels employed . . . at and about Jamaica" in 1797, Vice-Admiral Sir Hyde Parker, was usually to be found at Cape Nicolas Mole, at the western end of Santo Domingo (now Haiti), a small anchorage which was ridden with yellow fever and swarming with mosquitoes. The Mole's purpose was entirely martial: it had recently been captured from the French and for the commander-in-chief was strategically better placed than Port Royal, in Jamaica. It had no social life; the captains of the warships nominally based there could expect leisure and equable company only when their ships needed dockyard refits at Jamaica, where the society of Port Royal and Kingston could be relied upon for invitations to dinner at the homes of rich planters, and the choicest food and wines would be served by immaculately uniformed Negro servants and eaten in the company of beautiful women. This emphasized the dreariness of a captain's normal existence afloat, when an invitation to the first lieutenant and the doctor to join him at his table constituted a social occasion, and everyone knew and was probably heartily sick of the others' jokes and foibles.

Normally there was nothing but the usual habour routine to occupy Captain Hugh Pigot's thoughts during his infrequent stays at Cape Nicolas Mole in his frigate the *Success;* he would sit in the hot and humid solitude of his cabin dealing with the paperwork, or pace the windward side of the quarterdeck (which was shaded by canvas awnings and specially reserved for his use). However, on January 19, 1797, as the frigate lay at anchor at the Mole he had plenty of time to reflect on the furore which he had caused because he had lost his temper with the captain of an American merchant ship, a certain Mr. William Jesup, some six months previously. Indeed he was being forced to reflect, since he had to set down his explanation in writing.

To Captain Pigot, who though only twenty-six years old was a post captain, the whole wretched business was a matter for surprise, since all he had done was to order a couple of boatswain's mates to give the damn'd fellow a "starting" with a rope's end. A few stripes across the back was little enough for Jesup to complain about considering his behaviour and the way he had handled his ship, which was one of several Pigot had been convoying.

Pigot was prepared to agree that he had been rather hasty; that his anger with the "Jonathan" had clouded his judgment. But further than that he would not go; nor indeed had the commander-in-chief then desired it. But now—that very day—Sir Hyde had been forced to order a court of inquiry . . . simply because of a Yankee skipper whose behaviour, Pigot thought, had certainly shown him to be a fool or a knave, and perhaps both; whose behaviour had hazarded the *Success* and whom Pigot had punished accordingly.

Pigot's hasty action had certainly landed him in deep water. Apart from the diplomatic relationship between Britain and the

United States, which at that time was far from friendly, on a more prosaic level the masters of American merchant ships, although only too willing to trade with British ports, had an active and sometimes understandable dislike of the Royal Navy.

This had sprung up against the ever-present background of disagreement between the two nations over Britain's claim to the right in wartime to board American ships on the high seas and take off British sailors. The rights and wrongs of this will be discussed later, but it must be remembered in turn that the masters of many neutral ships could be a nuisance to nations at war. They were always ready to protest but, in the opinion of the Royal Navy, seldom cared to give credit when it was due—when, for example, a British warship rescued and set free (without making any claim against her owners) an American merchantman which had been captured by the French because she was allegedly carrying a cargo to or from a British port.

Such bickering was natural: it had always existed in previous wars and was to continue in wartime for the next century and a half. Any combatant country expecting a neutral's thanks for an act of kindness in time of war was naïve, and any neutral skipper who failed to grumble and protest at every opportunity was a rare and tolerant prince among seafarers.

Nevertheless convoying a motley bunch of British and neutral merchant ships, all of different size and seaworthiness and whose masters were invariably rugged individualists, was a thankless and temper-fraying task for even an experienced and patient frigate captain, which Hugh Pigot certainly was not. No one in authority commented if the convoy arrived safely; but if even a single ship was lost to the enemy, her owners made wrathful protests to the Admiralty, blaming the escorting warship for what was often the master's stupidity, or the result of their own notorious frugality in not allowing a large enough crew (which had probably been further depleted by a press-gang) or sufficient new sails and cordage. Sailing with a very small crew, reefing down too much at night through habit or over-cautiousness and falling far behind the convoy (the master of a merchant ship was freed by the convoy system of the need to hurry into port to be first at the market place with his cargo, since his rivals were usually in the same convoy)—all these, and several more, were the faults to which many of the charges of a harassed frigate captain were prone.

Captain Thomas Pasley, of the *Glasgow*, provides typical examples. "The *Mary Agnus* was leaky and sinking for want of men to pump her . . . came out so badly manned that at Bluefields he applied to me for men to weigh his anchor; I think him a rascal but could not see him sink—so gave him four men," he wrote about one of his charges. "The damn'd mule her captain stood on till 6 o'clock ere he put about, not paying the smallest attention to the signal," he said of another. ". . . How can I pretend to answer for the safety of ships commanded by such a set of mules? Thus is a captain of a man-of-war's character sported away, who happens to have the misfortune to command a convoy."

THE INCIDENT which had forced Sir Hyde Parker to order an inquiry into Captain Pigot's behaviour had occurred in July 1796, just before the Spaniards joined the war on the French side. The British had earlier captured Port au Prince, a small French town sprawled on a plain at the far end of the long and ever-narrowing gulf at the western end of Santo Domingo. The coastline for dozens of miles on either side of the gulf consisted of jungle interspersed with isolated villages and small towns, most of which were still held by small French garrisons and hardly worth the bother of attacking. One town, Leogane, which gives the gulf its name and is only twenty miles short of Port au Prince, was a flourishing base for French privateers, so that British merchantmen bound up the gulf for Port au Prince had to be escorted.

Pigot in the *Success* had been convoying a dozen of them on the short voyage from St. Marc, sixty miles away, when the incident happened. Pigot knew the Leogane privateers were a constant menace—not because they were powerfully armed, but they were small enough to be propelled by oars: dangerous opponents in an area where the wind often dropped suddenly, leaving sailing ships wallowing in a flat calm. The Frenchmen were so bold that in such a calm they would dart out and, skimming across the water like lissome flying fish, seize and tow away some fat merchantman as she lay helpless and out of gunshot from the escorting frigate, whose sails, starved of wind, would be hanging down limply like so much laundry.

For the whole of this particular voyage one American ship in the convoy had been a continual nuisance, according to Pigot. Badly sailed and usually out of station, she repeatedly ignored shouted orders and requests from the *Success*. She was the brig *Mercury*, of New York, and was being handled in such a lubberly fashion that in broad daylight she had run up so close under the *Success*'s stern that her jib-boom had nearly stove in the frigate's jolly boat in the stern davits.

This had been alarming enough, in Pigot's view; but that very night, July 1, despite frequently shouted warnings, she had rammed the *Success* amidships, and her jib-boom had poked across the waist of the ship like a clumsy giant's lance before being snapped off short by the frigate's main shrouds.

To Pigot, roused out of his sleep by the crash of the collision, and whose frigate formed the convoy's sole protection, there seemed to be only one immediate explanation for the *Mercury*'s strange and dangerous behaviour: with Leogane only a few miles to leeward it seemed obvious the American captain, William Jesup, was in the pay of the French and had deliberately rammed the *Success* to disable her, leaving the flock of merchantmen to the mercy of the enemy privateers.

The *Mercury*'s crew, Pigot had told Sir Hyde Parker, did little or nothing to help separate the two ships; and it was after Jesup had been called on board the *Success*—where he had made several unhelpful remarks—that he was given a "starting."

Pigot was probably justified in being angry that the collision had actually occurred; but he was not the man to act with restraint or foresight: his impulsiveness and lack of judgment stopped him realizing that for the captain of one of His Majesty's ships to order an American skipper to be "started" with a rope's end was bound to be regarded by even the British Government as an insult to the American flag. It was just the type of provocation, insignificant yet humiliating, which was bound to anger the sensitive Government of a new and proud country and give powerful ammunition to its considerable anti-British element.

PIGOT'S TROUBLES had begun officially when the *Mercury* arrived at Port au Prince and Jesup went on shore to register his protest with the American Consul, Mr. L. MacNeal, who helped him draw up a petition to the British authorities. Addressed to "His Honour R. W. Wilford, Commander of His Majesty's Forces at Port au Prince," it gave Jesup's version of the whole episode. According to him the fault was with the *Success,* which "wore ship and ran foul of the *Mercury.*" Captain Pigot had then "ordered his people to cut away everything they could lay their hands on," and also told them to bring back to the frigate the *Mercury's* jib and foretopmast-staysail, saying "they would do to make trowsers" [*sic*].

Jesup's petition said that he "begged Captain Pigot for God's sake not to cut any more than he could avoid, or words to that effect. Captain Pigot forthwith commanded his people to bring the d—d rascal that spoke on board the frigate, where he remained for a few minutes till the vessels were cleared. Pigot thereupon desired the boatswain's mates to give the d—d rascal, meaning your Petitioner, a good flogging.

"They took hold of your Petitioner, and inquired who he was—it was told them, he was the Master of the *Mercury.* Well, said Captain Pigot, 'flog him well and let him flog his officers.' These orders were instantly obeyed in so severe and cruel a manner that your Petitioner was nearly bereft of his senses. During the time your Petitioner was thus so brutally beaten and ill-treated, he, your Petitioner, made use of no offensive language, or no kind of resistance—but only begged they would have compassion on him . . .

"Your Petitioner arrived here same day, when he exhibited the marks and bruises of his shocking treatment to a number of the most respectable inhabitants and others in the town of Port au Prince, who all impartially pronounced it an outrage of the most brutal and unmanly kind, as the certificate annexed to this paper abundantly testifies."

Jesup requested that his petition, dated July 4, three days after the *Mercury* arrived in port, should be put before the proper authority so that he could obtain "justice and satisfaction." The certificate attached to it bore the signatures of thirty-seven of the "most respectable inhabitants" who had "seen and viewed the marks and lashing inflicted on the body and person of Captain Jesup . . . by the order of Captain Pigot," and "give it as our candid opinion that the dangers to be apprehended from such wanton and barbarous treatment, is of the most imminent and alarming nature to the life and person of Captain Jesup, revolting to humanity, degrading and dishonourable in the highest degree to the commander of a ship of His Britannic Majesty."

Consul MacNeal also signed the certificate and added a paragraph saying that he too had "viewed the body and arms of Captain Jesup, and that it appears to me, that he had been severely flogged, beat and bruised, by some person or persons unknown to me."

On July 8, possibly in reply to a counter-allegation by Pigot, the nine passengers who had been in the *Mercury*, including a Frenchwoman, Mme. Gumaire, signed another certificate saying that at the time of the incident they "did not hear Captain Jesup utter or say anything of an irritating or offensive nature, but [that he] behaved in the most passive and forebearing stile [*sic*] in his answers when hailed from the *Success.*" When he left the *Mercury* for the frigate he appeared to be "in perfect health"; but when he returned he was "in a very suffering condition" owing to "the sore beatings and bruises whereof his body and arms, which he exhibited to us, bore the most convincing proof . . ."

The petition and certificates were duly forwarded to the British commander-in-chief, Sir Hyde Parker. There is no record whatsoever that he took any action when he received them: certainly he neither noted the incident in his journal nor wrote to the Admiralty. (Under the *Regulations and Instructions,* a commander-in-chief's dispatches were to tell the Admiralty of his fleet's activities "and of all other circumstances worthy of notice," and he had to keep a daily journal recording all such information.) Parker appears to have been satisfied with Pigot's explanation and description of the episode.

Pigot was convinced that he had been perfectly in the right, and Sir Hyde had behaved very well so far, in his view: there had been no unnecessary nagging and carping. His confidence seems to have been well founded, for there must have been a tacit understanding with the admiral that the whole episode should be ignored—unless demands for an explanation arrived from Their Lordships in Whitehall. Anyway, for many days after the arrival of Jesup's petition all was quiet; but unknown to Pigot or Sir Hyde, copies of the petition and certificates had been sent to the United States, where they were immediately published in the newspapers. The reaction was instantaneous and noisy.

At that time the American Press and the British Government viewed each other with mutual suspicion—within a few months Lord MacDonald was to write to the Secretary of State in London that "half a dozen books are not certainly published in any one year.

. . . The printers are employed in the universal business of newspapers and . . . the consequence is that the opinions of all classes arise from what they read in their newspapers; so that *by newspapers the country is governed.*" He added that "the newspapers which abuse or slight us most, sell best."

Even allowing this was an exaggeration inflated by outraged indignation, it goes far to explain the extent of the uproar when Mr. Jesup's story was published. Within a few days copies of newspapers from the Southern states were delivered on board Sir Hyde's flagship at Cape Nicolas Mole, and Pigot found the dog—indeed, a large pack of them—still worrying the bone.

It did not take long for the first of the swell waves heralding the storm's approach to travel eastwards across the Atlantic from the United States and lap along the shores of Whitehall. The episode had happened on July 1, the latest date on the Jesup certificates was July 8, and on July 25 the *New York Diary,* among many other newspapers, had published its first full account of Jesup's story. By September 22 the Lords Commissioners of the Admiralty—otherwise known as the Board—were reading a copy of the *Diary* in London. This gave them the first news of the incident and since Sir Hyde Parker had made no mention of it in his dispatches—a major tactical error—Their Lordships instructed the Secretary to the Board, Mr. Evan Nepean, to write to him at once demanding information.

With scant regard to the spelling of names, Nepean's letter told Sir Hyde that "I am commanded . . . to transmit to you the enclosed extract from the *New York Diary* of 25th July last relating the particulars of the very extraordinary behaviour of Captain Pigott of His Majesty's ship *Success* towards Captain Jesup of the ship *Mercury* and to signify Their Lordships' direction to you to call upon Captain Pigott to report a full and circumstantial account of the transactions above alluded to, which report you will please transmit to me for Their Lordships' information."

The letter was sent at once to Falmouth for dispatch to the West Indies by the next packet. (There were nine packets maintaining the service between Britain and the West Indies and America.) However, before the ship sailed the Board had to send another letter to Sir Hyde about the same subject, but written in much stronger terms.

The reason was that Mr. Robert Liston, the British Envoy

Extraordinary and Minister Plenipotentiary in the United States, had of course read Jesup's account in the newspapers. From Philadelphia he had written an indignant report to the Secretary of State, which arrived in London after the Board's first letter to Sir Hyde had been sent off to Falmouth. Basing his judgment solely on the newspaper accounts, Liston wrote on August 13: "It is with great concern I observe that the complaints of acts of injustice and insult committed by our officers against American citizens continue and increase . . . A deep impression has in particular been made upon persons of all ranks by the enclosed statement of an outrage offered to Mr. William Jesup . . . which has been published in every newspaper in the United States.

"Although the petition of the injured party does not probably explain in its full extent the nature of the provocation given to Captain Pigot," Liston admitted, "yet the number of respectable names which are subscribed to the certificate annexed appear to leave little or no doubt as to the facts of the cruel treatment. And the matter is such that it seems to merit the most serious attention on the part of the King's Ministers."

Lord Grenville received this letter and an extract from a newspaper at the beginning of October. After showing it to the King he returned to Downing Street and wrote to the Admiralty, enclosing an extract from Liston's letter, saying, "I am to signify to Your Lordships His Majesty's pleasure that a particular inquiry be immediately made respecting the conduct imputed to Captain Pigot, and the circumstances of the transaction."

The Admiralty, who had of course already seen the *New York Diary* a week or two earlier, instructed Mr. Nepean to send the second letter to Sir Hyde, this time in harsher terms, saying that the Secretary of State had sent them documents "relative to the outrageous and cruel behaviour of Captain Pigot," and signifying the King's pleasure that an inquiry should be held "into this very extraordinary proceeding, transmitting to me without delay a full statement of the case as you shall find the same to be, in order that Their Lordships may take such measures . . . as may appear to be meet and proper."

BY THE TIME the packet reached Cape Nicolas Mole after her long southward sweep into the Atlantic to pick up the trade winds which carried her across to the regular landfall at Barbados, Their Lordships' second letter was six weeks old. The Jesup episode had occurred five months earlier, and for the whole of that time Hugh Pigot had lived in a state of ever-increasing uncertainty.

Sir Hyde Parker may well have reflected that his efforts to hush up the whole business had been the worst mistake he could have made, since in any dispute the first person to protest to authority with boldly-phrased and well-documented allegations secured considerable tactical advantages. Now—well, Pigot must face a court of inquiry, and the Admiralty, not Sir Hyde, would then decide if Pigot should be court-martialled.

Such a court of inquiry was not authorized by law; its existence was based on custom. Usually it comprised three captains whose task was to investigate and see if there were sufficient grounds for a court-martial. Sir Hyde gave orders on January 19, 1797, that Commodore John Duckworth, with Captains James Bowen and Man Dobson, were to "inquire into the conduct of Captain Pigot." There was a safeguard for Pigot in Sir Hyde's order because the next phrase said the inquiry was to be based "on the evidence of such officers and seamen as he [Pigot] may choose to bring before you." Thus Pigot could, if he wished, make sure that no one likely to give unfriendly or potentially dangerous evidence would be heard.

Pigot selected his witnesses, but the master of the *Success*, who had been on watch at the time of the collision, was now in hospital at Jamaica, the gunner was also at Jamaica in a prize, and the ship had had only one lieutenant on board at the time.

Captain Pigot's cabin in the *Success* was prepared as a courtroom, and the day after Sir Hyde issued his order the commodore and two captains arrived on board the frigate with all due ceremony. With their clerk taking the minutes, they began the inquiry. On either side of the cabin, looking like a squat bulldog, was a 12-pounder cannon, the barrel gleaming black on its buff-painted carriage. The light from the skylight overhead was diffused by the white canvas awning stretched over the quarterdeck and poop, but where it streamed in unshaded through the stern windows it was harsher, giving more than a hint of the heat outside. The cabin was low—a man of average height had to duck and hunch his shoulders to avoid hitting his head on the beams. The cabin bore signs of Pigot's occupation— a white-handled, light cavalry sword hung from a hook in its scabbard; a brass speaking trumpet, bell-mouthed, and highly polished, hung nearby; and a telescope sat in its rack. The silverware on the sideboard showed Pigot was not a poor man.

The commodore ordered Captain Pigot to be called in, and the clerk first read out Sir Hyde's order to hold the inquiry, followed by Mr. Jesup's petition and the accompanying certificates. Pigot had been busy writing in the hours before the inquiry, and when asked for a statement describing his side of the affair he handed Commodore Duckworth several sheets of paper covered in his large handwriting.

This was then read out to the court. Headed "Circumstantial account of the American ship *Mercury* running on board the *Success*," it said that Pigot had been asleep at 1 A.M. on July 1, when he was wakened by the master calling out, "Put your helm hard a'starboard or you will be on board of us." Pigot said that while he was dressing he heard the master "repeat these words very distinctly four or five times; and when the ship he was hailing had approached so near as to make it impossible for her to wear clear of the *Success*'s quarter, I likewise heard him repeatedly call to them to throw all a'back." [thus stopping the ship].

The other ship, the *Mercury*, was close to the wind on the larboard tack, said Pigot, while the *Success* and the rest of the convoy were on the starboard tack [the *Mercury* was approaching the *Success* from the frigate's right-hand side]. The *Mercury* "struck the *Success* with all her sails full on the starboard beam, her bowsprit passing through the *Success*'s main shrouds."

Pigot added that "fortunately for both the wind was slight, and not much swell. Our people were immediately employed endeavouring to clear the two ships.

"I must here observe that to the best of my knowledge and belief they did not cut away more of the rigging or anything else belonging to the *Mercury* than was absolutely necessary to disengage the two ships from each other. I, as well as the officers of the *Success*, repeatedly called to the people on board the *Mercury* . . . pointing out many other necessary steps to be taken to prevent her yards catching the rigging of the *Success*. . . . I can confidently say that from the time she was first hailed until she struck the *Success* and during the time she was on board her, not a soul belonging to the

Mercury made the smallest effort (in the first instance to avoid it) nor afterwards in endeavouring to clear the ships of each other."

Pigot listed the damage to the *Success,* and said that although it blew a strong easterly wind next day he saw the *Mercury* "carry as much sail as any other ship, and to be one of the first beating into Port au Prince." He recalled that on the morning before the collision the officer of the watch in the *Success* "hailed this ship and cautioned her against keeping so near us, as she had narrowly escaped several times falling on board of us," and added that "the circumstances already mentioned, added to the many instances I have been witness to and experienced, of the incivility of the Americans to His Majesty's ships officers, and the partiality shown by them to our enemies, led me firmly to believe the *Mercury*'s running on board the *Success* was not accident but design," so that the *Success* would be damaged and would be forced to leave her convoy at the mercy of the French privateers from Leogane.

"So firmly was I impressed with this idea, which was strengthened by their want of exertion in endeavouring to clear the ships . . . that passion overcame my reason, and I am sorry to acknowledge, on the Master of *Mercury* coming on board the *Success,* I immediately ordered him to be punished by the boatswain's mate with the end of a rope; however," Pigot admitted, "I now feel sensible that in the heat of passion I was led to exceed much the bounds of propriety by inflicting that or any other punishment of the kind."

It must have taken a great deal of effort on Pigot's part publicly to admit having been even that much in the wrong; but he was almost certainly acting under advice—advice which told him that without a complete apology for the flogging it would be impossible for the Admiralty to avoid a trial. However, Pigot qualified his statement by adding: "I feel it equally necessary for my own justification to declare on my word of honour (and I may say if further proof is wanting I can call on the officers and ship's company under my command to certify) the circumstances as related in the American papers is for the most part—particularly by that relative to the severity of the punishment inflicted—fraught with the greatest falsehood and malice, and I can take it upon myself to say I do not believe the Master of the ship would himself have taken any notice of it, had he not been urged to do so by the Americans at Port au Prince with the hope of extoring money from me, as they offered to come to compromise, but gave out it should not be for any small sum."

As soon as his statement was read, Pigot handed Commodore Duckworth a list of his witnesses. The first one was the *Success*'s first lieutenant, William Hill, who described the collision and continued, "The Master of the *Mercury* then said we had better take his ship and destroy her, than to leave him in that situation, and murmured greatly at our people when on board [the *Mercury*] assisting him to get clear of us: he likewise said to our people when on board his ship that he was fearful of their stealing from him. On that expression Captain Pigot called him on board and . . . desired him to remain aft on our quarterdeck. . . . During the time we were employed clearing the ships of each other, the Master of the American still murmuring and abusing our people on board his ship, Captain Pigot directed me to send two boatswain's mates aft, and ordered them to thrash him, and I suppose he received about twenty strokes with a rope's end on his back.

"Captain Pigot then ordered him into the jolly boat, at that time alongside, to go on board his own ship. When going down the ship's side, he [Jesup] swore and said he would pay his Mate for that, and thought himself very well off in escaping so well."

The three officers forming the court then questioned Lieutenant Hill. "Do you recollect Captain Pigot giving directions to his people to cut away the *Mercury*'s jib and foretopmast-staysail and bring them on board the *Success* to make themselves trowsers?" they asked. "I did not hear it," said Hill.

"Is it your opinion, as a gentleman, officer and man of honour, that the cause of the *Mercury*'s getting foul of the *Success* arose from negligence and inattention, or appeared to be from design?"

"It appeared to happen from negligence and inattention," said Hill, "as that ship was frequently hailed and no person answered . . ."

"Did Captain Pigot express any apprehension that the American ship had acted by design, to disable the *Success?*" asked the court.

"Captain Pigot did express those sentiments to me immediately on the Master of the *Mercury* going from the *Success,* and likewise in the morning watch, being then opposite to the enemy's post of Leogane."

The next witness was the surgeon, Mr. John Crawford, who told the court that Captain Pigot had said the American ship might have intended to disable the *Success,* and he had "mentioned a circumstance which had happened to the trade [i.e., merchant ships] we had last convoyed to Port au Prince, of a gunboat coming from Leogane and attacking a brig in a calm, not more than two gun-shots off . . ."

"Do you know," inquired the court, "that Mr. Jesup . . . was so cruelly beat on board the *Success* as to be nearly bereft of his senses?"

As a medical man, Crawford was of course an expert witness; but more important was his considerable experience in patching up men after they had been flogged on Captain Pigot's orders. "I do not think so," said Crawford, "and I heard the punishment, and did not consider at the time it could injure him materially."

With this assurance ringing in their ears, the court adjourned for the day, and when they met again their first witness was a young master's mate, Mr. John Forbes, who had been on deck at the time of the collision. In answering the stock question whether Jesup was beaten in such a manner as nearly to have deprived him of his senses, Forbes said no: he had received from twenty to twenty-four strokes, "and in going into the jolly boat said that he would be damned if he did not give his Mate the same."

Finally the name of Thomas Jay was called: he was one of the two boatswain's mates who had actually administered the "starting" to Jesup. Did he give the American such a severe beating, inquired the court, that the man was nearly deprived of his senses? "No I did not," declared Jay.

"What sort of rope was it that you gave the strokes with?"—"It was a piece of one of the main ratlines, cut for the purpose of disentangling the ships from each other."

The court—which had already read in Jesup's petition that Pigot was to blame for the collision—had now heard Pigot put it squarely on Jesup, denying the American's story that he was forcibly taken on board the *Success.* And although Pigot said he thought Jesup deliberately tried to disable the *Success,* his four senior witnesses had all considered it was an accident.

The court when it met again did not take long to draw up its written report, which was soon on its way by boat to Sir Hyde on board the *Queen,* to be followed later by the minutes of the inquiry evidence.

For both the commander-in-chief and his hot-tempered captain the findings were not unsatisfactory. The *Mercury,* the report said, "instead of being run foul of by His Majesty's ship *Success,* was from negligence and inattention, or from wantonness and design, evidently run on board the *Success,* when it might have been avoided if the person directing the *Mercury* had only complied with the seamanlike suggestions offered to him by the Master of the *Success.* . . .

"After this extraordinary act was committed it fully appears . . . that the two ships were extricated from the alarming situation . . . with most officer-like dispatch by the crew of the *Success,* under the directions of Captain Pigot, and in the performing of the essential and momentous piece of service, it does not appear that any wantonness in destroying the sails and rigging of the ship *Mercury* was committed . . . or any kind of plunder authorized by Captain Pigot, or any language such as might appear indignant to the nation the vessel belonged to, used; nor was the said Mr. William Jesup seized and brought on board of the *Success* by force, but came on board without being touched. . . ."

"We must," continued the court, "give due praise to Captain Pigot's conduct thus far in the proceedings, but we must (as Captain Pigot in his statement of proceedings doth) most truly lament that the agitation and torment produced in his mind by this act of negligence and inattention, or wantonness or design, had so put him off his guard, as an officer and a gentleman, that he did improperly and in a manner not to be justified, direct the said Mr. William Jesup to be punished with some stripes with a rope's end across his shoulders, though it does not appear that in this act there had been the least premeditation, as there were no orders for stripping the said Mr. William Jesup, nor does he appear to have been so confined as to prevent him using his endeavours to avoid the strokes by moving about. . . .

"We therefore feel that Captain Pigot's situation was a very particular one, and trust it will clearly and evidently appear that the warning given to the *Mercury* on the morning previous to the accident, as well as the Master's again hailing her directly antecedent to her running on board of the *Success*, had impressed Captain Pigot's mind with a full conviction that it was committed by design, which with his admitted and known zeal and ardor [*sic*] for His Majesty's service, and considering his honour and character as an officer blended in the protection of the vessels under his convoy, which had he been disabled would most probably have been captured . . . had created such warmth and irritation in his mind, as by the impulse of the moment to make him lose sight of what he owed to Justice and his own character: but it appears to us as evident during the whole transaction that Captain Pigot had not in his thoughts the most distant idea of any national offence, or disrespect to, the States of America, and that act could only be applied to the individual aggrieved, and consequently we experience great distress of mind that Mr. Liston, His Majesty's Minister in America, should in an extract of his letter, say that the complaints of acts of injustice and insult committed by His Majesty's naval officers against American citizens continue and increase, as with great truth and confidence, we can assert during our service in this country [the West Indies] the reverse has been the case . . ."

Sir Hyde, after reading the report, wrote to the Admiralty that he had the honour of transmitting the minutes and result of the inquiry, "and trust that however unjustifiable [Captain Pigot's] conduct may appear to Their Lordships, they will be of opinion with me, that it is proved to be far, very far, more favourable than what has been represented either by Mr. Liston or the party aggrieved, and most sincerely hope that His Majesty will be graciously pleased, when the papers are laid before him, to see and consider it in the same manner or light as I do."

His Majesty's views were never recorded; but it is certain neither he nor Sir Hyde knew that in a file at the Admiralty containing official letters from captains was one from Pigot, dated two years earlier and written within a month of him obtaining his first command, the sloop *Swan*. Pigot complained to the Board of "the insolent conduct of the master of the *Canada*, West Indiaman, towards me." The *Swan* was part of the escort of a convoy which included the *Canada*, and the senior officer of the escort ordered Pigot to "enforce the sternmost of the merchant ships . . . to carry more sail and attend to his signals." But, complained Pigot, "I received for answer from the master of the *Canada* that he would make what sail

he thought proper and desired me to fire at him at my peril . . .
Upon my firing a shot across his forefoot [i.e., bow] he set his
maintopgallant sail and made use of some insolent language . . ."

Then, wrote Pigot, a few hours later, when the sloop was lying-to
reefing sails, the *Canada* collided with her, "and I am strongly of
opinion purposely." All the time Pigot and his men strove to free the
two ships, "the master of the *Canada* stood upon the bowsprit of his
ship and addressing himself to me made use of the most insolent
and provoking language . . ."

The Secretary of the Admiralty noted on the letter, "Sent copy to
the Master of Lloyd's Coffee House" for the *Canada*'s owners, hop-
ing they would not condone such behaviour. By chance the next
letter written by the Secretary referring to Pigot concerned the Jesup
affair.

APART FROM the official aspects of the Jesup affair, the episode
had caused Sir Hyde considerable personal distress because of all
the officers serving under him, Hugh Pigot was one of his favourite
captains: indeed, the young man's father had once been the commander-in-chief of that very station. However, the admiral had no
way of knowing—until he received their reply in three or four
months' time—whether or not the letter he had just written to the
Admiralty pleading in the young man's favour would have any
effect. There was undoubtedly a very definite risk that Pigot would
be court-martialled and cashiered to placate the Americans, the
King, and the Opposition in Parliament, or even the First Lord of the
Admiralty.

This delicate situation had also produced an urgent operational
problem for the admiral: he had written his letter on January 24, but
a convoy already assembling at the Mole was due to sail for England
on February 14, and the *Success* had to be one of the escorts because
she was under Admiralty orders to return to England.

But with Pigot involved in a scrape, Sir Hyde clearly regarded it
as an inopportune time for him to return to England: once there he
would have no champion and no one to shelter him from the immediate and direct wrath of the Admiralty, Parliament and the newspapers. Undoubtedly Pigot was safer in the West Indies: whatever the
Admiralty decided to do, Sir Hyde could up to a point argue and
temporize for a considerable time. With letters taking weeks to cross

the Atlantic, he could delay things long enough for tempers to cool and for the whole episode—at least as far as Parliament and Press were concerned—to have been forgotten.

But the *Success* herself had to sail for England: that could not be avoided. Fortunately there was an easy solution—Pigot could exchange ships with another captain. Sir Hyde as commander-in-chief had full authority to agree to such an exchange—though he could not force it on anyone. By chance there was a captain commanding a frigate of the same size as the *Success* who was quite willing to change: he was Philip Wilkinson, of the frigate *Hermione*.

While there is no surviving documentary evidence which says in so many words that Sir Hyde arranged the exchange solely to keep Pigot in the West Indies the motive is obvious, and it is known that up to a few days before the convoy was due to sail, Pigot expected to go to England in the *Success,* and his crew were aware of this. Then suddenly the exchange was arranged, and Pigot told more than a score of his men (while appealing to them to transfer with him to the *Hermione*) that he was disappointed that he would not be going to England with the *Success.* That Sir Hyde was deliberately protecting Pigot appears to be the only possible explanation—although one for which written evidence is unlikely to be available.

II

Islands of Death

—〰—

THE WEST INDIES meant all things to all men in Hugh
Pigot's day: for the ambitious naval officer, whether a pim-
ply junior lieutenant or a senior post captain, there was the
frequent chance of a swift promotion since fatal tropical diseases
created plenty of vacancies, while admirals with even moderate luck
could reckon on a small fortune from prize money. For the British
Government, however, the string of islands were a perpetual headache, since their defence was a never-ending drain on the Treasury
and on the supply of men for the Army and Navy, whose resources
were invariably overstretched. They were frequently a distraction
for the politicians, who all too often counted the haphazard propaganda value of a dispatch in the *London Gazette* announcing the
capture (at an unrevealed cost) of some wretched spice island as
more important than a long-term strategic plan for operations in
Europe. For the first few years of the war they stamped on the
enemy's toes under the impression they were slowly crushing his
whole body.

However, they were regrettably correct in the assessment of the
propaganda value of their spice-island strategy since to the powerful

merchants in Britain and the plantation owners the islands were an apparently inexhaustible well of wealth and political influence.

The long semilune of islands loosely called the West Indies form a 2,500-mile-long barrier (the distance from Gibraltar to the Arctic Circle) enclosing the Caribbean, and are swept along their length by the trade winds, blowing from between north-east and south-east. The difficulty of sailing eastward against the prevailing winds and current from Jamaica and the other western islands meant that the Admiralty had to divide the Caribbean into two commands, the Leeward Island Station covering the eastern area, and the more important Jamaica Station to the west.

We have seen that at the beginning of 1797, at the time of the Jesup affair, the commander-in-chief of the Jamaica Station had his headquarters at Cape Nicolas Mole (also variously called Mole St. Nicolas and St. Nicolas Mole), at the north-western end of what was then Santo Domingo (now Haiti). The Mole, not much more than a good anchorage, was well-placed by Nature as a sentry box at one side of the Windward Passage, a natural gap forty-five miles wide between Santo Domingo and Cuba, which was one of the main exits through the barrier of islands for ships bound to Europe. This highly-important sea highway—indeed, with convoys for Britain forming up at the Mole it was more of a cross-roads—had to be guarded by the Royal Navy and the Mole was the obvious base for their operations.

Single ships and convoys coming to the West Indies from Britain were bound to certain routes by the trade, or prevailing, winds, and usually reached Barbados, at the south-eastern end of the islands, after five or six weeks at sea. If not bound for the southern ports in the Leeward or Windward Islands, a ship then turned north-west inside the barrier of islands.

". . . It is of the utmost importance to prevent any great alarm arising on account of our West Indies interests either in Jamaica or the Leeward Islands. So much property is embarked in both these quarters, any disaster in either would produce disagreeable convulsions at home"—so wrote Henry Dundas, the Secretary of State, to Earl Spencer, the First Lord of the Admiralty, in January 1801. Spencer had earlier written that the capture of the Dutch island of Curaçao would be popular with the Government as well as "our merchants who are never backward in availing themselves of any fresh opening for their speculations."

Both Dundas and Spencer were hard-headed politicians; and the tragedy was that to retain popularity and placate the West India merchants a succession of ministers squandered the lives of thousands of men for the security of what was, except for sugar, basically a luxury trade. For example, at this time in Britain the price of bread was rising disastrously; but the West Indies' exports did not include an ounce of grain. Strategically, after America gained independence, Jamaica would have been sufficient as a base; though for the purpose of trade the islands absorbed much of Britain's exports.

The Navy's task in the West Indies was easy to define but difficult to carry out effectively. Most important was the need to protect the "trade," in other words the merchant ships, while at the same time prevent French and Spanish merchantmen and warships arriving in or departing from the islands or the Spanish Main.

The situation was complicated by the fact that French- and Spanish-owned islands were scattered haphazardly among those belonging to Britain; and in Santo Domingo, where Sir Hyde Parker had his base, all three nations were in occupation—Spain in the eastern portion and France in the western, with Britain occupying several ports and anchorages, such as Cape Nicolas Mole and Port au Prince on the west coast with French troops often less than a score of miles away. Almost every island had plenty of hiding places along its coastline for the privateers of all three nations, so that each of the trio had to convoy its merchantmen—if it had sufficient escorts available—against the privately-owned vessels licensed by their Governments to act against the enemy.

Yet despite the fact that Sir Hyde was (like every other commander-in-chief) always short of ships, his greatest enemy, against whom he and his officers waged a constant but losing battle, was sickness: disease in the West Indies killed thousands more British sailors and soldiers than the French and Spanish. The islands were among the unhealthiest spots in which at this time the Navy and Army were called upon to serve. At the island of St. Lucia in May 1796, for instance, the 31st Foot consisted of 776 men, but seven months later only fifteen were reported fit for duty—the rest were dead, dying or seriously ill. In Grenada in the nine months up to February 1797, when Pigot was facing the court of inquiry, the 57th

Regiment lost fifteen officers and 605 men, while the 27th Regiment, in the same period, lost twenty officers and 516 men.

These are not examples of exceptional losses: in the West Indies as a whole the figures are almost as bad. In the year ending April 1796, out of an average total of 15,881 white troops, some 6,480 died from sickness: 40 per cent. In the next year 3,760 died out of an average force of 11,500: 32 per cent. Most of them fell victim to yellow fever.

For private soldiers and NCOs, a draft to the West Indies was all too frequently a sentence of perpetual banishment and eventual death; but they were not the only victims: the Navy suffered dreadful casualties. In the campaign against Santo Domingo in 1794, forty-six masters of transport ships and 11,000 of the men in their ships died of yellow fever, according to the biographer of the man who was Agent of Transports for the West Indies.

Captain John Markham of the 74-gun *Hannibal*, a son of the Archbishop of York, writing home from Santo Domingo in 1795 said, "Since my arrival [two months previously] six of my people are dead, and every man in the ship has scurvy in a degree." Within a few weeks Markham was himself invalided home and a month later his former first lieutenant wrote: "Since you left us . . . 170 have been buried already, and many more must go, I fear." The *Hannibal* eventually lost more than two hundred men in six months. The *Raisonable*, in a voyage of less than 300 miles from Jamaica to Port au Prince, buried thirty-six of her crew on the way.

Yellow fever was, in the West Indies, clearly much more dangerous for a ship's company than war, and it struck impartially. By comparison, casualties in battles were light: at Trafalgar, for instance, the heaviest British losses were to be in the *Victory* (fifty-seven killed) while the most in a ship of a comparable size to the *Hannibal* were the forty killed in the *Colossus*. The deaths from yellow fever in the three ships already mentioned totalled more than 260; the total British killed at Trafalgar, when twenty-seven British ships captured or destroyed eighteen French and Spanish ships, was only 449.

A young midshipman serving in the West Indies at this time was William Parker, later to become an admiral of the fleet. His biographer, who served with him, wrote: "Blockading and chasing strange sail gave full occupation, but the yellow fever made its terrible ravages . . . None can realize, except those who have witnessed it, the effect of this terrible infliction in a ship, when men are seized by day and night with a poison from the atmosphere . . . The alarm engendered by this state of peril leads frequently to drinking on the part of those exposed to the danger; some feeling, or fancying, that extra stimulus is most desirable in such a climate, are unable to draw the line at moderation, while the old heathen feeling, 'Let's eat and drink, for tomorrow we die' actuates others who are reckless . . .'

The other two major problems facing Sir Hyde Parker were finding enough seamen to replace those who were killed or permanently invalided by disease, and repairing his ships. The first was the most difficult—the Admiralty in London had too much trouble manning ships based in Britain to concern themselves with sending out replacements, despite direct requests to do so. The result was that every merchantman arriving in the West Indies could be sure that a press-gang would soon be on board to take off as many men as possible, leaving just enough to navigate the ship. Repairing warships was hampered by the fact that Port Royal, in Jamaica, was the only available dockyard and it was invariably short of almost every type of stores, particularly masts and spars, and guns.

So much for an outline of the difficulties and dangers facing everyone from seamen to admirals in the West Indies. For the officers at least, the rewards were in proportion. Earl Spencer, the First Lord of the Admiralty, telling Sir Hyde Parker that he was being recalled to England after three years in Jamaica, hoped he would regard it solely as "a change of service which may naturally be looked for after so long a term as you have enjoyed of the most lucrative station in the service."

It is obvious why it paid rich dividends to be a favourite captain of the commander-in-chief. There were two main tasks to be carried out by the frigates—convoying merchantmen, and cruising in search of enemy ships. When the commander-in-chief allocated his tasks, he would be only human if he sent his favourite captain cruising in the most profitable areas, with the less profitable going to the less favoured. For those captains who found no favour or patronage (not necessarily through any fault of their own) there were convoys to escort . . .

An example of what Sir Hyde could do for young captains is

given by his secretary at that time, the Reverend A. J. Scott. He referred to one capture by the *Amphion* and *Alarm* "whose invoice amounted to nearly £200,000, and that Admiral Parker and the two captains would at least have each £25,000." Scott was, as the admiral's chaplain and confidential secretary, in a good position to know the figures.

The numerous deaths through disease meant there were plenty of vacancies for promotion, so that an admiral could quickly advance those he favoured. And the First Lord, too—Lord Spencer, recommending a certain captain for promotion, told Sir Hyde, "He is the son of . . . a friend of mine."

Although social position and "influence" was in this sense inherited, "patronage" could be acquired: a brilliant young man (Nelson is an example) would, if he was lucky, obtain the patronage of a senior officer who would ensure his promotion. As the senior officer scaled the heights, so would he advance his protégés. Sir Hyde provides an example of this when, after being sent unexpectedly to command the Jamaica Station, he told the First Lord of "my own peculiar situation, being estranged from all my own officers, who have been following my fortunes, and some of them looking up to me from their childhood." He would, of course, find new protégés in the West Indies, as well as favourites, who would look to him for advancement.

III

Taking the Strain

—✺—

A ROPE CAN BEAR a heavy load for a long time without apparently being overstrained; then suddenly and usually without warning (although an experienced eye can sometimes detect the signs of stress) it breaks, often with disastrous results. Why does it happen at one moment and not another? Why can it bear a strain of perhaps ten tons and yet break when only a tiny extra load is applied? And why does it part at one point along its length and not another?

The story of the dual tragedy of Pigot and the crew of the *Hermione* bears a curious similarity to a rope under a heavy load which, with only a slight warning, broke under the strain of but an extra ounce.

To understand how and why the tragedy occurred it is essential to examine the background of the men and the events for the same clues one would seek when trying to discover why a particular rope parted in certain circumstances when apparently similar ropes did not. It is very important to know the strains to which it had earlier been subjected.

In the case of the *Hermione* and her men these factors are not difficult to investigate and are only slightly complicated—but not obscured—by the late arrival on board of some men—including Captain Pigot—from the *Success*. They were few enough in numbers, but continuing the rope simile, they weighed just that much more than an ounce.

Because Pigot served in the *Hermione* for only eight months—from February 1797 until the tragedy occurred in the following October—one might suspect that the captain whom Pigot succeeded, Philip Wilkinson, had some responsibility for the subsequent behaviour of the crew, particularly since he had been commanding the frigate for the previous two and a half years. Was it a case of a kind captain being succeeded by a cruel one? Or a cruel man being replaced by one even more cruel? The affair of the *Hermione* was not something that happened overnight: it has in fact all the elements of a Greek tragedy: one small and apparently unimportant incident after another increased the tension almost imperceptibly, yet each made the bloody climax more inevitable.

Philip Wilkinson was the son of a barber in Harwich and, in a Navy where the social position was most important in securing promotion, he had obviously done well in obtaining the command of a frigate. The man who helped him was Commodore John Ford, then senior officer on the Jamaica Station and who in September 1794 gave Wilkinson the command of the frigate *Hermione*, so that he became a post captain. (A commanding officer's rank depended on the size of ship: a man commanding anything smaller than a sixth rate would be a commander or less in rank. Command of a sixth rate, like the *Hermione*, was a post for a captain.)

The two log books kept on board a warship—one by the captain and one by the master—are usually taciturn accounts of day-to-day events in a ship. The amount of information they gave depended on the individuals keeping them, and fortunately those for the *Hermione* and *Success* give a good picture of events. But there is also a detailed description of Wilkinson—albeit a prejudiced one—by a man who served under him five years after Wilkinson left the *Hermione*.

John Wetherell, of Whitby, served his apprenticeship at sea in one of the collier brigs sailing between Newcastle and London, carrying to the capital the "sea coal" needed for its hearths. He was then caught by a press-gang and taken on board the frigate *Hussar*, commanded by Wilkinson.

From his account it is clear that Wetherell hated Wilkinson; but better a biased witness than none at all, particularly when much of what he wrote about the *Hussar* bears out conclusions drawn from the *Hermione*'s log for the period of Wilkinson's command. He portrays Wilkinson as a brutal man (who had apparently learned nothing from the *Hermione*'s fate) and describes several episodes which are, unfortunately, impossible to confirm or deny. On one occasion, when the frigate was with the Fleet off Brest, Wetherell says that several members of the crew were so oppressed by Wilkinson's cruelty that they wrote a letter of petition to the admiral commanding the Fleet "beseeching his fatherly aid requesting his honour to snatch us from the paws of our tyrannical prosecution [*sic*]."

About a week later, when the *Hussar* was at Plymouth, a fight between a young midshipman and a seaman resulted, according to Wetherell, in Admiral Sir Robert Calder coming on board to investigate. After hearing both sides of the story, says Wetherell, Sir Robert criticized Wilkinson in front of his crew for his behaviour, saying he had received a hint from Admiral Cornwallis "concerning your ship and crew," and telling Wilkinson to "look back on the unfortunate *Hermione*."

There are various other acts of cruelty described by Wetherell. The *Hussar*, under Wilkinson's command, was finally wrecked and the survivors were taken prisoner. After Wilkinson was exchanged by the French there was the usual court of inquiry over the loss of the ship, but in the absence of witnesses it reached no conclusions. Nevertheless Wilkinson spent most of the rest of his life on half pay, indicating the Admiralty probably had reservations about him, although by stepping into dead men's shoes he eventually became an admiral.

HAVING SEEN Wetherell's account of Captain Wilkinson in 1803, we must put the clock back to 1794, when in the West Indies Wilkinson was appointed to the *Hermione*. From September that year, when he took over command, until early December, the frigate did not move more than a few score miles from Port au Prince. One can imagine Wilkinson's relief when he was ordered to Jamaica, and on

December 6 he wrote: "At anchor in Port Royal Harbour, refitting and taking on stores." The ship stayed there until February 1, 1795, when she sailed back to Port au Prince once again and operated in that area for the rest of the year.

However, we are more concerned with what was happening *in* the *Hermione* than what was happening *to* her. Obviously no log can indicate in precise terms whether the men in a ship were contented or unhappy; but the crimes committed and punishment given can be important clues in the hands of someone who has read a large number of logs, since certain types of crimes were more prevalent in a discontented ship than those in one whose captain was stern but just. Frequent cases of "insolence" and "neglect of duty" are, curiously enough, usually more indicative of an unhappy ship than odd cases of "mutinous behaviour." Seamen preferred a taut and just captain to someone who was free and easy—the latter unwittingly left them at the mercy of cruel officers.

Wilkinson's logs therefore allow us to look back into the past and, to a certain degree, glimpse the kind of life led by the men in the *Hermione* for the last year he was in command. It is unfortunate that for the last half of 1796 the master's log is missing, since this would help confirm the punishment ordered by Wilkinson: there is every reason to suppose, from the curiously spasmodic way floggings were recorded, that Wilkinson did not note down every case in his own log. Nor was there any regulation requiring him to do so.

Since the floggings which Wilkinson listed are given in Appendix B on page 341, there is no need to go into them in detail, beyond noting that he ordered a total of 408 lashes between January 25 and October 12, and it appears strange that although three men received a total of five dozen lashes on April 27, apparently no one was flogged again, if the log is to be believed, until August 16, when three men were given a total of one hundred and eighty lashes.

Much of the trouble on board was due to drink, and while the idea of a drunken seaman collapsing in a besotted heap beside a gun, clawing at the deck in an effort to stop it spinning, is not an edifying one, it is understandable. Most of the *Hermione*'s crew had served on board for more than three years, and the majority had not been allowed on shore for leave for one moment since the day they had set foot on board and been "read in."

Except for the weeks recently spent at Port Royal, when the ship was refitting and taking on stores—back-breaking work beginning before dawn and ending after dusk, often in the blazing sun—they had been cooped up in their tiny ship in fetid, damp heat. Their only amusement—if Captain Wilkinson allowed it, and not every captain did—was an occasional dance to the scraping of a fiddle. They were deprived of the company of other men, for ship to ship visiting was discouraged, and of women. For year after year the men were held in their wooden prison and, what is psychologically more important, they had no idea when—if ever—they would be free again. (Perhaps they were fortunate in not knowing the war was to continue, with only a few months' break, for the next twenty years.)

It was in these conditions that a benevolent Government allowed each man in one of His Majesty's ships of war a free issue of a quarter of a pint of rum in the morning (mixed with three gills of water), and another quarter of a pint (also mixed with three gills of water) in the evening. A man might—and often did—horde his morning tot and add it to the evening's, using half a pint of rum to make himself more pot-valiant or mellow. Hoarding grog was forbidden by regulations which were largely ignored; indeed, a man's tot was valid currency on board—the stake for a wager, payment for a good deed, or as a bribe. But over-indulgence meant a flogging, which was a severe type of punishment.

Although the cat-o'-nine-tails was a terrible instrument of punishment, since the ship's company was always mustered to watch a flogging one must assume that authority intended it should also be a deterrent—both to those flogged, and those who watched. In the *Hermione* under Wilkinson it appears to have been no deterrent; and under Pigot the more flogging there was, the more crimes there were committed on board.

An example of its failure as a deterrent was Walter St. John. Wilkinson ordered him to be given two dozen lashes on April 27 for drunkenness and quarrelling, followed by three dozen lashes on August 16 for neglect of duty. Then on October 24, his back laced with scars, his shirt was once more stripped off and a muscular bosun's mate laid on another couple of dozen lashes—this time for "neglect of duty and insolence."

The almost inevitable progression can be clearly seen. His first crime, getting drunk and quarrelling, had earned him twenty-four lashes. If he had never been flogged before (there is no record of this being the case) and was a man of average sensitivity, when the scars on his back would be much less important than those which remained in his mind: he would have been humiliated and his pride damaged, if not destroyed, and he would probably bear a grudge. His only way of working off this grudge—without being openly mutinous, which was to risk death—would be to do his work slowly or badly (or both). This may have been the reason for the second flogging—thirty-six lashes for neglect of duty. But did those five dozen lashes so terrify or deter him that he did his work properly in the future? Apparently not, for fifty-nine days later he was punished yet again for neglect of duty, only this time it was aggravated by insolence, although he was fortunate to get only two dozen lashes. It had all started with drinking the grog which was issued to him free in over-large quantities. Would it have ended up, after seven dozen lashes, with mutinous conduct if Walter St. John had not been transferred to another ship soon afterwards?

It is worth noting that although according to regulations captains could not order a man to be given more than a dozen lashes without asking the commander-in-chief, a number of captains ordered a great many more without seeking permission (which was often impossible because they were at sea) and never hesitated to enter the fact in the log, a copy of which had to be sent off to the Admiralty every three months. The Admiralty clearly did not enforce the regulation: indeed in 1806 the limit of a dozen was removed from the *Regulations and Instructions.*

FOR THE LAST MONTH of 1796 the *Hermione* spent most of her time at anchor in St. Marc Bay, carrying out a partial self-refit. "Employed overhauling the topmast rigging . . . Sent a gang wooding," the log records for the 13th. Wooding (which, as its name implies, was simply collecting firewood for the ship's coppers) and watering were the only opportunities that the men had of setting foot on shore, and even then they were always working under the watchful eyes of marine sentries, who stood with their muskets primed and bayonets fixed.

On December 27 Captain Wilkinson received orders to raid a village north of St. Marc, whose inhabitants were proving troublesome. The log reports laconically: "At 8 A.M. run inshore and fired a broadside at Coridans Salt Pans. $^1/_2$ past 9 a lieutenant and two master's mates with the boats manned and armed went on shore and set fire to the village. Rowed along the shore and took possession of two boats and finding the enemy collecting very numerous they returned with the boats they had taken. Hoisted in the boats and tacked ship." By noon on New Year's Eve the ship was back at anchor in St. Marc Bay.

So the year 1796 passed. For Wilkinson and the *Hermione*'s crew it had been one of boredom: not a penny in prize money, and the only action had been the miserable raid on the village. Yet for most of the men the only thing that made up for the perils of yellow fever and the heat was the chance of prize money.

On January 14 a cutter arrived with orders for Wilkinson from Sir Hyde Parker: a storeship was soon due and the *Hermione*, after taking on stores from her, was to sail for Cape Nicolas Mole, arriving not later than February 4.

The promised storeship duly arrived, and while Captain Pigot was facing a court of inquiry at the Mole over the Jesup episode, Captain Wilkinson noted in the *Hermione*'s log, "Received a quantity of Gunner's, Carpenter's and Boatswain's stores . . ."

A few days later the *Hermione* sailed for the Mole, arriving on the afternoon of February 4. Wilkinson saw that the anchorage was crowded with heavily-laden merchantmen waiting to make up a convoy for England, while others, their paint worn and blistered and the rigging slack after a long Atlantic crossing, had obviously just arrived from England.

Wilkinson's barge was lowered and soon he was on board the *Queen*, reporting to the commander-in-chief. Sir Hyde (who had of course received the report of the Pigot inquiry into the Jesup affair and was faced with the problem of the *Success*'s return to England) appears to have recalled the *Hermione* purposely to arrange for Wilkinson and Pigot to exchange ships. Since Wilkinson had spent two and a half fruitless years in the *Hermione* without finding a worthwhile prize, and probably realized that he could expect no patronage or advancement from Sir Hyde, it is unlikely he had any regrets at leaving both the ship and the West Indies in favour of the Channel.

It is clear that Philip Wilkinson's major shortcoming was that his leadership was based on the Articles of War, not on his own personality, assurance and talent. A born leader had no need to use the Articles, save in exceptional circumstances. However, we must now move on to the man who inherited the *Hermione,* and made her name and his synonymous with sadistic cruelty.

IV

In Father's Lee

—ɯ—

I F NEPTUNE EVER SMILED on a young boy, he must have done so when Hugh Pigot stepped on board His Majesty's ship *Jupiter* on Sunday, May 5, 1782, to start his naval career at the age of twelve and a half. His father, who had brought him to Plymouth, where the *Jupiter* lay at anchor in the Hamoaze, preceded him on board and on the quarterdeck was greeted by a Captain's Guard. While a marine officer bellowed "Present your arms" to the neat scarlet-jacketed men, a band struck up a march and a large blue flag was broken out at the maintruck.

The individual details of this colourful ritual were no doubt lost on the boy, but its significance was not, for his father was Admiral Hugh Pigot, who was carrying with him an Admiralty Commission, immaculately inscribed in copperplate handwriting and embossed with a great seal, appointing him in time-honoured but melodious phrases, "Commander-in-Chief of His Majesty's ships and vessels employed or to be employed at and about Jamaica and the Bahama Islands, etc."

Pomp and ceremony, stirring marches and deferential salutes— these were the boy's first glimpses of the Navy as he stood watching his father acknowledging all the honours due to an admiral with such an exalted appointment, and undoubtedly they were to condition his whole future attitude to the Navy. But before seeing how the boy fared at sea in the lee of his illustrious father, it is worth noting what traits he had inherited, for better or worse, from his family.

The most important among them were his father and two uncles, George and Robert, who were the sons of Richard Pigot, of Westminster, and his wife, Frances. This trio, all of whom were to find fame and fortune, mostly by their own unaided efforts, were brought up without the discipline a wise father imposes during childhood, and the help, assurance and guidance he can offer to youth, because Richard Pigot died when only forty-seven years old.

George, in addition to being the eldest and the most turbulent, is the one who, as the narrative will later show, yields the most clues to the character of his nephew. In apprenticing him to the Honourable East India Company as a writer when he was seventeen years old, Frances Pigot had made a wise choice for her son, since India—in the form of "John Company," as it was generally called—usually gave a generous reward to those of its employees who survived the natural hazards of service.

By the time George was thirty-two he was—with the help of a young lieutenant named Robert Clive—helping relieve the British garrison besieged at Trichinopoly by a native army of 8,000; at thirty-six he was Governor and commander-in-chief of Madras and father of the two daughters presented him by his mistress, who died shortly afterwards. But despite native revolts and French attacks, George Pigot's main enemy was himself: his methods were autocratic and bullying and they made him many enemies among men with whom daily he had to work. He clearly loved power, and when it was given to him at the age of thirty-six he made bold decisions with no fear of the responsibility. But his judgment was poor and he frequently acted too hastily, seldom giving a thought for the consequences of his actions.

When the long war with France ended in 1763 George Pigot was forty-five and rich, so he returned to England, where—as became a rich nabob—he was created a baronet and became a Whig Member of Parliament. An Irish barony followed and he took the title of Baron Pigot of Patshull in the County of Dublin. He bought the Patshull estate in Staffordshire to go with it, reputedly paying Sir John Astley £100,000 for it. He also took another mistress, Mrs.

Catherine Hill, of Pepper Hill, Shropshire, who presented him with three sons in succession.

India was still a troubled continent, and by the time his third son was born Lord Pigot was on his way back to India. However, his Lordship's twelve-year absence in England had not mellowed him; nor had his autocratic and bullying methods changed, and he was soon involved in quarrels. But he made a grave mistake in the course of one dispute, trifling in itself and too complicated to deal with here, by arresting a member of the Council and putting him in jail. He miscalculated the effect on the other members, some of whom imprisoned him and freed his former prisoner. Not unnaturally his Lordship's activities caused a stir in England. Pigot had both friends and enemies among the General Court of the East India Company, which finally resolved that he should be restored to his position as Governor, but nevertheless his conduct on several occasions had been "reprehensible," and that powers he had taken were not authorized by charter or warranted by any orders or instructions.

The court worked out a face-saving formula by which it restored him as Governor by a commission dated June 10, 1777, and at the same time ordered him to give up the Governorship a week later. But Pigot's enemies in Madras had kept him in prison while all the controversy was going on in London, and he fell ill, dying on May 11 at the age of fifty-eight.

Lord Pigot left the Patshull estate to his brother Robert, who inherited the baronetcy, but the Irish title lapsed, since his sons were illegitimate. The other tangible sign of wealth that his Lordship had found in India was the huge Pigot Diamond, weighing 188 grains and which he left to his two brothers and sister, who sold it by a lottery for £23,998.

While George had been in India, his second brother Robert, who was two years younger, was having a successful career in the Army. At the age of twenty-four he fought in his first battle, Fontenoy, and was to become a lieutenant-general. The third brother, Hugh, had in the meantime entered the Navy. Obtaining his first command, the fireship *Vulcan*, at the age of twenty-three, he was "made post" by being given temporary command of the *Centaur* (for the rank went with the appointment). His first real command was the 44-gun *Ludlow Castle*. In the next few years he saw a good deal of active service:

he was commanding the 60-gun *York* in the highly-successful assault on Louisberg in 1758; a few months later he commanded the *Royal William* under Admiral Sir Charles Saunders. But, with the end of the Seven Years War early in 1763, Captain Hugh Pigot went on shore. His turbulent brother George had just resigned as Governor of Madras and was on his way home. Hugh was then forty-two years old, and his wife Elizabeth had borne him two children, Isabella, who was then thirteen (and destined to be a friend of George IV and Mrs. Fitzherbert), and Henry, a year younger. With the Navy being drastically reduced there was little chance of further employment, and he settled down to the life of a country gentleman.

When George arrived back from India and became a Member of Parliament and a baronet, Hugh began to take an interest in politics as a Whig, like his brother. His domestic life, however, was upset by the death of his wife; but he soon married again, this time to Frances Wrottesley, a daughter of Sir Richard Wrottesley, Bt, whose brother-in-law was to become the Marquis of Stafford. Hugh thus became linked by marriage to one of the most powerful of the Staffordshire families and one with strong naval connections and political influence. His brother George had in the meantime bought the Patshull estate.

In 1769, Hugh's second wife presented him with a son, the subject of this book, and on September 5 he was christened at the parish church of Patshull, being given the name of Hugh, after his father and his great-grandfather. He was two years old when his father was given the command of the *Triumph* but did not take up the appointment. Nevertheless it did not affect promotion because, of course, progress up the captains list was automatic: admirals dying meant everyone else moved up the appropriate number of places.

Finally in March 1775 (a few days before his brother Robert fought at Lexington in the opening round of the American War of Independence) Captain Hugh was promoted Rear-Admiral of the White, second from lowest of the nine grades of admiral. The jump over the first was due to the fairly rapid expansion of the Navy in anticipation of the war, and in December he became Vice-Admiral of the Blue, four steps up the nine-rung ladder to the highest rank the Navy could offer. His previous experience had been as the captain of an 84-gun ship, which hardly equipped him for his present rank; but for the time being it was no handicap because, although the

American War was in full swing, the Whigs had fallen and the To-ries—the "King's Friends"—were in power under Lord North, whose leadership was mostly confined to acting as horse-holder for the King. Whig admirals like Pigot could not expect employment; but no Government could stop his promotion, because providing he lived he stepped into dead men's shoes.

Only Robert Pigot was engaged in the war, which slid from one calamitous situation to another. General Burgoyne surrendered at Saratoga in 1777; France joined the Colonists in 1778, followed by Spain in 1779, and Holland a year later, while Prussia and the north-ern powers formed an "armed neutrality." Britain staggered on in isolation, a cantankerous King at the wheel and a sycophantic gov-ernment manning the pumps.

Although the years sped by, Vice-Admiral Pigot received no summons from the Admiralty. His brother George died in India, but the admiral and his family continued to live at Patshull, looking after George's three sons (the eldest was within a few months of the same age as his own boy Hugh, and all four were playmates at Patshull).

Finally Cornwallis, besieged at Yorktown, had to surrender, thus ensuring that America was lost—or won, depending on one's view-point. The long-overdue collapse of the "King's Friends" followed, and with the Tories routed the Whigs formed a new government in March 1782. Hugh Pigot's fortunes changed with equally dramatic suddenness: on March 30 Admiral Lord Keppel became the new First Lord of the Admiralty and on the same day he made Pigot a Lord Commissioner—in other words a member of the Board—and a few days later promoted him to be Admiral of the Blue.

Pigot was still digesting his good fortune when Keppel made him commander-in-chief in the West Indies to replace Sir George Brydges Rodney, whose Tory politics had, of course, put him com-pletely out of favour with the new Government. Pigot's meteoric rise in less than a month is a good example of the powerful and utterly disastrous part that politics played in the Navy; but it was also useful to him since it solved the problem of a naval career for his second son, Hugh, who had just passed his twelfth birthday.

Since the admiral was about to sail for the West Indies, young Hugh would go as well. As the commander-in-chief's son he would be assured of the best of everything, ranging from food to the deference of his captain, but excepting the sound training in the vagaries of human nature which the knock-about life of the midshipmen's berth would have given him. For him there would be none of the misery that usually greeted a youngster on first going to sea; no one would dare bully him overmuch with Admiral Pigot in the offing. The rough-and-tumble discipline which made a man out of a youngster, teaching him assurance and tolerance, and demonstrating what real leadership entailed at all levels, would be missing from young Hugh's early, formative months at sea.

Admiral Pigot and his entourage arrived at Plymouth, and on May 5 he hoisted his flag in the *Jupiter,* comfortably accommodated under the watchful eye of her captain, a far from dour Scot named Thomas Pasley. On May 18 the *Jupiter* sailed. ("Ship very much lumbered by the vast quantities of stores, chests and etc, brought on board by the Admiral . . . and croud [*sic*] of followers," noted Captain Pasley in his private journal.)

As Admiral Pigot settled into his cot that night he was no doubt delighted to be at sea again; but his departure was a dreadful example of political expediency. The command in the West Indies was then one of the most important in the Navy: Rodney, whom Pigot was replacing, commanded a fleet which included six 90-gun line-of-battle ships, twenty-one 74s and nine 64s. Pigot, it will be recalled, had not been to sea for nineteen years and had never served in any higher capacity than captain of an 84-gun ship.

Captain Pasley unwittingly added an ironic postscript to the situation in his journal next day: "Weather blustery and disagreeable. The Admiral and all his youngsters most heartily seasick owing to his not having been at sea for nineteen years."

But while the Pigot family were united in their misery, and Pasley noted "uncommonly cold for the season of the year—such as old men does not remember," the admiral's departure had caused a major crisis in Whitehall, and even as he retched his way out of the Channel, a cutter was flogging her way to windward in an effort to catch him up to deliver urgent orders from the Admiralty—orders which told him not to sail.

THE CRISIS was caused by the arrival of a dispatch to the Admiralty from the West Indies telling them that within a few hours of Pigot being given his commission as the new commander-in-chief in the West Indies, the man he was to replace, Rodney, had won a decisive victory over the French Fleet at the Battle of the Saintes, capturing five French line-of-battle ships, including the huge flagship, the *Ville de Paris*.

London—indeed the whole of Britain—would go mad with joy when Rodney's news was published and the Government, knowing Pigot was on the eve of sailing (if he had not actually left), could visualize the mob's reaction when they heard their new-found hero had just been sacked. . . .

The First Lord hurriedly drafted new instructions ordering Pigot not to sail to the West Indies, and sent them off by a special messenger who was told to deliver them at all cost. The man galloped to Plymouth, where he found that although the *Jupiter* had sailed twenty-four hours earlier, there was just a chance that a fast cutter could catch her before she left the chops of the Channel. He put to sea, but ran into the same bad weather that was disturbing the admiral and had to turn back.

While London rejoiced, the King and Parliament hastily prepared to shower Rodney with praise, pension and a peerage. The *Jupiter* meanwhile bore the Pigots across the Atlantic and Captain Pasley wrote some illuminating comments in his private journal. "The Admiral seems the perfect gentleman, affable and agreeable, which makes the service I am employed on the more agreeable," he commented after Pigot had been on board four days.

Nor did the passing days—which did not bring them the right winds—make him change his first impressions: by the end of June he still found the admiral "pleasing, affable, good company," and he wrote, "I do not think any admiral can be more pleasing in service or to serve than Admiral Pigot." He had but one reservation: "I have my fears when he comes to command so large a fleet: in that line he can have no experience, and from what I have seen a change must be worked to cutt a figure—but let me not judge rashly."

On July 10 the *Jupiter* arrived at Port Royal, Jamaica, where a startled Admiral Pigot, unaware of the recent battle, saw an extraordinary sight. "We found Admirals Sir George Rodney, Rowley, Sir Samuel Hood and Drake, thirty-seven ships of the line besides frigates, and the French ships taken," wrote Pasley. ". . . Such a Fleet, or such a number of flags, never was seen before in this Western World."

The fleet soon had more news from London—news which must have dispelled some of the bitterness over Rodney's sudden displacement by Pigot: Rodney himself had received a peerage (and by the time he returned to his house in Hertford Street, Mayfair, Parliament had voted him a pension of £2,000 a year, to pass on to his heirs: this must have been welcome to a man who had once spent four years in France owing to debts). Hood, too, had received a peerage.

Hood did not return to England with Rodney: instead he stayed on in the West Indies as second-in-command, and he left his opinion of Pigot on record. In his view Lord Keppel had been most unpatriotic "in placing an officer at the head of so great a Fleet who was so unequal to the very important command through want of practise." Pigot, he said, had neither foresight, judgment nor enterprise, otherwise "he might have had a very noble chance for rendering a good account both of the French and Spanish squadrons."

THE COMMANDER-IN-CHIEF'S INEXPERIENCE had no effect on his son Hugh, who stayed in the flagship with his father for the next few months. However, negotiations for peace which had begun early in 1783 were concluded by the end of the year and the admiral hauled down his flag and returned to England, leaving Hugh behind. Within a few weeks the Government changed, and with it the Board of Admiralty, of which the admiral was still a member. He retired to Bath, his career as a sailor finished.

His young son Hugh, however, stayed at sea: he was sent from the West Indies to the *Assistance* on the America Station, staying in her for two years before being transferred to the *Trusty*, which brought him back to the West Indies. On August 31, 1789, he passed his examination for lieutenant. Under the regulations he had to be twenty years old before he could serve as a lieutenant and he had only a day or two to wait before his birthday. But the lad had been out of England for more than seven years, and he received permission to return for leave. (Many of the dates for Pigot's appointments and promotions are given wrongly in the *Dictionary of National Biography*. See note on pages 353–54).

After seeing his father, mother and two sisters, he set off the next July to join the 74-gun *Colossus* as fifth lieutenant. She was commanded by a friend of his father's, Captain Hugh Cloberry

Christian, who had served under the admiral in the West Indies. With Britain at peace, the Navy was being cut down. Lieutenants and captains—even experienced ones, men who had several times distinguished themselves in battle—were two a penny; indeed, many were serving in merchant ships. It needed influence to get an appointment—particularly in a ship like the *Colossus,* and Lieutenant Pigot was fortunate since he did not lack that commodity.

Within a couple of months Captain Christian was replaced by Captain Henry Harvey, and either the young fifth lieutenant impressed Harvey or influence was at work, because within a few weeks Hugh was made fourth and, on January 7, 1791, third lieutenant. He had been on board six months and two days, and his promotion had been rapid. However, he remained third lieutenant for the next fifteen months, until April 24, 1792, when he suffered a demotion, being transferred to the 50-gun *Assistance,* a much smaller ship, as fourth lieutenant.

His father died in December of that year, and he had to wait nine months—until January 28, 1793—before he was made third lieutenant again. But on February 1 the great war with Revolutionary France began, and the Navy hurriedly expanded: ships were rushed into commission and officers were recalled. On April 5 Hugh was once again a fourth lieutenant, but this time it was a promotion because the ship was the 98-gun *London,* commanded by Captain Richard Keats. His new appointment did him little good as far as experience was concerned because the *London* spent a long time in the dockyard being fitted out as a flagship. This was unfortunate, for Hugh might have learned a great deal about leadership and the handling of men from that staunch Devonian Keats, who was a close friend of Nelson.

Pigot's next appointment was in January 1794, as first lieutenant of the 38-gun frigate *Latona.* It was at this point, it seems, that interest really went to work to help him along the road of promotion, and it probably came from the direction of the Leveson-Gowers and his uncle, Lieutenant-General Sir Robert Pigot. Hugh had been the *Latona*'s first lieutenant only a month when he was given command of the fireship *Incendiary;* but this was simply a device to make him a commander, and eleven days later, on February 21, he was given command of the 18-gun sloop *Swan,* which had been built at Plymouth two years before her new commanding officer had been born.

Pigot was now twenty-four years old, and apart from the brief month as first lieutenant of the *Latona*, his previous highest appointment had been as third lieutenant in the *Colossus*. His new command was at Jamaica, and he had to cross the Atlantic to join her.

He arrived in the West Indies and took over the *Swan* in April. Within a fortnight he was writing the letter to the Admiralty, referred to earlier, complaining of the language used by the master of the *Canada* after she collided with the *Swan*; within six months he was "made post" and given command of the frigate *Success*. The *Swan*, of 300 tons and armed with eighteen guns, had a crew of about eighty men. The *Success* was roughly twice her size, with thirty-two guns, plus carronades, and a complement of 215 men. Thus, with at the most twenty weeks' experience of command, he now had the power of life and death over ten-score men. The order appointing him to the *Success*, signed by Commodore Ford, was dated September 4, a day short of twenty-five years after he was christened at Patshull. By coincidence, Commodore Ford next day appointed Captain Philip Wilkinson to command the frigate *Hermione*.

In Hugh Pigot's case, history was repeating itself with a vengeance: his father, Admiral Hugh, had arrived with his young son in the West Indies in 1782 to take over Rodney's great fleet with no greater experience than that of captain of an 84-gun ship; now, twelve years later, his son, relatively even less experienced, had been given a frigate.

V

The Red Baize Bag

—∞—

HIS MAJESTY'S FRIGATE *SUCCESS* was anchored in
Port Royal when Captain Pigot went on board to take
command on September 4, 1794. In pouring rain, with a
strong wind whipping it across the decks, he read to the ship's
company Commodore Ford's order appointing him to her. He had
not been in the ship more than a couple of hours before a boat came
alongside and two hungry, rain-soaked men were brought on board
under guard and handed over to the master-at-arms. They had deserted from the ship a few days earlier, but their taste of freedom
had been brief.

The *Success*, built at Liverpool between 1779 and 1781 at a cost of
£13,759 16s. 9d., had an official complement of 215 men. This was the
number the Navy Board regarded as necessary to sail and fight the
ship. But a ship's official complement was, in time of war, usually
just a number: most captains had to make do with many fewer men.
Hugh Pigot's first task in his new command was therefore one of the
most difficult that continually faced a captain in wartime: finding
enough seamen so that he could report to the commander-in-chief in
the time honoured phrase that the ship was "in every respect ready
for sea."

The muster book was brought to him, so that he could read the figures written against the phrases, "Total borne considered as complement," and "Short of Complement." The book told him a dreary but familiar story, particularly the column headed "D, D.D., or R," which were three abbreviations indicating the only ways a seaman could leave His Majesty's service. "D" stood for "Discharged"—to another ship, to a hospital or for some other officially endorsed reason; "D.D." was the gruesome way of reporting that a man had died, either from illness, accident or in battle, and had thus been "Discharged Dead." The third abbreviation, "R," stood for "Run," the Navy's way of saying a man had deserted.

Captain Pigot's first orders were to prepare the ship for sea: certain rigging had to be repaired—and more men had to be found. He told the surgeon to report how many of the *Success's* sick in the hospital were sufficiently recovered to be brought back on board, and three days later was told there were a dozen. A boat was sent off to fetch them, but the *Success's* net gain was only eleven, because while the boat waited at the quay one of its crew managed to slip away and vanish among the streets of Port Royal.

For the rest of September, life on board the *Success* was comparatively uneventful, if Captain Pigot's log gave a fair picture. He watched the men at work and gradually came to know them, singling out certain men for promotion. Henry Croaker, for instance, who came from Plymouth, was made Yeoman of the Powder Room on September 13. It meant little in terms of his pay, which was increased by a shilling to 26s. a month, but it was a position of great trust, since Croaker would have, under the gunner, responsibility for the storage of the gunpowder. Pigot's choice of Croaker was the first example of his unerring—and, as far as the *Success* and later the *Hermione*, were concerned, fatal—instinct for putting his trust in the wrong people.

September soon came to an end, and with it the first twenty-six days of life in the *Success* under Captain Pigot. No floggings had been noted in the log, and only one man had deserted. However, for most of the crew of the frigate, October marked the beginning of twenty-seven months of bullying, misery and dejection, when (with the exception of the captain's favourites) many of the men were to be treated like criminals and driven to the limits—but for the time being not beyond—of mental and physical endurance. Although Pigot was still busy trying to get more men for the ship, the month began with a series of desertions. On the 3rd he had to go on shore, and while his barge was waiting one of the crew seized the opportunity to desert. This loss was more than balanced by a haul of four men brought in by a press-gang that Pigot sent the same day to search some merchantmen anchored nearby. Finally in the first sixteen days of October Captain Pigot had obtained ten men from his press-gang, lost four trained seamen by desertion, and had another deserter brought back.

On October 22, Pigot showed his teeth: he ordered five men to be flogged, and the day was rounded off by a man who had been sentenced to be flogged round the fleet being brought alongside the *Success* so that one of her boatswain's mates could administer the *Success*'s share of the punishment.

Since the cat-o'-nine-tails and flogging enter into this narrative with painful frequency, both must be described if the significance of the subsequent events is to be understood. The cat was used in both the Navy and the Army, although the Navy type was a lot heavier and, according to one of the leading authorities on naval jurisprudence writing in 1813, "It has been the ancient practice and usage in the Navy for the commanders to have the cat-of-nine-tails made of a cord of a certain weight and texture, that the same force or power applied to one lash, is equal to four of the common cat used in the Army." He declared that "one dozen of lashes, according to the present mode of discipline, applied to the bare back by a boatswain's mate, furnished with a naval cat-of-nine-tails, is equivalent to at least fifty lashes laid on by a drummer with a military cat." The explanation he gives for the difference in the sizes and weights of the cats is simple: since the naval captains were by regulation limited (before 1806) to ordering a maximum of a dozen lashes, they used heavier tails.

The naval cat-o'-nine-tails consisted of a handle about two feet long, usually made of rope but sometimes of wood, and an inch in diameter—about as thick as the average broom handle. To one end of the handle were secured the nine "tails," each two feet long and made of line a quarter of an inch in diameter—a fraction less than the thickness of a normal pencil. The tails were never knotted unless the man was being punished for theft, in which case each tail was knotted every three inches or so.

A rope-handled cat weighed between thirteen and fourteen

ounces. These dimensions and weight were general and probably varied slightly: one of the last cat-o'-nine-tails used in the Navy— on board H.M.S. *Malacca* in 1867—is covered in red baize and is two feet long. Each tail is also two feet long and a quarter of an inch in diameter. (Experiments made recently with a cat of these dimensions are described in Appendix A, page 339.)

When wielded by a strong man one lash from the cat would knock down the victim from the sheer impact, and the boatswain's mate, who had to put all his strength into each blow, was replaced after he had delivered only a dozen lashes.

Obviously the cat-o'-nine-tails, being of a standard weight, was administered with roughly the same power; thus the effect of a dozen lashes varied only with the type of victim; some men were more sensitive to pain; others had more pride, a sense of honour, which was damaged. Three dozen lashes could kill one man; another would survive 200. Probably the greatest indictment of indiscriminate flogging was that the number of lashes were ordered on the assumption that every man had the same kind of physique and personality, making no allowances for the sensitive man or the type who was by nature tough and brutal and who would be a criminal in any age or environment.

Since each was different it is understandable that we get diametrically opposed descriptions of what flogging felt like. To one man it was "nothing but an O, a few O my Gods, and then you can put on your shirt"; but another man, a soldier and flogged with a lighter cat-o'-nine-tails, wrote that after the first two or three strokes "the pain in my lungs was more severe, I thought, than on my back. I felt as if I would burst in the internal parts of my body . . . I put my tongue between my teeth, held it there, and bit in almost two pieces. What with the blood from my tongue, and my lips, which I had also bitten, and the blood from my lungs, or some other internal part, ruptured by the writhing agony, I was almost choked, and became black in the face."

An eyewitness said that after two dozen lashes (which was Pigot's normal punishment for drunkenness) "the lacerated back looks inhuman; it resembles roasted meat burnt nearly black before a scorching fire." One authority said that "some captains boasted of having left-handed boatswain's mates who could cross the cuts made by the right-handed man."

The reasons why the Admiralty abolished the limit of a dozen lashes when the *Regulations and Instructions* of 1790 were revised in 1806 have never been given; but in their wisdom, the Board probably saw little point in continuing a regulation which they knew was being openly flouted—so openly that captains recorded the fact in their logs.

Courts-martial could, and of course did, award large numbers of lashes for serious crimes. Normally both captains and courts awarded them in dozens, up to eight or nine dozen; after that they were usually given in hundreds. On comparatively rare occasions captains ordered the extra half-dozen, and a few cases are recorded of less than a dozen being given.

It has already been pointed out that the lonely life of a captain and the strain under which he lived led to the danger that his character and judgment would become warped, and William James, one of the most respected and accurate historians of the war at sea against Revolutionary France, who knew a great many contemporary officers, wrote of flogging: "Captains there are who seemingly delight in such work; and who, were the cruise long enough, would not leave a sailor with an unscarred back."

Only a year after the Admiralty had abolished the dozen limit, a lieutenant at Bombay ordered three men to be flogged and, Sir Samuel Romilly wrote, "the punishment was inflicted with such horrible severity that they all three died in less than twenty-four hours after it was over." Such cruelty was rare, although plain harshness was more frequent. But the majority of captains were just and popular: the crew of the *Vestal*, for example, having heard in 1794 that their captain was being appointed to another ship, petitioned to be allowed to sail with him.

Any judgment of the seaman's conditions in Pigot's day would be unbalanced without considering the way the seaman's civilian brother lived on shore. As far as justice was concerned—if that is not using too strong a word—the civilian was far worse off since he could be, and frequently was, hanged if he committed one of nearly two hundred offences. It was a brutal age: that factor must be borne in mind all the way through this narrative. The gibbet, the whipping post and pillory were all there for the errant civilian; and every hanging in Britain was public, attended by a noisy and jostling crowd who behaved as if it was a prize-fight, cheering the condemned man who stepped bravely to the scaffold and jeering at the reluctant.

Justice at sea under the Articles of War, if fairly administered, was considerably more merciful than justice on land under the laws of England. The trouble was that the life at sea gave more scope for both wrong-doing and the unfair administration of justice. Like all rules and regulations, they were only as good as the men who administered them. In the hands of Pigot the Articles merely licensed sadism; in the hands of a reasonable man they were a good rule-of-thumb method of providing immediate and rough justice.

ON OCTOBER 22, 1794, after he had been in command of the *Success* for six weeks, Captain Pigot ordered the first lieutenant to send all hands aft to witness punishment. The boatswain's mates were soon at the hatchways, their calls shrilling and the ship echoing to the shouts of "D'ye hear there: all hands aft to witness punishment! D'ye hear there . . ."

In the *Success*, and later the *Hermione*, men to be flogged were lashed to the capstan: their arms were tied along one of the bars which radiated from the capstan drum like spokes of a wheel lying on its side. (In most ships it was more usual to up-end a wooden grating at the gangway.) The boatswain's mates had not finished piping and shouting the order at the hatches before the men started to run on deck, to gather in groups near the capstan, which was just forward of the wheel. The marines with muskets and bayonets clattered up the ladders, perspiring freely in uniforms which were ill adapted for any climate, least of all the tropics; the doctor joined the officers standing in a group on the starboard side. The master-at-arms then brought his five prisoners on deck, helped by the ship's corporal and a marine armed with a musket.

In a moment there was silence in the ship: in front of Captain Pigot, as he faced forward, were the solid row of red-coated marines; to his right a small knot of officers; to his left were the five prisoners; on both sides were the seamen. Pigot was in full uniform of dark blue, with lapels edged with gold, and an inappropriate white-handled cavalry officer's sword, which however had the virtue of lightness, hung at his left side.

Pigot glanced down at the sheet of paper he had been holding. He read out the first of five names written on it. "John McWilliam!"

One of the five prisoners shuffled forward, the master-at-arms at his side. Pigot wasted no time: the man was accused of drunkenness and showing contempt to his superior officer. Had he anything to say? McWilliam's answer, if indeed he made one, is not recorded. However, the captain was prosecutor, defence counsel, jury and judge, so that no time was lost in deciding if McWilliam was guilty.

The seaman, his eyes still bloodshot from the previous night's ill-considered assault on his hoarded grog, was led to the capstan, and Pigot gave the order for McWilliam to strip. The man pulled off his shirt, so that he was bare from the waist up, and then stood with his arms outstretched along a capstan bar and his legs wide apart. The boatswain's mates then lashed his wrists to the bar.

"Seized up, sir," reported the master-at-arms.

Pigot then opened a copy of the Articles of War, and started reading from number thirty-six (the so-called Captain's Cloak) which covered "All other crimes not capital, committed by any person or persons in the Fleet, which are not mentioned in this Act . . ." While the Article was being recited everyone, including Pigot, had removed their hats. Pigot concluded: ". . . shall be punished according to the Laws and Customs of such cases used at sea." He then announced the sentence—two dozen lashes.

A boatswain's mate produced a red baize bag, took out a cat-o'-nine-tails and shook it, so that the tails fell free. "Do your duty," Pigot ordered.

Standing behind and to one side of McWilliam, he swung the cat back to the full extent of his arm then, like a suddenly released spring, brought it down on the man's bare back.

"One," counted the master-at-arms.

Again the cat swung through the air. "Two," intoned the master-at-arms. At roughly twenty-second intervals the cat fell. The surgeon watched to see that the man did not lose consciousness; Captain Pigot watched to make sure the boatswain's mate was using all his strength.

When the last of the two dozen lashes fell on McWilliam's back, the seizings holding him to the capstan bar were cut and he was taken below to wait for the surgeon to attend to him—it was well known that even the slightest cut tended to suppurate in a tropical climate. The next name was called and the second of the five men stepped forward. For the third and fourth men the floggings were the first of a series that were to last for almost a year.

Finally Pigot told the first lieutenant to dismiss the men; but the day's floggings had not finished, and the next session was to be the worst. The previous day, Captain Pigot had received an order from Commodore Ford saying, "When the signal for punishment is made tomorrow morning, you are to send a lieutenant with a boat manned and armed from the ship under your command to His Majesty's ship *Europa* in order to attend the punishment of John Omeburg, private Marine, pursuant to the sentence of a court martial."

In other words, Marine Omeburg—whose crime had been mutiny—was to be flogged through the fleet, receiving 300 lashes (if he did not die before the last one was administered). The total of 300 had been divided equally among the warships in the anchorage, each captain being told the number of lashes his boatswain's mates would be responsible for administering.

Flogging through the fleet was a spectacle which for magnitude and sheer horror would have made many a Roman emperor jealous. Port Royal anchorage was a vastly more impressive amphitheatre than the Colosseum in Rome, and even Nero could not have set in motion with the flutter of a signal a comparable ceremony as that in the great warships when their guns began booming and a procession of boats bore the victim to receive his punishment.

The men had already drunk their morning ration of rum and eaten their dinner when, promptly at 1 P.M., a gun was fired from the *Europa* and a yellow flag fluttered at the foretopmast head. From every warship in the anchorage, including the *Success*, a boat commanded by a lieutenant, and carrying two armed marines in addition to its normal crew, was sent off to the *Europa*, whose launch was already alongside, a grating rigged up vertically amidships.

Eventually the launch, followed by a procession of boats from the other ships, arrived alongside the *Success,* a drummer in the bow beating the lugubrious "Rogue's March." Marine Omeburg, who had already been flogged alongside several vessels, was lashed to the grating once again.

All the men of the *Success* were in the rigging or standing on the nettings; and one of the boatswain's mates, clutching a red baize bag, climbed down into the launch. The provost marshal—who acted as the squadron's chief of police—then read out in a stentorian voice the sentence of the court that had tried Marine Omeburg. Finally Captain Pigot bawled down from the gangway, "Boatswain's mate! Do your duty."

For the sixth time that day the men of the *Success* heard the dull swish of the cat, and saw the wounds it inflicted on a spread-eagled man. Finally, the *Success*'s share of the 300 lashes having been laid on, the marine was cut down.

On the day just described, when Captain Pigot began flogging in the *Success*, he had been in command for forty-seven days. Although the operations carried out by the frigate for the rest of his command do not concern us, it is important to know the way he treated the frigate's crew.

His log, the only one to survive, begins when he joined the *Success* on September 4, 1794, and ends on September 30, 1795, the last flogging being on September 11. The punishment the log records is most revealing, both for its severity and inconsistency.

From the time of the first floggings in October 1794 until the last entered in the log is a period of forty-six weeks; but it is probable that for more than eight weeks between June 3 and August 3, when the ship was at Port Royal, Pigot was not actually on board, because no floggings are recorded. In the preceding twenty-one weeks the longest gaps between recorded floggings were thirty-three, seventeen and eleven days, although the usual space was between two and seven days. It is likely that Pigot was also on shore for the thirty-three-day period, since the ship was also in Port Royal at that time.

However, for an examination of the floggings ordered by Pigot only the longest period, eight weeks, has been subtracted from the forty-six weeks he was in command. During these thirty-eight weeks, Pigot recorded eighty-five separate floggings, when he ordered a total of at least 1,392 lashes to be administered—a weekly average of two floggings totalling thirty-eight lashes. In that period there were between 160 and 170 men on board the frigate, so that Pigot had flogged the equivalent of half the crew.

However, several men were flogged more than once; and the total of 1,392 lashes is also on the low side, because Pigot actually logged 1,272 lashes but in noting ten other floggings he omitted to mention how many lashes were given. He would not have ordered less than a dozen—as mentioned earlier, there are very few recorded instances of less than a dozen being given by anyone, and certainly Pigot is not responsible for any of them—so 120 lashes have been added to his total of 1,272, although in all probability there were many more. A complete list of all the floggings for the period with which we are concerned, October 22, 1794, to September 11, 1795, is given in Appendix C. The following table gives details of the men who received the *most* punishment during that period.

TABLE I

Name	Date		Crime	Number
William Morrison	Oct.	22, 1794	Drunkenness, contempt	12
	Dec.	6	Disobedience and contempt	24
	Dec.	8	Disobedience and contempt	24
	April	11, 1795	Gambling	12
	May	4	Disorderly behaviour	12
John Charles				
(died Sept. 26)	April	25, 1795	Disorderly behaviour	12
	May	4	Disobedience	12
	May	21	Insolence and contempt	12
John Finney	Dec.	26, 1794	Not given	12
	Dec.	31	Sleeping on his post	12
	March	25, 1795	Neglect of duty	12
Jeremiah Walsh				
(died Sept. 30)	Aug.	4, 1795	Neglect of duty	24
	Sept.	11	Drunkenness and contempt	12
Martin Steady	Nov.	26, 1794	Neglect and contempt	12
	March	5, 1795	Disobedience	12
	March	23	Disorderly behaviour	24
	April	2	Disobedience	24
	May	21	Drunkenness	12
	June	4	Mutinous behaviour	24
	Aug.	3	?	?
	Sept.	11	Drunkenness	12

Name	Date		Crime	Number
Michael Clifford	Dec.	8, 1794	Disobedience and contempt	24
	Feb.	26, 1795	Disobedience and contempt	12
	March	23	Disorderly behaviour	24
	Aug.	10	Drunkenness and gambling	12
	Sept.	10	?	?
John Bowen	Jan.	12, 1795	Uncleanliness	12
	April	11	Disobedience	12
	April	21	Reptd disobedience to orders	36
	May	21	Attempted desertion	48
Luke Keefe	Oct.	22, 1794	Drunkenness and contempt	12
	April	14, 1795	Disobedience	12
	Aug.	3	?	?
	Sept.	11	Disobedience	24

It will be seen that John Charles was given a dozen lashes on April 25, another dozen nine days later, and a third dozen seventeen days after that. It was impossible for the wounds to heal between each flogging; and in fact it took Charles just eighteen weeks to die as a result of the punishment. The table also shows that Jeremiah Walsh was given twenty-four lashes on August 4 and another dozen on September 11. He was perhaps luckier than Charles, for he was dead by September 30.

Although the cat-o'-nine-tails killed both these men, they were given comparatively few lashes compared with some of the crew: Martin Steady, for instance, who was flogged eight times in ten months. On one occasion Pigot did not log the actual number of lashes, but in those ten months Steady was given at least 132 lashes. Steady was twenty-three years old and an Irishman from Cork, and for "mutinous behaviour," his sixth crime, he could have been flogged round the fleet, so he might be considered lucky getting only a couple of dozen. But from the dates of the five previous floggings it is obvious that for the eleven weeks between March 5 and May 21, Steady's back must have been continually raw, except perhaps the short period after April 2, when it would have had a chance to heal slightly before the dozen on May 21.

Was Steady a bad character? The *Success*'s muster book shows, from the way he was promoted, that he was not. He joined on February 24, 1793, as a landsman—the lowest possible rank for an adult, which meant he was no seaman. Yet by June 3 he was an ordinary seaman and on February 4 the next year rated an able seaman by Pigot's predecessor, who had obviously thought him a good man. The answer is probably that Steady was unlucky and a victim of Pigot's obsessive hatreds.

Another seaman, John Bowen, received 108 lashes in eighteen weeks and, like Martin Steady, is another example of crimes becoming successively worse the more a man was flogged. One can be forgiven for speculating what his behaviour would have been had he not been flogged for the original crime of uncleanliness, which was so insignificant that it could have been punished by stopping his grog, giving him extra duty, or in a dozen other less brutal ways than using a cat-o'-nine-tails.

Flogging, although a dreadful punishment, thus seems to have had little deterrent effect. One man who saw the last days of the cat-o'-nine-tails commented that after being flogged "a bad man was very little the better; a good man very much the worse. The good man felt the disgrace and was branded for life. His self-esteem was maimed, and he rarely held up his head or did his best again."

However, the striking thing about Pigot's punishment—apart from the ominous frequency—is the complete lack of balance. For *attempting* to desert one man was given a dozen lashes while another received forty-eight; for *actually* deserting one man received twelve while another had thirty-six. Likewise Pigot gave twenty-four lashes for mutiny—which, apart from murder and treason, was one of the worst and rarest offences in the Navy—and twenty-four for drunkenness. It is curious that six out of fifteen floggings ordered by Captain Wilkinson in the *Hermione* were for fighting, quarrelling or rioting, while not one of Captain Pigot's eighty-five floggings in the *Success* was for any of those three offences.

VI

The Favourites

—ᗰ—

THE MAN described in official letters as "Sir Hyde Parker, Knight, Vice-Admiral of the Red and Commander-in-Chief of His Majesty's ships . . . at and about Jamaica, etc., etc." was a widower of fifty-eight. As a commander-in-chief he was a competent administrator but (as events were to prove at the Battle of Copenhagen four years later) an indecisive and uninspired leader.

Like his protégé Hugh Pigot, Sir Hyde when a youngster had powerful interest to help him get to windward in his career: at the time he was appointed commander-in-chief at Jamaica he had reached the same position as his father, whose Christian name he also bore.

On the Jamaica Station Sir Hyde had little opportunity to distinguish himself in battle; but as we have seen, there were financial considerations which made up for any lack of martial glory. The mob's cheers for a hero died as the sun set; but a few score thousands of pounds in the Funds continued to bear interest. . . .

For any commander-in-chief, one of the most important men on his staff was his secretary, and when he came out to the West Indies Sir Hyde had been fortunate in persuading a young parson, the

Reverend Alexander John Scott, to become his chaplain and confidential secretary. Scott, then twenty-eight years old, was a keen bibliophile and had a remarkable talent for languages, speaking fluent French, German, Spanish and Italian. (He later became Nelson's secretary, and it was in his arms that the great admiral was to die at the close of the Battle of Trafalgar.)

With only a tiny staff (Scott, some clerks and writers) Sir Hyde was always kept busy with a great deal of paperwork, particularly when a convoy or a packet was about to sail for England. There were always many official letters to write—to the Admiralty, Navy Board, Sick and Hurt Board, Pay Office and Victualling Office, among many others. Surveys and reports had to be made on sick ships and sick men; details of prizes captured, requisitions for shot, powder, provisions, masts and spars, rigging and paint—all these had to go through the commander-in-chief.

We have seen how a commander-in-chief could enrich his favourite captains by sending them to patrol areas where there was the best chance of finding prizes. In Sir Hyde's own command at this time the plums were going to three young captains, William Ricketts, Robert Waller Otway and Hugh Pigot. Ricketts had powerful interest to back him up—he was the nephew and heir of Admiral Sir John Jervis who, within ten days of Wilkinson and Pigot agreeing to exchange ships, was to win a great victory off the Cape from which he took the name of the earldom a grateful King bestowed on him, St. Vincent. Otway was the son of a rich Irishman, Cooke Otway, of Castle Otway in Tipperary. Both these young men had considerable ability as well as interest. Nevertheless, an example of the advantage conferred by interest is a comparison of the tasks allotted to Ricketts and to Philip Wilkinson for the last two months of 1796—Ricketts in the *Magicienne* captured an 18-gun French corvette on November 1, a couple of coasters on November 9, two laden schooners on December 1, and a large sloop on December 3. During that time the *Hermione* had been at anchor at Cape Nicolas Mole or patrolling off Port au Prince, and had captured nothing.

ON WEDNESDAY, February 8, 1797, two days before Pigot and Wilkinson were due to exchange ships, the sun rising over the Black Mountains was hidden by low cloud and Cape Nicolas Mole was gloomy and humid. The crews of all the vessels in the harbour, both warships and merchantmen, were about to be treated to another public display of justice at work. Michael Supple, a seaman on board the 74-gun *Valiant*, had been found guilty of mutiny and Sir Hyde had directed that he should be hanged on board his own ship at 8 A.M. on the 8th.

A few minutes before eight o'clock, Captain Pigot appeared on the quarterdeck of the *Success*, and tucked under one arm was the familiar slim volume containing the Articles of War. At the same time, on board the *Valiant*, Michael Supple was led up on to the fo'c'sle by the provost marshal with a guard of marines, followed by the chaplain.

Then the ship's bell sounded the four double strokes for eight bells, 8 A.M. The ominous silence that had fallen over all the ships was suddenly shattered by the heavy thud of a gun firing on board the *Valiant*. The cloud of smoke which swirled up finally blew away in the wind, revealing Supple's body hanging lifeless at the yard-arm.

On board the *Success* Captain Pigot—as did every other captain, including Wilkinson in the *Hermione*—then read to his crew the 19th Article of War, the one that Supple had broken, followed by an "admonition" written and signed by Sir Hyde explaining why Supple had been executed, and warning them to take heed, because such punishment was the inevitable sequel to mutiny.

After half an hour Supple's body was lowered from the *Valiant*'s yardarm and the boats returned to their respective ships. In the *Success* the crew went back to their work and Captain Pigot walked below to his cabin, ordering that the muster book should be brought to him.

THE REASON WHY PIGOT sent for the muster book was that he was preparing to transfer to the *Hermione*, and under the *Regulations and Instructions* a captain exchanging ships in the same port was allowed to take a certain number of men with him. Pigot could have his own cook, steward, clerk and coxswain—who were in effect his personal entourage—and another fourteen men, of whom five could be petty officers.

Pigot and Wilkinson no doubt made an agreement beforehand, because Pigot took more men from the *Success* than Wilkinson did from the *Hermione:* no doubt Wilkinson was prepared to help out Pigot, since seamen were so hard to find in the West Indies, while the *Success* would be paying off as soon as she arrived back in England.

So Pigot sat at his desk and read through the names in the muster table to refresh his memory, and started drawing up a list in his large and characterless handwriting. He was not taking his steward, so the first name was that of his cook and then his coxswain. He added nearly two dozen adults and two boys—one the cook's son—to the list, and then sent for the first lieutenant.

By this time every man in the *Success* knew from rumour that the ship was due to sail for England in a few days. For most of them England—the British Isles, at least—naturally meant home, and they must have been delighted at the prospect: many of them had been in the West Indies for two or three years. In reality it would make little change in their way of life: they were unlikely to be allowed leave—though women would be brought off to them by the boatload, and some of them might even be the legal, as well as self-proclaimed, wives of the men.

However, more than a score of them soon received a rude shock: as soon as the first lieutenant arrived, Pigot gave him the list he had just drawn up and told him to send all the men named in it down to the cabin.

When they arrived—startled, no doubt, at this invitation to otherwise forbidden territory, for at the door to the captain's quarters there was always a marine sentry on guard—Pigot was affable. One of the men, describing the scene later, wrote (omitting all punctuation) that the captain said: "My men I am going to inform you of my leaving this ship but I should be glad to go home as well as you but I dare say you know the reason* I would wish to carry you along with me if you are agreeable not that I can force you against your inclination so I'll leave you for a day or two to consider."

Pigot did not have to wait: all but two men agreed to go with him to the *Hermione.* But if Pigot was so cruel, why did these men, with two exceptions, agree? The answer is quite simple: Pigot had his favourites, in the same way he had his victims. In addition the men

*If the seaman intended a full stop at this point it shows Pigot was implying they knew he was being kept in the West Indies as the result of unexpected orders, which would obviously have been the aftermath of the Jesup affair.

had prize money owing to them, thanks to the *Success*'s previous good fortune, and if they went back to England under another captain they could say good-bye to the money.

They knew, however, that if they stayed with Captain Pigot he would make sure that he wrung the money out of the prize-agents—apart from any other consideration, he wanted his own two-eighths, and there was Sir Hyde Parker, waiting for his eighth. When the rates of pay are borne in mind—they had not been changed for a century: since the days of Charles II—it is clear that the lure of even £10 in prize money was a big one, since it was almost a year's pay for an ordinary seaman, who received 19s. a month.

A written statement by one of the men, Richard Redman, confirms these conclusions. The relevant passage (without any punctuation) comes immediately after his description of Pigot's appeal for volunteers, referred to earlier, and gives his response: "With gratitude I couldn't deny him with any properity [propriety] for he behaved to me very kindly in several respect even in every port he whuld endeavour to get whatever prize-money be due to us."

Since Redman was one of the first to turn on Pigot a few months later, and a dozen more of the twenty-one adults were to be among the ringleaders in the *Hermione* plot, it would be fascinating to know exactly what made Pigot choose them from among the 175 men then serving in the *Success*. His list is another—and the most disastrous—example of his unerring instinct for picking the wrong men. Had the Devil been his advocate, Pigot could not have chosen his own executioners with more skill.

SINCE SUCH A HIGH PERCENTAGE of the men were subsequently to become murderers and traitors, and because the Irish have—quite wrongly—been blamed by some naval historians for being the ringleaders, it is worth noting that of the twenty-one men twelve were English, three Irish, three Scottish, one a Manxman, and two American.

Among the more important men that Pigot took with him were his cook, John Holford, a mild-mannered, almost timid man of forty-four who came from Epsom in Surrey (Holford's son, aged thirteen, was also in the ship, and usually helped wait on Captain Pigot at table); a boatswain's mate, Thomas Jay, thirty-three years old and born in Plymouth; and his coxswain, Patrick Foster. Listed as "Foster" in the *Hermione*'s muster table and "Forster" in the *Success*'s, he was an Irishman—a "Patlander" in the contemporary naval slang—born in Galway thirty years earlier. A captain's coxswain held a curious position in a ship: a first-class seaman and responsible for the crew of the captain's barge, which he always steered, he was also a personal and highly-trusted servant, a mixture of butler (though not valet—that was the steward's job), bodyguard and major-domo.

In addition to the twenty-one petty officers and seamen, Pigot had also arranged to take with him to the *Hermione* a lieutenant, a master's mate and a midshipman. The lieutenant was Samuel Reed, who had joined the *Success* in the previous July, and from his rapid—and apparently unmerited—promotion in the *Hermione*, he seems to have been one of Pigot's favourites. The master's mate was John Forbes, and the midshipman John Wiltshire, a Londoner who was eighteen years old and had been in the *Success* for only nine weeks. A midshipman often had some link with his captain—one of his family, or the relative of a friend or patron—but there is no indication of any such connection in Wiltshire's case.

VII

"At Your Peril . . ."

—⁘—

THE YOUNG FIRST LIEUTENANT of His Britannic Majesty's frigate *Hermione*, John Harris, had said his farewells to his old commanding officer, Captain Philip Wilkinson, and now he was waiting at the after end of the starboard gangway on Friday, February 10, ready to welcome the new one. He was hot and sticky, because although the spotless canvas awnings stretched over the quarterdeck took the worst of the heat out of the scorching Caribbean sun, his uniform was not designed for such weather, and the cocked hat, worn athwartships, had no brim to protect his eyes from the glare.

But the sun and the uniform were not the only reasons why he was perspiring freely: his present anxiety was focused on the boat which had left the *Success* and was being rowed briskly towards the *Hermione*, because it was bringing the frigate's new captain on board. In a few moments he would appear at the break of the bulwarks, hot from his scamble up the ship's side and—if gossip and rumour in the fleet were anything to go by—ill-tempered and critical, and as safe to deal with as an overheated gun.

Grouped round Harris were a motley collection of men: the one boatswain's mate stood ready, his call in his hand waiting to pipe the new commanding officer on board; the marines in red jackets, their cross-belts smoothly-coated with pipe-clay, stood as stiff as the ramrods in their muskets; and the sideboys stood at what everyone but the marine sergeant would call attention. The commission officers were represented only by Harris himself: the second lieutenant had gone to the *Success* with Captain Wilkinson, and Captain Pigot was bringing his replacement. The commander-in-chief was due to appoint a new junior lieutenant and a marine lieutenant. The senior warrant officers were represented by the master, surgeon and purser, and the junior by the gunner, carpenter and boatswain.

Finally the barge was alongside, and Harris gave a quick signal to the boatswain's mate as he glimpsed the top of a gold-braided cocked hat coming up the ship's side. By the time Captain Pigot stepped on to the deck the call of the boatswain's mate was shrilling and twittering, sounding more like the jittery outcry of an agitated bird than a salute. The marine sergeant gave a signal and, as the drummer beat out a ruffle, the marines presented arms.

Pigot saluted the quarterdeck, and Harris stepped forward to introduce himself and welcome the new captain on board. Pigot told him he could present the officers. Since there were so few on board, it did not take long. The master was due to leave the *Hermione* very soon; the gunner, Richard Searle, had served in the ship for four months and a day; the surgeon, H. T. Sansom, had been on board seven months. The boatswain, Thomas Harrington, had served in the *Hermione* for four months and Wilkinson had found him satisfactory; but he and Pigot appear to have taken an instant dislike to each other. No doubt Harrington knew that Pigot had only a few weeks earlier arrested the boatswain of the *Success* and brought him to a court-martial, which had sentenced him to be dismissed the ship. Harrington probably felt resentment over this episode: a resentment which he took no pains to hide judging by his subsequent behaviour.

The carpenter, Richard Price, was a twenty-five-year-old Welshman and one of the four men who had served longest in the ship. The next man in seniority was the master's mate, William Turner, who had been in the ship more than two years. He appears to have failed his examination for lieutenant and was later described by one who shared a cabin with him for eight months as a "clever, disappointed man."

Captain Pigot shook hands with each man, and before going below told Lieutenant Harris to turn up the hands. Swiftly the boatswain's mate hurried about the task of assembling the men on the quarterdeck, his shrill piping—which earned such men the nickname "Spithead Nightingales"—interspersed with shouts of "All hands! All hands!" and followed by hoarse threats concerning the fate of the last men to appear on deck.

Soon Pigot appeared like the leading actor in a play, a parchment scroll in his hand, and looked around him. Seamen in tattered shirts, with their faces deeply tanned, looked as if they really belonged in the ship. The marines, drawn up once again, neat but perspiring, muskets at their sides and bayonets fixed, looked smart but incongruous, as if their natural element was a smoothly-cobbled parade ground.

Pigot then unrolled the scroll and began reading the large, copper-plate writing. It was the commission "from Sir Hyde Parker, Knight, Vice-Admiral of the Red," dated February 6, and addressed to "Hugh Pigot, Esquire," appointing him to the *Hermione* and "willing and requiring you forthwith to go on board and take upon you the charge and command of captain in her accordingly; strictly charging and commanding all the officers and company of the said frigate to behave themselves jointly and severally in their respective appointments, with all due respect and obedience unto you, their said captain."

Most of the men had heard such a commission read before: it was worded in the time-honoured way, and although it ordered officers and seamen alike to obey, it also contained a warning to the commanding officer. Pigot was to carry out the General Printed Instructions and any orders and instructions he received and, he read, "hereof, nor you nor any of you may fail as you will answer the contrary at your peril . . ."

Pigot had now "read himself in," thus lawfully establishing himself as the commanding officer of the *Hermione:* he was king of all he surveyed on board the frigate, with power of life, death, health and happiness over more than eight-score men. He would be, if he carried out the spirit as well as the letter of the *Regulations and Instructions*, counsellor to his crew, as well as captain; the man who helped them when they had personal troubles, as well as punishing them when they misbehaved. Embodied in him should have been all that real leadership entails: the knowledge that his men were human beings, with hopes and fears, problems and pride, and that if they had a leader they respected, whose discipline was just even if rather harsh, who displayed humanity and not vanity, then they would follow him anywhere.

Rolling up the scroll, Pigot ordered the crew to give three cheers for the admiral and, after telling Harris to dismiss the men, went below to his cabin, where his personal furniture, clothing, food and wine was being stowed. He had yet to choose his steward, and he picked—wisely, it transpired—John Jones, a man who came from Shrewsbury, in Shropshire, and was then twenty-four years old. The men from the *Success* were brought on board, and from then on the *Hermione* had two boatswain's mates—one more than she was officially allowed.

The fact that Pigot did not have a clerk was a nuisance, because there was a great deal of paper work attached to exchanging ships. In the *Success* he had to leave for Wilkinson attested copies of unexecuted orders, signal books, muster book and many other documents which were needed if the administration of the Navy was to run smoothly and the voracious appetite of its bureaucrats be satisfied. On joining the *Hermione* Pigot had to check and sign similar papers. A captain signed warily, because his signature meant that he accepted as a fact the various stores were on board and the documents recording the quantities were in order. He would be answerable for any deficiencies.

Pigot was pleased, therefore, when from the remoteness of the lowerdeck he received a neatly-written and polite note from a young boy who had been press-ganged and brought on board the *Hermione* a few days earlier. The boy, William Johnson, had taken the bold step of writing to the captain "representing . . . my situation and my not being used to seafaring life," and he expressed the naïve hope that Captain Pigot "would not insist on keeping me." Young Johnson's knowledge of writing and grammar, and the innocent revelation in his letter that he had been trained as a clerk in a countinghouse, made Pigot send for him. Any hope that Johnson still had of being set free was dashed by Pigot telling him that as he had no clerk, Johnson could serve as a writer. According to Johnson, Pigot told him that "in a short time I should be preferred if I merited it." A captain's clerk held an important post, receiving the same pay as a midshipman or master-at-arms, and had a cabin to himself. A writer, however, was just what his title implied; indeed, "copier" would be more accurate, since his main task was to copy orders into the order book, and letters into the letter book.

William Johnson, aged fifteen, and the captain's writer, was a good example of the wide scope and impartial tyranny of the press-gang. A year earlier he had been living in England, and by his account he was probably an orphan, since "friends" found him a job in the countinghouse of a firm in Port au Prince and paid his passage across the Atlantic.

"On arrival there I was settled accordingly," Johnson wrote later. But within a short time his firm had some business to be done at Kingston, Jamaica, and it was entrusted to the young clerk—probably because his superiors regarded the short voyage as dangerous owing to French privateers, rather than as a tribute to the boy's commercial ability. Their wary wisdom was justified because Johnson's ship was captured by the French less than twenty-five miles from Port au Prince and he "suffered a long and severe imprisonment."

It was the custom for the British and French to exchange prisoners from time to time, and eventually Johnson and several others were freed in return for some French captives in British hands and put on board a cartel, or exchange, ship. Unfortunately the sight of a cartel arriving at Cape Nicolas Mole brought out press-gangs like wasps discovering a honey pot, and the young clerk found himself on board the *Hermione,* just as much a prisoner as he had been in the hands of the French, but with all the added dangers and hardships of being at sea in one of the King's ships in time of war.

Within a few days several more men joined the *Hermione.* One of them, however, Midshipman David O'Brien Casey, was familiar to several of the older members of the crew and takes a leading part in this narrative. Casey had just been sent over from the *Ambuscade* to fill one of the vacancies in the *Hermione.* This meant demotion because he had been serving as an acting lieutenant. (His rank of lieutenant could not be confirmed since he was only nineteen, but a youth of less than twenty could serve in the acting rank.) For Casey the *Hermione* was a familiar ship, since he had served in her before.

Joining the Navy as an eleven-year-old boy Casey, who came from Kinsale in Southern Ireland, had been in the *Hyena* when she was captured by the 40-gun French ship *La Concorde* off Santo Domingo. After narrowly escaping being killed in an insurrection by French Negroes, the *Hyena*'s men were exchanged for French prisoners in British hands. Within a few months Casey was transferred to a 64-gun ship as an acting lieutenant. As he was then only sixteen years old, he must have been a competent youth, because coming from a poor family he had no "interest" to help him on.

By the time he was seventeen he was an acting lieutenant in a 74-gun ship; but when Sir Hyde Parker arrived as commander-in-chief he had many young midshipmen and master's mates among his protégés who had reached the age of twenty and passed their lieutenants' examination, and he was on the lookout for vacancies. Since Casey was under twenty, he lost his post as acting lieutenant to someone with more seniority or influence, and was sent as a midshipman to the *Hermione* where, he wrote later, "I was received by Captain Pigot and all the officers in the kindest manner, all seemed to commiserate my late misfortune, even my old shipmates among the crew partook of the same feeling . . ."

Another newcomer to the gunroom was Archibald Douglas, who had been sent to the ship as the new junior lieutenant. The frigate now had her full complement of sea officers, although she was short of a lieutenant of marines and some warrant and petty officers.

ON SUNDAY, two days after Pigot took over command of the *Hermione*, and with the convoy due to sail for England on Wednesday, escorted by the 74-gun *Leviathan* and the *Success*, Sir Hyde spent the whole day—after Divine Service on board his flagship—dictating and writing letters "to the Admiralty and other naval Boards."

Although the *Leviathan* and *Success* were to be the convoy's only escorts for the actual Atlantic crossing, Sir Hyde proposed sailing in the *Queen*, with several more of his ships, to cover the convoy until it was well clear of the Windward Passage. He would then send some of his frigates, including the *Hermione*, on independent cruises, while he returned to the Mole with his flagship.

Wednesday's dawn brought a cloudy sky and a brisk northeasterly wind. The merchantmen began weighing anchor at daylight and by noon they were clear of the land and beginning to form up as a convoy, urged on by the hoists of flag signals from the *Leviathan* and the *Success*. By 1 P.M. the flagship, with the *Valiant*, *Quebec* and

Hermione in company, had also sailed and soon passed the convoy: Sir Hyde did not intend to stay with the merchantmen: instead he would keep to windward, patrolling along the north coast of Santo Domingo, where he could intercept any French or Spanish ships attempting an attack.

The four warships sighted the convoy occasionally on Thursday and Friday, but as night came strong winds and vicious squalls forced each of them to send down topgallant masts and yards to reduce the windage up aloft. It was hard work for the ships to keep together in the darkness, and the bad weather lasted until Saturday night. As it cleared up on Sunday morning the topgallant masts and yards were once again swayed up, while reefs were shaken out of the topsails.

But Pigot's fury can be imagined when shortly after dark on Sunday night, having kept the *Hermione* in station all through the bad weather, the officer of the watch reported the flagship and the rest of the squadron were not in sight. . . .

Unknown to Pigot he had little or no chance of finding the squadron again in the darkness because Sir Hyde tacked his ships an hour after the frigate lost touch, so that for the rest of the night they were sailing a different course from the *Hermione*. In the meantime Sir Hyde had been joined by the *Mermaid*, which was commanded by one of his favourites, Captain Otway. The admiral had intended to put Otway (who was junior) under Pigot's command, and send the two frigates away to cruise off Puerto Rico. Finally, with the *Hermione* still not in sight on Tuesday morning, he ordered Otway to go alone.

The *Hermione* did not find the squadron again until dawn on Wednesday—she had been absent for more than two days. "1/2 past 4 A.M. found H.M. Ship *Hermione* had joined us," wrote Sir Hyde. "Ordered Captain Pigot to proceed off the west end of Puerto Rico, where he will find the *Mermaid*, which he is to take under his command and cruise on that station as long as they have provisions and water, then to return to the Mole."

THE *HERMIONE* arrived off the western end of Puerto Rico on Friday, found the *Mermaid*, and began cruising along the coast searching for enemy ships. The two frigates made a well-matched pair; but the *Hermione* was a Bristol ship, having been built on the

River Severn and launched fifteen years earlier, while the *Mermaid* was a Kentish ship, built on the Medway and launched three years after her consort.

Although both captains shared Sir Hyde's favour, Otway was the more deserving. Then within a month of his twenty-seventh birthday, he had served at the Glorious First of June and in 1795, while commanding a 16-gun sloop, he had captured an 18-gun French corvette after an action lasting thirty-five minutes. He had been lucky with prizes, and his good fortune was to hold out: by the time he returned to England in 1800 after six years in the West Indies he was reputed to have captured or destroyed 200 enemy merchantmen and privateers.

Sir Hyde's orders to Pigot meant the *Hermione* and *Mermaid* had to patrol the Mona Passage, the seventy-mile channel separating Santo Domingo and Puerto Rico. Shoals of rock and coral reefs litter the coastline of Puerto Rico, some stretching as far as a dozen miles offshore. To add to the navigational hazards the Mona Passage, another of the sea highways linking the Caribbean with the Atlantic, was notorious for its sudden heavy squalls, which could shred the sails of a ship caught with too much canvas aloft.

By Wednesday, March 22, the *Mermaid* had parted company and the *Hermione* was patrolling off Desecheo, the tiny mountainous island sitting squat, like a sagged blanc-mange in the Mona Passage twelve miles off Punta Jiguero, the western tip of Puerto Rico.

As soon as the frigate rounded the island Captain Pigot gave orders for the master to steer the *Hermione* close in under Punta Jiguero, thinking that if he followed the coastline he might well find some French privateers sneaking round the headland, their outline hidden from seaward against the green of the palms and the jungle.

When Puerto Rico stretched ahead of the ship and curved round to the starboard beam, Pigot swung his telescope to the right and could just make out the village of Aguadilla. From there to Punta Jiguero surf broke on to a long sandy beach, looking in the distance like a thin white ribbon on the edge of the sea. Backing the beaches were scattered groves of coconut palms, and a few hundred yards behind them the hills begin, huge green rollers of forest surging inland to lap at the feet of Pico Atalaya, the western peak of the mountains. This stretch of the coast is not hospitable: it does not invite strangers close inshore. Sand bars extend seawards for several hundred yards, and rock and coral reefs radiate like giant claws, waiting to rip the bottom out of an unwary ship.

The *Hermione* was within five or six miles of Punta Jiguero when the low part of the Point began to lift above the rim of the horizon as the ship slowly sailed over the curvature of the earth. Suddenly the lookouts in the mastheads called down that they could see the masts of several ships close inshore under the southern side of the Point.

Pigot could safely guess the masts belonged to French privateers—and probably to some of their prizes. And if the French were using Punta Jiguero as a privateer base it would certainly be well protected, both by Nature and the enemy. Soon he could see at least sixteen vessels at anchor, one of them a large brig. She and many of the others were definitely privateers' prizes, and it was equally certain that hidden among the palm groves round the anchorage would be shore batteries.

The *Hermione* herself would be able to get in close enough to open fire, but there was only one way of successfully plundering the nest—sending in the *Hermione*'s boats to cut out the ships. It was the kind of operation at which the British seaman excelled: there was something in the boat's swift approach as he strained at his oar, and then the last-minute spurt, often with round shot and musket balls kicking up fountains of water round him, that put fire in his belly.

"Clear the ship for action," Pigot ordered, "and send the lieutenants down to my cabin."

While the master took the *Hermione* in closer, Pigot explained his plan in detail to the three lieutenants, Harris, Reed and Douglas. He was going to send in the *Hermione*'s six boats with boarders and marines. They would cut out as many ships as possible and tow or sail them clear of the land. The rest they would destroy. The only weapons for the boarders would be cutlasses, pistols and tomahawks (which were like the Red Indian tomahawk from which they were derived: the head—one side of which was an axe blade, the other pointed—was fitted on to a handle usually about three feet long). Pigot said that Harris, the first lieutenant, would stay in the ship while Reed would command the expedition.

Pigot went up to the quarterdeck: in a few minutes the *Hermione* would be within random shot of the shore battery. The ship was ready for action: it was time to send the men to the guns. Pigot gave the order to beat to quarters, and while the drummer thumped out his rhythmic call to arms Pigot's ears began to take in a strangely assorted symphony of sound—the leadsman's monotonous chanting of the depth of water; the squealing of ropes running through the gun tackles, followed by the dull rumbling of the carriages as loaded guns were run out, their muzzles poking through the ports in the ship's side; the raised voices of the boats' commanders as they detailed individuals for special tasks; and the harsh scraping of metal on a grindstone as men hurriedly put a better edge on tomahawks and cutlasses.

Seamen were hoisting three of the boats over the side from their stowed position amidships, while the three in the stern and quarter davits were already towing astern. With the *Hermione* less than a mile away from the anchorage, Pigot saw that the large brig and the rest of the enemy craft had been stripped of their sails: the French had taken precautions against just this sort of attack. He told Reed that they should first tow the brig clear: she was heavily laden and the most valuable prize.

Soon the leadsman's shouts showed the water was shallowing fast: less than ten fathoms, sixty feet. The *Hermione* had only her topsails set and Pigot ordered them to be clewed up. As the frigate glided along, gradually slowing down, he searched the undergrowth backing the beach with his telescope. Was there a shore battery or not? He could see plenty of activity in the ships: it looked as if the crews were quitting—they were so close to the shore the men could almost jump on to dry land: indeed, one might think that they had been beached deliberately . . .

"By the deep nine!" sang out the leadsman: his lead had touched bottom at nine fathoms, which was fifty-four feet. The *Hermione*, Pigot estimated, was about half a mile off the beach. No coral, no rocks—and no shore batteries so far. The boarders climbed down into the boats. Then suddenly there were three muffled thumps from the direction of the beach, as if someone was beating a big drum. Three puffs of smoke drifting away into the undergrowth on the breeze betrayed the position of the French guns. Three thin spouts of water leapt up from the sea, but the French artillerymen, unused to firing at a ship, had underestimated the range as usual.

The guns were no real danger to the *Hermione,* but they could smash the boats. However, a few broadsides of caseshot would soon persuade the French gunners to quit their guns. Each of the

Hermione's 12-pounders fired a case in which there were forty-six shot, every one of which weighed four ounces: for the human targets it was like being pelted with lethal iron eggs.

The French guns fired, and once again the gunners underestimated the range.

Slowly, as the *Hermione* turned parallel to the shore, the sights of her carronades—which could be trained round further than the cannons—began to traverse the length of the beach, approaching the undergrowth where the French battery was about to fire its third salvo. The captains of the carronades had permission to fire as soon as their sights were on, and a few moments later those on the port side tugged their trigger lines and the stubby little guns leapt back in recoil, spurting flame and smoke. Men sprang forward with wet sponges, fresh cartridges and case shot, wads and rammers. Like machines they went to work: in and out with the sponges to remove any burning debris left inside—in cartridges and ram home—in wads and ram—in case-shot and ram. . . . While that had been going on the captains had fitted new tubes and primed the carronades, which were then run out again. They were trained round a few more degrees—for the ship was still swinging to bring the broadside guns to bear—and again the captains tugged the trigger lines.

A few moments later the ship was far enough round for the 12-pounders on the maindeck to bear, and Pigot gave permission for them to open fire. There were a few swift last-minute adjustments in the aim—a couple of handspikes under a carriage to lever the gun round a few more degrees to right or left; a slight movement of the wedge-shaped quoin on which the breech rested, to change the elevation of the barrel. Then in quick succession each gun captain, kneeling well behind the gun, beyond the limit of the recoil, saw the sight was on, shouted a warning, and tugged the long trigger line in his right hand. One after another the guns flung back in recoil with a swirl of smoke and flame, to be held by the thick rope breechings. The fumes blowing back in through the ports started the men coughing—after a few more rounds the whole of the gundeck would be almost hidden in a fog of smoke, and the men, half blinded, as well as deafened by the noise, would load and run out the guns by instinct and habit rather than in obedience to orders.

As Pigot had guessed, the Frenchmen soon quitted their guns and vanished into the undergrowth: against the *Hermione's* broadsides, their own three guns were useless. Pigot gave the order to cease fire, and went to the taffrail to wave the *Hermione*'s boats on their way.

BY NIGHTFALL there was an imposing little squadron of prizes anchored round the *Hermione*. The brig, Pigot later wrote to Sir Hyde, which was from Bremen, was "loaded very deep and is a very valuable vessel." Of the fifteen other vessels, Reed and Douglas had managed to refloat thirteen and tow them out, but all their sails were missing. The remaining two were so hard aground that they could not be moved and Pigot had ordered Reed to stove in their bottoms so they would end their days on the beach, rotting and cracking in the sun, a happy hunting ground for land crabs and termites.

Two boats full of armed men rowed round the anchored ships all through the night, guarding against a possible counter-attack by the French, and at daybreak Pigot gave his orders. He had decided to keep the brig since the *Hermione* could take her in tow, but the thirteen other vessels without sails, which were smaller and much less valuable, would have to be destroyed: he had no way of getting them back to the Mole. The French battery on shore would be destroyed by a landing party.

While Lieutenant Reed took a party on shore the men in the thirteen small prizes began making piles of all the inflammable materials they could find, and opening all the hatches, ports and skylights to create a draught. In the meantime the *Hermione* had passed a hawser to the brig and was weighing anchor ready to take her in tow. At a signal from the frigate the men in the prizes set fire to the piles of materials, waited a few moments to see that they were burning satisfactorily, and then bolted over the side into the boats to get clear. With startling speed the craft burst into flames: the wood in their topsides was bone dry and the slight breeze blowing through the open hatches rapidly fanned the flames to such heat that they were almost invisible in the scorching sun. Above the blazing ships the air crinkled and shimmered, and the men watching could hear the gasping noise of the flames, and the crackling of burning wood sounded like the snapping of many brittle twigs.

VIII

A Pride of Prizes

—ᴍ—

THE *HERMIONE'S* CREW during the first seven weeks of Captain Pigot's command had slowly split into two almost antagonistic groups. The smaller comprised the couple of dozen seamen and petty officers who had come on board with Pigot, and they were referred to as the "Successes" by the second group, which was made up of the 150 men who had served under Captain Wilkinson and called themselves "Hermiones."

This was not because of any particular loyalty to the ship, although nearly every warship normally had a solid nucleus of men who stayed in her for several years at a time (in the *Hermione* at this period it numbered about forty, less than a quarter of the crew); but apart from this nucleus there was usually a fairly rapid turnover of men owing to sickness, death and desertion, and the steady drain of seamen and petty officers sent off as prize crews. The arrival of a couple of dozen Successes should not have caused any problem: normally they would be quickly absorbed, losing their separate identity.

Why, then, did the two groups form in the *Hermione*? The reason is not hard to find: Captain Pigot was treating the former Successes with more leniency than the Hermiones. At first this might have been due to the fact he had hand-picked the Successes and knew them well, whereas the Hermiones were strangers. But later he was succumbing to his penchant for playing the game of favourites. He was not the first person, whether captain, schoolmaster or politician, to try to use a small clique to increase and buttress his power, mistaking sycophancy for loyalty, and later discovering that he had been outmanoeuvred, and that the clique had been using him.

Richard Redman, a quartermaster's mate from the *Success*, wrote of this period: "There was a continual murmuring among the *Hermione's* [original] ship's company concerning his [Pigot's] followers and the usuage [*sic*] they had before Captain Pigot came on board." Since there is no doubt Wilkinson had been a harsh captain, and bearing in mind that Redman himself was one of Pigot's favourites, it is an important clue to the new captain's behaviour.

The Hermiones' jealousy was soon unwittingly fanned by Pigot, because when the frigate arrived in Port Royal with the captured brig and began a refit, he arranged for the ex-Successes to be paid some prize money owing to them. This was a perfectly normal action, of course, and was undoubtedly one of the reasons why the men had agreed to transfer to the *Hermione* with him. It certainly caused no jealousy among the Hermiones, but Pigot's next action did: as soon as the money was paid, he told the ex-Successes that they "could go on shore for a day's liberty," according to Richard Redman, but he put them on their honour "to come back on board at Sunset."

The jubilant men were rowed to the shore, the envy of nearly 150 original Hermiones, many of whom had hardly set foot on dry land for as long as four or five years, apart from brief wooding and watering expeditions. It is to the credit of the ex-Successes that they all returned on time: but they were picked men.

A few days later eight of the original Hermiones gained their complete freedom, thanks to the intervention of the American Consul in Port Royal, by claiming that they were American citizens. Among them was one man who enters the narrative later, Benjamin Brewster. He was twenty-three years old and came from Preston, Connecticut. From the day they were brought on board their claim to have been born in America was not disputed, since the "Where born" column of the muster book recorded their birthplaces in the United States.

The order to free the men came from Sir Hyde Parker, who had been involved in a long correspondence with Mr. Silas Talbot, the American Consul at Kingston.

On the same day that the Americans were discharged, the whole crew of the *Hermione* were mustered, and a check through the muster book shows there was still a cosmopolitan ship's company on board totalling 172 officers and seamen, plus six marines and three boys.

The birth-places of the fifteen warrant and commission officers are not given. Of the remaining men on board forty-seven were English, two Welsh, eighteen Irish, and ten Scots. Among the rest were four Americans, three Italians and three Swedes, and one each from Spain, Denmark, Norway, Portugal, Prussia, Nova Scotia, Hanover, France, St. Thomas and Barbados. Of those whose birthplaces were not listed, thirteen had foreign-sounding names.

WITH HER REFIT COMPLETED the *Hermione* left Port Royal to return to the Mole. She had lost eight trained seamen, thanks to the efforts of Mr. Silas Talbot, but at last Captain Pigot had found a clerk. When John Mansfield Manning joined the ship on April 7 he was rated an able seaman, but within a day or two Pigot made him clerk—a very welcome promotion which meant that he left the cramped life on the forward part of the lowerdeck, where he had the regulation width of fourteen inches in which to sling his hammock, for the comparative luxury of a tiny cabin just forward of the gunroom on the port side, sandwiched between that of the boatswain and the marine lieutenant. The boy William Johnson, who had been acting as Pigot's writer, was sent back to serve as a seaman.

The short voyage to the Mole was uneventful; but as the frigate came into the anchorage there was a man on board the storeship *Adventure,* anchored nearby, who watched her arrival with great interest. His name was Thomas Leech, and because he had just heard that Captain Pigot now commanded the *Hermione* he was trying to make up his mind what to do next. Leech was a seaman with an unbalanced personality and a guilty past, since over his head hung the grim wording of the 15th Article of War—"Every person in or belonging to the Fleet, who shall desert, or entice others to do so, shall suffer death, or such other punishment as the circumstances of the offence shall deserve . . ."

Leech was to become one of the leading characters in the tragedy of the *Hermione*, and his relationship with Captain Pigot was a strange one. He was a deserter—in fact a veteran in that dangerous occupation—but different from most deserters in two respects: he had twice been successful, and each time he had returned to serve in one of the King's ships.

He had started his career as a deserter three years earlier when serving in the *Success* which, in July 1794, was commanded by Captain Pigot's predecessor. One night while the ship was in Port Royal he had quietly climbed down the ship's side and swum to the shore. Eventually the letter "R" for "Run" was marked against his name in the *Success*'s muster table, and most of the officers and men forgot about him. Most, but not all.

Several months later, after Captain Pigot had taken over command of the *Success*, the frigate was at anchor off St. Marc when a sudden squall made a transport ship drag her anchors and crash alongside the *Success*. While the frigate's crew were busy trying to get her clear several of them saw Leech on the transport's decks, and far from trying to avoid being recognized, he chatted with them. He was soon spotted by John Forbes, the young master's mate, who promptly leapt on board the transport and went straight to her captain, claiming Leech as a deserter from the *Success*.

He was taken back to the frigate, where Captain Pigot listened to Forbes's report and questioned other warrant officers about Leech's character and previous behaviour under the former captain. He was a good seaman—they all agreed on that, and the descriptions they were later to give on oath are interesting. According to Forbes, Leech was "sober, attentive to his duty, and at all times obedient to command." The master-at-arms gave him a similar testimonial, adding that he "always did his duty cheerfully." Thomas Jay, the boatswain's mate, agreed, and described him as "a quiet man."

In view of the favourable reports and because Leech had deserted from the ship while she was under his predecessor's command, Pigot decided to give the errant seaman another chance, providing he promised never to desert again. Leech cheerfully gave his promise, was freed and his name restored to the muster table.

For a while all went well with Leech: Pigot was later to declare that he "always found him during the time he was under my command a sober, attentive seaman, and always obedient to command,

and his conduct gave me so much satisfaction that shortly after he was brought on board the *Success* I stationed him to do his duty as captain of the foretop." That alone indicated Leech was a good sailor because the topmen, who handled the sails on the upper yards of the three masts, were the most agile and expert seamen on board.

Clearly Pigot liked Leech, because the seaman's ability was not enough to account for the kindness and leniency with which Pigot was to treat him later. He must have been an engaging rogue who became one of Pigot's favourites—for a rogue he certainly was, and a murderous one at that.

Forgiveness and promotion were enough to keep Leech happy for a few weeks; but he soon began feeling restless again, and confided his thoughts to the yeoman of the sheets, William Brigstock, who came from New York. The pair of them decided to desert, and on the night of August 22, 1796, while the *Success* was at anchor at the Mole, both men left their hammocks and crept up on deck, intending to swim for the shore. Leech was the first to go over the side, but before Brigstock managed to strip off his clothes he was seized by the ever-alert master's mate, John Forbes, who was making his rounds of the ship, and arrested. When the ship's company was mustered at daylight there was only one man missing—the only one who had promised never to desert.

Leech had in the meantime safely reached the shore and signed on in a merchant ship aptly called the *Free Briton*, giving his name as Daniel White. She had sailed for Providence, Rhode Island, some 1800 miles away, before any Royal Navy officers had time to search her. However, by the time she reached her destination Leech was once again feeling restless. He was certainly not seeking his freedom on land—it would have been easy enough to get work at Providence; and only a little effort would have equipped him with a "protection" declaring he was an American. Or he could have stayed on board the *Free Briton*. What he actually did seems inexplicable.

Also in Providence at this time was a British warship, the 16-gun sloop *Lark*. One would have thought that to Leech she represented the very tyranny from which he had just escaped, since twice he had risked hanging in order to quit the King's service. If he was caught this time the chances were that he would swing by his neck from the yardarm.

Leech knew all this only too well; but instead of keeping out of sight he packed his seabag, left the *Free Briton,* and went across to H.M.S. *Lark,* where he reported to a master's mate that he was a deserter from the *Success.* . . .

The *Lark's* captain, who was bound to send him back to the *Success,* transferred him to the *Swallow* a few days later. By the time she arrived at the Mole in April 1797, the *Success* had already sailed for England and Pigot had exchanged into the *Hermione.* For the time being Leech was transferred to the storeship *Adventure* under open arrest until Sir Hyde decided what to do with him.

When the unpredictable Leech saw the *Hermione* coming into the Mole under Captain Pigot's command, he probably thought that having once been forgiven he might work the same trick again. He promptly went to one of the *Adventure's* lieutenants, John Copinger, who was standing on the quarterdeck, and explained that as his former commanding officer was now in the *Hermione,* could he be put on board her?

But while talking to Lieutenant Copinger he had already been spotted from the *Hermione* by the sharp-eyed John Forbes, who was at once ordered by Captain Pigot to go across and claim him. When Forbes boarded the *Adventure* he was greeted by Lieutenant Copinger who told him they had a man on board called Daniel White who had deserted from the *Success* while she was under Captain Pigot's command. Forbes, however, was intent on first getting hold of the man he knew as Leech, so he went to the *Adventure's* commanding officer, Captain W. G. Rutherford, and explained that he had just seen Leech on board.

Before Captain Rutherford and Forbes realized that White and Leech were the same man, Leech himself came along the starboard gangway and spoke to Forbes, saying he had given himself up to the *Lark* as a deserter some weeks earlier.

So once again Leech found himself under Captain Pigot's command. The ship was strange to him but, of course, there were several of his former shipmates from the *Success* on board—among them Archibald McDonald, the master-at-arms, who was waiting to arrest him.

WITHIN A WEEK of the *Hermione's* arrival at the Mole, Sir Hyde Parker managed to trap and destroy another *Hermione* which had been causing him a great deal of trouble. She was a French frigate which had been lurking about in the Santo Domingo–Puerto Rico area for some months, and as soon as a British frigate arrived at the Mole to report she had driven the *Hermione* into a bay a few miles up the coast, Sir Hyde sailed with three ships, and the French frigate was destroyed.

However, the enemy were about to suffer an even greater loss: the French *Hermione* had originally been based at Cape François, more than 150 miles along the coast to the eastwards, where the French forces were desperately short of supplies. The French authorities there knew that their privateers had captured several American ships loaded with provisions for British ports, and sent them into the French-held Port de Paix and also Juan Rabal, nearby.

Since the privateers dare not risk the 150-mile voyage to Cape François with their prizes, the French authorities had ordered the *Hermione* to go and convoy them back. Her captain had advised against the venture but he had been overruled. Her destruction before she even reached Port de Paix showed his wisdom.

It also left the French prizes still in the two ports, where Sir Hyde had spotted them while on his way up to find the French frigate. There were fourteen in Juan Rabal, most of them at anchor "half a musket shot from the shore" and protected by a battery of five 32-pounder guns.

". . . It appearing to me practicable to cut them out," Sir Hyde later wrote to the Admiralty, he ordered Pigot in the *Hermione* to take the *Mermaid*, *Quebec*, *Drake* brig and *Penelope* cutter, "and execute that service." Sir Hyde did not explain how he had allowed French privateers to establish themselves within twenty miles of Cape Nicolas Mole and capture fourteen prizes so near to a large British base.

The *Mermaid*, still under Otway's command, carried Sir Hyde's orders to Pigot, and at sunset on April 19 the four commanding officers were rowed over in the gathering darkness to the *Hermione* for a conference with Pigot. In addition to Otway there were John Cooke of the *Quebec*, John Perkins, who was commander of the *Drake* (like the cutter, she was too small to be commanded by a post captain), and Lieutenant Daniel Burdwood of the *Penelope*.

Pigot showed them his orders from Sir Hyde, and it is easy to imagine the enthusiasm of the five young men—for Pigot, at twenty-seven, was the eldest—as they sat round a table in Pigot's cabin discussing by lantern-light the best way of cutting out the ships. Pigot's plan was quite simple: he would approach Juan Rabal at night from the eastward, and when the squadron was within two miles of the anchorage the boats from all five ships would be sent off to cut out the prizes. The frigates, brig and cutter would then follow under easy sail, keeping about a mile from the shore. If and when the French shore batteries mentioned by Sir Hyde spotted the boats and opened fire—and incidentally revealed themselves—the squadron, hidden in the darkness further offshore, would reply and draw the French fire, allowing the boats through unscathed.

Pigot worked out the distance and realized that with the present light wind and the current—which was setting against them—there was no chance of reaching Juan Rabal before daylight. He therefore decided to head out to sea for the rest of the night and then turn back next day, timing it so that the squadron would arrive off the coast after dark the following evening.

The commanding officers returned to their ships. For the rest of the night, and until 3 P.M. next day, the squadron steered north-west, then turned back towards Juan Rabal. With the current running at an uncertain speed right across their course, it would be very difficult in the darkness to find Juan Rabal: if they could not see the anchorage they would not know whether it was to the east or west. The easiest way of making sure was deliberately to steer to one side, so that on finding the coast they would know which way to turn. Pigot chose a point to the eastward, planning to arrive there "before the land wind came off."

By midnight the squadron had closed the shore and were running down to the westward. So far everything had gone well: "We had succeeded to my wishes," Pigot recorded. Finding the anchorage was not too difficult: they could see the outline of Point Juan Rabal, which was low and prominent, and backed by a conspicuous mountain whose peak looked like a ruined castle. Having identified the Point, the rest was easy: the privateers and their prizes were in the anchorage two miles to the westward. Pigot therefore hove-to his squadron a mile offshore, far enough out to avoid outlying rocks but close enough to hear the weird yells and squawks of wild animals, and the half boom, half swish of the waves breaking fretfully on the beach. In each of the ships the order had been given to beat to quarters and their boats were towing astern.

Pigot ordered the prearranged signal to be made to the other ships for them to cast off their boats. Those of the *Hermione* went ahead, with the launch commanded by Lieutenant Reed leading and the rest followed on astern. Once again Reed, the *Hermione*'s second lieutenant, was commanding an expedition, instead of Harris, the first lieutenant. This appears an insignificant point; but in fact Reed was Pigot's favourite from the *Success*, while Harris was not.

Reed steered the launch for the shore until he judged he was only a few hundred yards from the beach and then turned to starboard to run down parallel with it until he found the anchorage. Meanwhile Captain Pigot, knowing the speed the boats would be able to row and allowing for the fact that the current against them would be weaker close inshore, where the water was shallower, ordered the squadron to proceed under easy sail so that he could keep level with the boats but a mile to seaward.

The next half-hour was a tense period for Pigot: it was so dark that he could not see the boats as they crawled along under muffled oars, playing their dangerous game of follow-my-leader. He had planned the attack, brought the ships to the prearranged position, and sent the boats off into the night: now he was entirely dependent on the men in those boats. Supposing the master-at-arms in one of the other ships had been slack in checking that none of the men had been drinking—a shout or laugh from a drunken seaman in one of the boats would raise the alarm. So would any noise if two boats collided, or one of them ran on to a rock. A chance encounter with a native fishing craft might result in the boarding parties mistaking it for a French guard boat. . . . Any one of these eventualities would rob of a cutting-out expedition's most effective weapon, surprise.

The squadron had run almost exactly two miles and, according to Pigot's reckoning, should have been abreast of the privateer's anchorage. Suddenly he saw a scattering of sparks, then several red flashes, as if huge furnace doors were being hurriedly opened and shut. A few moments later the faint popping of muskets echoed across the water, followed by the dull, booming overtones of heavy cannon, as the French 32-pounders opened fire. A few spurts of water, just discernible in the darkness, showed that the cannon were firing at the ships of the squadron, although the musket fire was clearly aimed at the cutting-out parties.

Pigot promptly ordered the *Hermione*'s guns to fire back at the French batteries and, as he had previously instructed, the guns of the rest of the squadron joined in. Their shot were unlikely to do the French any harm; but the tremendous ripple of flashes as they fired their broadsides would show the French that five warships were in the offing and might persuade them that, whatever the boats close to the beach were doing, the heaviest attack would develop from the warships offshore.

Soon Pigot discovered that the cutting-out expedition had taken the French completely by surprise: that by the time the enemy had spotted the boats and opened fire with muskets the boarding parties were already "in possession of many of the vessels and had one actually under way."

"At about four o'clock," he wrote to Sir Hyde, "the vessels were all in possession of our people and standing out with the land breeze, except two small row boats which were hauled up on the beach and could not be got off. And," he added, "it is with particular satisfaction that it has been executed without a man being hurt."

Soon after daylight a convoy of nine ships (including eight American merchantmen) was under way for the Mole, escorted by Pigot's little squadron. The names, home ports, destinations and cargoes throw an interesting light on the kind of trade being carried out, and the complete details which Pigot enclosed in his report to Sir Hyde are given as Table II.

TABLE II

Ship	From	To	Master	Owner	Cargo	Condemned or not*	Where captured	By	Rig
Polly	New Portland[sic]	Cape Nicolas Mole	Aliha Herrving†	Not Known	Lumber, 20 casks porter	Condemned	Off J. Rabel	L'Ventrurie privateer	Ship
Two Sisters	New York	Port au Prince	N. Shellar	John Davis	Flour and cheese	Papers sent to Port Francois	Off J. Rabel	L'Ventrurie privateer	Brig
Sally	Philadelphia	Cape Nicolas Mole	James Yardsly	Stewart and Co.	Bread and Flour	Papers sent to Port Francois	Off J. Rabel	L'Ventrurie privateer	Brig
Abiona	Baltimore	Cape Nicolas Mole	Isaac Isaacs	Not Known	Ballast	Papers sent to Port Francois	Off J. Rabel	Two row boats	Brig
Columbia	New Providence‡	Rhode Island	George Thomson	Lawrie Evans	Ballast	Papers sent to Port Francois	Off J. Rabel	Two row boats	Schooner
Juno	New York	Port au Prince	Samuel Wright	Foster Riley	Coffee	Cleared	Tortuga	Privateer	Schooner
Citizen Snow Hill	Baltimore	Marie Galante	William Nasey	Hith and Co.	Flour, dry goods and wine	Papers sent to Port Francois	Off J. Rabel	Privateer	Schooner
Industry	Newhaven (Conn)	Cape Nicolas Mole	Not Known	Hodskins and Co.	Ballast	Papers sent to Port Francois	Off J. Rabel	Privateer	Sloop
					A sloop brought in by the men of H.M. brig *Drake* supposes to have sailed from the Mole.				

*i.e., as prizes by the French. †Presumably Eliha Irvine. ‡In the Bahamas.

Note: The above table is taken from the report enclosed in Captain Pigot's letter to Sir Hyde Parker. The original spelling has been retained.

IX

The Shipwreck

—w—

A FEW DAYS after Pigot and his little squadron arrived at
the Mole with the convoy of prizes, Sir Hyde had to transfer
Otway from the *Mermaid* to the *Ceres*. The Admiralty had
ordered the *Mermaid* to follow the *Success* back to England for a
dockyard refit at Plymouth, and Otway naturally did not want to
return with her. Fortunately Captain James Newman of the *Ceres*
had no such objection, so they exchanged commands.

So far as the ships were concerned, the exchange made no difference to Otway since they were almost identical. However, when
Otway went on board the *Ceres*, read himself in and looked over the
crew, he received a shock. Reporting later in writing to Sir Hyde, he
said that "there was a great want of regularity in her; the ship's
company were accustomed in a great measure to do as they pleased,
and drunkenness seldom considered as a crime." He found that in
addition to their taste for liquor and distaste for discipline, a greater
part of the frigate's crew consisted of "old men, boys and foreign-
ers." Referring to the drunkenness, he told Sir Hyde that "having
been from my infancy trained up in the service with different ideas,"
he was "endeavouring to put a stop to such pernicious example."

By the middle of May Sir Hyde Parker had agreeable orders for both the *Hermione* and *Ceres*: Pigot was to take Otway and the *Ceres* under his command, and the two ships were to cruise along the Spanish Main off the coast of the province of Caracas (now Venezuela). Pigot's orders were to seek what would be called in modern jargon "targets of opportunity": any enemy craft—merchantmen, warships or privateers that he could find.

The actual voyage to the patrol area, some 750 miles, gave Otway and his officers an opportunity to get the *Ceres*'s crew into some sort of shape. In the *Hermione* the new master, Mr. Edward Southcott, who had recently joined the ship, was proving valuable: competent in handling and navigating the ship, he knew the Caribbean well, and he also had the knack of handling men.

The frigates arrived off the eastern coast of Caracas, finding it bold and mountainous, fringed with steep cliffs. Turning westwards they passed close to La Guaira, the entry port for the capital of the province, without sighting a single sail, and carried on past Puerto Cabello, heading north-westward towards the Dutch island of Curaçao. The mainland runs west and then north to Point Tucacas, forming the Gulf of Triste. It is well named, because for more than thirty miles the coast is low and sandy, backed by swamps of mangroves whose roots rear out of the water like tortured, arthritic limbs.

The coastline of the Gulf makes two sides of a triangle, while the frigates' course to clear Point Tucacas formed the third. Pigot wanted to pass twelve to fifteen miles to seaward of the Point, and he worked out a course of west-north-west, with five degrees of easterly variation to be allowed in the compass. This would keep them clear of the only navigational hazards in the area, which were three low-lying mangrove cays tucked just inside the far end of the Gulf and separated from the shore by a narrow channel. They should pass the Point next morning.

The course for the night was signalled to the *Ceres* keeping station a quarter of a mile away on the *Hermione*'s larboard quarter, and then with its usual almost dramatic suddenness, the sun set—there is little twilight in these latitudes—and some haze added its quota to what soon proved to be a very dark night. Meanwhile the usual routine on board continued without interruption. The log was hove and showed they were making five knots with the quartering wind, and in the *Hermione* the officer on deck for the first watch, from eight until midnight, was John Forbes, the master's mate. At midnight

Lieutenant Harris relieved him. There were no special night orders, and Forbes passed on the usual information and instructions: the course was west-north-west, "nothing to the westward, with the same sail set"; the captain was to be called if the weather changed; watch the *Ceres* in case she made any signals; and the captain to be called at daybreak.

With Lieutenant Harris on the quarterdeck were, apart from the man at the wheel, two quartermasters, Thomas Dugal, a Scot from Perthshire, who had come from the *Success*, and John Goodier, a young Irishman from Cork. In six different positions in the ship were lookouts, and on the ship's present course the most important of them was the one on the larboard bow, sitting on the cathead and watching an arc from ahead to forty-five degrees to larboard. This was the landward side, and the man placed there, William Watkins, later claimed that his eyesight was bad.

The wind stayed at east-north-east, so there was no sail trimming to be done. The log was hove from time to time, and every thirty minutes the half-hour sand glass was turned as the quartermaster struck the bell slung in the belfry on the fo'c'sle. Every twenty minutes, in obedience to Captain Pigot's standing orders, Lieutenant Harris called out to all the lookouts to make sure they were awake and alert.

One, two, and then three bells had been struck by Goodier, and finally, just before 2 A.M., he went to the fo'c'sle ready to strike four bells dead on the hour. The ship was still making five knots through the water, wallowing slightly with the quartering wind; and aloft the great yards creaked while the down-draught of wind from the sails arching overhead made the seamen shiver occasionally. The man at the wheel, his face faintly illuminated by the light in the binnacle, moved slightly from time to time as he turned the wheel a spoke or two, counteracting the butt of a wave on the bow or the wayward pressure of an extra puff of wind.

Beyond the narrow world of the ship it was so dark the sea seemed to merge into the night sky without a hint of an horizon. Suddenly Lieutenant Harris turned to Dugal and asked him if he could see land ahead. The quartermaster peered for a few moments, then said no: he thought it was only a cat's paw of wind (which, ruffling the surface of the sea and making it appear darker, often gives the illusion of land).

Harris was not satisfied and called out the same question to Watkins, perched on the larboard cathead over the creaming bow wave. Watkins shouted back that he could see nothing.

Harris was deciding whether or not to alter course—perhaps unwilling to seem foolish if what he had seen was only a cat's paw— when at that moment the other quartermaster, John Goodier, came back aft from the fo'c'sle, where he had just struck four bells. Harris went to meet him on the gangway.

"Can you see land ahead over there?" he demanded.

Goodier turned and looked forward over the bow. "I am sure it is, sir," he replied.

With this confirmation there was no time to see if it was only the loom of the land—more of a sensation of a distant coastline than a sight of it—or the actual shore only a few hundred yards away.

Harris gave a string of orders. "Fetch the master and call all the hands!" he told Goodier, while to Dugal he said sharply: "Quickly, take the wheel and put the helm hard a'port." This would turn the ship to starboard, away from the land. (At this period, incidentally, "port" was being used for helm orders although the old term "larboard" was retained for other purposes.)

While Dugal hurriedly spun the wheel, the seamen on watch ran to the sheets and braces, hauling the great yards round to trim the sails so that the ship could steer closer to the wind. Dugal could turn the *Hermione* some sixty degrees before the wind would be blowing too far ahead to fill the sails and keep the ship moving, forcing Harris to tack.

The ship was still turning when the first of the officers and offwatch seamen roused out of hammocks and cots by Goodier's stentorian "All hands on deck!" came scrambling up from below, bleary-eyed and bewildered. But the *Hermione* was not the only ship in peril: the *Ceres*, a quarter of a mile away on the larboard quarter, was that much nearer the land. "Tell the gunner to prepare a gun," ordered Harris. A shot would warn the *Ceres* that something was amiss, in case she had not sighted the land.

The first of the *Hermione*'s officers to reach the quarterdeck after Goodier's bellowing was Edward Southcott, the master. Harris swiftly explained the situation and ordered Southcott to take over while he went down to the captain.

Southcott ran to the wheel (he said afterwards he could see land about a mile off) and told Dugal not to take the sails aback—to sail as close to the wind as possible, which meant steering due north, but not to tack the ship.

The gunner, Richard Searle, was by now forward on the main deck getting a gun ready for firing (only the lashings had to be cast off and the gun primed, since it was kept loaded for emergencies) and John Forbes, the master's mate, had run to the fo'c'sle, which was his station at the order "All hands."

Lieutenant Harris in the meantime had gone down to warn the captain.

Pigot was awake in a few moments, and Harris reported: "I've seen land ahead of us, sir—very near."

Pigot at once sat up in his cot and was just swinging his legs out to stand up when, as he wrote later, "I felt the ship strike several times." But the noise of water gurgling past and the creak of the tiller ropes as Dugal moved the wheel showed that whatever the frigate had hit she was still under way and, what was just as important, her rudder had not been torn off.

He ran up on deck, closely followed by Harris, to find the seamen straining and grunting as they finished heaving round the yards and trimming the sails: Southcott now had the ship hard on the wind, beating out to the northward. Captain Pigot then glanced out over the larboard quarter (roughly in the direction the *Hermione* had originally been sailing) and, he claimed later, he could just see land. A gun then boomed out forward as Searle fired the warning shot for the *Ceres*, and Pigot listened to the steady chanting of the leadsman in the chains, telling him how much water the *Hermione* had under her keel. There was precious little, but very soon each successive call showed it was getting deeper.

After firing the warning shot, Searle walked aft along the starboard gangway towards the quarterdeck, glancing across the ship and out into the darkness on the larboard beam. He was surprised to see two cays: they were small, they were low like hummocks in a flat field, and they were close to the ship: there was no mistaking them, even though it was a dark night.

"Has anyone seen those cays?" he called.

"Where?" demanded Pigot, walking towards him, followed by Harris.

"Over there—on the larboard beam—two cays."

Neither Pigot nor Harris could see them at first, but Pigot put the night glass to his eye. "I see them! Two of them!"

A few moments later, still peering through the night glass, he exclaimed that there was a third.

Seeming no higher out of the water than the *Hermione*'s hull, they were in fact the three cays just inside the western end of the Gulf of Triste. This meant the *Hermione* was some fifteen to twenty miles too far south. . . . And had Harris not altered course, she would have run up on the cays or the mainland beyond.

As soon as Pigot assured himself the *Hermione* was heading for deep water, his next concern was for the *Ceres:* had she seen land or the cays in time to turn northwards to the open sea? Had she heard the *Hermione*'s warning shot? Or was she even then hard aground, or sunk after ripping open her bottom on some off-lying reef? She had not fired a warning shot; on the other hand she was not lighting flares.

The leadsman, by then soaking wet as he hauled in the line and cast again and again, was still regularly calling out the depths at which the lead touched bottom: eight fathoms . . . ten . . . and finally twelve. With seventy-two feet of water under her keel the *Hermione* must be clear of danger, and Pigot gave the order to anchor.

"I waited anxiously for the morning," he wrote later to Sir Hyde Parker, "with the hope that the *Ceres* had anchored, or been as fortunate as the *Hermione* in extricating herself from so perilous a situation."

THE *CERES*, however, had not been so fortunate—if fortunate is the appropriate word to describe the result of Lieutenant Harris's alertness. Otway's first lieutenant had been on watch with the usual lookouts stationed round the ship; but unlike Harris he had seen nothing. The first he knew of danger was when the frigate's easy motion was suddenly interrupted by a heavy thud as the *Ceres* hit the first of a series of reefs running parallel to the shore. Before the sheets could be let fly to spill the wind out of the sails or an anchor let go, more heavy blows hit the ship's hull in quick succession as she continued to buck herself across the reefs.

By the time Otway had rushed up on deck the ship was in an uproar. Some men were letting the sheets fly, although a few more shocks would send the masts crashing over the side. Otway kept his head and as the off-watch men streamed up from below began giving orders. The sails could be left to flog for the moment: first he had to let go the anchors to stop the ship driving across any more reefs and ending up on the beach. The carpenter had already hurried below with a lantern to see how badly the ship was leaking. But as Otway began giving instructions to get the anchors laid out he was startled to find that most of the crew completely ignored him: discipline had almost vanished. At the moment the carpenter came up to report that water flooding into the ship was gaining on the pumps, some of the seamen were already smashing down the door of the spirit room to steal enough rum to get themselves helplessly drunk. Seven other men, running up on deck and hearing the carpenter making his report, saw that a boat had already been lowered by some of the steadier sailors, ready to take an anchor out. Without a moment's hesitation they scrambled down into it and, before anyone could stop them, cast off the painter and rowed off in the darkness, heading for the shore.

As Otway later reported to Sir Hyde Parker, "Little or no attention was paid to my orders, not the smallest exertion [*sic*], the spirits broached and the greatest part of them drunk."

Amidst all this confusion, the ship herself was still being lifted by the swell waves and relentlessly thrust forward. Flung down on to a reef by one swell wave, she was lifted up bodily by the next and surged forward by a third on to yet another reef. The rocks tore at her keel and gouged her hull planking; the rudder was wrenched off and the pieces floated away in the darkness. Eventually, with a final lurch and thump, the frigate came to a stop, hard aground. Someone took a cast of the lead and reported she was in fourteen feet of water. Since she had been drawing well over fifteen aft, that alone showed how much the swell waves had lifted her.

Otway's feelings can be imagined: he knew that even if her hull could be patched up, the chances of getting the ship back over the reefs were slight, however much she was lightened by jettisoning guns and gear to reduce her draught.

EVENTUALLY PIGOT'S ANXIOUS VIGIL drew to an end: almost imperceptibly the black of night diluted into grey and he could see the waves more clearly, rounded pyramids which surged past, burnished by the dawnlight to the colour of steel, and seeming hostile, cold and cruel. Slowly the visible horizon widened—fifty yards, then a hundred, and soon a mile. Pigot saw the three cays lying in the water like turtles; then beyond the line of the shore, low and even, with the swell waves moving in relentlessly towards it. From the *Hermione* they seemed in the distance to be grey ripples possessed of their own concentric rhythm, flecked with white where they hit rocks and scoured over reefs.

Finally, in line with the cays and inshore of the reefs, close to the beach, Pigot saw the *Ceres*. She was inert, like a half-tide rock; she did not rise and fall as the swell swept past her. Either she was stuck on a reef or she had sunk and was resting on the bottom.

Within a few minutes one of the *Hermione*'s boats, with Pigot on board, was making her way inshore towards the *Ceres*, with a man in the bows heaving a leadline and calling out the depths—both captains would need to know them if the stricken frigate was to be salvaged. The boat's direct course from the *Hermione* to the *Ceres* took them within what Pigot was to call "a pistol shot" of the south end of the southern cay.

But they were still three or four miles from the *Ceres* when the leadsman's droning voice warned the water was shoaling fast. Pigot wrote later that until then he "flattered myself, however, from appearances I should be able to bring the *Hermione* to an anchor near enough to heave her [the *Ceres*] off without difficulty (as the wind was then moderate) before she received any damage [he was then unaware of the damage she had already received], but in this I was disappointed for on sounding I found we [the *Hermione*] could not approach nearer to her with safety than three or four miles."

Pigot returned to the *Hermione* and brought her as close to the *Ceres* as he dared before anchoring again. He then set off in a boat to join Otway. He climbed on board the *Ceres* to find his friend busy, with the men who were still sober, building a raft to carry out an anchor. Pigot gave orders to his party and then the two captains went down to Otway's cabin to plan the best way of salvaging the ship.

Otway told Pigot that the *Ceres* was making six feet of water an hour, but the main trouble was that although the pumps were clearing it aft, the limber holes (through which the water forward normally ran back to the pump wells amidships) were completely blocked up. This meant the whole forward part of the ship remained flooded under many feet of water, so that the limber holes could not be cleared. But the worst leaks were forward, and until the water was pumped out the carpenter and his crew could not repair them. . . .

No one could think of a way out of this seeming impasse until Midshipman Casey spoke up, "suggesting and strongly recommending (having been in a similar situation before) one or two of the hand pumps being removed forward." This, Casey wrote later, "was instantly done, with the desired effect." The main pump could clear about a ton of water a minute. The little hand pumps, used for washing decks, were similar to the old plunger type still found on village greens, with a long hose attached to reach down the ship's side to the water.

It took many hours of arduous pumping to achieve the "desired effect," and stopping the leaks was not enough: the ship was far too deep in the water to float back across the reefs. The only way of reducing her draught was to jettison as much heavy equipment as possible. Since dumping six tons of equipment would result in her floating only about an inch higher in the water, obviously Otway would have to be drastic.

Cutting the masts over the side and getting rid of the yards and spare topmasts and booms would save more than fifteen tons, with the standing and running rigging accounting for another twenty; the sails and spares could be transferred to the *Hermione,* saving more than three tons. The guns and carriages, powder and shot, would help by at least seventy-five tons. Jettisoning most of the provisions and fresh water represented more than fifty tons. It meant, in effect, gutting the ship of almost everything except the hull, but it would lighten her by at least 200 tons, reducing her draught by more than two and a half feet.

LEAVING HIS PARTY of men on board the *Ceres,* Pigot returned to the *Hermione.* He had a great deal to think about: he and Otway were facing a crisis in their respective careers. As senior officer, Pigot had been responsible for both the ships and the course they steered, while Otway was responsible for actually running the *Ceres* aground. Someone in authority might well blame Pigot because the ships ended up so close to Point Tucacas; but the Admiralty would also certainly want to know why, if the *Hermione* had sighted land in time to avoid running aground, the *Ceres* had not done so.

The obvious answer was of course that Lieutenant Harris in the *Hermione* had been more alert than his opposite number in the *Ceres*. That was indisputable and could clear Pigot of some of the blame; but at the same time it would put more responsibility on the shoulders of his friend Otway. . . .

Having worked out the exact position of the *Ceres*, and also made a note of various facts and figures from her log books to compare with his own, Pigot could now see that there had been a strong current setting into the Gulf of Triste. This meant, as Pigot later wrote to Sir Hyde Parker, that although the frigates had steered west-north-west "through the water," the current setting into the Gulf had diverted them on an actual course "over the ground" of south-west. In addition, "though by log we had only run twenty-seven miles" from the point off Puerto Cabello where they had altered course the previous afternoon, the present position of the *Ceres* showed they had travelled between forty-five and sixty miles "over the ground" thanks to the unexpected current.

Pigot did not consider himself in any way responsible—this is clear from his report to Sir Hyde Parker—but the fault was entirely his, since in laying off the course he failed to allow for a possible inset into the Gulf, although such an inset is common and to be expected anywhere in the world, and the currents in the Caribbean are notoriously unpredictable. With about sixty-six miles to sail from off Puerto Cabello to Point Tucacas, he deliberately laid off a course to pass twelve to fifteen miles to seaward of it. The ships were making five knots so he would reach the Point, if the wind remained steady, in thirteen hours. But since there was bound to be an inset, the current had only to sweep across his course at the rate of just over a mile an hour for that period and he was bound to hit the shore at the northern end of the Gulf. And to make matters worse his night orders had not mentioned the slightest possibility of sighting land. (Had he considered this likely, his orders should have referred to it.)

His letters and subsequent actions show that since Pigot did not consider himself, Otway or the *Ceres*'s first lieutenant responsible for the night's events, he felt he had to point an accusing finger at someone else: a man who could be loaded with enough blame to prevent awkward questions being asked about the navigation or about the lookout being kept in the *Ceres*. He did not look far for such a scapegoat.

It is not known for certain what parts Captain Otway and Sir Hyde Parker played in Pigot's final solution: all three could have been concerned in what can only be called a wretched plot; on the other hand Otway and Sir Hyde might have been unwitting partners. However, Pigot's own letters show that he was the prime mover in what followed, and they give a strong hint that Sir Hyde aided and abetted him.

WITHIN A WEEK of the grounding the *Ceres* had been sufficiently patched up for the *Hermione* to be able to leave her and return to the Mole. In the meantime Otway had heard news—possibly through the American Consul—of the seven seamen who had deserted the stricken ship in the barge: they had arrived at the Spanish port of Puerto Cabello. He sent a letter to the Governor under a flag of truce, politely requesting that they should be returned. He received a very prompt and equally polite reply: the seven men, the Governor claimed, were in fact American citizens; they had made the requisite declarations to the American Consul, who was satisfied and had put them under his protection. This reply, not unnaturally, infuriated Otway because apart from being cowards who had deserted an apparently sinking ship, the *Ceres*'s muster book gave a completely different and probably much more accurate account of the men's nationalities.

Just before the *Hermione* left, Otway wrote a report for Sir Hyde Parker. Enclosing a copy of the relevant entries in the *Ceres*'s logs ("which will inform you of the disaster that has befel the *Ceres*"), he wrote: "Should you, sir exhibit the smallest doubt that any blame is to be imputed to me . . . it will afford me the greatest satisfaction in your ordering my conduct to be publicly investigated." He described the condition of the *Ceres*'s crew when he took over command and concluded: "In short, sir, the ship never could have been saved if it had not been for the uncommon exertions of the *Hermione*'s men, Captain Pigot himself constantly assisting in person."

The *Hermione* arrived back at the Mole early on June 9 and Pigot reported personally to Sir Hyde, giving him three signed letters. The first was his description of the *Ceres* grounding; the second requested a court-martial on the *Hermione*'s boatswain, Thomas Harrington; and the third asked that Thomas Leech, the deserter, should also be court-martialled.

The letter concerning the *Ceres* told how the two ships were "imperceptibly drawn by a very strong current into the Gulf of Triste." He described how he went on board the *Ceres* to consult with Otway. "I cannot help expressing to you, sir, my admiration of the steady, cool, exemplary conduct of Captain Otway throughout the whole of the arduous task that fell on him, and though beset by a variety of difficulties.

"If, sir, there is any blame in this unfortunate business, from inattention to the situation of the ship, or imprudence in the course steered, as the senior officer (and consequently the senior ship), it must be laid to my charge; it therefore behoves me to lay before you as clear a statement of the situation on this subject as I possibly can."

After describing in detail the events he wrote: "I beg leave to add, sir, though my own conscience entirely acquits me of having occasioned any misfortune by any neglect or inattention on my part, from the course steered, I feel great satisfaction in meeting any public investigation you might think proper to direct."

Had he ended the letter at that point it would have been a reasonable report. However, although he had already claimed the grounding was due to being "imperceptibly drawn by a very strong current into the Gulf of Triste," adding that if there was any blame over the course steered "it must be laid to my charge," he then produced the person he now considered to be to blame for the whole episode. ". . . Having made inquiry respecting the lookout kept by the [*Hermione*'s] officers and people . . . I cannot bring to light at present any stronger proof of neglect in that respect, on their part, than from comparing the situation of the *Ceres* when aground with the course steered [when] it very clearly appears to me that we must have passed within pistol shot of the southernmost of the three cays . . ."

He did not consider the possibility that the *Ceres* might have been more than a quarter of a mile from the *Hermione*'s larboard quarter (which was probably the case). Instead, he declared: "From these circumstances I must confess I do not think a proper lookout was kept by the officer who had charge of the watch in the *Hermione*; that the misfortune which befell His Majesty's Ship *Ceres*, and the consequent damage she suffered, is in great measure to be imputed to neglect, and as it was so near proving fatal to both ships, I beg to submit to your opinion the propriety of a further inquiry on that subject."

So Lieutenant Harris, the man whose keen eyesight had saved the *Hermione,* was being offered as the scapegoat for the *Ceres* grounding. Neither Otway nor Pigot mentioned that the first lieutenant of the *Ceres* had seen nothing: that the first he knew of land being near was when the *Ceres* hit it, sailing at five knots under all plain sail. Indeed, no one on board the *Ceres* was to be blamed in any way, then or later.

Captain Pigot's second letter to Sir Hyde was commendably direct and brief:

> Thomas Harrington, Boatswain of His Majesty's ship under my command having on the 2nd day of April last, in Port Royal Harbour, disobeyed the orders of Lt Harris and treated him in an insolent and contemptuous manner . . . and having been repeatedly guilty of the same offence, as well as totally neglecting his duties, and since his confinement been repeatedly drunk . . . I am to request you will be pleased to order a court martial to try him for the above offences.

The third letter requested a court-martial to be held on Thomas Leech "otherwise known as Daniel White," and briefly outlined his various desertions and recaptures.

In the letter to Sir Hyde concerning the *Ceres* Pigot had begged "to submit to your opinion the propriety of a further inquiry," which indicates that a fourth letter Pigot sent to the commander-in-chief that day, June 9, was written after the two men met. This letter began by saying he had made an inquiry into the lookout kept by Lieutenant Harris, continued it with a long verbatim extract from his first letter, and concluded by quoting the last part of it, substituting Lieutenant Harris's name for "the officer" and then altering the final phrase that the damage suffered by the *Ceres* "is in a great measure to be imputed to neglect" to read "imputed to *his* neglect." He then asked for an inquiry into Harris's conduct—which was tantamount to asking for a court-martial.

Clearly Pigot would not have requested an inquiry into Harris's behaviour at the same moment that he asked for Sir Hyde's opinion whether or not there should be a "further inquiry," so it must have been the result of Sir Hyde's opinion. The point is important in determining Sir Hyde's role in what followed, because the whole episode was now, by accident or design, about to enter the realm of naval "politics."

The reasons for this are almost disgustingly simple. An act of Parliament laid down that no person commanding a fleet or squadron of more than five ships could preside at a court-martial abroad, "but that the officer next in command to such officer commanding in chief shall hold such court martial." Sir Hyde's next in command was Rear-Admiral Rodney Bligh, whom he detested (and who should not be confused with Captain William Bligh, formerly of the *Bounty).* Indeed, within a year Parker wrote to the Admiralty to "request Their Lordships will remove Rear-Admiral Bligh from under my command, or, that Their Lordships will allow me to resign from a situation which must be extremely unpleasant, finding myself so ill-supported by the person next to me in command in keeping up the discipline and subordination of this particular squadron." The Admiralty's view was expressed much later by the First Lord, writing to tell Parker he was being recalled: ". . . though in the course of your command a few circumstances have occurred in which I could have wished you to have acted differently from what you did, especially with regard to the business of Vice-Admiral Bligh, I can, however, assure you that it is not on that account that this arrangement [Parker's replacement] is made."

Against this unhappy background was set the affair of Pigot, Otway and John Harris: the first two were Sir Hyde's protégés, while Harris was Rear-Admiral Bligh's.

On receiving Pigot's letter concerning Harris, Sir Hyde wrote within twenty-four hours to Rear-Admiral Bligh, ordering him to assemble a court-martial on June 16 to try Harris "for his conduct in having . . . negligently performed his duty, as set forth more particularly in a letter from Captain Pigot . . ." Bligh was also ordered to try Boatswain Harrington and Thomas Leech.

X

A Snub for Pigot

—ɯ—

ARLY ON JUNE 16 the thud of a gun firing echoed across
the anchorage at the Mole and the Union flag was run up at
the mizzen peak of the *Brunswick*, warning that a court-
martial was about to be held. Soon the four captains who were to
form the court under Rear-Admiral Bligh were being rowed across
from their own ships, smart in full uniform with swords—Bligh's
order to them had said "it is expected you will attend in your uniform frocks."

In the *Brunswick* the wardroom had been fitted up as a courtroom, with a table running athwartships. Admiral Bligh sat at the
middle of one side of the table, his back to the windows of the stern
gallery, with the captains on his left and right. The Judge-Advocate,
Mr. James Griffith—in effect the clerk of the court—sat at the end of
the table on the admiral's extreme right. A chair for witnesses stood
in front of the table to the right; another chair to the left awaited the
accused officer.

At a signal from Admiral Bligh everyone concerned with the trial
was brought in. The Judge-Advocate began by reading out Sir
Hyde's orders for the trial and then administered the oaths. Then
everyone except the five members of the court, the accused and
Pigot were ordered out.

Admiral Bligh said to Pigot: "You will be the first to be interrogated by the court about what you know of the charge against the prisoner: after that you will be at liberty to stay in court and conduct the prosecution."

After Pigot had sworn that his evidence would be "the truth, the whole truth, and nothing but the truth," he began by making several claims: that a southerly current had swept the *Hermione* into the Gulf; that she had passed the three cays on her starboard side without Harris seeing them; that Pigot knew this because of the position of the *Ceres* when aground; and bearing in mind the *Ceres*'s position, the *Hermione* must have passed so close to the cays that Harris should have seen them.

Admiral Bligh then asked Pigot a series of questions.

"What height out of the water was those cays?"—"I suppose about the height of the hull of the ship."

"At what distance could you have seen those cays?"—"At about the distance of one mile."

Bligh then asked: "Do you suppose it possible, if you had passed between the cays and the mainland, you would have passed at a mile or more distant from the cays?"—"Not in steering the course we then did."

Here Pigot had, of course, made a slip: with the southerly current affecting the ship in the way he had claimed, the course steered would not represent the ship's track "over the ground"—she would be moving slightly crabwise. Admiral Bligh was quick to spot this.

"Was you not driven to the southward by an unaccountable current into the Gulf of Triste?"—"Yes, we were."

"Might not that current have drawn you nearer to the mainland than the cays, and on that account [you would] have passed nearer to the mainland than the cays?"—"As I understand the *Ceres* was a quarter of a mile on our larboard beam, I think if we had been a mile from the cays the *Ceres* would have struck on the other shore, or would have certainly have [sic] run aground more to the southward of where she did."

But no one thought to ask Pigot one vital question: was the *Ceres* in sight from the *Hermione*? If she had been a quarter of a mile away, as Pigot had ordered, it should have been possible to see her, since Pigot was blaming Harris for not seeing cays allegedly visible a mile away which were "about the height of the hull of the ship." Likewise the *Ceres* should have seen the *Hermione* suddenly turning to starboard—if she was only a quarter of a mile away.

Admiral Bligh's next question was intended to find out if Pigot had considered the possibility of sighting land. "What orders did you leave with the officer of the watch that night?"—"I left no other than the General Order."

Had he or anyone else an idea they would fall in with the land that night? "I had none; nor did any officer communicate his ideas to me on that head," Pigot replied.

That finished the court's questioning, and Harris said he had no questions to ask Captain Pigot, who then left the witness's chair and took over the role of prosecutor. He called the master, Edward Southcott, as his first witness, and after the usual routine questions he asked: "At the time you came on deck, what distance do you suppose we were from land?"—"About a mile."

How far off did he think the *Hermione* must have passed the southern cay? Half a mile, said Southcott.

Admiral Bligh then interrupted: was the channel between the cays and the mainland wide enough for the *Hermione* to have been *more* than a half a mile off the cay? Yes, said Southcott.

Might not the current have driven the *Hermione* more than half a mile south, since the channel was wide enough? "Yes," Southcott replied, "but from the bearing of the *Ceres* when aground, from the *Hermione*, we could not have passed much more than that."

Admiral Bligh asked: "Can you take it upon you to say with any precision what distance you passed the cay?"—"No," admitted Southcott.

The master's mate, John Forbes, was asked by Harris about the night orders left by Captain Pigot. Were not those orders usually given "when there is no idea of falling in with land or vessels?"— "Yes."

Would not others have been given "if there was any idea of being drove into the Gulf of Triste?"—"Yes, I suppose so," said Forbes.

When the quartermaster, Thomas Dugal, gave evidence he was asked by Admiral Bligh: "Who was the first person that saw the land the morning of the 24th May when the ship struck?"—"Mr Harris," said Dugal, who was a former Success.

Harris asked: "Was not the *Ceres* between us and the land when we struck, and if the officer of the watch on board the *Ceres* had kept that lookout which was kept on board the *Hermione,* have seen the land and got clear, in your opinion, as we did?''—''He must,'' declared Dugal, ''if he had kept a good lookout, as he was nearer the land than we was.''

Harris no doubt intended the court to be reminded that no witnesses were present from the *Ceres,* and his question was obviously a broad hint that the wrong first lieutenant was being tried.

The *Hermione*'s lookouts were the next witnesses: one man who had been on the starboard gangway swore that he did not see the land ''until long after Mr Harris had discovered it from the quarterdeck and the ship had struck''; a second emphasized that Lieutenant Harris had sighted it first.

Their evidence closed the prosecution case, and Harris called his own defence witnesses. He began by asking Forbes about a hypothetical situation. When Forbes came on deck he had difficulty in making out the land some time after Harris had already seen it, so did Forbes think that if he had been the officer of the watch he would have sighted it sooner?

''No,'' Forbes said firmly, ''I do not.''

''That being the case,'' said Harris, ''do you suppose the charge of not keeping a good lookout can in the smallest degree be attached to me?''

Forbes's immediate future depended on Captain Pigot, who was sitting watching him a few feet away. Nevertheless, Forbes declared: ''No, I think not: Mr Harris deserves credit for keeping such a good lookout, not knowing that land was there.''

Harris called no more witnesses and went straight on to make his defence statement. Captain Pigot, he said, had claimed that the damage to the *Ceres,* the fact that the *Hermione* touched, ''and what might and nearly did prove fatal to both ships,'' was ''in a great measure to be imputed to my neglect.''

But, he said, he had been the first person to sight the land—the evidence had proved that; and the lookouts and officers all proved the weather to be dark and hazy, and that it was impossible for them to see the land. The *Hermione* had received no damage when she touched ground—''for it scarcely deserves the appellation of striking.'' He then declared: ''If the First Lieutenant of the *Ceres* had seen the land as well as myself, she would not have been hurt.''

The starboard side was not the place where an officer could ex-

pect to see land; and if they had run within pistol shot of the southernmost cay, the man stationed on the starboard side had declared it
could not be seen. "Where the probability of seeing land was, I saw
it . . . therefore the blame, if any, must be on the men stationed on
the starboard side, but which I think there cannot be, as every member of this court must know the rapid currents of this country . . .
If, on the other hand, the low land on the main should or ought to
have been seen before, all the blame lay on the *Ceres,* who was a
quarter of a mile nearer to it than us; consequently must have seen it
plainly, but in fact never saw it till she was aground with the helm
hard a'starboard" [*sic*].

That ended the evidence and the pleas. Captain Pigot and Lieutenant Harris left the court with the rest of the onlookers; only the
Judge-Advocate, the four captains and Admiral Bligh remained to
consider the verdict. It did not take long and soon the word was
passed through the *Brunswick* that the court was reassembling. The
Provost Marshal brought Harris in, and the Judge-Advocate picked
up a piece of paper. "At a court martial assembled on board HMS
Brunswick . . ." he read, recounting names of the members, the
original order from Sir Hyde, and the charge, ". . . having heard
the evidence produced in support of the charge, and what the prisoner had to allege in his defence, and having maturely and deliberately weighed and considered the whole, the court is of the opinion
that the charge has not been proved against the prisoner, but on the
contrary, that every necessary arrangement was made, and such *a
good lookout kept* [underlined in the original] as to mark a judicious
good officer, and do therefore fully acquit the said Lieutenant John
Harris . . ."

The verdict must have been a violent blow to Pigot's pride: here
was the man whom he said was responsible for the *Hermione* touching and the *Ceres* running aground not only found innocent, but
actually given considerable praise by the court for the very behaviour which had led Pigot to ask for him to be tried. . . .

Lieutenant Harris "immediately quitted the *Hermione,*" recorded
Midshipman Casey, "and join'd his friend Admiral Bligh's ship; I
believe they were related in some way."

Leaving aside the background of the Parker–Bligh clashes, there
is no doubt at all, on the trial evidence, that the verdict was fair.
Even if he ignored the verdict, on the evidence alone Sir Hyde

should have ordered the *Ceres*'s first lieutenant to be tried for failing to keep a good lookout. It goes without saying that since Pigot had worked out the course to be steered without taking the elementary precaution of allowing for an inset into the Gulf, he should have been the first man to be brought to trial.

NEXT DAY Admiral Bligh and the same four captains held a court-martial on Boatswain Harrington. The case was a curious one. Everyone would have known that a few weeks before leaving the *Success* for the *Hermione,* Captain Pigot had brought the *Success*'s boatswain to trial and had him dismissed the ship; and within a short time of joining the *Hermione* he had requested a court-martial on her boatswain as well.

Harrington, in his defence, produced a certificate of good behaviour signed by Pigot's predecessor, Captain Wilkinson, covering the period from September 1796 to February 1797; yet the evidence of Pigot and his officers—including Lieutenant Harris—against Harrington was overwhelming. They all cited several instances when Harrington had been insolent, insubordinate, asleep when he should have been on duty, and drunk when he was under arrest. Since Pigot's evidence was backed by Harris, Forbes and Casey, there can be no doubt of Harrington's guilt. The court's verdict was not surprising—that "the charge had been proved, in part," and that Harrington was sentenced to be "dismissed from his office of Boatswain of His Majesty's Ship *Hermione.*"

Yet the next time that Harrington appeared at a court-martial connected with the *Hermione,* less than a year later, he was the second master of the 74-gun ship *Thunderer*: he had a much more responsible post and his pay was £3 10s. a month compared with the £2 a month he received as the *Hermione*'s boatswain.

That he had become the second master of a line-of-battleship less than a year after being dismissed as the boatswain of a small frigate indicates he behaved himself well enough after his dismissal, while Captain Wilkinson's certificate of good conduct shows he behaved well before Pigot joined the *Hermione.* Clearly Pigot had taken an instant dislike to him; and Harrington was contemptuous of Pigot: all the offences he committed tend to bear this out.

With Harrington dismissed, the court turned its attention to the case of Thomas Leech, alias Daniel White, and the first witness was

John Forbes, who related Leech's activities as a deserter. After various others gave evidence, Leech asked Captain Pigot "to speak to my character." Pigot, as we saw earlier, considered him a "sober, attentive seaman, and always obedient to command," and added that he was so satisfied with him that after his first return he had made him captain of the foretop, "and had he not repeated the crime of desertion I should have not brought him to a court martial."

The court found Leech guilty, "but in consideration of his having delivered himself up; and the general good character given him by Captain Pigot and others," sentenced him "to receive only three dozen lashes with a cat-o'-nine-tails on his bare back on board the *Hermione* whenever the Commander-in-Chief shall think proper . . ."

Thomas Leech was a lucky man: it will be recalled that John Bowen, a former shipmate in the *Success*, had been given forty-eight lashes by Captain Pigot for *attempting* to desert.

CAPTAIN PIGOT had to get a new first lieutenant and a new boatswain. He must have suggested the second lieutenant, Samuel Reed, who was his favourite, should be promoted to first lieutenant, and the junior, Archibald Douglas, made second, leaving a vacancy for a new junior lieutenant. Sir Hyde agreed, made out the necessary orders, and sent Lieutenant Henry Foreshaw to fill that vacancy. (Foreshaw's name was subsequently spelled in various official documents as Foreshaw, Fairshaw and Fanshawe. "Foreshaw" is used in this narrative.)

Since the *Hermione* also wanted a lieutenant of marines—she had been without one for some months—Lieutenant McIntosh was sent to her. The new boatswain was William Martin, and his arrival most probably caused a lot of lewd comment among the seamen because he was allowed by Captain Pigot to bring his wife on board. "Allowed" is not strictly accurate: Pigot was probably careful to remain officially in ignorance of Mrs. Martin's presence, since the regulations forbade it. It must have been an uncomfortable life for Mrs. Martin, since she had to share her husband's box of a cabin.

Samuel Reed's promotion to be the *Hermione*'s first lieutenant gave few people pleasure. He had very little experience—his appointment was dated exactly eleven months after he joined the *Success* as acting junior lieutenant and four months after he transferred to the *Hermione* with Pigot as acting second lieutenant. However, from Pigot's point of view he had a pliant personality. Midshipman Casey, who had already served with him for four months and was to serve with him for a total of seven, commented that Reed's appointment was "rather unfortunate, he being for many reasons unfit for the situation, particularly with such a person as Captain Pigot."

WHILE THE THREE COURTS-MARTIAL had been in session, several merchantmen had arrived at the Mole to wait for a convoy to Jamaica. A frigate was needed to escort them, and Sir Hyde chose the *Hermione,* telling Pigot also "to proceed to Port Royal for such things as you may be in want of, and return to this port."

Some days after the *Hermione* had arrived in Port Royal, Pigot was delighted to see the *Ceres* being towed in to the dockyard, and he was soon on board. Otway was, of course, very pleased to see him and as a token of gratitude for his help in salvaging the *Ceres* he presented Pigot with a silver teapot.

XI

The Last Farewell

—w—

THE *HERMIONE* ARRIVED back at the Mole on Tuesday, July 18, escorting the *Westmoreland* packet, which had brought out the mail from England. As soon as the commander-in-chief's correspondence from the Admiralty was taken on board his flagship, Sir Hyde began going through the official letters. There was one, marked "Secret" and bearing the fouled anchor seal of the Admiralty, which was dated May 3 and told Sir Hyde in measured terms that—

"Disturbances have taken place among the crews of His Majesty's ships at Spithead under the command of Admiral Lord Bridport, but which by the measures which have been pursued, are happily terminated." Their Lordships enjoined Sir Hyde to take every possible measure to prevent any disturbances in his squadron, "should any attempt be made for that purpose."

The *Westmoreland* had already delivered to Fort Royal, Martinique, a similar letter to the commander-in-chief of the Leeward Island Station, Rear-Admiral Henry Harvey, who had been able to reply at once that "at present there is not the least appearance" of any disturbance.

Fortunately the Board's letter to Sir Hyde was not a complete surprise: a few days earlier the frigate *Cascade* had arrived from England with a warning letter from the First Lord, Earl Spencer, saying it was "absolutely necessary to avail myself of the sailing of the *Cascade* to let you know the very disagreeable situation of things here." Her captain would give particulars of "the very extraordinary and alarming mutiny which has broken out at Spithead." Spencer said "a very liberal offer has been made to them by Government on the subject of the grievance they complain of," and he was enclosing a copy of the offer, the conditions of which "will be adopted whether the mutineers here should choose to accept them or not."

Lord Spencer's letter was dated April 21, and that from the Admiralty May 3, but unknown to Sir Hyde the Spithead mutiny had subsequently become worse, despite the Board's assurance it was "happily terminated," and then spread to the Nore, where the effects were much more serious. Nevertheless Sir Hyde knew that the complacent phrases in the Admiralty's letter, and the rather more alarmed note sounded by Lord Spencer, could not minimize the basic fact that the fleet had mutinied—the very fleet on which Britain's existence depended. To a commander-in-chief of Sir Hyde's staid temperament and isolated position, it must have seemed that the world he knew was likely to topple about his ears; that the bloody Revolution which had swept France was setting foot in Britain—or at least in her ships.

Far more important, however, was that he received the Admiralty's warning against the background of an ugly rumour which had just reached him—one which sounded horrible enough to be true.

"A report prevails," Sir Hyde wrote to the Admiralty the day after the *Westmoreland* anchored, "which I am very apprehensive is founded upon truth, that the crew of H.M. schooner *Maria Antoinette* mutinied, threw the lieutenant and another officer overboard, and have carried the schooner into Gonaives." He soon heard that the schooner's surgeon and five loyal seamen had survived and were prisoners in French hands.

Thus the seeds of mutiny had also grown in the West Indies. They had not spread from Spithead—the *Maria Antoinette*'s crew had murdered their two officers long before news of the Spithead mutinies reached the West Indies. The mutiny in the little schooner was a brutal, traitorous affair; a straightforward case of cold-blooded murder and treason, whereas the mutinies at Spithead and the Nore involved only accidental bloodshed, and the men's loyalty to the Crown was never in doubt.

The news of the *Maria Antoinette* affair must have reached the warships at the Mole within a few hours of Sir Hyde receiving a report; and no doubt some men were envious of the freedom they imagined the *Maria Antoinette*'s crew had found. These men in the past years and months must have had read or related to them, by the usual hotheads found in any group in any age, the heady sentiments, catch-phrases and slogans of the leaders of Revolutionary France; when words like liberty and equality fell as thick and fast as a petty officer's curses and—at the time—had about as much significance.

The trouble had begun at Spithead when, after several of the men's petitions had been ignored over a long period, the crews of sixteen line-of-battleships finally ordered their officers to go on shore. The Spithead men were simply asking for better conditions: their petition to the Admiralty made the following requests:

1. That their pay should be increased.

This was hardly unreasonable since it had been unchanged for nearly 150 years. In addition the men were always paid months and frequently years in arrears, and even then not in cash: they were given "Tickets" which could only be cashed at the port where the ship commissioned. Wives and parents sent tickets by the men had to go to that port to get the money, unless the men sold their tickets to quayside sharks (often at less than half the face value) in order to send home cash.

2. That the weight of their provisions "be raised to the weight of sixteen ounces to the pound, and of better quality; and that our measures may be the same as those used in the commercial trade of this country."

The first demand sounds ludicrous, but it was not: a purser's pound weighed only fourteen ounces, and sometimes less. A purser was a curious mixture of clerk, retailer and ship's "housekeeper," and cases of honest pursers have been recorded. A purser had to deal with large quantities of money and was responsible for all provisions—quantities of which often went bad. To allow for this and also ensure he was economical, the Admiralty allowed him an eighth commission on everything issued—equal to two ounces in every pound. On top of that, over the years it had become the tradition for him to issue provisions in pounds of fourteen ounces. Indeed, contemporary naval handbooks gave a scale of two weights, one "avoirdupois" and the other "Pursers Establishment," in which "one pound avoirdupois is fourteen ounces avoirdupois to the pound." A combination in which a frugal Admiralty forced economies on a dishonest purser meant only one thing: the seamen suffered.

3. That while in a *British* port (an example of the fairness of their reasoning) they should be given "a sufficient quantity of vegetables, and no flour should be served."

The dreadful scourge of scurvy was sufficient justification for the first request; and the reason for the second was that once a week in port flour was served instead of beef.

4. That the sick men on board should be better attended and given "such necessaries as are allowed for them," and these "be not on any account embezzled."

Like pursers, good and honest surgeons have been known; but if they were any good they were usually in private practice instead of in the Navy. They were notoriously fond of the extra items—wine, for instance—allowed sick men; hence the men's wish for safeguards.

5. That they should be given leave when possible in harbour—but at the same time suggesting "there shall be a boundary limited," and any seaman going beyond it should be punished. They also requested leave when a ship was paid off.

The claim was more than reasonable, particularly since they suggested sufficient safeguards.

6. That a man wounded in action should have his pay continued until he was cured and discharged.

In other words, after being sawn up and sewn by a possibly incompetent surgeon, he should not be discharged from the Navy while still with open wounds or unhealed amputations.

By the standards of any day these were reasonable demands, but the Admiralty behaved with almost incredible foolishness. Faced with sixteen battleships taken over by mutineers at Spithead in protest over conditions which should have been voluntarily remedied half a century before, the Board offered the men four shillings a month more for able seamen, and lower ratings in proportion. Every other plea—for fresh vegetables when available, better care of the sick, reasonable leave, continued pay for wounded men—was ignored. The men rejected the offer but on April 20, on the eve of writing to Parker, Lord Spencer agreed to make a purser's pound weigh sixteen ounces.

Although the Admiralty were to make many more foolish mistakes, and the mutiny was to spread to the Nore (where more than thirty line-of-battleships entirely controlled by mutineers had London at their mercy), it is important, having seen the demands, to know whether the two great mutinies were inspired by revolutionaries or men genuinely feeling they had been badly treated.

Two brief quotations give a fair idea of the answer. The first was written by a magistrate sent specially to Spithead to investigate and report to the Under Secretary of State for the Home Department: "I am persuaded from the conversation I have had with so many of the sailors that if any man on earth had dared openly to avow his intention of using them as instruments to distress the country his life would have paid forfeit. Nothing like want of loyalty to the King or attachment to the government can be traced in the business."

The second is from the official report by two magistrates after investigating the Nore mutiny. Writing to the Duke of Portland, they assured His Grace they "have unremittingly endeavoured to trace if there was any connexion or correspondence carried on between the mutineers and any private person or society on shore, and they think that they may with the greatest safety pronounce that no such connexion or correspondence ever did exist. . . . Neither do they believe that any club or society . . . have in the smallest degree been able to influence the proceedings of the mutineers."

The men knew what the Red Cap of Liberty was; and no doubt many of the Irishmen among them, bundled off by the authorities on shore to serve at sea, visualized it replacing the Crown on top of the Irish harp. But for most seamen it is clear liberty was not so much a lofty ideal as the chance of occasional leave and better conditions.

In the *Hermione*, though, it was becoming to mean a great deal more: liberty was—perhaps at this stage only subconsciously—

being seen as ceasing to live a precarious existence at the mercy of a wilful and capricious captain, whose smiles quickly became intemperate outbursts of uncontrollable rage.

THE *HERMIONE* NOW had a few days in which to prepare for her next cruise. The most important task was to careen the ship because the barnacles and weed growing on the copper sheathing covering her bottom were slowing up the ship, especially in light winds.

Since there was virtually no rise and fall of tide at the Mole, and of course no dry dock, the only way to get at the barnacles and weed was to careen the ship, securing her to the quay, and then hauling on the masts with tackles to heel her over. It was a thoroughly unpleasant business: hard work for the crew and uncomfortable for the officers.

In the confusion Jacob Fulga, an able seaman, managed to slip away and desert. He had joined the ship in March, having come from a prize. Although he was not to know it, he had chosen a particularly dangerous moment to quit—he had not been reported to the commander-in-chief as having "Run" before the *Hermione* sailed on her last voyage, with the result that officially he was still part of her crew when, two years later, he was put on trial for his life.

On August 6, while the *Hermione*'s crew were busy scraping and scrubbing and Jacob Fulga was lying low, the 16-gun brig *Diligence* arrived at the Mole under the command of Robert Mends. The last person of any importance to be involved in the rapidly-approaching tragedy, Mends had just arrived from Charleston.

The *Diligence* needed a certain amount of fitting out before sailing again. Getting new sails for old and bringing on board a quantity of stores kept Mends and his officers and men busy for several days. Finally on Tuesday, August 15, the *Diligence* was ready, but she was still short of sails. However, an appeal to the *Hermione* resulted in one of the frigate's spares being sent over as a makeshift.

For the time being Sir Hyde Parker was flying his flag in the storeship *Adventure,* having sent the *Queen* away on a cruise. The previous Saturday, August 12, he had given Pigot instructions to take the *Renommée* under his command, but later decided to give him as well the *Diligence*.

His orders were quite straightforward: Pigot's squadron was to patrol the Mona Passage for seven weeks, and then return to the Mole. The orders could not have been better if Pigot had been allowed to write them himself—the land on both sides of the Passage was Spanish-held; the Passage itself was their main highway between the Spanish Main and the Atlantic, and therefore potentially rich in prizes.

On Wednesday, August 16, the three ships were "in all respects ready for sea": they had sufficient stores to last more than three months, and although the *Diligence* would not have water to last the whole patrol she would be able to replenish her casks from the other ships, or from streams on shore.

At 4.30 that afternoon the little squadron weighed anchor and made sail. The *Hermione* had begun her last voyage under her own name; but as far as anyone in the little squadron was concerned, another routine patrol had started. It was an uneventful night for the three ships as they made their way south-westwards towards Cape Dame Maria, and an entry in the *Diligence*'s log next morning described the first of many similar incidents: "At 40 minutes past 7 answered the general signal to chase, made all sail. At $^1/_2$ past 9 hove to and spoke the English sloop *Catherine,* letter of marque from Kingston to Quibo with rum. At $^1/_2$ past 10 filled and made sail in company with the frigates."

AS THEY MADE THEIR WAY to the Mona Passage the ships constantly chased unidentified vessels as they appeared over the horizon: there was a constant stream of signals from the *Hermione* detaching one or other of them in pursuit. Those which the *Diligence* alone intercepted give an idea of the scope of American trade in the Caribbean at this time—an American sloop bound for Baltimore with coffee on Sunday, August 20; another Jonathan on Tuesday which needed "a shotted gun" to bring her to; and a third on Wednesday which also needed "a shotted gun" before she would stop (a piece of cussedness on the part of her skipper, one suspects, since she was on a return trip to New York in ballast).

Apart from the constant making sail and heaving to, there was the normal shipboard routine to be carried out. On the day he fired his first shotted gun, Captain Mends also had a more peaceful task: a large quantity of biscuit (officially called bread) was too rotten to eat, and he ordered the master, boatswain and master's mate to carry out a survey. They wrote that 1,344 lb. was "mouldy, rotten, stinking and unfit for men to eat," and all of it "we have seen thrown overboard into the sea."

The surgeon reported to Captain Mends on Wednesday, August 30, that the second Lieutenant, George Mallas, who had been ill for the past few days, was dying, and at 11.30 that night he returned to say that Mallas had died. Mends wasted no time over the funeral (Mallas had probably died of yellow fever) and the ship's log recorded: "At $^1/_2$ past 12 committed the deceased to the deep."

At daylight, after chasing another ship—a Jonathan which also needed a shot across the bows—Mends reported Mallas's death to Captain Pigot, who sent over the *Hermione's* master's mate, John Forbes, to be the new acting second lieutenant. Whether Pigot sent him because he was a favourite (he had been brought to the *Hermione* from the *Success*) or to get rid of him after he gave such favourable evidence on Lieutenant Harris's behalf at the recent court-martial, is not known; but it was a choice which saved Forbes's life.

On Friday, September 1, the squadron arrived at the southern end of the Mona Passage and took their first prize. The day began with a series of stiff squalls sweeping down the Passage and at daylight the *Diligence,* sighting a ship, gave chase, followed by the two frigates. The brig soon caught up with her and sent across a boarding party, who reported that she was a Spanish schooner from Puerto Rico bound for Santo Domingo. Captain Pigot sent over a prize crew from the *Hermione* to take her into port, and signalled Captain Mends to send a midshipman from the *Diligence* to command her.

So the cruise continued and the days slipped by. One would be calm, followed by another full of squalls. On Wednesday, September 6, a particularly heavy squall in the evening which sent the topmen aloft in a hurry to reef or furl suddenly cleared to show a vessel in sight to the eastward, and Captain Pigot ordered the *Diligence* to chase it. She returned next morning escorting the ship, which was a 6-gun Spanish packet with a crew of seventy-three, and which had surrendered after a spirited action against the brig.

A week later the squadron sighted a cartel ship bound for the Mole, carrying former British prisoners whom the French were exchanging. Since all three ships in the squadron were now short of men, having sent off prize crews, Pigot decided to impress some of the Britons and share them out among the squadron. Thus the last new names ever to be entered were written down in the *Hermione*'s muster table.

On Thursday a sudden squall caught the *Renommée*, damaging her masts and spars so badly that Pigot ordered her to return to the Mole, leaving the *Hermione* and the *Diligence* to complete the patrol alone.

XII

Mr. Casey's Crisis

—∿—

EACH EVENING the *Hermione* and the *Diligence* reduced sail by furling the courses—the lowest and largest of the square-sails—and reefing the topsails, so that they sailed under easy canvas during the night. It was a snug rig and a safe one, because in the darkness it was usually impossible to see the notorious "white squalls" approaching, but if they suddenly met an enemy ship it took only a few moments to set the courses and shake out the reefs in the topsails.

On Thursday evening, the day after the *Renommée* left, both the *Hermione* and *Diligence* were sailing with only their topsails set when the time came to reef down for the night.

In the frigate, Captain Pigot and Reed were on the quarterdeck, and the first lieutenant was soon shouting out the first of the orders. Most of the work would be carried out by the topmen, with the direct responsibility for its speedy execution falling first on the midshipman and then the captain of the top in each of the three masts.

On deck the topmen waited expectantly: the captain insisted that all sailhandling must be done as if the commander-in-chief was watching the *Hermione:* he demanded speed and smartness. No excuses were ever accepted for the slightest delay; Pigot's voice, issuing strident and brassy from his bell-mouthed speaking trumpet, would pursue them aloft, often searing in its anger and terrifying in its threats.

"Man the rigging," Reed shouted at the topmen—there were about a dozen at each mast—who leapt into the shrouds and waited for the next order, which would send them running aloft in an almost vertical climb of fifty feet.

Waiting in the fore rigging were Midshipman Wiltshire and the new captain of the top, John Smith, a Yorkshireman born at Callingham, twenty-two years earlier, who had taken over from the errant Thomas Leech. Among those in the main rigging were Midshipman Casey and the captain of the maintop, John Innes, a Scot from Galloway, a former Success, and twenty-seven years old. The only mizzentopmen worth noting were Midshipman Smith, who was thirteen years of age; William Johnson, aged fourteen, who had acted for a while as Captain Pigot's writer; a Negro youth Peter Bascomb, from Barbados, who was sixteen years old and had been brought over from the Success; and Francis Staunton, who was seventeen and had been in the frigate for more than eighteen months.

The topmen were not, of course, the only men concerned with reefing: there were the fo'c'slemen and the afterguard. The fo'c'slemen handling halyards, braces and headsails were usually prime seamen too old to act as topmen. The afterguard, who worked on the poop and quarterdeck, were less skilled: their task was to provide muscle to haul on sheets, braces and halyards.

Of all these men, speaking in a variety of languages and accents, the topmen were the best seamen in the ship: they were handpicked, because theirs was the toughest and most dangerous work on board.

"Away aloft," bellowed Reed.

While the topmen scrambled up the rigging to the tops, Reed's next series of orders were to the men on deck: the heavy topsail yards were hauled round until the wind ran along the edges of the sails, unable to exert any pressure on the canvas, and then lowered a few feet. Reed shouted to the topmen fifty feet above him and they scrambled out along the yards.

The most experienced and expert went first because the men at the outer ends of each yard had the more dangerous and difficult job. After the men on deck hauled on the reef tackles, pulling the top part of the sail up to the yard like raising a venetian blind, the topmen spaced themselves out along the yard, their feet on the horse, a thick rope strung beneath, and soon had the reefpoints tied. They waited for the next order.

"Lay in!"

The men scrambled back along the yards into the tops. The yards would then be hoisted up again to their original position.

Captain Pigot was, as usual, watching the men closely and getting more and more angry. He had already shouted several times, telling the men to hurry. He could see most clearly the maintop, which was almost above him as he stood on the quarterdeck, and was the responsibility of Midshipman Casey.

At the very moment that Lieutenant Reed was about to shout "Down from aloft," Casey saw that a reefpoint had not been tied—overlooked by one of the men in his haste—and a length of plaited rope called a gasket, used to secure the sail when furled, was hanging down untidily behind the yard, just where Captain Pigot would be able to see it.

Casey promptly sent a man out to tie the reefpoint and clear the gasket; but Pigot was by this time in a rage. According to Casey, the captain "appeared to be greatly excited [and] fancying I suppose that we were not as smart as usual (we were known and admitted to be a very smart ship) got into a violent passion."

The moment Pigot saw the man climbing out on the yard he "instantly in very harsh language desired to know the cause."

Casey called down ("in a most respectful manner") an explanation, but Pigot "instantly launch'd out in the most abusive and unofficer-like language, calling me a damn'd lubber, a worthless good-for-nothing, that I never did anything right, and used many other severe expressions that I cannot and do not wish to recollect, and which may as well perhaps be omitted, to all of which I made no reply."

There was, of course, no excuse for the reefpoint; but there was an explanation. In the half-light, with Pigot yelling and bellowing, every man was rushing his work, fearful of being singled out by Pigot for a "starting." But frightened men rarely work properly.

Casey was in an unenviable position: Captain Pigot had always been friendly and had on several occasions recommended him to Sir Hyde Parker for promotion. (Sir Hyde had accepted, promising to make him lieutenant after a year's probation.) Casey wrote that up to then Pigot had treated him with "mark'd attention."

So Casey was more hurt than angry over Pigot's outburst; but if he hoped that this violent humiliation in front of the whole crew had ended the incident, then he hoped in vain, and the reason was Pigot's own personality. His usual impulsiveness, poor judgment and lack of self-control had made him abuse Casey at the top of his voice in a manner out of all proportion to the incident: in a matter of moments it had assumed for him an enormous and obsessive importance. Without a thought for the significance of what he had done or was about to do, he pursued it, like a dog at a bone, his pride, his fear of loss of face and his lack of judgment driving him on and providing its own momentum.

Reed gave the order "Down from aloft." The point where Casey and his maintopmen scrambled from the rigging onto the bulwarks was at the quarterdeck; and it was on to the quarterdeck that they then jumped, to find Pigot waiting, his face florid, his body tense with anger. Casey wrote: "He again attacked me in similar language as before, when my feelings were so excited from his dreadful and unmerited abuse."

Casey was a spirited youth and certainly no coward. "I replied that I was no such character as he described, of which he and every officer in the ship was well convinced."

Pigot's pride hung on too slender a thread to accept such a spirited reply; in any case he had lost too much control to restrain himself or draw back. "Silence, sir!" he shouted, "or I will instantly tie you up to the gun and flog you."

To threaten to flog a midshipman, particularly one of Casey's age and experience, was extremely unusual. Casey of course knew this, and his sense of injustice and bewilderment forced him to answer when it would have been wiser to have kept silent. He said: "I hope not, sir. This is cruel treatment, Captain Pigot, and what I don't deserve."

"You are under arrest: go below to your berth," ordered Pigot.

Casey's thoughts can be imagined: he probably regarded his career as ruined, since a court-martial would seem to be inevitable.

By now it was dark, and a few minutes later Pigot went below to his own cabin. His steward, John Jones, brought him a lantern. He then considered the situation. We do not know what he thought; but from what he subsequently did we can easily reconstruct the way his mind was working. He was, because a seaman had failed to tie a reefpoint, committed to flog a favoured senior midshipman, one he had often recommended to the commander-in-chief. But it is unlikely Pigot saw it in that light, any more than when two months earlier he had accused Lieutenant Harris—and received a well-deserved snub in the court's verdict. Yet even as he sat in his cabin he seems to have wondered whether on this occasion he had gone too far and was undoubtedly looking for a way to extricate himself without losing face.

Finally he passed the word for the first lieutenant, the master and the purser. As soon as Reed, Southcott and Pacey arrived, he started questioning them about Casey's behaviour earlier. All three said they had seen nothing. He then sent for Casey, telling the others to stay in the cabin.

The course Pigot had decided on was as simple as it was crude: he would humiliate Casey publicly: that would be sufficient. Indeed Pigot no doubt considered public humiliation (which he himself so clearly dreaded) a far worse punishment than flogging.

As soon as Casey appeared in the cabin, Pigot delivered himself of a judgment which Casey recorded as follows:

"Mr Casey, I have sent for you before these officers to express my disapprobation of your conduct this evening, and to know from them if they observed it. They seem ignorant, otherwise I would try you by a court martial. I have also questioned them as to your character, and they give you the highest character possible, and I must say myself that your conduct since with me has given me the greatest satisfaction."

He went on to "express his sorrow for my misfortune," wrote Casey, saying "that he [had] pitied me, and treated me more like one of his lieutenants than a midshipman; but from that moment he would change his conduct and consider me the same as any other midshipman in the ship, with the exception that I should never dine at his table, and if I did not go down on my knees the following morning on the quarterdeck he would flog me most severely, and in the most degrading way possible.

"I endeavoured to express my sincere sorrow," Casey added, "and I commenced in the most respectful and submissive manner to make every possible atonement for any real or imagined offence. I also endeavoured to express my gratitude for all his kind conduct to me while with him. But it was all unavailing."

Pigot merely declared: "You shall and you must submit to my decision that you go on your knees tomorrow morning. You are still under arrest: leave this cabin and return to your berth."

Pigot, realizing that Casey was not likely to submit, dismissed the master and the purser but told Reed to stay. Pigot appears to have thought that if the wretched youth would not listen to his captain he might listen to the first lieutenant if Reed went about it the right way. He therefore gave Reed certain instructions.

Back in the midshipmen's berth Casey reflected on Pigot's ultimatum. It was to his credit that he had given Captain Pigot the only honourable reply possible.

Later that night Casey was asleep in his cot when one of the quartermasters came down and woke him: the first lieutenant wanted him on deck. Hurriedly dressing, Casey went up to find Lieutenant Reed with the officer of the watch, Lieutenant Douglas. Reed at once began carrying out the captain's instructions and acting as the Devil's advocate. He asked Casey if he was going down on his knees before the captain next morning. When Casey said he would not, Reed asked him if he realized the consequences, and pressed Casey to accept his advice as a messmate and a friend, which was to submit to the captain, because that was the only way of preventing the disgrace of a flogging.

Casey wrote later that "I indignantly refused, adding that I thought he knew me better."

"The poor fellow seemed greatly distressed at his failure, and at what I believe he considered my obstinacy," Casey added. "He well knew what would follow, and he was most anxious to prevent it."

Early next morning some of the other officers spoke to him privately—among them Lieutenant Foreshaw, and the master, Southcott. They all "endeavoured to change my resolution. They were all more or less apparently attached to me, and anxious to prevent my disgraceful punishment, but," Casey added significantly, "none would attempt to persuade the Captain to change his cruel intention: they all appeared to be greatly in dread of him."

Shortly before 11 A.M. the boatswain's mates appeared at the hatchways to pipe "All hands aft to witness punishment." The marines, hot and sticky in their scarlet uniforms, clumped up on deck, clutching their muskets, and the seamen swarmed aft, falling in round the quarterdeck. The officers stood in a group on the port side, and finally the master-at-arms, McDonald, brought Midshipman Casey up from the midshipmen's berth and stood beside him at the capstan.

Pigot appeared with the inevitable copy of the Articles of War tucked under one arm, and without any preliminaries began reading them in a loud voice. It took several minutes, but finally he reached the 36th and last. He then looked at the midshipman standing by the capstan with his hat under his arm. The helmsman at the wheel a few feet away eyed the luffs of the sails towering overhead; but more than a hundred and fifty men were watching the youth: men from Chatham, overlooking the mud flats and saltings of the Medway, and from the bogs of Ireland; from cloistered Canterbury and the slums of Lambeth and Liverpool, Genoa and Leghorn; from mountainous Norway, and the palm-fringed island of St. Thomas; black men, white men; men whose native tongue was Italian, German, Portuguese, Norwegian, French, Swedish and Danish: men with vastly different backgrounds and standards of behaviour, but all of them with two things in common, a hatred of Captain Pigot, and a liking for Midshipman Casey.

Pigot said in a loud voice to Casey: "For your contemptuous and disrespectful conduct yesterday evening, I insist on your going down on your knees and begging my pardon."

This would be the humiliation he sought; and he knew that in his search for it he had the powerful backing of the Articles of War. But Casey refused. He replied in a respectful manner; indeed, his voice was humble; but the words he used were firm. "I assure you, sir, that I had no intention of offering you the slightest insult: I am very sorry that you should think I did: I can only beg your pardon."

"I insist that you go on your knees," retorted Pigot.

But Casey refused. Pigot again insisted; Casey again refused. Pigot then declared that had Casey gone on his knees, he would have been the first to despise him—but that he would now never be able to continue in the Service.

By saying he would have despised Casey, Pigot seems to have been trying to imply that his demand had really been only a test of Casey's character. He may have suddenly realized that in the eyes of the ship's company the first round had clearly gone to Casey for, in the midshipman's own words, Pigot then "with an oath, or rather coarse curse, ordered me to strip, which I also declined, saying that I never stripped at a public place of punishment; that he might order whom he pleased to strip me, and I would not prevent him."

Pigot barked out an order to the master-at-arms and Sergeant Plaice: "Strip him and seize him up!"

They pulled off Casey's jacket, shirt and stock: finally, when he was naked from the waist upwards, they twisted him round and tied him to a bar of the capstan. William Martin, the boatswain, then took the red-handled cat-o'-nine-tails from its red baize bag. It was an unusual task for him: usually a boatswain's mate administered a flogging.

"Give him a dozen," ordered Pigot.

Martin balanced himself against the gentle roll of the ship, and then suddenly his arm shot diagonally across his body. The tails of the cat whined for a split second, and then thudded into Casey's back.

When Martin stood back after delivering the twelfth stroke, with the blood-stained cat still in his hand, Pigot snapped at McDonald and Sergeant Plaice: "Cut him down."

The midshipman was gasping, for each lash from the cat had knocked the breath from his lungs, and with blood running down his back from the network of cuts he stood to attention.

"You will quit the midshipmen's mess and do no more duty," declared Pigot. "And you will prepare to leave the ship at the first opportunity—and that will be as soon as possible." With that, he turned and went down the companionway to his cabin.

Casey picked up his jacket, shirt and hat, and went below: the pain from his back was probably no worse than the agony in his mind. He went to the midshipmen's berth to collect his sea chest. Just forward of the gunroom was the steerage, an open space with the cabins of the warrant officers on either side, and there Casey decided to sling his hammock, using his sea chest as a table.

"All the officers, as well as my unfortunate messmates, commiserated with me most feelingly," wrote Casey, "and all continued to treat me with great kindness and attention." But none of them dared talk to him openly. "My meals were regularly supplied from the gunroom, or my late mess, and some of the officers, as well as my late messmates, visited me occasionally, and sat and chatted with me by stealth."

He added that "I have reason to know from the best authority [presumably Lieutenant Reed] that Captain Pigot frequently after my punishment expressed his regret to some of the gunroom officers in very strong terms, and he was often heard to say that no circumstance of his life gave him more real pain than his very severe conduct to me, for he ever considered me much superior to any other midshipman in the ship, and indeed to do him justice, he gave me very strong proofs of his good opinion, until this late unfortunate circumstance."

So Pigot expressed his regret; but did he really mean it? It seems unlikely: more probably he sensed definite but necessarily unspoken criticism of his behaviour towards Casey among the officers, and therefore made a superficial and unfelt profession of regret in order to allay this criticism, and to imply that he had been unwillingly forced into that particular course of action by Casey's own stubbornness.

It had all started with a frightened seaman forgetting a reefpoint, and a gasket working loose. A reefpoint and a gasket: they were symbols of Pigot's power over the ship's company.

THE *DILIGENCE* HAD by this time used up most of her water and on Saturday, September 16, the day after Casey was flogged, she signalled the *Hermione* to ask for some. The frigate hove-to while the brig sent over empty casks in her boats to exchange them for full ones.

This took some time, since Pigot allowed Mends five tons, and there was plenty of opportunity for the *Hermione*'s men to laugh and joke with the crews of the *Diligence*'s boats as they lowered the casks, and plenty of opportunity for secret messages to be passed.

In charge of the brig's boats was John Forbes, the former master's mate in the frigate. When he went on board the frigate he heard about Casey's treatment, and no doubt breathed a sigh of relief that, temporarily anyway, he was out of danger of being involved in such an affair.

On Sunday night Pigot was walking on the quarterdeck talking to Southcott when a shadowy figure loomed up out of the darkness and bumped into them. As he apologized both the captain and the master recognized him as John Watson, an able seaman, and Pigot remembered seeing his name on the surgeon's sick list.

There were several men on board at this time who were partly blind at night. It was a common enough complaint (caused by a vitamin deficiency) and since it was hard to diagnose, could be shammed without difficulty, particularly by topmen who did not want to work aloft.

John Watson was a topman, and earlier in the day the surgeon had recommended to the first lieutenant that he should be excused duties. Reed had agreed and ordered that he should act as gunroom sentry. Accidentally bumping into the captain and master at night in these circumstances appeared a trivial incident; but like many other apparently trivial incidents at this time, it had a certain significance.

IN THE *HERMIONE* on Wednesday, September 20, five days after the flogging of Casey, the surgeon, Sansum, faced a busy morning: every day more and more men lined up to see him, and his "Journal of Physical Transactions," a copy of which he had to give Captain Pigot, contained an ever-increasing number of entries. Some of the men claimed they were lame; others that they were blind, partly or temporarily. John Watson, the man who had bumped into Pigot and Southcott in the darkness, once again reported sick and was excused going aloft, but had to continue doing sentry duty. Peter Stewart, an able seaman, was so lame that he sat on the deck and dragged himself along backwards, using his hands. In addition he reported that he was going blind, and Sansum put him on a special list for a ration of wine. James Duncan, a topman, reported he had hurt his toe, and was given sentry duty.

The men's bad health was due almost entirely to the complete lack of vegetables and fresh meat, and many had varying degrees of scurvy. A contemporary medical book shows that Sansum had no difficulty in diagnosing it: "The first appearances of this malady are marked by a languid, torpid state of body; the patient has a pale, bloated look; there prevails a dejection of mind; and the breathing is affected on the slightest exertion. In a short time the gums acquire a softness and swelling; blood exudes from them and putrid ulcers are formed . . . The heart is subject to palpitations . . ."

These, it should be noted, were only the "first appearances."

The patient causing Sansum most anxiety was the marine officer, Lieutenant McIntosh: the previous day he had suddenly collapsed with a fit of giddiness, complaining that he could not see. He had been taken to his cot at once and was soon covered in a cold sweat, followed by a high fever and a splitting headache. The most stupid man in the ship could have diagnosed the illness—yellow fever, the all too familiar "Black Vomit." Before long McIntosh's eyes were bloodshot, protruding and rolling wildly; then they turned yellow, and his skin also took on a yellow tinge. In fleeting moments of coherence he complained of violent pains in his back and the calves of his legs.

During the night he had calmed down, but the vomiting had started and he went into a delirium. The disease was following its usual course: there was little Sansum could do except administer opiates, since it was nearly always fatal. Sergeant Plaice, with commendable loyalty, was keeping a constant vigil beside McIntosh's cot. The sick man had to be left in his cabin and he vomited and raved away his last few hours of life separated from his brother officers by a thin canvas bulkhead as they ate their meals or slept in their cabins.

The surgeon was not a popular man in the ship: perhaps he was ruthless with malingerers, and there were plenty of them. Two men already mentioned, Watson and Duncan, for instance, were shamming.

At this time Sansum's servant, a fourteen-year-old boy named James Hayes, was full of a resentment against his master which he was only too willing to communicate to any of the crew who would listen. The reason was not hard to find—a few days earlier he had been caught stealing from the surgeon.

Sansum, however, was not the only unpopular officer. Archibald Douglas, the second lieutenant, was perhaps trying to ingratiate himself with Pigot; but whatever the reason, the men hated him. They also hated the youngest officer in the ship, Midshipman Smith, who was thirteen years old and had just caused a seaman named John Fletcher to receive a severe flogging for what they regarded a trivial offence. Fletcher, a Whitby man, had served in the *Hermione* for nearly five years—he was one of the half-dozen who had been with the ship since she commissioned in December 1792.

The first lieutenant, Reed, was not popular, but the men did not bear him any particular malice: he had a weak character, and they probably saw that he had a hard time trying to please the captain. Pacey, the purser, was disliked no more than any other of his calling; and the men seem to have had a genuine regard for the master, Edward Southcott, and the carpenter, Richard Price, a Caernarvon man who had first joined the ship nearly five years earlier as an able seaman.

So the morning of Wednesday, September 20, passed: Sansum dispensed his meagre medicines; Pacey served out the provisions at fourteen ounces to the pound; Lieutenant McIntosh's life ebbed away; and the *Hermione,* with the *Diligence* on her starboard bow, sailed along under easy canvas.

At 11 A.M. a fresh breeze sprang up from the north-east and a lookout suddenly spotted a sail dead in the wind's eye. It was only one of a hundred such sightings made in the previous months; but at the moment he shouted the news down to the quarterdeck, a shadow fell across the lives of more than 170 men on board the frigate.

Captain Pigot immediately ordered the signal for "General Chase" to be made to the *Diligence,* which was nearer to the stranger than the *Hermione.* By 1.15 P.M. the brig was close enough to see that she was another Jonathan, and a boarding party reported she was from Newport, Rhode Island. Her brief role in the forthcoming tragedy completed, the American ship got under way again as the frigate and brig turned back south-westwards.

But for their long chase after the schooner both the warships would almost certainly have missed a sudden squall which came up at 6 P.M. Pigot ordered the *Hermione's* topsails to be reefed, and the topmen ran to the bulwarks ready for the mad scramble up the rigging at the order "Away aloft."

This followed immediately and the men were soon up the wildly-gyrating masts and out on the yards, feverishly gathering up the canvas as the wind tore at it. As far as Pigot was concerned they were not working nearly fast enough, and with his speaking trumpet to his lips he aimed a stream of curses and threats at them. He had learned nothing from the Casey incident, and within a few moments he was in the grip of his usual impetuous rage.

He turned to the seamen on the mizzentopsail yard. Three of these, it will be remembered, were only youngsters—the former clerk William Johnson, the Negro boy Peter Bascomb, and Francis Staunton, who was eighteen years of age.

Pigot watched as they fought with the sail fifty feet above his head, trying to get the last of the reefpoints tied; but to him they appeared a lubberly bunch—slow and unskilful. He put his speaking trumpet to his lips and hurled up a threat which must have chilled their blood, since one of the eight or ten men on the yard was bound to suffer. Convinced that his order to hurry was being ignored, Pigot bellowed:

"I'll flog the last man down."

They knew this was no idle threat. Pigot and Reed watched them as they scrambled back in to the mizzentop, and nearby the master, Southcott, was standing just abaft the wheel and directly beneath the yard. Suddenly three figures became detached from the slender security of the yard and seemed to hang motionless in space for a split second before their screams clawed the air and they plunged downwards, like birds of prey. At the moment they hit the deck Southcott pitched forward with a grunt, struck on the back by a falling body.

The colour of his skin showed that one of the trio was Peter Bascomb. The second was Francis Staunton, but the name of the third has not been recorded.

Captain Pigot looked at the three bodies sprawled on the deck only a few feet away. Their grotesque attitudes, like rag dolls thrown on a rubbish heap, showed they were dead.

"Throw the lubbers overboard," he ordered.

The screams of the falling men had frozen everyone on deck and aloft, and when they heard Pigot's subsequent contemptuous order, which the wind had carried in the silence that followed, the men on the mainyard began to murmur in protest—the episode, wrote Casey, "caused a painful sensation when it was observed." The murmuring made Pigot glance up. When he saw the maintopmen staring down at him instead of wrestling with reefpoints or getting back into the top, he screamed at Jay and Nash, who were near him: "Bosun's mates! Bosun's mates! Start all those men!"

Jay and Nash scrambled up to the maintop, side-stepped out onto the yard, and lashed at each man in turn with their knotted ropes. The seamen could not protect themselves: each had to use an arm to cling to the yard, so that the starters smashed down on their heads and shoulders remorselessly, while from below Captain Pigot watched: he had not finished with them yet. In the meantime Mr. Southcott was carried below to his cabin.

When Jay and Nash, their bruising task finished, came down on deck again Pigot ordered that the maintopmen's names should be taken: the starting had not been a sufficient punishment for those murmurs of protest—which he obviously correctly interpreted as criticism—and he would deal with the men properly in the morning . . .

Midshipman Casey's comment is all the more valuable because he had previously been the midshipman of the maintop and wrote his verdict forty-two years after it happened. The men's death was "a melancholy circumstance . . . which greatly increased the previous dislike of the Captain, and no doubt hasten'd, if not entirely decided, the mutiny."

That it decided the immediate fate of Pigot and nine officers is certain, because it is clear from the evidence of several of the ringleaders that during the night an instinctive change came over many of the ship's company. Pigot's brutality in threatening to flog the last man down, which resulted in the death of three young mizzentopmen; his lack of compassion when they perished at his feet; and his crude behaviour in "starting" the maintopmen and making it clear he would flog them on the morrow, were things so alien and shocking to the men that their response could only be primitive.

Exactly what they discussed that night is not known for certain, except for the evidence of one man. But he was to become a leader, and he said, as will be recorded later, that several decided they "were going to take the ship." However, while Pigot and the rest of the officers—with the exception of one on watch—slept soundly in their cabins, the men's courage failed them. Dawn brought Thursday, September 21: a cloudy day with light and variable winds and a mass flogging of the maintopmen in prospect.

XIII

The Inevitable Hour

—ɯ—

THE BOAST of heraldry (and interest) had secured Hugh Pigot's promotion to captain, and he had made full use of the pomp of power for his own cruel ends. Inheritance and prize money had given him wealth; but now his inevitable hour was fast approaching, spurred on by the cat-o'-nine-tails and the starter. The reason, seemingly a strange one when set against the floggings and furious threats which put men in terror of their lives, was that discipline no longer existed in the *Hermione*.

The fault was entirely Pigot's. For months he had imposed a harsh, brutal and erratic discipline which finally defeated its own purpose because eventually it inhibited the men's response to it, as all over-strict discipline is bound to, in the same way that a man trapped in a snowdrift is swiftly numbed by Nature so that he does not feel the cold.

The Hermiones, basically the same men who had served under Wilkinson, were clearly no worse than those in any other British warship; certainly not as bad as those that Otway found in the *Ceres*. The offences the Hermiones committed under Wilkinson were, apart from the usual desertions, quite minor; and there is no evidence that they became worse under Pigot. But, because of the type of discipline he imposed, and the resentment his behaviour engendered, the pattern changed.

The conclusion is inescapable: the occasional minor and monotonously similar offences—drunkenness and quarrelling, for example—committed by some of the Hermiones were infinitely less harmful to the King's service than the brutalizing effect of Pigot's continually harsh punishment and bullying manner. Terrorized men fumble and forget—the untied reefpoint in the Casey episode proves that—or they hurry and fall, as in the case of the mizzentopmen.

Therefore in the *Hermione* discipline had been destroyed by the man charged with enforcing it, while at the same time the men were labouring under the stress of the climate, disease, and the cruise itself, now in its fifth week. Almost continuous sail-handling was a great strain on men already debilitated by the lack of fresh food, and even the slightest attack of scurvy left them breathless after the least exertion. A rain squall meant more than reefing and an entry in the log; it meant soaking clothes and bedding—with what spare gear the men had sodden by water dripping through the seams of the deck planking, which opened up in the heat of the sun and made the lower deck more fetid than usual.

Under a good captain who cared for his men, the stress of climate, disease and constant hard work was bearable; but with a harsh, thoughtless captain it was not. A hot, sultry day, when the sun and humidity were stifling, was for a contented man simply a quirk of the weather. To an oppressed seaman it was an intolerable burden, sapping his energy and destroying his spirit.

BY DRAWING on all the relevant contemporary official and private documents which could be traced, it has been possible to study and, where space allowed, relate Hugh Pigot's activities up to September 20, 1797, the day the mizzentopmen fell to their deaths. His actions, often described in his own words from letters and the questions and answers at courts-martial and the Jesup inquiry, have already revealed much of his personality. The statistics and incontrovertible evidence of the floggings in the *Success* point to him using the cat-o'-nine-tails as much to satisfy his sadistic instincts as to administer justice. But it is more important to understand *why* he flogged so much than to know how many lashes he ordered.

As he took the last impetuous, headlong steps toward his own destruction, it is possible to make an appraisal of his character, but before doing so it must be emphasized again that Pigot was far from being just a brutal captain: with two others, he was the worst in the Royal Navy's recorded history.

Brought up as a child in a family with a tradition of command and authority, Hugh had inherited more than his share of arrogance and autocratic behaviour from his uncle George, who was probably a hero to the young boy. Lord Pigot had been in England from the time Hugh was born until he was six, and much of the time had been spent at Patshull. The comparison between the boy's mild-mannered father and the forceful, blustering and arrogant uncle must have been very marked.

By entering the Navy under his father's wing we have seen that Hugh was at first shielded from the harsher side of a life which had a tradition of undeviating discipline and often equally harsh over-tones of bullying and petty despotism. The boy found, when he first boarded the *Jupiter,* that seamen old enough to be his father had to touch their hats to him; at a very impressionable age he realized there were virtually no limits to his behaviour, that he personally was someone set apart from the rest. He discovered there were very few limits to the exercise of power by anyone in authority. He could, by a wave of his hand, bring a grey-haired seaman running. The lowly boatswain's mates, under a slack or harsh captain, could bruise seamen with their starters without reason or reprimand. In turn, lieutenants could haze and harry the boatswain's mates, while the captain could bully them all. Obviously not many captains were bullies; indeed, the percentage was small. But the Articles of War and the customs of the service gave each of them the opportunity: like a sword in its scabbard, the weapon was always there when required.

So, for all his formative years, Hugh Pigot was in a privileged position, watching (but not understanding or learning) how men wielded power, often without restraint, or with only the restraint an individual placed on himself. Soon—all too soon—he was himself wielding power, power lawfully placed in his hands by the Articles of War and backed by the whole strength and majesty of the State: power which increased in scope with every promotion.

Only thirteen years after first going to sea at the age of twelve,

Pigot was commanding a frigate with the power of life and death over a nominal ship's company of 215 men. He had more crude, naked power over any one of his seamen than the King over his whole nation: the King could not order any man to be given even one lash, let alone a dozen; he could only reprieve, not condemn. Every commanding officer was an offending seaman's prosecutor, defender, judge and jury and, thanks to the all-embracing thirty-sixth Article of War, the so-called Captain's Cloak, lawmaker as well.

Anyone given such power needed to exercise considerable judgment, humanity and restraint; justice indeed had to be tempered with mercy. Since he was dealing with men for the most part simple, uneducated and superstitious, he should have more than a touch of father and confessor in him.

Most of the captains in the Navy fulfilled this role; but in Hugh Pigot the King had a bad bargain. Due certainly to his early environment at sea, and to his own basic personality, the youth and later the man had come to believe that he need never brook even the slightest hint of denial, contradiction or suggestion from a subordinate, that there were no limits to the methods he used.

While he was serving under Sir Hyde Parker he was quite correct in this assumption: almost all the official documents concerning Pigot's service still survive, and apart from the Jesup case there is not even a hint that he had ever been criticized, advised or warned that his methods were cruel, unnecessary or dangerous. Since most of the time he commanded a frigate he came under Sir Hyde, that worthy must bear some responsibility: under him, Pigot had in fact been able to bully his crew and even flog two men to death without comment. In fact Sir Hyde approved of Pigot's harsh methods—a letter proving this will be quoted later. For Sir Hyde, a United Irishman sworn to bloody revolution lurked behind every grumbling sailor who spoke with a brogue; if the man had an English accent then he was a member of the London Corresponding Society and therefore just as dangerous.

So far we have been concerned only with the way Pigot treated his own crew. But when, behaving more like an irresponsible drunkard than the captain of one of His Majesty's ships of war, he actually ordered the American master of a United States' ship to be flogged with a rope's end, what was the result? Did his commander-in-chief at once demand an explanation, institute an inquiry, express any surprise or criticism? No—Sir Hyde did not bother to mention it in the daily journal that he was by law required to keep, nor in his dispatches. And when brought to account for his actions—on the direct orders of the Secretary of State—Pigot was once again in a privileged position: on Sir Hyde's orders only Pigot's witnesses were called.

Even by the custom of the service Pigot should have faced a court-martial or a court of inquiry over the *Ceres* going aground; but he avoided it. The court's verdict in the trial of Lieutenant Harris, and the report of the Jesup inquiry, are the nearest things to criticism that Pigot was forced to endure.

Criticism: that word held at least one key to Pigot's personality, because criticism (however oblique, and whether actual, implied, or as in the Casey episode, completely unintentional) was anathema to him. Much of Pigot's behaviour appears to have been caused by the fact that within him, to be thrust away and denied whenever it tried to come to the surface, was a half-conscious recognition of his own inadequacy and inexperience; as if he realized, deep down, that in truth he was no leader; that the men did not respond to him spontaneously, obediently and loyally as they did to captains he knew were natural leaders.

His misgivings were probably justified: the influence which obtained him command of a sloop at the age of twenty-two had failed to give him confidence and ability. Nor did he have time to gain either before getting command of a 32-gun frigate a few weeks later.

To compensate for his own misgivings he seemed determined that his ship must appear the smartest in the fleet: thus every manoeuvre had to be carried out as if the admiral was watching, although he did not realize that flashy methods used while getting under way at the Mole might not be the best when a dangerous squall hit the ship in the open sea. Speed and blind, unquestioning obedience: these qualities he demanded from his officers and men, because they compensated for the inadequacies of his leadership. Making the common error of confusing speed with efficiency, and terrorized obedience with loyalty, he produced a ship which was not an effective fighting machine, though neither he nor Sir Hyde was intelligent enough to realize it. Real leaders produced seamen who were efficient, and speed was an automatic by-product; who were loyal because they were properly led, and were blindly obedient because of absolute trust in their leaders.

Yet since he was surrounded by brother captains who were both experienced and natural leaders, Pigot's own pride probably instilled in him a fear that he might appear weak or vacillating, undignified or undecided—shortcomings which he knew were unheard of in real leaders.

This fear almost certainly added to the rigidity of his mind: once he had decided on a course of action he could not change it: he pursued it to the bitter end, regardless of whether it was right or wrong. Making ill-judged and impulsive decisions and sticking to them rigidly, without a moment's thought of their effect on the future, meant he lived in the eternal "now"; he acted his part for today without realizing that there must inevitably be a tomorrow, a time of judgment, and of reckoning. So far in his career there had been no tomorrow, no judgment of any cruel, stupid or ill-considered action.

It was almost certainly a part of his sense of his own inadequacy that led to him becoming obsessed with the minutiae of discipline, so small-minded that he investigated the most trifling alleged failure of duty with an obsessive and terrifying thoroughness more usual in the Inquisition and the Star Chamber: the neglected reefpoint, for example, which had led to the flogging and (apparent) ruin of Casey. Forgetting the original trifling cause, Pigot became obsessed with the overriding need to humiliate Casey, and distorted and inflated the situation into a public trial of strength between himself and the youth. It is equally significant that he thought that such a demonstration of his power was necessary. But this was the "now"; he did not consider the "tomorrow," when Casey's career would be ruined over a trifle. (And it *was* a trifle: there were more than two dozen reefpoints per row in a topsail: leaving one untied would not damage the sail.)

By similar obsessive processes, Pigot had his favourites and his scapegoats, men against whom he had festering grudges. There is little doubt that Boatswain Harrington's downfall began originally because Pigot disliked him. In any ship the boatswain was usually the most skilled all-round seaman on board. Did Pigot fear unspoken criticism or contempt from such a man because of his own lack of experience? Did he need to provoke, and then break two of them, to prove himself?

It seems certain that the departure of Lieutenant Harris on June 17 removed the last restraint on Pigot. Up to then, Harris appears to have been a buffer between the men and Pigot. But after June 17 the events moved swiftly to their bloody climax, with Pigot utterly incapable of appreciating the dull anger and resentment, the bewilderment and fear that his ill-considered excesses and inconsistent punishments aroused.

The last vestige of discipline vanished in the *Hermione* as the three mizzentopmen fell to their deaths: at that moment the crew seem to have realized that Pigot had no regrets or scruples in sacrificing men's lives. And their reaction was the primitive "kill or be killed" response of the jungle: a response which society had, by its taboos, laws and culture, managed to train most of its members to renounce by offering them other means of obtaining equity and fair play.

However, in the *Hermione* the months of brutal treatment and injustice were strengthening the men's natural and deep-rooted instinct of self-preservation and, no doubt fed by revolutionary talk, it was becoming powerful and urgent; more than strong enough to submerge the tradition and habit of submissiveness to an apparently superior being.

On Pigot's behalf it can be argued that many of the men serving in the Navy at this time were lazy, idle, truculent, resentful of unpleasant conditions afloat and bad food. Those who had been pressed hated their loss of liberty. Yet, unlike Otway when he joined the *Ceres,* Pigot never once complained of the quality of his ship's company; and he inherited the ship from a captain who enforced a strict discipline. In any ship at that time a proportion of the men were thoroughly bad characters; but the vast majority of captains trained up highly efficient crews without constantly using the cat-o'-nine-tails. If other captains could handle their men without incessant flogging, why could not Pigot? There seems to be only one conclusion: the fault lay in Pigot, not in his crew.

However, we must not make the mistake of judging Pigot by today's standards, but by those of his contemporaries. Since it was his methods of punishment which give grounds for criticism, we can take a brief look at what was happening across the Atlantic in England on September 20 and 21, 1797, the day the mizzentopmen were killed and the day the maintopmen were flogged.

On the 20th at the Old Bailey in London, Robert Arnold was charged with "burglariously breaking and entering" a house and stealing "a cloth cloak and other articles," and was sentenced to death. Sarah Warwick, found guilty the same day of "privately stealing in the shop of Edward Evans a piece of printed calico," was also sentenced to death. Although Britain was at that moment fighting to free the world of tyranny, few Britons would have been shocked at these two sentences (which were carried out), for they were typical of those passed nearly every day that courts were in session.

Naval law was in fact considerably more lenient in practice than civil law, although its liberality may have been due to the Admiralty knowing that a man hanging by his neck from the yardarm meant the ship lost a seaman. The crimes for which the Articles of War prescribed the maximum sentence of death fell mainly into the categories of treason, mutiny, desertion and cowardice in the face of the enemy. By comparison, on September 21 at the Old Bailey Samuel Philips was found guilty of stealing "a flock bed and several articles" and was publicly hanged a few days later.

IN THE *HERMIONE* on September 21 at 10.30 A.M., just half an hour before all hands were called aft to witness punishment, the *Diligence* hoisted the signal for a strange sail in sight to the northwest. It would have been better if her lookouts had not seen it. The wind was easterly and light, and Pigot at once ordered "general chase." Both ships bore away in pursuit although, unless the wind increased, it would take several hours to catch up.

Promptly at 11 A.M. Thomas Jay and Thomas Nash went through the ship ordering the men aft to witness punishment, and McDonald, the master-at-arms, who had been given a list containing the names of more than a dozen maintopmen, marched his charges up on deck, where they were stripped and flogged at the capstan for their tardiness and murmurings the previous evening.

Midshipman Casey, recording the episode, wrote, "*A very severe punishment* [underlined in the original] of several men, I believe twelve or fourteen, took place in the usual way, at the public place of punishment."

While the men were being flogged, the frigate and brig continued to chase the strange sail, which appeared to be a schooner privateer. As the wind went round to the north it put them farther to leeward, and they tacked at 2.30 P.M., and again at 6 P.M., by which time the privateer was still well up to windward, bearing north-east. With night coming on Pigot knew his chances of catching her were slender: she had the choice of working out northwards through the Mona Passage, or doubling back southwards, passing them in the darkness. But deciding he would be more likely to intercept her if he split his force, Pigot signalled to the *Diligence* that she was to stand away on a different tack at 8.30 P.M.

With their guns loaded and run out in readiness, the two warships worked their way to windward in the light breeze, and Thursday, September 21, drew to a close. In the *Hermione* as twilight gave way to darkness the officer of the watch ordered the lookouts down to the deck from the mastheads. At 8 P.M. the boatswain's mates piped "Down hammocks" and the men collected them from the nettings along the top of the bulwarks and took them below to sling in their allotted positions. Lanterns were issued by the purser's steward's assistant; the watch was changed, the bells rung and the hour and half-hour glasses turned. Soon afterwards the boatswain's mates piped "Ship's company's fire and lights out": the only lights allowed in the ship now were in the gunroom (they had to be doused at 10 P.M.), those beside each sentry, and the dim light in the binnacles illuminating the compass.

At 10.15 P.M., when all the off-watch men and the day workers should have been asleep, Captain Pigot went to see Southcott. The master was still in charge of navigation, even though he had been in his cot all day after being badly bruised by the falling boy. The sentry stood to attention as Pigot walked into the gunroom—which was full of the sweet, nauseous yellow fever smell of Lieutenant McIntosh—and entered Southcott's cabin. He explained that the two ships were still chasing the privateer and he had told the *Diligence*, which had been four miles away to the west-north-west at 8 P.M., to stand away on the other tack at 8.30 P.M. She had done this and was now out of sight. Pigot then gave Southcott the usual routine night orders—he was to be called if the weather changed or if they sighted another ship, and in any case at daylight.

Pigot then walked back up to his cabin on the deck above and the sentry at the door, Private Andrew McNeil, stood to attention as he passed. In the cabin his steward, John Jones, helped him undress and gave him his long nightshirt to put on. Jones slept in a hammock just outside the cabin door, within a few feet of where McNeil stood on guard.

On the deck below the captain's cook, John Holford, was already asleep on top of the armourer's chest outside the gunroom door, and nearby his young son was also sleeping. In their cabins forward of the gunroom the captain's clerk, the gunner, carpenter, and Boatswain Martin and his wife slept soundly. Near Martin's cabin Midshipman Casey was in his hammock. Midshipman Smith was sleeping in the midshipmen's berth, but if anyone had looked for Midshipman Wiltshire in his hammock—for that was where he was supposed to be—they would have found it empty.

Opening off the gunroom, the surgeon and the first lieutenant occupied two cabins on the starboard side, while the third was empty—its owner, Foreshaw, was on watch. On the larboard side, the purser, master and second lieutenant were sleeping, while in the fourth cabin Lieutenant McIntosh was dying, with Sergeant Plaice still keeping vigil.

Forward of the gunroom and only a few feet from Casey's hammock, the sentry at the porter cask was James Duncan, the foretopman with a bad foot; and nearby James Perrett, the ship's butcher, was snoring in his hammock.

Up on the quarterdeck, his eyes straining in the darkness for a sight of the privateer they were chasing, was Lieutenant Foreshaw, the officer of the watch, and with him was William Turner, the master's mate. At the wheel, watching the dimly-lit compass and the luffs of the sails, was Thomas Osborn. Between the aftermost carronades on the larboard side, acting as a lookout, was James Barnett, one of the maintopmen who had been flogged that morning; and the lookout on the other side was one of the afterguard, James Irwin from Limerick. At the forward end of the quarterdeck a marine sentry, Private Robert Newbold, guarded the water cask—for water was strictly rationed, although a daily allowance was left in the scuttlebutt so that the men could occasionally refresh themselves.

In each of the tops there were men on watch ready to reef or set more sail: John Brown, a young Scot, was in the maintop with George Walker, a former jailbird. In the foretop, in addition to the men on watch, was Midshipman Wiltshire, who was bent on keeping out of the way after hearing certain rumours.

To the casual onlooker—and to the officer of the watch, Lieutenant Foreshaw—everything appeared in order: every twenty minutes the lookouts answered the lieutenant's hail by calling out that all was well. But they were wrong, or lying, for the inevitable hour of Hugh Pigot had at last arrived.

XIV

Time for Murder

—ᴍ—

AT 11 P.M. John Brown and George Walker were still on watch perched in the *Hermione*'s maintop fifty feet above the deck, when suddenly they sensed in the darkness that someone was clambering up the mainstay towards them. The only reason for a man coming monkey-fashion up the massive rope—which ran at a steep angle from the fo'c'sle to the maintop—would be to avoid being seen from the quarterdeck.

A few moments later, breathless and perspiring, David Forester scrambled off the stay and into the top. Forester, born in Sheerness and not yet twenty years of age, who had been in the ship for three years, wasted no time: the mutiny had begun, he told the two men. "Go down to the fo'c'sle: they want you there."

A startled Brown replied: "We can't go down there: it's our watch to take in the topgallants."

"If you don't go down, it'll be the worse for you," Forester said curtly, "and don't go down by the rigging: use the stay."

Brown already had an inkling of what was about to happen: he said afterwards that at noon that day Forester—who was, like himself, a maintopman—had asked the captain of the maintop, John Innes, "If he had heard anything of what was going on last night.

. . . That Innes replied 'No,' on which Forester said, 'They were going to take the ship last night, but they would do it that night.' "

Reluctantly Brown and Walker swung out of the maintop and, followed by Forester, went hand over hand down the mainstay to the fo'c'sle. There an extraordinary sight met their eyes: a group of men round a bucket of rum, like natives at a cooking pot, were "drinking and fighting." According to several witnesses some were half drunk. Among them were the captain of the foretop, John Smith, a Yorkshireman, and James Bell, a Scot, both former Successes; John Farrel, a fo'c'sleman from New York; and Joseph Montell, an Italian maintopman and one of the original Hermiones.

The bucket of rum from which they were gaining courage was not the result of hoarding their twice-daily tots: it belonged to the officers and had just been stolen from the gunroom by Lieutenant Douglas's servant, an Irish boy of fourteen named James Allen, and William Anderson, the gunroom steward, who was eleven years older and came from Canterbury.

Brown and Walker watched the group, and after listening to their chattering for a few minutes decided they did not sound like determined mutineers: Farrel and Smith, for instance, started wrangling and "making use of some oaths, that they were not fit to go through with the business," according to Brown, who was so unimpressed that he decided to return to his post in the maintop. He did not bother to go back up the mainstay; instead he went aloft by the main shrouds at the fore end of the quarterdeck, and no one asked him why he had left his post.

With Osborn at the wheel, the *Hermione* continued on her course, still chasing the privateer. As far as Lieutenant Foreshaw on the quarterdeck was concerned all was well: the frigate's masts and yards creaked in counterpoint to the working of the hull and the bubble of the bow wave, and blocks clattered as ropes tightened and slackened with the ship's roll. Suddenly Brown, back at his lofty vantage point in the maintop, heard a shout of alarm—it seemed to be from a marine on the maindeck standing at the foot of the ladderway to the quarterdeck.

PRIVATE ANDREW MCNEIL, the marine sentry guarding Captain Pigot's cabin, stood in the small pool of light cast by the lantern hooked on to the bulkhead and was surrounded by the grotesque black shadows it threw. McNeil had more than an hour to wait, with his musket by his side, the bayonet fixed, before he would be relieved. Apart from Captain Pigot, the only other person sleeping on the half deck was Jones, the steward, who was in his hammock only a few feet away.

Suddenly out of the encircling darkness, several men leapt at McNeil. One of them swung a cutlass, the flat side of which flashed for a moment in the lantern light and then hit the marine across the head before he had time to shout out. Dazed, McNeil collapsed to the deck, but as his mind slithered on the edge of unconsciousness he heard a voice which he recognized as that of a Negro, John Jackson, one of the captain's bargemen, who was saying, "Let the bugger alone—we'll go in and murder the Captain."

Joe Montell, the Italian, had in the meantime snatched up McNeil's musket and bayonet and in a few moments the group smashed down Pigot's door and vanished into the cabin.

The sound of splintering wood, punctuated by McNeil's groans, roused Steward Jones, who sat up in his hammock and saw McNeil sprawled on the deck a few feet away, blood spattered on the deck round him. Jones had no idea what had happened but ran across and knelt down beside him. McNeil gasped out that he had been attacked, and at that moment they heard heavy blows and men grunting in the captain's cabin. Jones helped McNeil to his feet and they scrambled up the companionway to the quarterdeck to raise the alarm.

Captain Pigot had woken to the sound of his cabin door being kicked in. Leaping from his cot—this took a few seconds since it swung from the deckhead—he snatched up a short dirk: there was no time to get his white-handled cavalry sword, which was on a rack fixed to the bulkhead.

By the time Pigot was on his feet, dirk in hand, the door had crashed down. He then saw several men, silhouetted against the lantern light outside, streaming into the cabin, crouching to avoid hitting their heads on the beams overhead. All armed with cutlasses or tomahawks—except for Joe Montell, who had Private McNeil's musket and bayonet—they included David Forester, two boatswain's mates—the Irishman Thomas Nash and the Cornishman

Thomas Jay—Thomas Leech, the deserter Pigot had forgiven, Richard Redman, the quartermaster's mate, and a young Dane, Hadrian Poulson.

As soon as they spotted Pigot in the darkness they began slashing at him with cutlasses and tomahawks. Pigot tried to ward them off with his dirk which, only two feet long, was little more than a large dagger. The men got in each other's way in the darkness and were unfamiliar with the cabin so that, still dressed in his long nightshirt, Pigot managed to fight them off while shouting for help.

"Where are my bargemen?" he cried.

"Here are your bargemen," yelled Poulson. "What do you want with them, you bugger?"

By now they were in a frenzy. Forester hit Pigot two or three times with his cutlass and Pigot, lunging back, managed to wound him in the foot with the dirk. Pigot's cot was slashed to ribbons and chairs were smashed and flung out of the way. Pigot, wounded several times and becoming faint from loss of blood, still shouted for help. His attackers, cursing and screaming as they tried to finish him off, were then joined by John Phillips, the Hanover-born sailmaker, and the American John Farrel, who earlier had been drinking rum on the fo'c'sle. Pigot managed to slash Phillips's hand with his dirk, but Phillips succeeded in stabbing him in the stomach with his cutlass.

Finally, gasping for mercy and bleeding from a dozen or more wounds, Pigot collapsed over the barrel of one of the 12-pounder cannons, his nightshirt torn and soaked with blood and perspiration.

In the meantime there was pandemonium on the quarterdeck above: Steward Jones and Marine McNeil had scrambled up the companionway, McNeil calling out, "Mr Foreshaw! Mr Foreshaw!"

The young lieutenant demanded: "What's the matter?"

"Sir—some men have broken into the cabin—I think they are murdering the Captain!"

Foreshaw decided he could not leave the quarterdeck. He told the master's mate William Turner: "Go down and see what's causing the noise in the cabin."

"If you want to know you can go down yourself!" retorted Turner.

At this, Foreshaw seemed at last to have realized the crew were mutinying and that the ship was in deadly danger. Knowing the nearest assistance lay with the *Diligence* away to leeward, he turned to Osborn, the man at the wheel, and ordered: "Put the helm up: wear the ship and steer for the *Diligence!*"

"I'll see you damned first," said Osborn.

Foreshaw promptly knocked him down, and Osborn yelled for help. At that moment a group of men who had previously been on the fo'c'sle—John Jones reckoned there were twelve or fourteen of them—ran aft along the gangway and seized Foreshaw.

Marine McNeil had by then gone back down the companionway to see what was happening in Pigot's cabin. Looking through the door he saw, faintly lit by the feeble glow of the lantern outside, "the Captain on the larboard side, leaning against the gun, with his shirt torn and his body all over blood."

Thomas Leech, Forester, Patrick Foster (who was Pigot's coxswain), the Negro Jackson and several other men were standing over on the starboard side, near the captain's desk, as if uncertain what to do next. At that moment they heard Osborn's cries for help coming through the skylight from the deck overhead.

Several of them, led by Nash and Farrel, immediately ran up to the quarterdeck, where they found that the group of mutineers from the fo'c'sle had seized Lieutenant Foreshaw. While some told him his life would be spared others were warning him to prepare for death. Two leading mutineers—John Smith, the captain of the foretop, and James Bell, a quartergunner—then hustled both Foreshaw and Turner aft, saying they had nothing to fear and their lives would be saved. John Brown, still up in the maintop, could clearly hear the alternate threats and reassurances above the shouting and yelling.

But as soon as Nash and Farrel arrived on the quarterdeck the fo'c'sle group asked them what they should do with Foreshaw.

"Heave the bugger overboard," ordered Nash.

Foreshaw, guessing that by now the mutineers controlled the whole ship, begged them to spare him: "I have a wife and three children entirely dependent on me," he said. John Jones heard him continually pleading with the men "to save him until next morning," but "they would not hear what he had to say."

David Forester walked over to Lieutenant Foreshaw and grabbed him. He was later to admit that if he had not seized Foreshaw then, he thought the lieutenant's life would have been saved. But his gesture was the signal for the men to go berserk: they "began to chop at him with tomahawks and bayonets," recorded Jones. Trying to ward off the blows with his arms, Foreshaw slowly retreated to the ship's side and when he could go no further climbed up on to the bulwarks, with the men still slashing at him, and then finally vanished into the darkness over the ship's side.

With the quarterdeck now under their control, Nash, Montell, Forester, Farrel and Poulson went down to the captain's cabin again and found that Pigot was still alive, leaning on a couch, his body soaked in blood.

"You bugger, aren't you dead yet?" exclaimed Farrel.

"No, you villain, I'm not," retorted Pigot, and held out his dirk to ward them off. Both Forester and Phillips had already been wounded by that dirk and hesitated, as did the rest of the men. But at that moment they were joined by William Crawley, who had a tomahawk in his hand and, miscounting the number of his confederates but probably fortified from the rum bucket, cried out: "What, four against one and yet afraid? Here goes then!" He attacked Pigot with his tomahawk, giving courage to Farrel, who slashed the captain across the head with his cutlass. Pigot collapsed on the deck, then struggled to his feet again, crying for mercy.

"You've showed no mercy yourself and therefore deserve none," shouted Montell, lunging with the bayonet fixed on the marine sentry's musket. The bayonet ran Pigot through, and he collapsed again, dropping his dirk. Some of the mutineers then picked him up while others started smashing one of the stern windows. In the faint light from the sentry's lantern Pigot, though barely conscious, recognized the face of one of his former favourites.

"Oh! David Forester—are you against me too?"

"Yes I am, you bugger," retorted Forester, and stabbed him once again.

By then there was a large enough hole in one of the windows, and the men grasping Pigot's body—which was slippery with blood—hurled him out into the sea. Some of them later claimed they heard Pigot's cries as he was left astern. The murderers then quit the cabin.

Forester saw John Jones at that moment—the steward was busy bandaging the wounded marine's head—and tapped him on the shoulder. "I've just launched your bloody master overboard," he said. "The bugger—I gave him his death wound, I think, before he went out of the window," and told him of Pigot's surprised cry. Jones was to remember that tap on the shoulder for more than five years.

THE ATTACK so far had taken little more than five minutes. The fighting in the captain's cabin almost overhead had finally roused Southcott, the master. He scrambled out of his cot and in his night-shirt ran into the gunroom, where he jumped onto the table to climb out through the skylight—it was the quickest way up and one always used in an emergency.

"Not conceiving mutiny," he said later, "I was in my shirt without arms." He had just grasped one side of the skylight and was heaving himself out when Richard Redman appeared on the deck above him crying out, "Here is one of the buggers coming up! Knock him down!" With that he lashed Southcott across the face and arm with a handspike—a long wooden bar tipped with an iron ferrule and used for heaving round the gun carriages.

Southcott collapsed, rolling off the table and falling on to the scuttle of the magazine. In the cabins round him and apparently still asleep were Lieutenants Reed and Douglas, the surgeon, and the purser. Sergeant Plaice was still with the dying marine officer while in the cabins forward of the gunroom the gunner, carpenter, captain's clerk, boatswain and his wife were either undisturbed or preferred discretion to valour.

Midshipman Casey, however, soon woke up. "On the first alarm," he related afterwards, "I was in my hammock asleep. . . . Being entirely unacquainted with what was the matter, and seeing some men near the gunroom, I called out to know what was the noise, or what the matter was, but received no answer.

"I then got up in my shirt and went up the after hatchway [to the half deck near Pigot's cabin] . . . I heard a dreadful noise issue from the cabin door, and I saw several of the crew running from the starboard side towards the cabin door.

"I again asked what the matter was, when two of the men, by the names of Farrel and Phillips, hearing me call out, inquired who I was. On finding who I was, told me that they were striking for liberty but they themselves wished me no harm and desired I would immediately go down below and stow myself away, or go to my bed, as they supposed some of the men would put me to death.

"Finding there was no resistance being made, and being unarmed, I went below. . . . I perceived the outside part of the gunroom surrounded with armed men, one of whom, William Crawley, [was] making use of the following language, 'That the first bugger who offered to move or make the smallest resistance they would immediately put them to death,' or words to that purport. Finding it was impossible to make the smallest resistance, I lay down in my hammock."

By this time there was chaos in the gunroom and Southcott had regained consciousness. "After I recovered, I ran to my cabin and got my sword, called for the officers in the gunroom and made all speed." He could hear men outside and on the deck above shouting "Hughie's overboard! Hughie's overboard! Hurrah—the ship is ours!" Southcott drew his sword from its scabbard and banged it against the cabins on either side—Lieutenant Douglas's forward and the purser's aft—to rouse them.

John Brown, the frightened maintopman, now climbed down the shrouds to the deck, thinking from the cries that the mutiny was over. He was sadly mistaken: hardly had he stepped out of the rigging before he found James Bell, the quartergunner, busy smashing open an arms chest with a tomahawk. As soon as the lid was prised off Henry Croaker, John Elliott and Patrick Foster, all former Successes, seized the muskets and started handing them round to the other men. At that moment Bell looked up and saw Brown.

"Here's one of them," he said. "What shall we do with him?" Both Leech and Smith, the captain of the foretop, said, "Let him go," so Bell thrust a musket into his hands and told him to guard the after hatch, and not to let anyone come upon deck "without knowing them." Brown later said he "felt obliged to take the musket to save my life."

The second man in addition to Casey who had been near the gunroom door at the beginning of the mutiny was James Duncan, the lame foretopman acting as sentry at the porter cask, which was near the midshipmen's berth. He later claimed that when the mutineers first rushed down the after hatch they knocked out his lantern and William Crawley swore at him, saying, "Damn your eyes, I'll

knock your brains out if you don't get out of my way: I don't know
friend from foe."

"For God's sake what's the matter?" asked Duncan.

At that moment John Holford, the captain's cook, who had been
sleeping on the armourer's chest a few feet away, woke up. Leaping
off the chest he shouted—as if in answer to Duncan's question—that
the ship was on fire; but quickly realizing his mistake he followed
the crowd to the gunroom door, where he heard them yelling,
"Where is he? Where is the bugger?"

The fourth man near the gunroom—the marine on sentry duty at
the door—was apparently unaware of the mutiny: he cried out
"Mercy" as the mob ran past Duncan at the porter cask, making for
the gunroom door.

The man they were hunting was Lieutenant Archibald Douglas;
but roused by Southcott's sword banging on his cabin, and then
hearing the shouts, he had leapt from his cot stark naked, and bolted
into the sick marine officer's cabin next door.

"When I first saw him, he was naked," said Sergeant Plaice. "He
said, 'Lord, Sergeant, what is the matter?,' then he crept under the
officer's cot." Douglas probably thought no one would dare come
near McIntosh, who was known to be dying, and whose cot was
soiled since he had no control over himself.

He was no sooner hidden under the cot than a crowd of mutineers, headed by Joe Montell, broke into the gunroom. Samuel Reed,
the first lieutenant, whose cabin was on the other side from the door,
ran out and leapt on to the table, intending to escape through the
skylight; but Montell, who had exchanged McNeil's musket for a
tomahawk, made a wild lunge and cut him across the face. Reed
dropped to the deck and was trampled underfoot as a swarm of
mutineers surged in behind Montell shouting, "Where is he? Where
is the bugger? . . . Where's Douglas—we can't find Douglas!" They
then shouted out for lanterns to be handed down through the skylight.

Southcott recorded that "I returned to my cabin, as I could get no
assistance; I hove my sword behind my [sea] chest and lay down in
my cot."

According to Sergeant Plaice, "At this time there were about
twenty or thirty of the mutineers" in the gun room, and many of
them went into Douglas's cabin "with tomahawks and bayonets and

different kinds of arms and cut his palampour and his cot down. I heard them say, 'The bugger is gone; we cannot find the bugger!' "

The mutineers then left the gunroom to search the ship and, said Plaice, "Mr Douglas went into his cabin again and took his bed gown down and brought it into our officer's cabin and put it on. Then he went under the cot again."

David Forester, having played his part in murdering Captain Pigot, then heard the men on the deck below shouting for Lieutenant Douglas and—as he later confessed—he seized a lantern and went down to the gunroom, but by the time he arrived the rest of the mutineers had just left. As he reached the door he suddenly heard the excited shrieks of "Here he is! Here he is!" from Lieutenant Douglas's fourteen-year-old servant, James Allen, who had apparently seen his master slipping back into McIntosh's cabin after getting his dressing-gown.

The boy's cries also brought the mutineers running back, a mass of bellowing men, many drunk, others frightened into a frenzy, and all ready to do what anyone they knew or trusted ordered. Forester was just in time to lead them.

"Come out, you bugger: we've found out where you are!" they cried as they converged on McIntosh's tiny cabin.

Douglas crawled out from under the cot and at the sight of him the mutineers went berserk. Describing the scene three years later, Sergeant Plaice could not keep the horror from his account: "I suppose there were twenty tomahawks, axes and boarding pikes jagged into him immediately in the gunroom," and within a few moments Douglas had "more than twenty wounds." They took him out "and I saw no more of him, except his lifting his right arm and singing out for mercy. They cried out, 'You bugger, we will show you mercy.' "

As they dragged Lieutenant Douglas through the door, the boy Allen was lashing out with a tomahawk and screaming, "Let me have a chop at him: he shan't make me jump about in the gunroom anymore."

At that moment, however, Lieutenant Douglas managed to break free and, streaming blood, his dressing-gown slashed to ribbons, he ran forward past where Midshipman Casey was lying in his hammock. "On [his] getting abreast of the midshipmen's berth I saw him seized by several of the crew," Casey related afterwards. "Those men fell on him with different weapons and left him, apparently dead, on the gratings of the after hold." Casey did not see the final blows struck—"I was so shocked that I turned my head away."

David Forester then found the other person the mutineers were seeking, Midshipman Smith, who had caused John Fletcher to be flogged a few days earlier. Forester seized the boy, who wriggled out of his grasp and ran. Forester promptly lashed out with Pigot's sword and managed to hit him.

Several mutineers then chased the screaming boy, raining blows on his back and head with their tomahawks and bayonets until he collapsed near where Douglas had been left. Casey, having watched this, then heard the men on the maindeck above shouting down the hatchways, "Hand the buggers up! Launch the buggers!"

The men who had been chopping at Smith then seized Lieutenant Douglas—who groaned, giving Casey the first indication that he was still alive—and hauled him to a hatchway ladder. One of them climbed the ladder, dragging Douglas upside down by his heels, while others pushed from below. At that moment William Crawley, the Irishman who came from Kinsale, the town where Casey had been born, arrived with a tomahawk in his hand. "Where's the bugger? Let me have another stroke at him before he goes!" With that he smashed the pointed edge of the tomahawk down on Douglas's head with such force that the ash handle broke.

Steward Jones was also a horrified onlooker, standing in the shadows only a few feet away. He saw Forester run up and "chop at him several times with a cutlass or tomahawk. There were ten or a dozen round him, chopping at him." When Forester had not enough room to chop, said Jones, "He stabbed him; I saw the blood running down the Lieutenant's thighs. His shirt was stained also with blood."

Midshipman Smith was then dragged up the ladder after Douglas—"as though they had been two dogs," said Casey, and the mutineers were at the same time "making use of the most horrid language." He added that "on their getting under the halfdeck I again heard a great noise, saying 'Cut the buggers! . . . Launch the buggers! . . . Heave the buggers overboard!' "

On the halfdeck outside the captain's cabin John Holford was a terrified spectator of what followed. Lieutenant Douglas, an almost completely crimson figure and by then bearing little resemblance to a human being, was dragged to a port by the excited group of men and pitched out past the muzzle of the gun and into the sea.

David Forester and John Fletcher then seized Midshipman Smith. For Fletcher, who came from Whitby and had been in the *Hermione* for nearly five years, this was the moment of revenge for his recent flogging. Together they flung the boy out of the port.

There was a short pause while the mutineers collected their wits and lit some more lanterns. No leader had emerged to give orders and co-ordinate their murderous work—indeed, Osborn was still at the wheel and steering the frigate in chase of the privateer because no one had told him to do anything else. There were dozens of men still utterly bewildered and uncertain what to do: men like John Holford, who was still standing under the halfdeck near Captain Pigot's cabin with some mutineers nearby.

One of them glanced round and suddenly saw something moving near the ship's side, which in the darkness, looked very much like a ghost.

"Who is that coming in that port?" he called excitedly, pointing with his cutlass.

Another of the mutineers took a pace or two towards the shape. "Why it's Foreshaw!"

The prospect of a conversation with an officer supposed to be dead did not deter a third man. "Let him come in and hear what he has to say for himself."

And indeed it was the third lieutenant: "When I saw Mr Foreshaw come in at the port, the blood was streaming down his face from his head," said Holford.

Faint from loss of blood and shock, Foreshaw had not plunged into the sea when the mutineers on the quarterdeck had forced him over the side: instead he had fallen into the mizzen chains—the broad and thick planks projecting horizontally from the ship's side abreast and abaft each mast, to which the shrouds were fitted. They had provided Foreshaw with a resting place. Having recovered his strength, he had then climbed down on to the barrel of a gun and scrambled in through a port.

As soon as he saw the men running towards him, shouting threats, he clapped his hands together and cried, "Good God, men, what have I done to harm you, that I should be treated in this manner?"

Several of them, impressed by this appeal, answered that they would try to save his life. Meanwhile the news that Foreshaw was still alive travelled swiftly and Thomas Nash and John Farrel soon came running down from the quarterdeck, Nash grabbing Foreshaw by his right wrist.

"Foreshaw, you bugger," he cried, "are you not overboard yet? Overboard you must go, and overboard you shall go!"

At that moment Farrel lashed at Foreshaw with a tomahawk, cutting off one of his hands at the wrist. He and Nash then seized the shrieking officer and dragged him up the ladder to the lee gangway, where they pushed over the side and watched his body splash into the water. For the moment the first bout of slaughter was over, and the death roll so far was Captain Pigot, Lieutenants Foreshaw and Douglas, and Midshipman Smith.

XV

The Dead and the Drunk

—ω—

MIDSHIPMAN CASEY, after going back to his hammock for the first time on the advice of Farrel and Phillips, found that "several of the crew at different times shook my hammock in a noisy manner and wishing to know who I was . . . after some little consultation among themselves they told me to lay still, as they did not wish to hurt me. Some of them wished that I would either go on deck or go into some more secure place that I might not be murdered."

A few minutes after seeing first Douglas and then Midshipman Smith attacked and dragged away, Thomas Nash had told him he had better get dressed and go on deck "as I would be much safer than lying in my hammock as probably by continuing there I might be put to death."

Casey took this advice and went up on deck, but "seeing them in great confusion and not thinking myself safe, I again went down to my hammock. I was again visited by a number of people, one of whom was Nash, who insisted that I should drink with him.

"I was talking to the Boatswain for a short time, who was then in his cabin, during which time Thomas Nash pressed me very much to join in the mutiny and told me the ship's company were determined to appoint me their lieutenant, which I refused. He made answer, 'Suppose we make you do it: how can you help yourself?'

"I told him if they insisted on it, it could not then be helped, but begged he would desist from anything of the kind. He said no more to me at the time."

Casey was in a dangerous position: if he refused the mutineers' demands they would probably kill him; yet if he agreed he became a mutineer himself. His choice was whether he should risk being murdered in the King's name, a loyal officer, or executed later in the name of the King, a traitorous officer. If he refused to join the mutineers, nearly every man's hand in the *Hermione* would be against him—and almost every hand held a tomahawk or cutlass. If he did join the mutineers, then outside the *Hermione* every British hand would be turned against him, holding a noose.

Meanwhile Nash and Richard Redman, unworried by the practical difficulties of remaining loyal to the King and yet remaining alive, had gone up to the quarterdeck where the master's mate, William Turner, who so far had not been active in the mutiny, apart from refusing to obey Foreshaw's order to go down to Pigot's cabin, was continuing on watch as though nothing had happened.

Redman, however, now went to him and said, in the hearing of Pigot's steward, "Officer, here you are," as if giving him command of the ship.

Leech, John Elliott and Farrel were already on the quarterdeck, and after a discussion with Nash and Redman they decided for the time being to turn south—Osborn was still steering the ship on the northerly course. No leader had yet come forward, but Nash was slowly emerging as the man taking most of the decisions: he told Thomas Jay, his fellow boatswain's mate, to pipe the order, and Jay went through the ship crying, "Every man to his station: about ship."

This order was one of the most decisive given: up to then only about forty out of the ship's company of more than 150 had been active mutineers: the rest had kept out of the way, either through loyalty or because they were frightened or confused.

Now, however, a familiar order was being shouted by a familiar voice and the bewildered men's natural reaction was to obey, without realizing that once they lifted so much as a finger in answer to the order, they too became mutineers. Technically they had all broken the 20th Article of War, since they had failed to use their "utmost endeavours" to suppress mutiny or sedition.

With all the men at their stations, Turner gave the necessary orders, and the *Hermione* turned southwards, away from the *Diligence*, to run before the wind down the Mona Passage. There was much to occupy the ringleaders' attention: much drinking to be done, many decisions to be taken and, as far as some of them were concerned, several more people yet to be murdered.

Leaving Thomas Jay and James Bell in charge on the quarterdeck, sixteen mutineers then went down to Captain Pigot's cabin for a meeting. These eighteen men now emerging as ringleaders (and listed in Appendix D, page 345) were a curious cross-section of the ship's company. Eight of them had been handpicked by Pigot and brought over from the *Success*. Of the remaining ten, Nash and Michael Whatman had served in the *Hermione* for four and a half years; a topman, William Clarke, for four and Turner for three years. The birthplaces of all but two of the eighteen are known: nine were English (five from Kent), two Irish, three Scottish, another Danish and there was one American.

Pigot's cabin, in the light of their lanterns, was a macabre sight: chairs were smashed, the cot torn to pieces, and the couch and deck soaked in blood. The gaping hole in one of the stern windows was a reminder of the recent fate of the cabin's rightful owner. It was an appropriate setting for the major decision the men had to take. It was on the face of it a fairly simple one: should they kill the rest of the officers and warrant officers? There were ten—Lieutenant Reed, Mr. Southcott, Sansum the surgeon, Pacey the purser, Searle the gunner, Price the carpenter, Martin the boatswain, Midshipman Casey and, for good measure, Manning, the captain's clerk, and McIntosh, the marine lieutenant, who was dying anyway.

The discussion ended without a clear cut decision being made. From their subsequent actions it seems Richard Redman had spoken against more killing (with, as we shall see, one possible exception); Forester was for killing them all; and Nash was at that time in agreement but wanted to spare Midshipman Casey.

Yet they seem to have been in no hurry. After talking and arguing some returned to the quarterdeck and others wandered through the ship. Redman went up to the quarterdeck, but then he said he was going below and would leave the charge of the deck to Turner and Farrel.

WHILE THE SIXTEEN MEN had been arguing in Pigot's cabin, most of the men whose lives were under discussion were in their cabins round the gunroom on the deck below, unaware of the debate but convinced their last hour had come. Each faced the prospect in a different way.

John Mason, the Belfast-born carpenter's mate who had come to the *Hermione* from the *Success*, claimed that he had been in his hammock when woken by "a terrible noise of hurrahing." Swinging out of his hammock in the darkness ("there were no lights to be seen") he felt his way up the ladder to the main deck, but someone pushed him down again, so he went to the gunner's cabin. His reason, he explained later, was that "I was frightened and wanted to get out of the way."

But he found little in the cabin to reassure him; both the gunner, who was sitting naked on his cot, and Mason's superior officer, Richard Price, the carpenter, were weeping. According to Mason, the three men had stayed in the cabin while outside the blood-chilling chorus of both the murderers and their victims was punctuated by strident cries of "Hand them up!"

Southcott, in the meantime, had been lying in his cot listening first to the search for and then the savage attacks on Lieutenant Douglas and Midshipman Smith. He had heard their desperate pleas for mercy; he had recognized—and remembered—the voices of several of their attackers. He had assumed he would be the next to be killed, but the mutineers had left the gunroom, returning some minutes later to search through the cabins again. They saw Southcott and some cried out, "Here's the Master!" while others shouted, "Don't harm him!"

When several came into his cabin and saw by the light of their lanterns that his head was bloodstained, they asked who had been responsible, and tried to reassure him that he would not be hurt. But as an indication that there was little or no control or agreement among the mutineers, they appointed four of their number—including John Elliott, who had just helped to murder Captain Pigot—to guard Southcott: not to prevent him escaping, but simply to stop their own people from killing him. They then sent for the surgeon to bandage him.

Sansum had already been busy patching up Lieutenant Reed, the victim of Joe Montell's attack. When Redman visited the gunroom later and saw that Reed had been hurt, he went over to him and shook him by the hand, saying, according to the carpenter, that he "was sorry the Lieutenant was hurt, for they did not intend to hurt him, who never hurt them."

Southcott received more news when Sansum was brought to his cabin under an escort of mutineers. "He informed me," Southcott said, "that the First Lieutenant was wounded and his head was cut open in two or three places with a tomahawk, and he had been sewing it up."

Just after Sansum, in the master's own words, had "put a plaister on my face," a mob of men streamed into the gunroom once again and started shouting at Southcott's door that they would kill him. While the four sentries refused to let them in, more mutineers appeared at the skylight overhead and added to the confusion by yelling down that no one else was to be killed.

The mutineers in the gunroom—heeding the shouts from overhead—now ordered Sansum, Pacey and Lieutenant Reed to sit in chairs by the mizzenmast, which passed through the cabin just abaft the table and skylight. William Clarke, who had been one of the sixteen meeting in Pigot's cabin, stood over them as sentry. The three prisoners were then joined by the gunner and the carpenter, both still weeping. That meant that all the officers and warrant officers were now in the gunroom with the exception of the dying marine lieutenant, Midshipman Casey, who had returned to his hammock, Martin, the boatswain, who was still in his cabin with his wife, and Manning, the clerk, who was next door.

The majority of the ringleaders then went up to the quarterdeck. The *Hermione* was completely under their control, although their fellow mutineers were certainly not. All the officers and warrant officers were either dead or under guard, with the exception of Turner, the master's mate, and Midshipman Wiltshire, who had both joined the mutiny.

Leech, Elliott (who had handed over his task of guarding Southcott to someone else) and William Turner then went down to search through Pigot's possessions. They could not open the bureau in which Pigot kept his papers, so they sent for Steward Jones, who arrived in the cabin nervous and apprehensive.

"What money had the Captain got?" demanded Leech. "And where are the keys?"

"I don't know," replied Jones. "He kept the keys and his money himself in his waistcoat pocket."

"Damn the keys," said Leech, "we'll let everything stand till tomorrow morning and clap a couple of sentries on the door."

With that they left the cabin to go below, warning the sentry, Walter Brooks, not to let anyone else in. Leech told Jones, "You are to attend the gentlemen ['That is, the officers that were to be,' Jones later explained] and get dinner tomorrow as usual."

A few minutes later Jones heard Redman calling his name. "I went to Redman," said Jones. "He still had a sword drawn in his hand. He called me a bugger and asked me for some of the Captain's wine. I told him if he would allow me I would go and fetch the keys, and he bid me follow him down to the store-room."

The store-room was on the orlop deck, below the gunroom. Pigot naturally had a well-stocked wine store and Jones said, "I unlocked the door and [Redman] told me to give him some of the best wine. I told him there were different sorts and it was all good, and he told me to hand out a bottle of any sort.

"I gave him a bottle of Madeira. He knocked off the head of it with his sword and drunk about half a pint or more, and gave it to some more men who were at the door. He told me to give him two bottles more of Madeira, which he took up with him to the Boatswain's cabin."

Once there he poured some wine and water into a mug and carried it through to Southcott, the mug in one hand and the remains of Pigot's sword (he had broken it earlier when he hit it against the bulkhead of Southcott's cabin) in the other. Southcott, thankful for the wine, had no difficulty in recognizing the sword by its large silver guard.

By the time Jones had locked the wine store and returned to the lower deck he was in time to hear Redman, Nash and Farrel once more "disputing whether they should save the lives of the Doctor and Purser. They all swore as Hughie (meaning the Captain) was overboard they should all go, adding that they might as well be hung for a sheep as a lamb."

Midshipman Casey wanted to join the rest of the officers, and went to the door, begging the sentry "to allow me to go into the gunroom," which he did. "After having spoken to most of the officers who were there, [I] was going to sit down at their request, when Thomas Nash came in, making use of very bad language, and desired the Purser and Surgeon to prepare themselves for death against the next morning, for the ship's company were determined against letting them live.

"During the time I was at the Boatswain's cabin door," continued Casey, "Nash had frequently said that the ship's company were determined to put the Purser and Surgeon to death. Finding Nash was a friend of mine and wished to save me, I remonstrated with him and endeavoured to save their lives, but he told me they were determined to put them to death."

There was now a brief lull in all activities except drinking. Several men went back to the fo'c'sle to finish off the bucket of stolen rum, as well as various bottles they had later found in the gunroom. Richard Redman, who had sunk a good deal of the captain's Madeira, was half drunk and beginning to feel lecherous. This boded ill for Martin, the boatswain, because apparently Redman had been thinking about Martin's wife while arguing with Nash and Farrel whether or not the purser and surgeon should be killed.

Soon John Holmes, a young seaman from Lambeth, London, arrived outside the gunroom door and told the sentry that a seaman suffering from scurvy, John Evans, was very ill, and asked for the surgeon.

The mutineers agreed to let Sansum attend Evans and three men formed themselves into an escort: Holmes, armed with a tomahawk, William Crawley, who helped kill Midshipman Smith and had found a cutlass to replace the tomahawk he had smashed on Lieutenant Douglas's head, and William Marsh, who so far had not been an active killer—an omission he was soon to make good.

Thus escorted, Sansum left the gunroom, where he had just been sentenced to death, to help save a life. On his way he saw another seaman lying ill in his hammock and recognized him as William Bower (so Bower claimed afterwards) and asked how he was. Bower told him, and Sansum commented that he was himself about to die.

"What for?" exclaimed Bower.

"It's none of your business," interjected Marsh, and Crawley warned Bower: "Hold your tongue, or we'll serve you the same way!"

Sansum went on to see Evans, did what he could for him, and was then marched back to the gunroom. Lieutenant Reed had in the meantime been allowed to lie in his cot because he was feeling faint from his head wound.

By then a large number of men had, in the absence of any sort of discipline, gone below and broken into the spirit room where, stowed in squat puncheons, hogsheads and barrels, were nearly a thousand gallons of rum. The men lost little time in knocking in the bungs and serving the raw spirit in buckets, mess kits, mugs and any other receptacle handed to them.

But the men drinking the greatest quantities and getting viciously besotted were not the original group of mutineers. These—numbering some forty or fifty men, according to an estimate by Midshipman Casey—were staying comparatively sober because they had work to do. The men getting really drunk were those who knew nothing of the mutiny until it burst on them and had then, through caution or confusion, hesitated until it was clear the mutiny had succeeded. Then, filling themselves with liquid bravado, they set out to prove to the ringleaders that they too were true mutineers. Like most converts, they were to display more zeal than the original protagonists.

And, coinciding with all this, a new and powerful figure was about to come on to the scene: a man who so far had stayed in the shadows but whose smooth tongue and revolutionary talk may well have stirred the ringleaders into starting the mutiny. He was a man whom Captain Pigot had, within a day or so of taking over command, promoted from able seaman to surgeon's mate. He might not have known much about nostrums or surgery, but he seems to have had a demagogue's flair for striking at the psychological moment.

XVI

"Kill Them All"

—◊—

THE SURGEON'S MATE of the *Hermione* was Lawrence
Cronin, an Irishman born in Belfast thirty-five years earlier.
He owed his presence in the frigate to the unfortunate coincidence in June 1795, which brought the merchant ship in which he
had been serving and the *Hermione* together in Port Royal. Cronin
was taken on board the frigate and although marked down in the
muster book as a volunteer, he was almost certainly pressed but, as
was usual, given the chance of "volunteering" to qualify for the
bounty. Since Cronin was rated an able seaman, this amounted to
£5.

He remained an able seaman for the next twenty months; then
the day after Pigot took over command of the *Hermione* he made
Cronin the surgeon's mate. This was a considerable promotion—his
pay rose from £1 4s. a month to £2 10s. but, what was almost more
important, it allowed him to shift his hammock from the forward
end of the lowerdeck, where he had the regulation width of fourteen
inches in which to sling it, to the comparative comfort of the midshipmen's berth. It was there that Midshipman Casey got to know
him well, and after spending more than seven months with him,
gave his verdict that Cronin was "a treacherous, drunken, infamous

character; he was in many instances worse than the worst of the mutineers.''

By comparison with the other seamen Cronin was an educated man: he could write well and persuasively, whether it was notes for a haranguing speech to a mob of mutineers or a letter seeking favours from a Spanish governor.

His sense of timing would have done justice to a good actor: he came on to the stage to take his part in the *Hermione* mutiny dramatically, emerging from the darkness forward to stride aft along the lowerdeck to the gunroom, shouting for all the men to gather round the after hatchway and the skylight.

From the rum bucket on the fo'c'sle, from the spirit room below, from the gangways and the quarterdeck, the men streamed to the stage that Cronin had chosen. And he had chosen it with care, because by standing on the gunroom table he would be halfway through the skylight and able to dominate both the lowerdeck—for he towered over the prisoners in the gunroom—and the halfdeck forward of the captain's cabin. The mutineers crowding round the skylight and afterhatch would be able to see the prisoners, and for what Cronin had to say the juxtaposition was important.

As the men gathered round, Cronin leapt on to the table and called for someone to hold up a lantern. Taking a piece of paper from his pocket, he smoothed it out and held it up to the light. The men waited expectantly.

''I have something to read to you,'' he announced. It had been written before the mutiny began, he said, and concerned the conduct of the officers. He began by declaring, ''I have been a Republican since the war,'' adding that the *Hermione*'s people were doing a very right, a very good thing. That set the men cheering, and as soon as they were quiet again he continued that *all* the remaining officers must be put to death, or it was no use putting one of them to death.

Southcott, describing Cronin's speech later, said, ''I heard great parts of it as I lay in my bed.'' To Midshipman Casey, lying in his hammock a few feet away, ''The scene now became dreadful, and the greatest confusion prevailed. All were more or less inflamed and excited by spirits, except about forty or fifty of the principal mutineers, who kept sober and steady, and opposed to taking any more lives; but the majority of the crew prevailed against them . . .''

As soon as Cronin finished his speech there was again uproar:

from the men on the halfdeck there were bellows of "Hand 'em up! Pass the buggers up! Kill them all!"

At that moment the flimsy gunroom door crashed open and a small group of men burst in, shouldering aside the sentries. They included Joe Montell, William Marsh, David Forester, Adam Brown—a recent arrival in the ship—and two marines, Patrick Field and another known as "Happy Tom." Before any of the sentries could stop them, they seized the purser, Stephen Pacey, and dragged him up the ladder to the quarterdeck, stabbing and punching him viciously as he cried out for mercy. As soon as they reached the gangway several of them, led by Marsh, lifted Pacey up and flung him over the ship's side into the sea.

They then ran back down to the gunroom again, where Sansum waited, white as a sheet, beside the mizzenmast. Jumping up and down round the surgeon like a jackal and taunting him in a shrill voice was his fourteen-year-old servant, James Hayes. Earlier, as men had shouted down the skylight for the officers, Hayes had been repeating their cries, parrot-fashion, shrieking, "Hand them up! Hand the buggers up!"

The group, still led by Forester, Montell and Marsh, seized Sansum and dragged him out of the gunroom, stabbing, punching and kicking him at the same time, with Hayes a screeching demon dancing round. They took him up to the gangway and he too was thrown into the sea, still alive. Southcott, who had heard and seen all but the last few moments of this episode, said later that Hayes "boasted of having been the occasion of putting his master to death, and the rest of the mutineers said that [Hayes] was the great cause of the Surgeon being put to death." The fact that Hayes had been punished for stealing from the surgeon, Southcott added, "was the occasion of his persuading the people to put his master to death; to be revenged, he called it."

The same group, apparently acting independently of the rest of the mutineers, had not finished: it was now the turn of the first lieutenant. Reed was still slumped in his cot with a bandage round his head covering the stitches so carefully sewn by Sansum. The mob, already perspiring freely from their efforts in hurling Pacey and Sansum overboard, rushed back to the gunroom, seized Reed and dragged him up to the gangway, where they threw him over the side.

By now Richard Redman had other things than mutiny and murder on his mind: he was apparently thinking of the boatswain's wife—a woman, and a white woman into the bargain, and there was only one man standing in his way. . . . He went below to the lowerdeck and, striding up to Martin's cabin, exclaimed, "By the Holy Ghost, the Boatswain shall go with the rest!"

He dragged the protesting Martin out of his cabin, forcing him to go up the ladder to the maindeck. He then hauled him over to one of the gun ports and pushed him out. Sergeant Plaice said later that he "heard the Boatswain cry out when he was overboard." Redman then went down to the boatswain's cabin, watched by John Jones, who noted that he "remained in the cabin with the Boatswain's wife, and I saw him no more that night."

But even though the captain, the three lieutenants, surgeon, purser, boatswain and a midshipman had been murdered up to then, many of the mutineers were still not satisfied. "The language, noise and scene altogether was horrible, as may easily be imagined," wrote Midshipman Casey.

Once again the dreadful cry of "Hand the buggers up!" echoed through the ship; once again a mob swarmed down to the lowerdeck. This time their quarry was Captain Pigot's clerk, John Manning, who was still in his cabin next to the one now occupied by Redman and Mrs. Martin.

John Brown, the maintopman, was horrified to see a mob dragging Manning up the ladder. Among them he noticed James Hannah, Adam Brown, William Marsh and David Forester, all of whom helped push Manning out through a gun port.

There was, however, still more killing to be done: still some grudges to pay off. Marine Patrick Field, his comrade in arms "Happy Tom," James Hannah and one or two other men went down to the gunroom again and thrust their way into the cabin of the marine lieutenant, McIntosh, whose death throes were still being watched by Sergeant Plaice. McIntosh, in the last stages of yellow fever, was foaming at the mouth, his eyes rolling, his whole body jerked by convulsions. "The Doctor did not expect him to live that night," according to Sergeant Plaice.

The marines seized the ends of the blanket on which McIntosh was lying, lifted him out of the cot and carried him from the cabin. By the dismal light of the lanterns they saw the livid blotches covering McIntosh's body which showed them they would only just beat Nature in the race to kill him.

They had great difficulty in getting the alternately limp and convulsing body up the ladder, but finally struggled over to a gun port. Then, with a "one, two and heave!" they slung McIntosh out into the sea; the tenth man to die that night.

The mob, still in a frenzy, were joined by several more men as they ran below to fetch up their next intended victim, Mr. Southcott. The sentries left on guard at his cabin door tried to stop them, but they were outnumbered. "There were eight or ten men in my cabin to take me out," said Southcott, "and the gunroom was full of them." But just as they seized Southcott and began to drag him out, more mutineers appeared at the skylight overhead and "they called out upon deck to stop their hands, not to put any more to death."

"The Master," said Casey, "was principally saved by two of the principal mutineers placing themselves as sentinels at his cabin door, and by his servant boy, quite a youth . . . going through the ship crying, and begging of the crew most piteously that his life might be spared."

But the fact that Southcott had been saved—temporarily, at least—did not mean that the others—Midshipman Casey, the gunner and the carpenter—were to be left in peace: all three were ordered to go up to the quarterdeck, where they found "a greater part of the ship's company present."

There was a great deal more yelling and arguing, and "after some little consultation, they agreed to save our lives," said Casey. Undoubtedly one of the men who spoke up on Casey's behalf was Thomas Nash, who by then appears to have been gaining a measure of control over the mutineers. Nash, it will be recalled, helped kill Pigot and told the men to "launch" Foreshaw, and with the American John Farrel, threw the lieutenant over the side after he had climbed inboard again. After that neither man took part in any more killings, and Nash several times did what he could to help Casey. Now, however, his friendship was about to prove an embarrassment to the midshipman.

With the mutineers agreeing to reprieve the three men, Nash acted quickly. Whether it was to seize the initiative in front of the whole ship's company and prove himself their leader, or because he knew or sensed they already accepted him in that role, there is no way of knowing for certain, but the evidence points to it being the former case.

William Turner, the master's mate, was standing near Nash, who turned to him and announced: "Mr. Turner, you are to consider yourself captain of the ship while she is in our charge, and you, Mr. Casey, are to be the First Lieutenant."

Casey, however, refused and much to his relief was allowed to go below to his hammock.

An argument then broke out over where they should take the *Hermione.* Should they make for an enemy port in Santo Domingo or Puerto Rico, or sail to the Spanish Main? The nearest important port on the Main was La Guaira, about five hundred miles southwards across the Caribbean.

The French and Spanish ports in the islands of course were much nearer; indeed some could be reached within a few hours. But the more intelligent of the mutineers must have realized that any island was likely to become a trap: the news of their arrival would reach Sir Hyde Parker, and he would blockade the island. The chances of escaping in a French, Spanish or neutral ship without being intercepted by a British frigate would then be slender.

The Spanish Main seemed a much better proposition: it was farther to sail, with more chance of being intercepted by a British ship—but she would have no suspicion that there was anything wrong on board the *Hermione,* and the mutineers had Captain Pigot's secret signal books. By going to the Spanish Main they would also have a better chance of getting to the country that some of them wanted to adopt as their own—the United States.

So the men finally voted for the Spanish port of La Guaira, and a few minutes later the sentries were knocking on the door of Southcott's cabin, demanding that a messenger be allowed in. "It's Captain Turner's orders that you tell him where the ship is," he explained.

"I can't tell him," replied Southcott. "I wasn't on deck yesterday."

The man was back a few minutes later asking for Southcott's log book and "Day's work"—the rough notes of the course and distances the ship had steered the previous day. Southcott handed them over. (It is believed the mutineers destroyed the captain's and master's logs before entering La Guaira: there is no trace of either in the Spanish State and naval archives, nor are they referred to in Spanish official correspondence. The muster book was destroyed for reasons which will soon become apparent.)

Despite the mutineers' reprieve at the quarterdeck meeting earlier in the night, Southcott, Casey, Price and Searle were still in grave danger of being murdered by various drunken mobs who in the darkness were still ranging through the frigate like packs of wolves. "My life was repeatedly debated," wrote Casey, "and for some hours in the scales. I was subsequently told by my friends that I was twice or thrice condemned, and on the point of suffering [death], and that it was with the greatest difficulty that I was saved; two or three of them always kept near me during the night, as a protecting guard, and removed me occasionally from place to place for more safety."

Southcott was also having an anxious time: describing the period after the quarterdeck "reprieve" he said that "a great many different times during the night until half past eleven o'clock next morning—I suppose twenty times—they attempted to take me out and put me to death, and were stopped by others desiring them not to do it." Among the "others" was the quartermaster John Elliott: but the names of the rest who acted as sentries to save the lives of both Southcott and Casey are not known.

The reason for Price's reprieve, according to Casey, was his long service in the *Hermione*. A Welshman, he had joined the *Hermione* in December 1792 as an able seaman, while the ship was commissioning at Chatham, and had the fourth longest service in the ship. He was promoted to carpenter's mate and then, through Captain Wilkinson, obtained his warrant as carpenter, which meant he had probably served an apprenticeship with a shipwright—perhaps at some small shipyard on his native Menai Straits.

AS DAYLIGHT FILTERED through the *Hermione* it lit up parts of the ship that by then looked more like a slaughterhouse. Captain Pigot's cabin was naturally bloodstained, while on the deck below, the gunroom and its furniture had first been splashed with the blood of Southcott and Reed; then Lieutenant Douglas and Midshipman Smith had been attacked in there, as well as Sansum and Pacey. Outside the gunroom, between the door and the after ladder, it was even worse, since both Douglas and Smith had lain there, badly hacked about, before being dragged on deck. A bloody trail left by Reed, Douglas, Smith, Sansum, Pacey and Manning led up the ladder to the half-deck, and then to various gun ports and the gangways, where the men had been thrown over the side. Even on the quarterdeck there were ominous stains showing where Foreshaw had been attacked.

However, the mutineers seemed unworried about these sanguinary signs of the recent massacre; for many of them daylight meant only that they could see what they were drinking, for few of them had been to sleep. Richard Redman emerged red-eyed and bleary from the boatswain's cabin after his sojourn with the newly widowed Mrs. Martin. But if his face looked debauched, he made up for it sartorially. "I saw him dressed with a ruffed shirt and white waistcoat," reported the watchful steward John Jones.

It is not known whether Redman had added rape to his crimes or whether he found Mrs. Martin acquiescent; but it is perhaps significant that with seven men passing her cabin door on their way to be murdered, and her husband dragged from her side by Redman and flung into the sea, not one witness (including Southcott, Casey— who was in his hammock less than a dozen feet away—and John Jones, who saw most of what went on that night near the gunroom) ever reported hearing her evince alarm, cry for help or ask advice. Jones heard no feminine protest when he saw Redman go into the cabin with the obvious intention of spending the night with her—yet she knew that Redman had killed her husband.

Few people except Redman had time or inclination to worry about Mrs. Martin's chastity, but Southcott, in the midst of the constant sallys into the gunroom by groups of mutineers intending to murder him, had time to notice young James Allen, the servant of Lieutenant Douglas, swaggering about. "He had one of his master's rings on his finger," said Southcott, "a fancy ring with hair in it, and he had some of the officers' shirts on, and was cutting the legs off one of his master's pairs of half-boots to put on as shoes."

With daylight the perils of the mutineers in the *Hermione* increased a thousandfold—particularly the danger of discovery and interception. No ship could be regarded as friendly—even in the unlikely event of a meeting with a Spanish or French warship, the chances of a disastrous misunderstanding were great. None of them was safe until they had arrived at La Guaira and arranged their terms with the Spanish authorities.

So at daybreak Turner ordered the topgallants—the third highest of the square sails—to be set, to help speed the *Hermione* southwards. With the northerly breeze she had a soldier's wind—it did not need much sail-trimming skill to keep her sailing fast.

The men then returned to their drinking. One bucket of rum and another of wine under the half-deck were of absorbing interest to a group of mutineers who included several marines, among them John Pearce. Dipping his mug deeply was James Duncan, the foretopman whose alleged bad toe had led him to being made sentry at the porter cask. According to Steward Jones, he was "very much in liquor." The mutiny and the liquor had apparently cured him in a way previously unknown to medical science, since "he seemed very active among the people, very lively and contented. He had not walked about for some time on account of qr[his] sore toe, but after the mutiny he walked about very fast."

Another ostensibly sick man was William Bower, who had been on the surgeon's wine list. When Mr. Southcott saw him he was "active with the rest and seemed to be rejoiced at what had happened, and was dancing, singing and drinking." John Jones reported him, with an unconscious pun, as being "lively and full of spirits."

WITH THE MUTINY OVER and the men settling down to some serious drinking, it is possible to analyse the roles played by various individuals during the recent lurid hours, which have been described in detail entirely from eyewitness accounts. At the last muster on board the frigate of which a record remains, the ship had a crew of 168. It is unlikely this total changed much during the following six weeks.

A close study of all the documents concerning the mutiny, including several confessions and examinations, shows that there were sixty-two known active mutineers, i.e., men who committed specific acts, as distinct from the rest who obeyed the leaders' orders. Of these sixty-two (who were also named later by loyal men and are listed in Appendix D, page 345) the nationalities of forty-six are known for certain. Twenty were English, ten Irish, three Scottish, three Swedish, one American, two Danish, two Italian and there were one from each of the following countries: Germany (Hanover), Portugal, St. Thomas, Spain and France. Of the sixteen ''unknowns,'' one was coloured and West Indian, twelve had British-sounding names and three were definitely foreign. Among the sixty-two there was the nucleus of eighteen men referred to earlier who actually plotted the mutiny, or took leading parts immediately it began, and can be considered the ringleaders.

Just how loyal had proved the men that Hugh Pigot hand-picked in the *Success* and brought over to the *Hermione*? Of the original twenty-one petty officers and ratings and two boys, the Negro boy Peter Bascomb perished in the fall from the topsailyard. Of the twenty-one adults, eight were among the eighteen ringleaders (and included Jay and Redman) and they and four more were among the sixty-two active mutineers. Of the remainder, only two are known to have definitely remained loyal (Pigot's cook John Holford, and the son). Midshipman Wiltshire, who was not included among the twenty-one adults, was at least sympathetic towards the mutineers.

To round off the statistical aspect of the mutiny we can see who had been the main killers so far. Eleven men are known to have taken an active part in killing two or more people, and curiously enough only one of them, Redman, came from the *Success*. Three of the men who helped kill Pigot were Successes.

Far ahead of the others on the list of killers was David Forester, who had helped murder seven people (Pigot, Douglas, Smith, Pacey, Sansum, Manning and Reed); Montell and Hannah, each with five victims; Marsh and Adam Brown with four; William Crawley, Marine Field and ''Happy Tom,'' each with three; Nash and Farrel with the same two (Pigot and Foreshaw); and Redman with two (Pigot and Martin). Thomas Jay, Thomas Leech, Hadrian Poulson, John Phillips, Patrick Foster and John Jackson had also helped kill Pigot, while in addition Redman had wounded Southcott, and Montell had wounded Marine McNeil and Lieutenant Reed. Only one mutineer, Redman, had been solely responsible for one murder—his victim was, of course, the boatswain, Martin.

Nash and Farrel seem to have had enough of actual killing after dealing with Pigot and Foreshaw. Forester, however, never tired— he was active at the first and the penultimate murders.

The events already described by eyewitnesses, and those about to occur, indicate the mutiny was not the work of one man, rather that a crowd of men helped by a bucket of rum finally decided to make the first move, planning to attack in two groups: one would go aft along the maindeck to kill the captain and then the officers in the gunroom below, while a second group would secure the quarterdeck.

The first group—which included Jay, Nash, Montell, Redman, and Forester—left the fo'c'sle and dashed aft to Pigot's cabin, where their gruesome task probably took longer than they anticipated. The second group was delayed—whether because they lost their nerve or had a disagreement is not known—and they arrived on the quarterdeck several minutes late, if their attack was supposed to coincide with the other group's.

It might be asked why Lieutenant Foreshaw, on watch on the quarterdeck, did not hear the arguing, fighting and heavy drinking on the fo'c'sle immediately before the mutiny began, and which was described by the maintopman Brown. The explanation is simple enough: the distance from the fo'c'sle to where Foreshaw would have been standing on the quarterdeck, and from the fo'c'sle to John Brown in the maintop, was the same—between eighty and ninety feet. Brown, by his own account, knew nothing of the brawling until, after David Forester's threats, he climbed down the mainstay to the fo'c'sle. If Brown in the maintop had heard nothing, then it is unlikely that Foreshaw would have done. The men who were quarrelling and drinking would have realized that Lieutenant Foreshaw must not hear them, whether or not they were going to take the ship (and at that time John Farrel and John Smith were cursing and saying the men were "not fit to go through with the business," according to Brown). And of course a square-rigged ship beating to windward makes a good deal of noise. (One or two brief accounts of the mutiny say that the men rolled shot along the decks before the mutiny began. This is not borne out by evidence, and was clearly impossible since every officer was taken by surprise.)

The lack of a single leader caused a good deal of confusion and probably much more bloodshed than the original mutineers intended. It is significant that Nash, who finally emerged as a real leader, and the American John Farrel, who appears to have been his right-hand man, took part in no more killings after the murder of Pigot and of Foreshaw, and although Nash warned the purser and surgeon to prepare for death, he did not help kill them and was

instrumental in getting a reprieve for Southcott, Casey and Price—
for the time being, anyway.

THE MORNING after the mutiny passed slowly. Displaying recur-
rent paroxysms of rage, like men obsessed with a murderous
grudge, a gang of mutineers constantly appeared at the after ladder,
howling for Southcott and Casey to be brought up and killed. Each
time they were calmed down and talked out of it by others acting as
sentries in the gunroom.

After each sally the gang returned to their bottles and buckets of
liquor, becoming more drunk and more determined. Some were
probably aware they had been tardy in taking up their tomahawks
and were more than anxious to prove that they were loyal to the
mutiny. Others had let a sickening mixture of rum, wine and blood
reduce them to the level of wild animals. They talked and argued
among themselves about the unreasonable attitude of their leaders
and the sentries down in the gunroom. Of course, the master and
that puppy Casey must go; and the gunner and the carpenter too.
Cronin was right—they must all go!

Finally by 11.30 A.M. they had soaked up sufficient liquor and
noisy argument, and waved their tomahawks enough times to stir
themselves to action, only this time they would not be talked out of
it. With a series of bellows they rushed down to the gunroom, thrust
aside the protesting sentries, and seized Southcott. As several of
them dragged him up to the quarterdeck, the others went through
the ship shouting to everyone to come aft to "see the Master put to
death." Southcott thought once again his last moment had come:
after more than twenty attempts they had finally managed to get
hold of him.

Seamen ran, staggered and lurched to the quarterdeck: many
were so drunk they could see two or three Southcotts, and most of
them were shouting and cheering, taking up the old refrain of "Kill
the buggers! Hand the buggers up!" Southcott was unceremoni-
ously dumped on the grating abaft the capstan. From the position of
the sun he could see the frigate was being steered south: that told
him they were probably making for the Spanish Main. However, his
eyes and ears warned him that it was a voyage he would not be
making as the monotonous chorus of "Kill the buggers!" slurred
now as the men became more drunk, swelled through the ship.

Some of the mutineers sat on the carronades; others perched in the mizzen shrouds and on the nettings. The shouting finally became a babble; then they stopped talking, waiting for something to happen. At that point, Southcott said afterwards, "The principal ringleaders, Redman among them, those that were petty officers in the ship before, spoke to the others."

But the bewildered master could hardly believe his ears because, speaking forcefully, these men asked the rest of the mutineers "if they saw any occasion to put me to death in cold blood after they had got the ship so long, and those who had a mind to save my life should hold up their hands."

Southcott looked round: more than 150 pairs of eyes were watching him. More than 150 men, many of them very drunk, were about to pass judgment and signal whether he would live or die: a judgment based on the way he had treated them since he had joined the ship five months previously. Had he been just and reasonable, trying to be fair despite Pigot's harshness? Or had he taken the easiest course and toadied to a sadistic captain? Had he hazed and bullied just one man? For it only needed that man to speak out now. All this was being put in the balance, and in addition there was the danger that just one man, soberer or more intelligent than the rest, would point a finger and say that if Southcott was allowed to return alive to British soil, he would be the witness that would hang any mutineer who fell into British hands; that with Southcott, Casey, Searle or Price living, none of the mutineers would know a moment's peace for the rest of his life.

But no one pointed a finger—an omission which would in time leave several of them dangling by their necks from the yardarms of various of His Majesty's ships: instead, to Southcott's surprise, "a great part of them held their hands up," and, what is more, "They gave three cheers and I was ordered below and carried into the Captain's cabin and confined there."

The "principal ringleaders" whom he describes as having saved his life were not identified, except for Redman, other than being the ship's former petty officers; but they probably included Nash, Jay and Elliot.

The reprieve included Casey, the gunner and the carpenter. Casey was taken to the captain's cabin, given a chair and made to sit between two guns on the starboard side, while Southcott was put in another chair on the larboard side. Both men were told they could talk to each other on condition they spoke loudly enough for the guards to hear; but private conversation was forbidden. They would be allowed to walk about the deck for exercise in due course, but for this they would be separated and escorted by their guards. The gunner and the carpenter were confined in their own cabins with sentries on the door.

What these four men saw during their walks on deck gives a good picture of how the mutineers of the *Hermione* spent the first few hours of what they regarded as their new-found liberty. Southcott, for example, saw marine John Pearce, who had spent the forenoon drinking, heave into the sea his red, blue and white uniform, complete with pipeclayed cross-belts and gaiters, consigning it to the deep with a string of equally colourful oaths.

Carpenter Price came across John Williams, a lame member of the gunner's crew, sitting on a gun, and noticed he could not walk and "seemed very low spirited." Before the *Hermione* had sailed from the Mole Williams had given the carpenter some money for safe-keeping, and now Price took the opportunity of returning it, "for which he thanked me."

James Perrett, the ship's butcher, saw Price and, ignoring the guards, "came up to me crying, saying he had a wife and family in England, and that he was sorry for what had happened." Perrett seems to have been prone to tears because Steward Jones also reported seeing him crying the same day. "I often saw him crying when the people have ordered him to kill the stock and when he was at work at it." However, Southcott saw him in a different light, both metaphorically and in reality. He "used to come into the cabin with the lantern every night . . . He always appeared very cheerful, speaking very disrespectfully of the officers who were killed, saying what big rogues they were."

Apart from Perrett, only two men spoke to any of the four officers regretting the mutiny, and they were George Blakeney Chapman, who came from Derby, and William Carter, who talked with Price. Nevertheless, certain individuals had not regarded themselves as mutineers right from the beginning, and among them were Sergeant Plaice, Steward Jones, John Holford, the captain's cook, and the ship's cook, William Moncrieff, the man from Orkney who had served longest in the *Hermione*.

While taking exercise, Casey sometimes came in for abuse from the mutineers, particularly James Bell, the Scot from the *Success*. "Bell frequently abused me," said Casey, "calling me 'Puppy,' and other things, and he was stopped by some of the other mutineers."

A few of the leading mutineers—who were by now calling themselves "lieutenants"—frequently spoke to Casey, and nearly always on the same topic: they "pressed me to enter the Spanish service, assuring me that on my doing so they would get me either lieutenant or captain of a frigate, saying they were certain I should never return to England."

This offer, obviously made with the best motives, is one of the clearest indications of the basic naïveté of the mutineers: an insight into the simple way in which they saw their problems and the solutions.

XVII

The Oath of Secrecy

—⟡—

STEWARD JONES had been mindful of Nash's instructions
the previous night that next day he was to "attend the gentlemen and get dinner," which was the midday meal. He had
told Perrett, the tearful and reluctant butcher, to kill a goat, and
Holford, the former captain's cook, had prepared it.

But the violent debate over whether or not Southcott, Casey and
the other two men should be killed had delayed the meal. Finally
three leading mutineers—James Farrel, Bell and John Elliot—who
were now styling themselves "lieutenants," decided that Jones
should serve their meal on the quarterdeck under the awning.

They also decided to invite—perhaps order would be a more
appropriate word—Mr. Southcott to join them. He was brought up
and seated at their table for a meal of fried goat's meat. He was not a
willing guest—perhaps he found it a bizarre experience to be dining
a few feet from where, an hour earlier, his hosts had called for a
show of hands to decide whether he lived or died. Questioned about
the meal later he declared, "I was forced upon to eat with them."

In the afternoon all the men on board were ordered aft again: the
surgeon's mate, Lawrence Cronin, had been busy once more with
pen and paper. He had realized that most of the mutineers when

they reached La Guaira would eventually go to sea again in Spanish or neutral ships, either to earn a living or because they wanted to get to America. With more than 150 men scattering to the four winds, the main danger of any of them being captured by the British and hanged as mutineers would come from them gossiping, bragging in their cups or informing on each other. The British Government was certain to offer large cash rewards for information leading to arrests. To ensure the identity of the mutineers stayed a secret forever, Cronin had drawn up a special oath which he proposed administering to every man in the ship.

It may seem strange that he should expect men to keep an oath who had just mutinied, committed a series of extremely brutal murders, and were adding treason to the list; but his reasoning was perfectly sound. The British seaman of the period might be reckless with his money on shore—if he was given the chance; it might be impossible to leave liquor within his reach and expect him to stay sober; he might under pressure admit to having a wife in more than one port. He was, however, extremely superstitious and, more important, usually set great store by an oath. Once he took it, he generally regarded it as absolutely binding.

With the ship's company assembled on the quarterdeck (Southcott, Casey, Price and Searle were also brought up to take part) Cronin administered his oath: they had to swear "Not to know one another in any part of the globe, man or boy, if they should meet, nor call each other by their former names," and they had to declare "This is my oath and obligation, so help me God."

The maintopman John Brown noticed that "some were willing and some were not," but it made no difference: everyone had to take it. To make sure of the four officers, Cronin administered the oath to each of them separately, and Southcott later declared he had no option because they said they would save his life only if he promised "not to discover the mutiny at any part of the world." They did not realize that in law an oath taken under duress was not binding, not worth the breath expended in reciting it.

As night fell, with the *Hermione*'s bow wave creaming up in the darkness and her sails bellying, the mutineers relaxed once more: the wind was still north, and southward lay the Spanish Main: with a fair wind they were steering, so they thought, for liberty. Astern lay the sadistic oppression of men like Pigot: also behind them—so

Cronin no doubt persuaded them—was the tyranny of a corrupt monarchy apparently in the last stages of decay. As a Republican he had probably described the freedom that was to be theirs—while the ship sailed for asylum in La Guaira, an outport belonging to a nation which made no pretence of being democratic and was ridden and ruined by a highly-centralized, corrupt and inefficient bureaucracy presided over by His Most Christian Majesty Carlos IV, who had, in all but title, abdicated his absolute powers to Manuel Godoy, a man more than suspected of being the Queen's lover and who basked under the absurd title of Prince of Peace.

But for the moment the mutineers could dream: free of the threat of the cat-o'-nine-tails, and with gallons of free wine and rum at hand and no discipline, there was plenty of time to drink and brag. Freedom and potent liquor transmuted their sordid and vicious murders into glorious blows which they had struck for liberty.

There were plenty of men to brag, and much for them to brag about. Young James Allen was proud of the ring he had stolen from his late master, Lieutenant Douglas, and of the boots he had acquired. He related to anyone who would listen how he "had a chop" at Lieutenant Douglas, and how he had found him hiding under the marine officer's cot. The boy Hayes boasted how he had had his master, the surgeon, put to death. The foretopman James Duncan, who had claimed that he was lame, said in Southcott's hearing that "If the buggers were living—meaning the officers—that he should never have had his toe well."

The mutineers finally decided to liven up the evening with some music, and Steward Jones was the man they wanted to provide it. "They ordered me up to play the flute for them, that they might dance on the quarterdeck," he reported later.

He sat on the capstan and while his nimble fingers picked out their favourite tunes he watched the dancers and the drinkers and stored up their names and activities in his memory. There was John Watson, for instance, one of the gunner's crew, who had claimed to be blind at night. Jones noted that now Watson was "dancing with the people, very much in liquor. . . . He seemed to me to be always stupid with liquor." Southcott was able to explain Watson's apparently miraculous cure because he heard him say, "I was not blind then: they [the officers] thought I was blind, but they were mistaken."

Southcott added that "he spoke it to let me know that nothing was the matter with him at the time. Some of the mutineers made answer that the mutiny had cured the blind and the lame: nobody was blind at that time: they were all well."

Another man cheerful and drinking his fill was William Crawley, who had killed Midshipman Smith—described as "a little boy" by Steward Jones when telling how he heard Crawley "make his brags about it several times."

So the mutineers danced, sang and drank the night away. They were men of little or no education, and most of them completely unsophisticated and naïve. They thought they had achieved their liberation, little realizing that most of them would live the rest of their days in terror of a tap on the shoulder, a knock on the door or the sight of a familiar face in a strange ship or in a strange street. Yet a tap on the shoulder, or a familiar face, was to bring many of them the "one-gun salute" signalling an execution as long as ten years later.

But however sophisticated and educated the men might have been, it would have been hard for them to accept that, whatever the conditions had been in the *Hermione,* the hard fact was that Britain was fighting, and fighting alone, a desperate struggle against the French. The Revolution in France had started with fine words and loudly expressed hopes of liberty, brotherhood and equality; but it had soon become a tyranny where its leaders, still crying freedom as they set up more guillotines, sought to enslave the world: already it was a tyranny stretching from San Domingo—now several leagues astern of the frigate—to India; and, within a year or two, from Spain to the burning sands of Egypt and the ancient cities of the Levant; from the shores of the Channel, in sight of the Dover cliffs, to the very gates of Moscow.

When one small nation—for Britain, in manpower, was small— had to fight such a massive power (and Britain was the only nation that fought consistently from the beginning of the war in 1793 until its end in 1815, for the peace of 1802–3 was only a breathing space for both sides) it was inevitable that occasionally a wretched series of circumstances should place a man like Pigot under a commander-in-chief like Parker in a place like the West Indies.

One can understand and sympathize with the majority of the men for the terrible predicament in which they found themselves;

but by venting their sense of injustice on Pigot and nine other men who were comparatively or completely innocent, they had gone too far for any man's hand to help them—least of all, as they were soon to discover, a Spaniard's. Even when all excuses have been made, the fact is that in ridding themselves of a tyrant they had made themselves tyrants and immediately established a far worse tyranny. The revolution they had staged in the *Hermione* was, ironically, a microcosm of the French Revolution; a venture which began with high hopes, but fell victim to man's greed, jealousy and moral weaknesses: the all too familiar shortcomings which only fools and vote-catching politicians can ignore when planning a better world.

However, the mutineers stand condemned for the senselessness of the murders. Pigot might have been a brute—but Martin was killed only because Redman lusted after his wife. Midshipman Smith might have been a spiteful little sneak—but what justification was there for throwing a dying Lieutenant McIntosh over the side? Lieutenant Douglas might have been a captain's toady—that was no excuse for the senseless slaughter of Foreshaw, Sansum, Pacey and Manning.

Only two put up a real fight, Pigot and Foreshaw. But even before they had been tossed over the side the mutineers had control of the ship, so it was not necessary to kill anyone to ensure the mutiny's success. Yet eight more men were killed, and every one of them in cold blood. Was it because "dead men tell no tales"? No, since the leaders allowed four other officers to be reprieved, and clearly all four would tell a lot of tales the moment they had the opportunity. Why were the officers not put off in one of the ship's boats and allowed to row to an island—as the *Bounty* mutineers had served Captain Bligh and eighteen loyal men? Alternatively they could have been allowed to live and, like Casey, Southcott, Searle and Price, handed over to the Spanish as prisoners of war when the ship arrived at La Guaira.

The mutineers would not have greatly increased the chances of *being* captured by showing mercy, since the identity of most of the men would be discovered from previous muster books, and they could be identified in a court by such people as John Forbes, now in the *Diligence,* and Lieutenant Harris. In any case the Admiralty, knowing most men had their price, would soon find a former mutineer willing to turn King's Evidence in return for a free pardon.

Why then, since the men all knew of the *Bounty* mutiny, did they kill ten of the *Hermione's* officers? The *Bounty* mutiny had happened ten years earlier; but the mutiny in the little *Maria Antoinette,* when her captain and another officer had been thrown over the side, had occurred only a few score miles away and only a few weeks earlier: perhaps the methods used were fresher in their minds. But more important is the fact that Pigot's behaviour had made the men revert to the law of the jungle.

ON SATURDAY, September 23, the second day after the mutiny, the *Hermione's* new "captain," William Turner, was far from sure of the ship's position, so the mutineers decided Mr. Southcott should be made to take some sights. They went down to the captain's cabin "to desire me to go on deck to take an observation. I went on deck carrying my quadrant, and after that Redman came down twice or three times into the cabin with Turner." They worked out the sights, put Southcott's charts on the table and laid off a new course for La Guaira, allowing for the current which flowed up from the south-wards along the South American coast into the Caribbean and was sweeping the *Hermione* some sixteen miles to the westward every twenty-four hours.

From time to time when Turner and the "lieutenants" wanted to talk together in secret they used the captain's cabin, ordering the guards to take Southcott and Casey for a walk on the quarterdeck. At one meeting they had to decide what to do with the officers' possessions: they had collected and locked away a considerable quantity of loot. Captain Pigot's tableware alone made a sizeable list—apart from fifty silver spoons of various types, there were such items as a couple of silver porter mugs, the silver teapot given to him by Captain Otway after the *Ceres* grounding, and a silver cruet. There were also two pairs of silver shoe buckles and a pair of knee buckles, two watches (one in gold, another pinchbeck), a pair of silver-mounted pistols, a gold ring and eighty dollars in cash.

A search through the possessions of the other officers, both mur-dered and prisoners, yielded 368 dollars, three more watches, and a quantity of clothing. The "lieutenants" decided to dispose of the clothing (after taking for themselves the more luxurious items like silk shirts and stockings) by dividing them up between the messes, of which there were more than twenty-five in the frigate, each comprising six or more men.

The crew were once again ordered aft to the quarterdeck, watched this time by Casey and Southcott. "They got all the Captain's clothing and placed [it] on the deck and shared [it] out," Casey said later. "They then fetched the officers' chests and overhauled them for papers."

But the silver, watches and other valuables, the leaders decided, should be shared out among those who had taken major parts in the mutiny. The articles would be made up into roughly equal shares, and given to the men who, according to John Holford, "entered their names for that purpose." The articles were heaped on and round the capstan—a silver gravy spoon, five watches, silver porter mugs, twenty-three tablespoons, a gold pencil case, a silver teapot . . .

The money was made up into piles each of sixteen dollars, and Turner prepared for the share out, doing it in the usual seaman's way. "I saw Redman have a list in his hand from which the names were called . . . and I thought it was a list of the principal persons concerned in the mutiny," said Jones. According to John Holford, it was Turner who held up an article and called out to William Anderson, the gunroom steward, "Who shall have this?" and Anderson who was facing the other way, read out a name. "Those so named," Holford said, "were the principal mutineers."

Nash, Leech, Joe Montell, Smith, Marsh and Elliott were among those who each had sixteen dollars, while those receiving individual articles included Jay, Forester and Redman. But the share out did not satisfy everyone. "Thomas Jay . . . claimed a silver teapot which had been Captain Otway's present, saying he thought he deserved it," recorded Steward Jones. When Forester, who had certainly helped to kill seven of the ten officers (Southcott later testified that "I heard him say he had assisted to murder the whole of the officers"), came away from the capstan Jones noticed he had "two or three silver spoons in his hand, and some gold." He was far from happy and was "disputing with Croaker, the Gunner's Mate, about the share of the prize-money, that he had not received what he deserved, as he thought he was a principal in the murders or massacres."

Sartorially the mutiny had brought about a great change in the ship's company. David Forester had some of the captain's clothing: Southcott noted he was wearing one of Pigot's shirts, while Jones, previously responsible for the captain's laundry and who knew every item in the wardrobe, saw that Forester was also wearing a pair of Pigot's white stockings.

Young Allen added one of Lieutenant Douglas's shirts to his kit which, of course, already included the pair of cut-down half-boots; and Redman was still rigged out in the white ruffed shirt and white waistcoat in which he had left Mrs. Martin's cabin. Undoubtedly clothes made the man, for Jones reckoned that Redman "seemed to act like an officer."

AS THE *HERMIONE* approached La Guaira the men began making preparations for going on shore: for many of them—particularly the gunroom steward William Anderson, the ship's cook William Moncrieff, and an American seaman, Isaac Jackson, from Boston—it would mean leaving a ship which had been their home for nearly five years. They would have to take all their belongings with them—clothing, blankets, hammocks (each man had two) and any other prize possessions or loot they had accumulated. Many of them needed new bags to carry their gear, so John Slushing, now acting as sailmaker in place of John Phillips, who had more important work, fetched up some rolls of canvas from the sailmaker's store and issued out lengths to anyone who wanted them.

Once the men went on shore from the *Hermione* they would of course begin a new life: Lawrence Cronin's oath would start to operate. The *Hermione*'s previous muster book would give Sir Hyde Parker the identities of most of them because every captain had "at the expiration of every two months, to send to the Navy Board a full and perfect muster book . . ." This contained (or should—some captains and pursers were lax) many details about each man in the ship. Except for officers, it was supposed to state the man's name, place of birth, age and rating.

The last muster book sent in by Pigot was for the period ending July 7, 1797, but unfortunately for Sir Hyde it had by then been forwarded to the Admiralty, and until he could get it sent back again it was no help. The one then on board, beginning July 14, should have been sent in on September 14, but of course the *Hermione* was at sea. Sir Hyde would therefore eventually know the names of everyone in the ship up to July 7, but not those who had joined after then (the former prisoners that Pigot had taken out of the cartel, for instance) or had left the ship.

Clearly every mutineer in the *Hermione* would have to change his name—even those who had joined after July 7, since their real names were known to Forbes in the *Diligence,* and to the four officers. The leaders had already anticipated all this: the muster book must be destroyed, but since the Spanish authorities would want to know of everyone in the ship, a list giving their new names would have to be drawn up.

The task was given to Redman, who went down to the captain's cabin, ordered Southcott and Casey to be taken out, and sat himself at Pigot's bureau with pen, ink and paper. Every man in the ship— with the exception of the four prisoners—was sent down to him one after the other and asked what name he wanted to adopt. Thomas Nash favoured Nathan Robbins for himself, while the unpredictable Thomas Leech went back to the name he had adopted when he deserted from the *Success,* Daniel White. The Dane Hadrian Poulson became Adiel Powelson while the murderous David Forester chose Thomas Williams as his alias. The Frenchman Pierre D'Orlanie be-came Peter Delaney and the surgeon's servant James Hayes changed his name to Thomas Wood.

One of the men who made the least change in his name was Richard Redman: he merely became John Redman.

Lawrence Cronin, the self-avowed Republican, then took over the pen and paper: the mutineers would need a letter or petition to present to the Spanish Governor explaining why they had been forced to mutiny, and why they had brought the ship to a Spanish port.

XVIII

The White Flag

—ᴍ—

EARLY ON Sunday morning, September 27, when the devout Spanish folk on shore were dressing themselves carefully to attend early Mass and celebrate St. Damiano's Day, the Spanish Main was sighted from the *Hermione*. The blue-grey blur in the distance soon came into focus and resolved itself into the great range of the Caracas Mountains. There were two useful landmarks—Monte de Avila, three miles inland from La Guaira, and the huge Silla de Caracas, the Saddle of Caracas, to the westward. Farther along the coast more peaks faded into the distance, like half-forgotten memories.

As soon as they could distinguish the port of La Guaira—it stands on a narrow coastal plain between two great masses of rock—three of the ringleaders, Leech, Elliott and Turner, sent for the steward. They "desired me to get a razor and shave them, as they were going on shore, which I did, and tied their hair," said Jones.

Although Nash had appointed Turner the "captain" of the *Hermione*, his task was simply to navigate: a position similar to that of Southcott as the master under Pigot. By then power rested in the hands of five or six men, of whom Nash and Leech had emerged as the strongest.

The anchorage at La Guaira was then simply an open roadstead in front of the town and defended by several fortresses, one of which was still under construction. The leaders decided to heave-to the frigate a mile or two from the shore and send a deputation to the town. The launch was prepared and the crew chosen. They were, for the most part, Captain Pigot's former bargemen, and John Jones said that one of them, the Dane Hadrian Poulson, was "dressed clean with a white ruffed shirt on." He also noted that included in the crew were "the people who could speak different languages." Certainly talking with the Spanish authorities would present no problem because Antonio Francisco, who had come to the *Hermione* from the *Judith* merchantman, was a Spaniard, and he was ordered to get ready to go with the party and act as their interpreter.

With the leaders shaved and combed, and the launch ready, there was a small incident which showed the position of Turner in the present situation. The ship's company was assembled on the quarterdeck when, according to Brown, "the ringleaders of the mutiny ordered Mr. Turner on shore to make terms for carrying in the ship." He was to be their spokesman.

The launch was lowered and the crew climbed in, followed by Antonio Francisco, Turner (who carried Cronin's letter to the Governor), Leech and Elliott. They took with them "an English Jack and a Spanish ensign, but did not hoist them when they left the ship," according to John Mason, who was watching their departure, but Steward Jones saw that they put up a white flag—a flag of truce—as they neared the shore.

Remaining in charge on board the *Hermione* were Nash, Farrel, John Smith and Bell. This clearly indicates the real leaders, since Leech and Elliott obviously went on shore to keep an eye on Turner and in fact conduct the negotiations, using Turner as a mouthpiece.

DON JOSÉ VASQUEZ Y TELLEZ, the Spanish Governor of La Guaira, was very puzzled when it was reported that a British frigate had arrived off the port and one of her boats was coming in flying a flag of truce. He was even more puzzled when guards brought into his office four men from the boat.

One of them, Antonio Francisco, then introduced the other three to the Governor and explained that they had brought a letter for him to read. The original letter has not survived, but fortunately it is known what the Governor learned because his superior, the Captain-General of the province of Caracas, later wrote a letter to Sir Hyde Parker, describing the men's visit. The relevant section is worth quoting in full.

"When the frigate came into the port of La Guaira," the Captain-General wrote, "he who appeared to be its commander [i.e., Turner] declared that he and the rest of the crew had found themselves reduced to the sad necessity of liberating themselves from the severe treatment and chastisement which they met with from the Captain and certain of the officers, at the same time that the provisions indisputably necessary for the support of life were extremely scarce, and those given them of the worst quality, on which account, and also being naked from not having for a long time received any pay, they found themselves oppressed from such united misfortunes that no other remedy remained than that of obliging the said officers to quit the ship, which they did in the principal boat belonging to her, at the distance of ten leagues [thirty miles] from Puerto Rico, together with their equipage and a supply of provisions.

"He added that the crew under these circumstances had resolved to come to the dominions of the King my Master, and in case of not being received in them, to repair to some one of the islands belonging to the Dutch or French . . ."

Although the Captain-General omitted to refer to it, one of the conditions imposed by the mutineers before handing over the *Hermione* was that they should not be given up to the British.

The mutineers' letter appeared sincere and honest enough as far as the Governor of La Guaira was concerned—particularly the reference to sending the officers away in a boat (though had he checked he would have found the frigate still had her full complement of boats on board).

The Governor was impressed with the men's petition and wrote a brief note, enclosing the mutineers' letter, to his superior Don Pedro Carbonell, who held the posts of Captain-General of the Province of Caracas, Field Marshal and President of the Royal Court of Justice. He was at the city of Caracas, six miles from La Guaira as the crow flies, but in fact more than twenty miles away by the dusty, twisting road which climbed up the mountains to the capital.

In the meantime, the Governor explained to Turner, until the Captain-General's orders had been received the four delegates should stay in La Guaira: accommodation would be provided for them and for the crew of their boat.

NEXT MORNING a messenger returned from Caracas with the Captain-General's preliminary reply. The Governor then summoned the harbourmaster, and with the four British delegates went down to the frigate's boat: Don Vasquez would announce in person to the *Hermione's* crew the Captain-General's immediate instructions and proposals.

The men, who had been waiting anxiously on board since the previous afternoon, saw the boat returning, and through telescopes could make out several strangers sitting with Turner in the stern-sheets. Judging by the magnificence of their dress they were important officials, and the men lined the bulwarks and climbed up the ratlines to get a better view. When he saw Turner give an unmistakable signal Nash ordered the ship's company to give three cheers, and the strangers in the launch gave three in reply.

Soon Don Vasquez, followed by the harbourmaster and other officials, was stepping on to the quarterdeck of the *Hermione*, followed by Turner, Leech and Elliott. Nash called the hands to attention and Turner made a brief speech describing his talk with the Governor, saying that he had to go to the city of Caracas the next day to settle the details with the Captain-General. He then introduced the Governor.

Don Vasquez, pausing from time to time to enable his words to be translated, told the assembled mutineers that for the present the *Hermione* would be received at La Guaira and was to be moored off the harbour, until he received more instructions from the Captain-General authorizing him to negotiate further terms. In the meantime they could go on shore in parties and would be paid the wages due to them.

At this the men gave him a cheer and he was escorted to the gangway. The harbourmaster stayed behind to give Leech—who, according to Southcott, was officer of the watch—instructions for piloting the ship into harbour, while Turner and Elliott went back on shore with the Governor. By nightfall His Britannic Majesty's former frigate *Hermione* was moored under the fortresses of La Guaira.

As soon as he returned to his office Don Vasquez wrote a report to the Captain-General on his visit to the ship. Leech came on shore next day to join Turner and Elliott, and the trio then went up to Caracas to see the Captain-General in person.

Once they had covered the twenty miles of mountainous road to the city they found it bright and cool—for it is 3,000 feet above sea level—with palm trees lining squares which were almost gaudy with colourful flowers and shrubs. They were soon repeating their story to Don Carbonell. By now convinced the whole business was genuine, he was sympathetic, and anyway it was a double victory for Spain, since she had simultaneously gained a 32-gun frigate—and one was badly needed, since British warships and privateers were reaping a rich harvest along the whole of the Main—while depriving the British of a valuable warship.

The cost of whatever he now did for her crew was insignificant compared with the value of the ship. He therefore ordered (as he later wrote in reply to a stern letter from Sir Hyde) that "money be given to those that were naked in order that they might clothe themselves and relieve their wants."

He wrote a letter for the delegates to read to their shipmates, and then settled down to draw up orders for Governor Vasquez, saying that until he heard from the King about the British seamen's future—and it would take some months to receive a reply from across the Atlantic—they were to be kept in the province of Caracas, paid twenty-five dollars for subsistence and housed in a barracks at La Guaira. In the meantime there would have to be a council meeting in Caracas before the *Hermione*'s future could be decided.

As soon as the delegates returned to the *Hermione* they were surrounded by an excited throng and Turner read out the Captain-General's letter containing, as Southcott later reported, his "proposals." The main point that interested the listening mutineers was that the Captain-General undertook not to hand them over to the British.

Turner was soon followed on board by the Governor, who had received further instructions from Don Carbonell. He said many of them would be able to go on shore next day to live in barracks, and that arrangements were being made to pay them an advance of twenty-five dollars. This prompted William Carter (who had previously spoken to the carpenter about his wish to suppress the mutiny) to speak up. Why were they being given the money? he asked suspiciously. It was "a present to subsist on," the Governor replied.

After the Governor left the ship several Spanish officers came on board to make various arrangements. There were certain sick men to be taken to hospital—among them John Williams, the lame seaman—and Southcott, Casey, Price, Searle and the ship's cook, William Moncrieff, had to be put on shore since they insisted on giving themselves up as prisoners of war. A list of the five names had already been given to the Governor by Turner.

In the meantime the Captain-General had called a *junta* for October 3 to decide what to do with the *Hermione*.

THE *JUNTA*, or council meeting, which met in Caracas on October 3, started off a running battle between the Spanish bureaucrats which was to last for two years and, as far as the *Hermione* was concerned, have ludicrous results. It provides the only amusing episode in the story of the frigate.

It is necessary to understand how the Spanish dominions were administered in order to see how easily the *Hermione* was immobilized. The man who ruled the province of Caracas in the King's name was the Captain-General, Carbonell. To help him he had a complicated set of ordinances and the tradition of more than two centuries of Spanish occupation. The ordinances had been altered or amended over the years, and successive kings had issued various decrees to the viceroys and captains-general which by 1797 had reached formidable proportions, there being 156 huge volumes for New Spain alone.

The Captain-General of Caracas—in common with the rulers of other Spanish dominions—was not allowed to use much personal initiative: when in doubt he had to write to the King (or rather to the premier, Godoy, the Prince of Peace) asking for instructions. It took months to get a reply from wherever in Spain the Court happened to be residing.

Over the centuries the viceroys and captains-general had become loaded down with work—they dealt with everything, ranging from commerce and defence to the quarrels and grievances of the native Indians. The constant stream of detailed instructions, demands, and decrees from the Court in Spain—which, as always, poked its finger into every pie, however small—added to their troubles and, stultifying all initiative, resulted in complete inefficiency.

Eventually the intendant system was started. The intendant (in Caracas he was Don Estevan Fernandez de Leone) was in effect the treasurer of the province. Previously the viceroy or captain-general was responsible for the departments of finance, war, justice and administration (which covered everything from keeping an eye on the people's morals and town planning to commerce and irrigation). Under the new system the intendant took over the finance department completely and was given a good deal of control where money was concerned in the other three, as well as stamping out smuggling (which was rife), and defence.

In the naval and military sphere the intendant was supposed to deal only with the financial aspect, leaving actual operations to the captain-general and the various commanders. But—and it was a big but—he was equal in rank to the captain-general. He was supposed to carry out the instructions of a *junta* formed by the captain-general, intendant and other senior officials of the province; yet he had the right to correspond direct with the King—at this time through the Prince of Peace—so that without actually refusing to carry out an order of the *junta* he could delay matters for a very long period.

WHEN THE *JUNTA* MET on October 3 those present were the Captain-General, Don Carbonell; de Leone, the Intendant; Brigadier Don Joaquin de Zubillaga, commanding the infantry in the province; and Brigadier Don Mateo Perez, who commanded the artillery. The major item on the agenda was of course the question of "the crew of the English frigate of war named the *Hermione* of 40 guns who laid hands on her and gave her up to His Majesty in the port of La Guaira." (The Royal Navy regarded her as a 32-gun ship because carronades—she carried eight—were not included in the total.)

The Captain-General decided that each member of the *junta* should record his vote in writing on the following specific questions: (a) Should they accept the frigate? (b) Should they give protection and asylum to the crew? (c) Should the crew be accepted as subjects of the King?

The members all voted in favour of each question, but decided that until the King's approval had been received, the crew should be kept in the province. The ship herself should be refitted as soon as possible.

Then they chose a new name for the *Hermione*: while under the red and gold flag of Spain, she would be the *Santa Cecilia*. (The previous *Santa Cecilia*, a 36-gun frigate, was burned with three Spanish battleships on February 17 that year in Shaggaramus Bay, Trinidad, to prevent her falling into British hands.) As for manning her, they were very short of seamen and, according to a report just received from La Guaira, they would need at least twenty-five of the British sailors in addition to every available Spanish seaman. Don Carbonell decided that for the time being the *Santa Cecilia* should be taken to Puerto Cabello, where there were piers and it would be easier to work on her.

After the *junta* Carbonell drew up the necessary orders: to Don Vasquez, the Governor at La Guaira, instructing him to leave twenty-five picked British seamen on board, and then send the ship round to Puerto Cabello; to the Governor at Puerto Cabello, Don Miguel Marmion, telling him to expect the ship and that she was to be refitted; and also to Intendant Leone who, although he had been present at the *junta*, needed written instructions.

With a ship due to leave for Spain with dispatches within a day or two, Carbonell later wrote two letters to the Prince of Peace, one on October 5 and the other the next day, explaining what had happened, and in each one concluding that "I beg your Excellency to think it worthy to give the account to His Majesty, and communicate to me his Royal Approval." By the time his letters reached Spain the Court would have moved up into the wild Sierra Guadarrama, to the dismal grey-stoned palace of the Escorial, more than 3,000 feet above sea level and from where, near the tombs of his long-dead forebears, Carlos IV would rule his vast Kingdom until December 10, when the ritual move to Madrid would take place.

AS SOON AS Turner heard from the Governor that twenty-five of the mutineers were needed to stay on in the *Hermione* the leaders met to discuss the matter. Of the ringleaders Nash, Jay, Bell, the American Farrel, McReady and Turner, all decided they would stay in the ship, but Leech, Redman and several others agreed they wanted to go on shore. Turner was therefore instructed to call for volunteers to make up the twenty-five, and from them he chose among others Midshipman Wiltshire, Antonio Marco, Hans Christopher, a Dane, and Peter Stewart.

Turner was also told to send the rest of the men on shore to the barracks. At this point Steward Jones, who had not been treated as a prisoner of war—perhaps the "lieutenants" wanted him to wait on them—went to Turner "and got liberty . . . to go on shore, and was never with the ship's company afterwards." He joined Southcott and the rest of the officers.

With the exception of the twenty-five mutineers remaining in the ship, the *Hermione*'s former crew were marched off to the barracks and a few days later told to go to a street near the dock gate, where they would be paid the twenty-five dollars promised to them by the Governor. They trooped off there to find a large table had been set up, with Spanish soldiers on guard. A Spanish official sitting at the table had a pile of money before him and a copy of the list of names—in effect aliases—which Redman had drawn up. Each man in turn was called up to the table, paid twenty-five dollars, and a tick put against his name. "Mr Turner said he would take the money for the people in hospital," noted Perrett.

After the seamen had been in La Guaira a few days the Spanish authorities ordered them to be moved inland to Caracas. No reason was given, but it was probably because the *junta* had decided that until they received the King's approval of their decisions, a port offered too many opportunities for the men to slip away in merchant ships.

At this point six of the *Hermione*'s marines, headed by Plaice and Corporal Nicholas Doran, and including McNeil, the sentry wounded while guarding Pigot's cabin, Robert Newbold, who had been sentry at the water cask, and William Macey, who was in hospital, tried to give themselves up as prisoners of war; but the Governor declared—as befitting La Guaria's chief bureaucrat—that he could not accept them: their names were not on the original list of prisoners given to him by Turner, and they would have to surrender as prisoners when they reached Caracas. So, leaving Macey behind in hospital, the remaining five marines prepared for the march to Caracas.

The loyalty of these six marines had never been in doubt; but some actual mutineers, both leaders and those who had simply obeyed, were beginning to have misgivings. No doubt a few were disillusioned because the Spaniards had not treated them like heroes—indeed, one Spanish captain of a merchant ship said later they were "held in the utmost detestation: the scorn and contempt of everyone."

Richard Redman was one who had doubts. He had to go to

hospital, where he was seen by the carpenter, Price, who had been released from arrest to receive medical treatment. Price recorded that Redman "said he had had no hand in the mutiny. He likewise questioned me what the Master and Midshipman [Casey] had to say against him. I then told him they had nothing to say, and [I] begged him to go home to England" [i.e., give himself up as a prisoner]. Redman, however, "told me he would go to America and from there to England."

Mrs. Martin, the boatswain's widow, had been brought on shore from the frigate. It is not known if her presence had any effect on Redman's decision not to stay in the ship; but she was soon to leave the mutineers.

While visiting the hospital the carpenter also saw John Williams, the lame seaman who was receiving treatment for his legs, and expressed sorrow for what had happened. "He then cried and said he would go to England and give himself up."

Just as the mutineers began their march to Caracas Mr. Southcott—who, with the rest of the prisoners, was being kept at La Guaira for the time being—heard that William Carter "wanted to speak to me, but the Spaniards would not allow him to give himself up." Carter was the man who spoke to Southcott after the mutiny, disclaiming any responsibility for what had happened, and later asked the Governor of La Guaira why they were to be given the twenty-five dollars.

James Perrett, the butcher, afterwards described how he and another seaman also wanted to give themselves up as prisoners. "I tried myself through Mr Turner . . . and he got me and William Innes put in the guard house for it, and we lived three days on bread and water. They [the Spanish authorities] told us if we wanted to give ourselves up we should have done so to the ship's company before we came in."

With the men disappearing up the road to Caracas, half-hidden in the dust thrown up by their tramping feet, the former crew of the *Hermione* were beginning to scatter to the four winds.

Even among those who had not tried to give themselves up as prisoners there were men who, on the evidence of people like Southcott, had not originally joined the mutineers but were forced to obey their orders since the alternative was instant death. Yet because they did not know that once in La Guaira they had a right to surrender as prisoners (or did not dare) they were for the most part doomed to remain wanted men to the end of their lives.

A FEW DAYS LATER the *Santa Cecilia* sailed from La Guaira for Puerto Cabello. The Spanish schooner *San Antonio* had been moored nearby taking on a cargo of cheese, soap and cocoa destined for the Spanish garrisons in Santo Domingo. With British warships patrolling round the island her captain knew it would be a dangerous voyage.

He had been more than surprised when he saw the *Hermione* arrive off La Guaira on September 26, and for the next couple of weeks he had heard a series of rumours—some of which had grown in the telling—about what had been happening on board her. Indeed, for some time he seems to have been better informed about what had actually happened to her British captain and several of her officers than the Captain-General, who apparently continued to believe Turner's story about them being put off in a boat.

Finally with the *San Antonio*'s cargo stowed, the hatch covers put on and the anchors weighed, she set off on her long and lonely voyage, her crew no doubt saying a few prayers that they would successfully run the gauntlet of British privateers and warships.

XIX

Bad News for Sir Hyde

—m—

THE *HERMIONE'S* CONSORT, the *Diligence*, had been
steering to the northwards on the other tack while the mutiny had been taking place. Her officers had seen no definite
sign of the frigate during the night after 8 P.M., when she had been
four miles away to the east-south-east. Half an hour after midnight a
sail was seen in the darkness on the same bearing and "supposed to
be the *Hermione*" by Charles White, the master, who noted in his log
that half an hour later they "lost sight of the sail."

That was to be expected, since the *Diligence* and *Hermione* were to
stand on different tacks at 8.30 P.M. However, when daylight came
next morning there was no sign of the privateer they had been chasing, nor of the *Hermione* but, as Captain Mends noted in his log, to
the south-east they "saw a strange sail," and the *Diligence* "made
sail in chase."

By 8 A.M. the strange ship was six or seven miles to the south-east
but drawing away fast. Mends continued the chase until noon but
the stranger was gaining all the time, and with the wind becoming
lighter he knew there was no chance of catching her. He tacked
northwards once again and at 4 P.M. noted, "No sail in sight." The
"strange sail" had almost certainly been the *Hermione*, though of

course Captain Mends did not realize it at the time, and never approached close enough to recognize her as a British frigate. He continued the patrol, expecting to sight the *Hermione* a few hours later.

Hours merged into days and Mends became increasingly alarmed as they swiftly added up to a week. Should he leave the patrol area and search for her? That would risk the *Hermione* returning from another direction and finding him missing. He could be blamed whether he stayed where he was or went off on a search, since the *Hermione* might be stuck on a reef, badly damaged and waiting for his assistance, or chasing an enemy ship, confident that Mends would maintain the patrol.

By September 29 the frigate had been absent eight days and Mends's luck had vanished. Until then he had been fortunate with prizes; but for this period, when any error of judgment would probably have been overlooked if he had a couple of prizes to his credit, he saw only a succession of British ships or Jonathans.

The last of the brig's water was almost gone by the 29th, and Mends decided to take her into Ocoa Bay, on the south-west coast of Santo Domingo. It took three days—from September 29 until October 2—for the *Diligence*'s boats to bring off full water casks.

All that time Mends had the worrying thought that in the meantime the *Hermione* might have returned to the Mona Passage—which was some fifty miles away—and, not finding him there, left again in search. He was thankful to be under way again, and the *Diligence* was soon back on patrol. But his luck did not change: there was no sign of enemy ships; nor was there any sign of the *Hermione*. Pigot's little squadron had reached its patrol area on September 4, and Sir Hyde's orders told him to patrol the Mona Passage for seven weeks and then return to the Mole. The *Hermione* and *Diligence* should begin their voyage back to the Mole on October 16. It was by then October 3, with thirteen days left before the patrol was due to end.

By the evening of the 15th Mends was in a state bordering on desperation: the *Diligence* should sail for the Mole next morning; in the meantime he had sighted neither prize nor consort. Finally dawn came on the 16th, and it was time to set a course for the Mole. But, as Mr. Charles White, the master, noted in his log, at daylight the lookouts "saw a ship in the east quarter." She was not far away and Mends hurriedly set more sail and started to chase. By 7 A.M. she had hoisted French colours; by 8 A.M. the *Diligence* had "fired a shotted gun at the ship, when she hauled down her colours."

The brig's boarding party reported that she was in fact an American ship, the *Sally*, of Norwich, captured by the French privateer *Pandora* while on her way from New London to Jérémie with a cargo of horses and naval stores, and that they had the French prize crew of a dozen men under guard. The prisoners were brought over to the *Diligence* and Mends left one of his officers in command of the schooner, with a crew of four seamen.

Since the *Diligence* had to return to the Mole, Mends kept the schooner in company and the two ships turned back south-west-wards.

Next morning at daylight the *Diligence*'s lookouts spotted another schooner, and a boarding party discovered she was American and bound for Jacmel with a cargo of flour and provisions for the French from Boston. Instead of following the example of the French privateer *Pandora* and seizing the ship Mends contented himself with putting the French prisoners on board her. They were eating his stores and drinking his precious water: let the Jonathan feed them for the next day or two, until he arrived in Jacmel.

With the *Sally* in company, the *Diligence* sailed south-westwards for the next three days; but at daylight on October 20, after a squally night, the lookouts reported three ships in sight. Leaving the *Sally*, the *Diligence* chased the nearest one, which proved to be a Danish sloop bound for Santa Cruz, so the brig set off after the second ship, which was a schooner. Three hours passed before the *Diligence* was close enough to fire a shotted gun at her. She hoisted Spanish colours but held her course, and it took two more shots across her bows before, as Mr. White noted in his log, "the chase hauled down her colours."

He added, "Boarded and took possession of her. She proved [to be] the Spanish schooner *San Antonio* from Caracas to St Domingo with cheese, soap and cocoa, eight days out. Took her in tow." When the Spanish captain arrived on board the *Diligence* he was taken down to the cabin: he had some important news which he was anxious to pass on to Captain Mends in private.

The news was the most shattering that Mends had ever heard, for the *San Antonio* was of course the schooner which had sailed from La Guaira after the *Hermione* arrived there. But the Spanish captain, after solving the mystery of the frigate's whereabouts, told him that from what he had heard, the *Hermione's* mutineers had been in correspondence with the men in the *Diligence* (presumably while the brig took on water casks from the frigate), and that Mends had better watch out.

The report which Mends wrote for Sir Hyde Parker a week later related the story the *San Antonio's* captain had told him. Part of the story was incorrect and exaggerated:

"It is with inespressible [*sic*] pain I inform you of the fate of His Majesty's ship *Hermione*," Mends wrote, "the uncertainty of which to me had long been a source of mortifying reflection, now ascertained beyond all doubt to have been such as mocks our warmest passions, and remained for these times to produce.

"By the master of a Spanish schooner which I captured on the 20th . . . I am informed that the *Hermione* arrived at [La Guaira] on the 26th of last month at 3 P.M. having been run away with by her crew; who not content in such atrocity, added to it the last, the most horrible of all human actions, a general indiscriminate slaughter of their captain and officers, excepting the Surgeon, and one of the master's mates, who concealed themselves, most of the Marines, six women, and in all some forty souls: it appears that Captain Pigot, about the time of going to bed, was murdered by his coxswain, who was nominated commander afterwards, and in that character delivered her up with all papers, signals and instructions to the Spanish Governor on conditions of arrears of wages being paid; to be considered as Spanish subjects; and not given up to the English when the war is over . . ."

From what the mutineers said at La Guaira, there had been a correspondence with the *Diligence's* crew to involve them in the mutiny, said Mends, and "had we not separated they would have taken us along with them.

"The Master of the schooner charged me to take care of myself when he related this. Having weighed this part of the information against the truly gallant, good-tempered disposition of my people, I called them together and fairly related the case in all its circumstances: never could any body of men be more shocked at hearing of such unexampled barbarism, nor was indignation marked stronger than when they were told of the intention of breeding mutiny in, or seizing the *Diligence* by force. To a man I was assured that had we been in company when this fatal catastrophe took place, that they would have retaken the *Hermione* or perished alongside her.

"The Master of the Spanish schooner informs me that the mutineers are held in the utmost detestation at La Guira [*sic*]; the scorn and contempt of everyone; their offer of going to sea in the ship under Spanish colours being rejected by the Governor."

Mends was courageous. One of his lieutenants was in the *Sally*, and another in the *San Antonio*; Spanish prisoners on board were occupying the attention of his few marines, and the nearest enemy port was less than fifty miles away. Yet he did not hesitate to call his men together and tell them that the *Hermione*'s crew had mutinied and killed the officers. Had they been planning a mutiny, it would have only needed one man to shout "Come on boys, let's do the same!" for Mends to have been tossed over the side.

Now that he knew the *Hermione*'s fate, Mends's immediate duty was to warn the commander-in-chief. He gave orders for the *San Antonio* to be taken in tow, and a signal was made to the *Sally*. At 11.30 A.M. the brig "filled and made sail." The Mole was still more than 300 miles away.

AT THE MOLE Sir Hyde Parker was flying his flag in the *Queen* once again after his few weeks' stay in the cramped old storeship *Adventure* and planning to sail almost at once with the *Carnatic* and *Valiant*. However, for the moment he was worried because, as he related in a letter to the Admiralty, his original fears—heightened by the *Maria Antoinette* affair—had been justified: he had just discovered that ripples from the great mutinies at the Nore and Spithead had at last crossed the Atlantic and reached the West Indies.

One of the twenty-six ships whose crews had mutinied at the Nore was the storeship *Grampus*. She had not been badly affected, and of the 412 mutineers later court-martialled only six were from the *Grampus*. She had then been sent to the West Indies, but not before four mutineers from other ships had been put on board. The *Grampus* arrived at the Mole early in October, and the first sign of trouble on board was described by her captain, Charles Carne, in a letter to Sir Hyde written on October 19. Explaining how he returned on board one night to find the mainyard hanging by the main tackles, he said he ordered some men to secure it in case a swell came on, and while this was being done "Colin McKelly and Abraham Mason (seamen) behaved themselves in the most contemptuous manner to me, their captain, and endeavouring to stir up the ship's company to mutiny; for which I have to request you will be pleased to order a court martial . . ."

Sir Hyde ordered the trial to be held next day, so that at the same time Captain Mends, 300 miles away in the *Diligence,* heard about the *Hermione* mutiny, five captains at the Mole heard the evidence against the two seamen from the *Grampus,* and sentenced them to death. When Sir Hyde read the minutes and sentence of the trial he decided to reprieve one of them.

Therefore on Monday, October 23, Colin McKelly was hanged from the yardarm of the *Grampus* and Abraham Mason received his reprieve. Earlier the same day Sir Hyde had written to all the captains telling them to "acquaint their respective ship's crews with the execution of this day for mutiny, which I hope will be an awful lesson to them, to avoid, by their good conduct, a similar punishment." The next sentence of Sir Hyde's letter was a direct result of Admiralty concessions during the Spithead mutiny: the captains were to tell the men "that I have ordered a full allowance of all species of provisions to be issued to them on the first of next month, agreeable to His Majesty's Order in Council of 18th May last." From then onwards there would be sixteen ounces in a pound, officially anyway.

Only one other action by Sir Hyde on the particular Monday concerns this narrative. Some days earlier, knowing the *Hermione* and *Diligence* were due to complete their patrol and leave the Mona Passage on October 16, he had sent the *Magicienne,* under Captain William Ricketts, and the *Severn,* to take their place.

Now Sir Hyde drew up some special secret orders for Ricketts "to proceed upon a particular service." They would be sent to Ricketts by the *Regulus.* The "particular service" was a strange one. When reporting on the *Grampus* court-martial later to the Admiralty, Sir Hyde said that "some proofs have appeared that the seeds of the late wicked mutiny [i.e., at Spithead and the Nore] were not wholly exterminated in that ship," and that they had been "in a great measure revived" by putting "four marked mutineers from other ships" on board before she sailed from England. However, it was discovered after the incident which led to McKelly being hanged that "so strong was the spirit for mutiny in the *Grampus* that immediately on their arrival [at the Mole] they began tampering with the crews of the ships then in port, and, from information, the Valiants and Adventures were inclined to adopt their measures, the Queens and Carnatics positively refused to have anything to do with them.

"Two men having been pointed out by Captain Carne as great promoters of the mutiny, although sufficient proof could not be adduced to bring them to trial, I have put them on board the *Magicienne* and *Regulus* [i.e., sent them in the *Regulus* to the *Magicienne*], with orders to Captain Ricketts to put them on shore near some Spanish settlement . . . as characters unworthy of remaining in His Majesty's service, with certificates annexed to their discharges of the crimes with which they are charged. These examples, I trust will damp the infection that appears to have been so near taking place, of the destructive licentiousness which threatens the very existence of the Navy . . ."

Two days after he wrote that dispatch, and a few hours before the packet *Princess Royal* sailed with it for England, the Admiral received an even greater shock—one which made the activities of the *Grampus*'s men look like children's games. As he noted in his journal for Tuesday, October 31, "At 2 A.M. arrived the *Diligence* . . ."

IMMEDIATELY the brig anchored Captain Mends had himself rowed across in the darkness to the *Queen* and within a few minutes was relating to the commander-in-chief the story of the *Hermione*'s fate as reported by the captain of the *San Antonio*. Sir Hyde acted promptly: he realized there was no chance of getting the Spanish to return the *Hermione* herself, since the two countries were at war; but he guessed that the Spanish authorities would have little sympathy with mutineers. They also had crew problems—press-gangs had to roam the streets of Spanish towns to man the ships of His Most Christian Majesty. The Spaniards would realize that large rewards given to British mutineers might well encourage their own men to desert to the British in the hope of similar treatment.

His strongest case lay in asking the Spanish authorities to hand over the mutineers because they were murderers, so he dictated a letter to the Governor of La Guaira "demanding the crew of the *Hermione*," as he phrased it in his journal. Since the man who delivered the letter would probably have to negotiate with the Spaniards, he chose Captain William Ricketts, who was one of his favourites as well as being a nephew of Admiral Earl St. Vincent, and his ship, the *Magicienne,* was well placed geographically. Orders would have to be sent quickly, since the *Regulus* had already sailed to deliver to him the two would-be mutineers from the *Grampus* and the admiral's order to maroon them.

Sir Hyde dictated instructions for Ricketts saying that he enclosed a letter for the Governor of La Guaira. Ricketts was "to proceed thither and use his best endeavours to procure the company of [the *Hermione*], and in the case of success, to distribute them on board his ships and join me off Monte Christe [*sic:* Cristi] or, in case of failure, to dispatch the *Diligence* to me with an account of the proceedings."

His instructions to Mends were simple enough: he was to sail at once in the *Diligence* to find the *Magicienne,* deliver the letters to Ricketts, "and follow his orders for your further proceedings."

With Mends on his way Sir Hyde wrote to the Admiralty describing what had happened and what he had done. Fortunately the packet *Princess Royal* was ready to sail for England, so the dispatch was sent across to her, and the frigate *Ambuscade* ordered to escort her well out into the Atlantic.

Sir Hyde sailed later the same day with the *Queen, Valiant* and *Carnatic* for the north side of Santo Domingo, but his departure had nothing to do with mutiny or war: a few days earlier yellow fever had broken out on board each ship, and Sir Hyde believed that the best way of dealing with such outbreaks was to get to sea. A fortnight later he was writing to the Admiralty that in the *Queen* twenty-four men had died and fifty more were still on the sick list but he trusted "the violence of the disease has subsided; the other two ships have not suffered in proportion."

THE PACKET *Princess Royal,* under the able command of Captain John Skinner, which had left the Mole on October 31 with Sir Hyde's dispatch reporting the *Hermione* mutiny, managed to avoid marauding French privateers, and arrived safely at Falmouth after a voyage of just over forty days—about a week longer than usual.

Sir Hyde's dispatch was soon in a coach rattling its way along the 266 miles to the Admiralty, where it was opened by Mr. Evan Nepean, the Secretary of the Board. On December 15 the Admiralty made the news public. The *Evening Mail,* among other newspapers, had already reported on December 13 the safe arrival of the *Princess Royal* from the West Indies, and on the 15th announced that "it is with much regret we have to relate a circumstance of the most daring and sanguinary mutiny that the annals of the British Navy can record. The particulars, we believe, are not known; but a most melancholy event has happened on board His Majesty's frigate the *Hermione,* of 32 guns, Captain Pigott [*sic*], son of the late Admiral, who with every officer of the ship except the surgeon, has been either killed or wounded, and the frigate carried into a Spanish port.

"It is hoped," added the newspaper (having no doubt received a suitable hint from the Admiralty), "that the characteristic honour of the Spanish nation will deliver up these detestable villains, that they may meet the reward due to their enormity . . ."

A few days later, on board his huge flagship the *Ville de Paris,* which was off the Portuguese coast, Admiral Lord St. Vincent also wrote an urgent letter to Nepean at the Admiralty. Dated December 22, from off the Tagus, it said:

> My dear Nepean,
>   The Spanish post is just come in, and Commissioner Coffin has sent me the enclosed, which I do not give entire credit to, because of the distance between Porto Bello and La Guayra (all in the wind's eye), but so many of these disgraceful events have happened, that I shudder for the fate of Pigot, who is a very promising officer and a spirited fellow.

The enclosure was a letter to the Admiral which said: ". . . I have this instant received a letter from Cadiz wherein they [say] yesterday arrived a Spanish brig from La Guayra [*sic*] which brings the account that the English frigate the *Hermione* was carried in there by the crew—the mutiny was in consequence of a man being on board in confinement either under sentence of death, or to be tried for a crime which would have had that effect—and the crew wished to rescue him—in the scuffle the captain is said to have been killed—the people fearing consequences, landed the officers at Porto Bello and took the frigate into La Guayra."

This letter was soon followed by a visitor to the *Ville de Paris,* who reported to Lord St. Vincent in person. The visit is described by a second letter. "The young man who arrived from Cadiz . . . and had the honour to wait on Lord St Vincent yesterday morning, is the person who gave the information [the details of] which he confirms by saying that the account given by the master of the vessel arrived from the said place is very full and circumstantial . . ."

The young man's report is interesting if only because it shows the captain of the Spanish brig from La Guaira knew Captain Pigot had been killed; but the dispatch he carried from the Captain-General to the Prince of Peace said, it will be recalled, that Pigot and the officers had been put off in a boat.

XX

The Cost of Freedom

—ɯ—

J UST TEN WEEKS after the *Hermione* appeared off the port a
warning was sent to the Governor of La Guaira that two more
British warships were in the offing, a frigate and a brig. This
was followed by the news that a boat had left the brig flying a flag of
truce, and soon Captain Robert Mends was explaining to the Governor that his senior officer, Captain Ricketts, had sent him to deliver a
letter from Admiral Sir Hyde Parker.

The letter was handed over, and Mends was asked to wait while
it was read and translated. When Mends was recalled, Don Vasquez
made his apologies: the matter was outside his jurisdiction. The
whole question of the *Hermione* was now in the hands of the Captain-General, to whom he would immediately forward Sir Hyde's
"reclamation," and would Captain Mends—he pronounced and
later wrote it 'Menzs'—please return next day for the Captain-
General's answer?

The letter arrived in Caracas that evening, December 6, and the
Captain-General called a *junta* for the next morning to consider the
reply. Don Carbonell was in a quandary: when the mutineers first
told him they had sent off all the officers in a boat he had believed
them (he would have known of the famous precedent of Captain

Bligh and the *Bounty*) and agreed to their condition that they should not be handed over to the British. But since then ugly rumours had reached his ears, supplemented by reports from La Guaira, that in fact the men had murdered the officers, with the exception of the four under guard at the port. Yet he could hardly go back on his word . . .

Next morning the *junta* met, and the minutes record that Carbonell told them how "a British frigate and a barquentine of war" had arrived and sent on shore under a flag of truce a letter from "the Vice-Admiral of the Naval Forces of His Britannic Majesty at the Jamaica Station." This letter, Carbonell said, "claimed the crew of the former British frigate *Hermione*, to punish them for the grave acts of piracy and assassination that he says they committed against the officers, and for seizing the ship."

The minutes add that "having read attentively and discussed the petition with the mature thought that the case required, it was agreed that the Captain-General . . . replies that having already sent an account to His Majesty, it is necessary to await his Royal decision; and without touching on the request to deliver up the crew, say that at the time the ship came into La Guaira the crew said they had sent the officers away in a boat" because of the treatment they had received.

As soon as the eight men had signed the minutes Carbonell drafted a reply to Sir Hyde Parker and sent it by messenger to the Governor at La Guaira for him to deliver "to the subordinate officer awaiting my reply."

In the meantime Carbonell's answer to Sir Hyde was given to Captain Mends, who took it to Captain Ricketts in the *Magicienne*. The two ships then sailed, the *Diligence* to join the commander-in-chief off Monte Cristi and deliver the reply, and the frigate to resume her patrol in the Mona Passage.

WHILE HIS LETTER to the Governor of La Guaira was being delivered, Sir Hyde was busy making plans to capture the mutineers should the Spaniards not hand them over, and which he described in a dispatch to the Admiralty. "Conceiving it impossible for the perpetrators of that horrid act to be at rest, and therefore most probably will ship themselves on board neutral vessels to America and these islands, I have sent narratives [of the mutiny] to all governors and to His Majesty's Minister Plenipotentiary in America [Mr. Liston, the envoy who had complained over the Jesup affair], and suggested to them the propriety of offering a reward and pardon to any (the principals excepted) who shall turn King's Evidence for bringing the principal actors to justice—having found the plots of all these disobedient plans confined to a very few—the greater part being led away by fear, not knowing when the execution of the plan takes place, [or] who to put confidence in, more particularly in this case after the destruction of the whole of the officers.

"It being of such importance to the salvation of the naval forces of Great Britian, that the cruel perpetrators of the piracy should be brought to condign punishment, and made most exemplary examples of, I trust his Majesty's ministers will see it in the same point of view, and make it a particular object with the Court of Spain to have the villains delivered up, as neither sound politics nor religion can induce any state to keep oath with pirates and murderers."

Although Sir Hyde had shown a shrewd insight into the workings of a mutiny—the situation of "the greater part" of the men in the *Hermione* had, of course, been as he visualized—he was soon to be disappointed by the Spanish authorities. The *Diligence* arrived and Mends delivered the Captain-General's letter, which Sir Hyde gave to his secretary, Mr. Scott, to translate. That worthy linguist soon appeared with three sheets of paper covered with his neat writing, the last one inscribed at the bottom left hand corner, "Translated literally according to the sense, signed A. J. Scott."

Don Carbonell's letter, quoted earlier, described the circumstances of the *Hermione*'s arrival, and that "he who appeared to be its commander" said that because of the conditions they had been living under, that they had been forced to send the officers off in a boat. "The said crew have ever since remained in this province, and an account of the matter has been transmitted to His Majesty in order that his sovereign will may decide therein." Don Carbonell concluded: "As soon as I receive it I shall punctually communicate it to Your Excellency . . . Everything that comes within my power Your Excellency may command. God preserve Your Excellency a thousand years."

Sir Hyde was naturally far from pleased with the Spanish reply: his report to the Admiralty lamented "the false policy which has actuated the Government of that country in the protection of these atrocious villains who, I find, as I suspected, are dispersing themselves to different parts; and unless sound policy induces the United States of America to exert their power in apprehending these criminals, I much fear they will escape the punishment which the heinousness of their crimes so justly merits."

Yet if the men did escape, it would not be Sir Hyde's fault. He soon heard from the Governor of Jamaica that proclamations offering rewards for the capture of the mutineers had been issued in the island and posters put in in Kingston, Port Royal, Port Morant and a dozen other places. At Cape Nicolas Mole notices were stuck wherever there was a suitable wall; in various other British-held ports in Santo Domingo walls and tree trunks broke out in a rash of posters. In addition the captains of all the ships in the squadron—and those of Rear-Admiral Harvey at the Leeward Island Station—had been warned to search neutral and British merchant ships.

Because of the difficulty of identifying the mutineers there seemed only a slight chance that even one would be caught; yet a few days after Sir Hyde received Don Carbonell's reply the first of them fell into his hands and was only too anxious to write a full description of what happened on board the *Hermione*.

THE MUTINEERS soon discovered their newly-won freedom was not the same freedom they had talked about when cooped up in the frigate under the autocratic rule of Captain Pigot. In the *Hermione* the conditions had been bad: the work was hard but they were paid for it, albeit little and late; the food was bad—but free—and what did not fatten at least filled. The twice-daily issue of grog was also free.

Now that they were at liberty on shore, however, nothing was free: on the contrary everything was very expensive. They had to pay for their food, and once they left the barracks to find work they had to pay for accommodation as well. Their twenty-five dollars "subsistence" soon vanished, and far from being regarded as heroes, they found most people contemptuous.

After being marched to Caracas the mutineers were later allowed to return to La Guaira and given permission to go to other towns and villages nearby where there was any chance of finding employment. Work was the most immediate problem and one which soon became desperate, particularly since they were under orders not to leave the province until permission arrived from Spain.

For the majority of the men there were only two types of work available—carrying stones for a new fortress being built on a hill above La Guaira, or pounding salt at the little village of Macuta, three miles eastwards of the town, where there were salt pans. No wages were paid for either job—only a ration of food. Such work in the glaring sun just ten degrees north of the equator was little removed from slavery. The alternative was to join the Spanish army, but since the few that did were mostly marines it seems the vacancies were few, and there was also the problem of language.

When the mutineers were brought back to La Guaira from Caracas several applied to the Governor for passes to go to America. In some special cases these were granted provisionally, but the men were told they would not be able to leave for some weeks: until, presumably, the Captain-General received approval from Spain.

With the exception of the twenty-five men working on board the *Santa Cecilia* at Puerto Cabello, and the others at the fortress and the Macuto saltpans, the rest stayed at La Guaira, wandering the streets searching for work. However, one day in November they were alarmed to find Spanish troops searching the town and arresting all the *Hermione*'s former seamen. As soon as the mutineers were locked up in jail they discovered one of the reasons: the embargo which had hitherto prevented American ships from leaving the port was to be lifted temporarily next day, and obviously the Governor was not going to risk the mutineers escaping.

Next morning a number of the men in jail—including James Irwin, John Holford and his young son, and James Barnett found out the second reason for the arrests: they were marched out of the prison and down to the quay, put on board a schooner and told they were being taken to Puerto Cabello. Barnett protested that he was "one of the salters at Macuto" and was released. When the schooner arrived at Puerto Cabello the men were imprisoned in the local fortress, and three days later taken before the Governor, Don Miguel Marmion. He ordered them to work on board their former ship, now the *Santa Cecilia.*

According to John Holford, several of the men protested that they had been granted passes for America and were wrongly arrested in La Guaira, and when Holford himself flatly refused to work on board the ship the Governor ordered him and his son to be taken back to jail. Later in the day a second batch of Hermiones arrived from La Guaira in another schooner and were sent to work on board the frigate. Among them was James Barnett, who had been rounded up a second time and his protest that he was a salter ignored. Barnett, too, refused to work in the *Santa Cecilia* and was sent on board her as a prisoner at large. He later reported that he escaped from her within two hours, but he had neither money nor food.

Holford described how he met Barnett after his escape. "He was in distress, and I kept him near a fortnight at my own expense, having brought sixty-nine dollars prize money out of the *Hermione*; but thinking himself under too much an obligation to me, he went to work at Macatee [*sic*: Macuto] for his bread."

This agreed with Barnett's explanation. "Without money, which was taken from me during the night, I was driven to great distress, and had it not been for the kindness of Holford I must have starved. At length I was obliged to go back to La Guaira, and there was under the necessity of pounding salt for my victuals only."

Holford said later that Barnett was weary in his mind about the mutiny, as he "could not venture with safety home, not knowing the consequences of what might happen if he was taken."

James Irwin, a young Irishman from Limerick, told a similar story: he worked in the *Santa Cecilia* because of "absolute necessity. I could get no other work then, for if I had not done it I must have starved." This was also confirmed by John Mason, the carpenter's mate. "There was no other employment to be had, except going to work at a fort on the top of a hill [at La Guaira] to carry stones." Those working in the *Santa Cecilia* were not given provisions by the Spaniards, but were paid. "It was called twelve dollars but some stoppages were taken out of it."

But by no means all the former mutineers had been taken to Puerto Cabello: leaders like John Phillips, the murderous sailmaker from Hanover, had joined the Spanish army with some marines. John Pearce, who Southcott had seen throw his uniform into the sea, "entered into the Spanish service, into the train of artillery," reported Sergeant Plaice. "I saw him in their dress." Others, according to Mason, were "doing duty in the garrison at La Guaira and the environs by their own consent."

Joe Montell, the Italian, said only eight or ten men received passes from the Spanish authorities to go to America. Lawrence Cronin, the glib Republican and former surgeon's mate, did not bother to apply: according to Montell he had "settled in La Guaira in professional business, encouraged by the Spaniards."

Mrs. Martin, the boatswain's widow, went to America—but not with Redman who, as soon as the men could leave Caracas, signed on in a ship. Many of the former Hermiones—as Sir Hyde Parker predicted—did this as soon as the Captain-General gave permission; and although it will take us ahead of the narrative, we can follow the fortunes of some of them. The step they took in signing on in Spanish, French and neutral ships was inevitable: seamanship was their only trade, and once the work on the *Santa Cecilia* was finished, the alternatives were carrying rocks or pounding salt.

John Holford and his son—who had only just passed his twelfth birthday—went back to La Guaira overland as soon as they were released from jail at Puerto Cabello, and again met Barnett, worn out and starving after his work as a salter. For three weeks the trio walked the streets looking for employment, but they were unlucky. Then they heard that a ship at Cumaná wanted seamen. "As we could get no passage from La Guaira," said Holford, "six of our party . . . went to Commana [*sic*] in an open boat." With them was James Bell, a former Success.

This voyage gives some indication of the men's desperate plight: Cumaná was the capital and port of entry of the province which bore its name and was more than 150 miles east of La Guaira—a long voyage in an open boat solely on the strength of a rumour that jobs were available.

Once they arrived, said Holford, "we got employed on a Spanish xebec [small and fast three-masted vessels, often used as privateers] for our victuals, but no wages allowed." Barnett and James Bell soon left the xebec. "From thence, after three weeks hard labour," said Barnett, he went to Barcelona, a small port nearby, and boarded a Danish schooner bound for St. Thomas, east of Puerto Rico. Staying there some time, he then went to St. Vincent, one of the Windward Islands, and on to Halifax, Nova Scotia, "where I was to have delivered myself up, but dreaded the consequences." From there he went overland to the Bay of Fundy and then sailed to Jamaica. After serving in other ships and sailing as far south again as Antigua, he "shipped on board the American schooner *Polly* out [of] which I was pressed by an officer of the *Maidstone.*" Thus Barnett's freedom, which had in fact been nearly two years of fear, came to an end.

Several other former Hermiones managed eventually to get berths in ships going to Curaçao, the Dutch island 150 miles to the north-west of La Guaira. Among the first to go in one schooner were John Mason, John Elliott, the Kentish quartermaster who had helped kill Pigot and then guarded Southcott, and William Brigstock, the American from New York, all of whom had originally come from the *Success;* and John Evans.

At Curaçao the men heard that the French privateer *La Magicienne* wanted men, so Mason and Elliott signed on—for a twenty-four-dollar advance and a share in the profits. The privateer then sailed for the port of Santo Domingo. Soon after arriving there she was joined by another French privateer, *L'Espoir,* which had some more former Hermiones on board, three of whom decided to quit her and join *La Magicienne*—the Italians Joe Montell and Antonio Marco, who had helped fit out the *Santa Cecilia* for the Spaniards, and the Frenchman Pierre D'Orlanie.

They left on board *L'Espoir* the murderous David Forester, as well as Simon Holmes, the former cook's mate, and two other mutineers. Mason later recalled that he had heard that George Chapman and William Carter—both of whom are known to have been against the mutiny—and a third man were also at Curaçao. *La Magicienne,* with five former Hermiones among the eighty-three men on board to help serve the guns and share the spoils, then left Santo Domingo to search for some richly-laden British merchantmen. But *La Magicienne's* captain was singularly unfortunate in his choice of a hunting ground.

Young William Johnson, the former clerk at Port au Prince, had developed a bad ulcer on his left foot at the time the mutineers had taken the *Hermione* to La Guaira. He was so young at the time, he explained later, that "I suffered myself to be carried to the house of the Commandant," where a Spanish surgeon attended him. As soon as the ulcer was cured he followed the other men to Curaçao, but he had no intention of going to sea again: he had quite enough of a sailor's life and his counting-house training helped him in "finding an advantageous situation . . . as clerk to the American Consul."

William Bower, from Chesterfield, was another needing medical treatment at La Guaira, and he later claimed that while still in hospital tried to give himelf up as a prisoner of war, but the Spanish authorities would not accept him. He then signed on in an American ship bound for Philadelphia, but at Charleston, her first port of call, Bower was alarmed to find posters on the wall offering one thousand dollar rewards for the capture of *Hermione* mutineers.

Two of the *Hermione*'s coloured seamen, the African Thomas Diamond and John Jackson, the bargeman who helped murder Pigot, joined a coasting vessel and faded into the anonymity which their colour afforded them in the West Indies.

Of the other important mutineers, whose adventures will be dealt with more fully later, Thomas Nash signed on an American ship and went to Charleston, and soon set that South Carolina seaport humming, with its newspapers, attorneys and leading citizens lambasting each other, and finally involved the President of the United States in his affairs.

Four others, the Scotsman William Benives, who had been partly blind at the time of the mutiny, John Brown, the maintopman called down to the fo'c'sle by David Forester before the mutiny started, William Herd, who had won a watch in the lottery for the officers' valuables, and John Hill, a foretopman, finally went to Curaçao. There they managed to get on board a cartel ship going to Guadeloupe and, according to a story told by Benives and Hill, captured her from the Spaniards "and carried her into Port Morant Bay, Jamaica."

The Irishman James Irwin, who had been taken to Puerto Cabello with John Holford and forced to work in the *Santa Cecilia*, finally managed to get back to La Guaira and in April 1798 joined an American schooner bound for New York. He made an unfortunate choice.

James Duncan, the foretopman who had declared in Southcott's hearing that "if the buggers [the officers] were living he would never have had his toe well" had been over-optimistic about the curative effect of mass murder, since later he had to go to hospital for three months. He recovered about the same time as a fellow-patient, John Williams, the man who had cried in the presence of Price, the carpenter.

Both Duncan and Williams then spent several weeks trying to find work, but without success. As soon as they were allowed to leave, they signed on in a Danish brigantine bound for Santa Cruz,

Duncan telling Williams that he wanted to get home if he could. Both men were to have many adventures before they were called to account for their behaviour in the mutiny.

Thomas Jay, the other boatswain's mate of the *Hermione,* was reported to have joined a Spanish gunboat at La Guaira. However death claimed some of the men: John Luxton, a Bristol-born able seaman who had voted to kill all the officers and later received sixteen dollars at the share-out of the valuables at the capstan, was one who died from illness; William Allen, a Devon man from Lynmouth and named by John Brown as a "principal mutineer," also died in hospital. They were, perhaps, lucky to meet death in this way: many others were to be less fortunate.

XXI

On Board a Corsair

—ᨆ—

A T NOON on March 1, 1798, more than five months after the mutiny, Sir Hyde Parker was cruising in the *Queen* with the *Valiant* and *Carnatic* in company. Up to that moment the admiral had not succeeded in capturing even one of the *Hermione*'s mutineers: his only knowledge of what had happened in the frigate came from the captain of the *San Antonio*. He still believed that of the officers only the surgeon survived.

Shortly after noon the *Queen*'s lookouts reported a strange sail in sight. Sir Hyde gave his orders, and the signal to chase, with the *Valiant*'s number and the bearing of the strange sail, was hoisted and a single gun fired to draw Captain Crawley's attention to it.

Soon both the strange ship—which had taken to her heels—and the *Valiant* were out of sight of the flagship. Five hours later the *Valiant* was hove-to windward of the chase which, Captain Crawley could see, was a 16-gun French privateer.

Since one broadside from the *Valiant* would have reduced her to so much driftwood, the privateer hauled down her colours without firing a shot, and a lieutenant with a boarding party took possession. She was *La Magicienne* from Curacao, and within a few minutes her crew were lined up ready to be ferried across to the *Valiant* as prisoners. However, one of the prisoners, who spoke perfect English, told the lieutenant he wanted to speak to the *Valiant*'s captain. The reason he gave was described by Captain Crawley in a report to Sir Hyde.

"It being hinted to me that James [*sic* John] Mason, late carpenter's mate of His Majesty's ship *Hermione*, was one of the corsair's crew and was desirous of relating what he knew concerning the mutiny, murder and piracy committed on board His Majesty's ship *Hermione*, I thought it proper to avail myself of the opportunity of bringing to light such an atrocious act."

He called to his cabin as witnesses his two senior lieutenants, and Mason was marched in under a marine guard. Captain Crawley began questioning him and was startled to find that Mason had not been the only former Hermione on board *La Magicienne*: there were four others among the prisoners, now in the *Valiant*, all intent on keeping their identity secret. The questioning was interrupted while Anthony Mark (who was Antonio Marco), John Elliott, Joseph Mansell (Joe Montell) and Peter Delaney (Pierre D'Orlanie) were weeded out from the other prisoners and put in irons under the watchful eye of the *Valiant*'s marines.

Captain Crawley finally had a written statement drawn up in the form of a deposition which Mason signed. In it he named nine officers and the midshipman killed by the mutineers, and listed the other officers and men who were prisoners of war at La Guaira. He added that several other Hermiones were on board another privateer, *L'Espoir*.

Rejoining Sir Hyde Parker next day, Captain Crawley gave him Mason's deposition and his own covering letter. Sir Hyde, delighted at the prospect of hearing for himself at first hand all the details of the murderous affair, ordered Mason to be brought over to the flagship. After a prolonged questioning, the facts that Mason had given were drawn up as another statement, which Mason signed.

They were just the facts that Sir Hyde needed—particularly the names of "the leading characters," whom Mason listed as Turner, Nash, McReady, Farrel, Bell and Lawrence Cronin. There had been only one woman on board, said Mason; no firearms had been used (i.e., no shots had been fired); he "saw a great quantity of blood in the Cabin window and at the afterhatch leading from the Gun Room"; and he had heard "repeated groans and screeches from the officers when murdering [*sic.*" The colour of the *Hermione's* hull, he added, was black with white mouldings.

But if Sir Hyde knew of the harsh way Captain Pigot had habitually treated the majority of his men—and it is inconceivable that he was unaware of it—then the last four lines of Mason's statement were significant. "The night before the mutiny two men [but he lists three] fell off the mizen topsail yard and were killed, their names are Francis Statton [Staunton], a Negro boy Peter, another (name unknown). There was punishment for several days previous to this and no appearance of mutiny."

As soon as Sir Hyde satisfied himself that Mason, if not necessarily innocent, was the least guilty of the five prisoners, he decided he would use him as the main—and indeed the only—prosecution witness against the other four.

HOWEVER, even before Sir Hyde signed the order for the court-martial he was horrified to discover that the crew of at least one other frigate, Captain Rolles's *Renommée,* had been on the verge of a similar sort of mutiny while at sea.

Sir Hyde later reported to the Admiralty that "a plot was discovered on board His Majesty's Ship *Renommée* just in time to prevent its execution. The intention was to perform the same tragedy as that in the *Hermione,* by murdering all the officers and carrying the ship into Havanah."

Sir Hyde added that, "the man who first warned Captain Rolles of his danger is one of so insignificant character as not fit to be rewarded by promotion. I therefore submit to Their Lordships' consideration whether a pension for life might not be attended by a general good as an example to hold out for the encouragement of men coming forward upon similar occasions."

While the four would-be mutineers of the *Renommée* were kept in prison at the Mole under a heavy guard, Sir Hyde gave orders for the court-martial of the four actual mutineers from the *Hermione,* appointing Captain Bowen the president and sending him three documents—copies of Captain Mends's letter from the *Diligence,* Captain Crawley's report on the capture of the men in *La Magicienne,* and John Mason's deposition. The other members of the court were Captains Edward T. Smith, John Ferrier, Man Dobson and John Crawley, and the trial began at 9 A.M. on March 17 on board the *York*. Mr. William Page acted as Deputy Judge-Advocate and brought the Articles of War, the Bible, a Crucifix and law books with him.

As soon as Captain Bowen gave the order the four prisoners, manacles securing their arms, were marched in under a marine guard. Once the witnesses were all present, Mr. Page stood up and read out Sir Hyde's order to try the men "upon an information contained in a letter from Captain Mends . . . and also a deposition of John Mason, late Carpenter's Mate of His Majesty's Ship *Hermione* . . . representing the said Anthony Mark, alias Antonio Marco, John Elliott, Joseph [Mansell Montell] and Peter Delaney, alias Pierre D'Orlanie, were a part of the French privateer *La Magicienne* . . . and were actually on board His Majesty's said Ship *Hermione* at the time the mutiny, murder and piracy were committed on board her; and for being taken in arms against His Majesty." (On this and subsequent occasions the real names and aliases were transposed in the charge.)

After Page had administered the necessary oaths, he read out Captain Mends's letter. To the two Italians, the Frenchman and the Man of Kent the scene must have appeared entirely unreal: the drone of Page's voice as he read Mason's deposition; the cold, impersonal glances of the five captains in full dress; the solemn ritual of the trial itself—all so remote from that wild night six months earlier when they had shouted and cheered and wielded cutlasses and tomahawks to kill the tyrannical Pigot and secure their liberty.

What had then seemed just and reasonable was now given a sinister turn: slinging Hughie over the side had become murder and mutiny; going into La Guaira with the *Hermione* was piracy; signing on in *La Magicienne* was being "in arms against His Majesty . . ."

Three of the four men might have protested that they owed no allegiance to His Britannic Majesty: D'Orlanie could have been accused by the French Government of being in arms against France, while as far as Marco knew, his allegiance was to the Republic of Genoa (although in fact three and a half months earlier it had become the Ligurian Republic). Montell's birthplace in Italy is not known, but his allegiance was to one of more than a dozen states. Yet had the men made that protest they would have been reminded of the oath of allegiance they had taken when, as pressed men or volunteers, they had first entered the Royal Navy—an oath to "His Sovereign Lord King George the Third," promising to serve him faithfully "in defence of his person, Crown and dignity against all his enemies and oppressors whatsoever."

All except the first of the witnesses were ordered out of the court, and the four accused sailors recognized the man in lieutenant's uniform who held the Bible while Page administered the oath as Lieutenant John Harris.

"Did you know any of the prisoners as belonging to the *Hermione*?" asked Captain Bowen.

"Yes," replied Harris, "since the 17th of June last, when I left her, they all belonged to her."

One witness was probably lucky not to be manacled with the other four men. He was John Kelly, a Catholic, who took the oath on the Crucifix before testifying that he had been in the *Hermione* on her last cruise until sent away in a prize. At the time he left, he said, the accused men were members of the crew.

A copy of John Mason's deposition was then produced in court and the former carpenter's mate signed it, whereupon "he was sworn in to give evidence against the prisoners." Mason, who was thirty years old and came from Belfast, also swore on the Crucifix as a Catholic.

"Inform the court," ordered Captain Bowen, "what you know of the transaction relating to the mutiny, murder and piracy which took place on board the *Hermione*."

"It was about ten o'clock at night," said Mason. "I was in my hammock and I heard the ship's company cheering and saying that the ship was their own. . . . I went down between decks and saw the Gunner sitting in his cabin, stripped and crying; the Carpenter likewise. The whole cry of the ship was 'Hand them up,' meaning the officers . . ."

From time to time Captain Bowen and other members of the court interrupted with questions to clear up points as Mason went on to describe how the ship was taken to La Guaira. But he gave no evidence whatsoever about the role the four accused men had played in the mutiny, although he described how they had served with him later in the French privateer.

When the four accused men were asked "separately and

severally" if they had any defence to offer, they said they had none, and Captain Bowen ordered the court to be cleared. The onlookers left; the marines closed in round the four prisoners and shuffled them out. The five captains did not take long to reach a verdict and decide on the sentence. The Deputy Judge-Advocate wrote it out in the time-honoured formula and the court was opened once again. The four men were marched in to hear Page read out the court's findings.

"At a court martial assembled and held on board His Majesty's Ship *York*, Mole St Nicolas . . . the Court . . . having heard the evidence . . . and very maturely and deliberately weighed and considered the several circumstances . . . and the prisoners having no evidence to produce, or anything to offer in their defence, the court is of opinion that the charge of mutiny, murder and running away with His Majesty's Ship *Hermione* and delivering her up to the enemy; and being found actually in arms against His Majesty and his subjects, on board *La Magicienne,* a French privateer, are fully proved . . ." The four men were "to be hung by the necks until they are dead, at the yardarms of such of His Majesty's ships, and at such times, as shall be directed by the Commander-in-Chief.

"And as a further example to deter others from committing, or being accessory to, such shocking and atrocious crimes, that when dead their bodies be hung in chains upon gibbets on such conspicuous points, or headlands, as the Commander-in-Chief shall direct . . ."

Unfortunately the first half of the court's verdict was sheer rubbish. The men had not been charged with "mutiny, murder and running away with His Majesty's said Ship *Hermione* and delivering her up to the enemy"; yet the court "fully proved" this non-existent charge. The charge in fact said *"and were actually on board . . . at the time the mutiny, murder and piracy were committed on board her,"* which was a completely different thing.

Secondly, even if they had been charged with mutiny, murder, running away with the ship and delivering her up to the enemy, the court never heard one word of evidence to prove it. Witnesses testified the four men were on board the *Hermione* as late as September 4, seventeen days before the mutiny, while Mason's oral evidence in court never once mentioned any of the quartet by name. The only evidence linking them with the mutiny in any way was in Mason's written deposition, which said the four men "were actually on board His Majesty's Ship *Hermione* at the time of the above-mentioned murder, mutiny and piracy."

This, of course, covered the actual charge drawn up by Sir Hyde; but men cannot be condemned to death for crimes not mentioned in a charge. However, in this case there is no need to waste any sympathy on the men, since justice was done, albeit by accident. They were four of the worst mutineers; and the second part of the charge, *"being found actually in arms against His Majesty and his subjects,"* was fully proved, and for that alone the death sentence was inevitable.

As soon as Sir Hyde received the minutes of the court-martial, he ordered some large posters to be printed. Beginning "At a court martial . . ." they went on to describe the trial and ended up with the stark wording of the sentence. As soon as the posters were ready, they were pasted up in ports the length and breadth of the Caribbean.

The execution of the four men was arranged to take place on board the *York* and Sir Hyde ordered a chaplain to attend them. The chaplain was Mr. Scott, the commander-in-chief's secretary, and the episode is described in his biography. "When he was in attendance on them after they were condemned, they exhibited so much good feeling that he was greatly interested for them. They were, moreover, all young, and in person the finest models of seamen that he had ever seen of any nation."

Promptly at 9 A.M. on the 19th a yellow flag was run up at the mizzen peak of the *York* and a gun fired. Boats came across from all the other warships. "Nothing could be more distressing to Mr Scott than the necessity of being present," wrote his biographers. "He described it as awful. The firing of the signal gun—the smoke rising to conceal the death struggles—and, as it cleared off, the lifeless bodies swinging from the yardarms."

Soon the bodies were lowered and taken on shore, where hastily erected gibbets were waiting in a conspicuous spot—well in sight of every ship that entered the anchorage. The bodies were slung from the gibbets in chains, so that the skeletons long remained to be a grim warning to would-be mutineers.

Later that day a document was handed to Sir Hyde: Joseph

Montell had left a confession, written an hour before he was hanged. In it he admitted—according to a report which Sir Hyde sent to the Admiralty—that "he was a principal, and [also] the principal in the massacre of the officers in that ship." It went on to say that he and three other men (whom he named as Bell, Draytenham and Farrel) obtained a bucket of rum and then, with "about four or five or six more" went into the gunroom in the darkness "and were the murderers of those in command." Having then gone forward again, they later "burst a second time into the Gunroom and fully completed the murder." In the confession Montell admitted hitting the first lieutenant on the head with an axe; and then later replying to Captain Pigot, who cried out for mercy, "You have shown no mercy yourself, and therefore deserve none," after which he "ran him through with a bayonet or a musquet."

But the last paragraph was the most interesting: "He believed that Elliott, the Quartermaster of the *Hermione* . . . saved the life of the Master of the *Hermione*, standing sentry over him sick in his berth the whole transaction, and that Delaney [D'Orlanie] who was executed with him suffered innocently."

NEXT MORNING the four seamen of the *Renommée* were brought to trial, and by nightfall the sentences had been pronounced—three were to be hanged and one was jailed for three months.

With the information about the *Hermione* mutiny supplied by John Mason and Joseph Montell Sir Hyde could write a second and more specific letter to the Spanish authorities. Instead of addressing it to the Captain-General, he again wrote it to the Governor of La Guaira.

"Providence having put me in possession of five of the pirates and murderers of His Britannic Majesty's late Ship *Hermione*, whose confession before their execution has furnished me with the names of most of the principal actors and murderers in that horrid transaction," he said, he was now writing "not only from a supposition you must have by this time received instructions from your Court," but also because His Excellency "must also be convinced of the impropriety which all Europe must view the politicks [*sic*] of the Court of Spain in protecting the persons of pirates and declared murderers from that exemplary punishment which it is the general interest of all nations to bring such atrocious villains to; and I am still surprised that a nation so marked in history for its national honor [sic] and justice should have adopted the contrary line of proceedings in confining the five officers that escaped the massacre, and allowing the perpetrators of these bloody acts to be at large, and even giving them rewards."

He concluded that "I do therefore, Sir, once more demand of Your Excellency in the name of His Britannic Majesty the bodies of these men marked in the enclosed list, as principals in the piracy and murder . . . as also . . . those gentlemen named as lately officers, and that Your Excellency will deliver them up to the officer charged with this dispatch."

Sir Hyde's demand was certainly written with a full charge of indignation, but unfortunately it went off with only a slight fizzle when it reached La Guaira. The reason was that on April 4, four days before Sir Hyde had dictated it, Captain Ricketts had again arrived off La Guaira in the *Magicienne* and, apparently acting on his own initiative (no orders appear among Sir Hyde's papers), sent his first lieutenant on shore under a flag of truce with a letter which Ricketts had written to the Governor, claiming "the murderers of Captain Pigot and his officers," adding that he would "return within three days for an answer."

The Captain-General's reply was sent to the Governor to await Rickett's return. It said that "The Most Excellent Sir Hyde Parker" had previously written demanding the men and claiming they had murdered their captain and part of the ship's company, "the which was unknown at the time of the said frigate's being received." The King had approved of the reception of the men, but no reply had yet been received from Madrid in answer to Sir Hyde's demand. At the time he first heard from Sir Hyde, Carbonell said, he had replied that he would communicate "with punctuality and despatch the resolution of the King my master," and "when it comes to hand I will forward it to His Excellency with the least possible loss of time."

The *Magicienne* was due to return for the reply on April 7 but did not appear until the 23rd, and when her first lieutenant, John Maples, came on shore once again under a flag of truce he did not ask for it: instead he delivered Sir Hyde's letter dated April 8, based on Mason's deposition.

This was at once taken to Don Carbonell, who read it with some irritation, judging from his reply. He said he had answered Sir Hyde's previous demand by saying that as soon as he heard from Madrid he would write again. "I am at a loss to know," he wrote primly, "whether or no this said answer has reached the hands of Your Excellency."

Now Sir Hyde had demanded "some individuals . . . as being officers and others as being principally guilty in the murders said to have been committed on board that ship. In reply I am to inform you that those in the enclosed list considered at their own request as prisoners of war were sent with others not belonging to the said frigate on the 30th March to be exchanged at the island of Granada."

As far as Sir Hyde's other points were concerned, Carbonell declared that "equivocal information has been given Your Excellency that some of the officers . . . had been imprisoned and others of the crew left at liberty and had had rewards given them. When I understood some disagreement had arisen amongst some of them I quartered them separately, which cannot be called putting them in prison; and I ordered money to be given to those who were naked in order that they might clothe themselves and relieve their wants, the which can with no little reason be called rewards." The list he enclosed gave the names of Southcott and the other loyal men.

The next letter Sir Hyde Parker wrote to a governor was as forthrightly phrased as the others. However, this time the recipient was a Dutchman, not a Spaniard—Herr Johan Rudolph Lausser, the Governor of the island of Curaçao. "Having received information that Your Excellency with great propriety to the interests of all maritime nations has secured in confinement three of the pirates and murderers that were a part of His Britannic Majesty's late Ship *Hermione*, and trusting that Your Excellency's sentiments coincide with the general policy of making exemplary examples of those atrocious villains, I have sent His Britannic Majesty's ship the *Magicienne* to demand in the King my Master's name, the bodies of these three pirates."

But poor Herr Lausser had done no such thing as put anyone in jail. "Some time ago some English sailors arrived here from La Guaira and Puerto Cabello, all provided with proper passports from the generals of those places . . . in order to be employed in the garrison service here," he replied, "yet on an assumption that these men might have participated in the piratical seizure of His Britannic Majesty's ship the *Hermione* I was not willing to receive them, and therefore immediately ordered them to quit the island. However, as I did not know for an absolute certainty that they were the crew of the *Hermione* they were not arrested or detained."

XXII

Southcott's Revenge

—〰—

THE NEWS of the *Hermione* mutiny had spread quickly through the Caribbean, and six weeks before Ricketts arrived in the *Magicienne* with Sir Hyde's second letter the crew of another British ship had mutinied and sailed into La Guaira. This time they were not seamen of the Royal Navy seeking freedom from the press-gangs and cat-o'-nine-tails; instead they were privateersmen, the toughest and most ruthless men afloat, little more than pirates with a licence, and they had quarrelled over the division of their spoils.

The ship was the 18-gun schooner *Kitty Sean*, whose crew of forty-three had been commanded by Captain George Ponsonby. Based at the island of Tortola, east of Puerto Rico, the schooner's men were on a share-of-the-profits basis. This was usual, and one of the reasons why privateersmen fought more desperately than most, since their reward was usually proportional to their courage and daring.

The *Kitty Sean* had been cruising off Cape Codera, sixty miles east of La Guaira, when they sighted a Spanish sloop which had left that port a few hours earlier loaded with a cargo of goods belonging to Don Jacinto Gutierres. They captured the sloop without difficulty:

the trouble began after the prize had been secured when, as Don Carbonell later reported to the Prince of Peace, some of the crew "had differences with the captain over the division of the cargo. Also they complained of the captain's maltreatment and cruelty."

Half the crew sided with the captain but the others, headed by the boatswain and master's mate, mutinied and made prisoners of Captain Ponsonby and the loyal men. With the *Kitty Sean* and her prize in their possession they decided to make for La Guaira, following in the wake of the *Hermione.*

Describing their arrival in his report, Carbonell wrote: "It seems that news of the welcome that the crew of the Royal Navy frigate *Hermione* received has encouraged other ships to surrender themselves. On the 9th [of March] an English privateer schooner came in sight of La Guaira. . . .

"Two of her sailors, named Arturo Andersol [Arthur Anderson] and Juan [John] Stapleton came into the port in a boat as spokesmen and told the Governor that they would hand over their ship on condition that the crew would be free to go to North America, and that each of them would be given a reward based on the value of the *Kiteyschean* [*sic*]." The ship, wrote Don Carbonell, "is as new and has very good sailing qualities, and can be valued at nine or ten thousand *pesos.*"

The Governor, he continued, "accepted the proposal, made her anchor in the harbour, disembarked the British crew, put on board a Spanish crew and informed me immediately.

"Straight away I called the council which I have set up to deal with matters of this nature, and it was agreed to bring all the crew to this capital to find out the details of the whole episode and make our decisions accordingly."

Having first discovered that the mutiny had been caused by the quarrel over Don Jacinto Gutierres's cargo, the council decided that the mutineers should be rewarded. The boatswain, master's mate, Anderson and Stapleton would each get eighty *pesos*, while each of the rest of the mutineers would get fifty *pesos*. They would be sent "with the greatest expedition to North America or any other friendly or neutral colony."

The *Kitty Sean* would be employed in privateering and had been sent to Puerto Cabello to provision and man her before resuming her former activities, only this time under the Spanish flag. "I have no

doubt that she will be useful because of her excellent sailing qualities," Don Carbonell assured the Prince.

Don Carbonell had struck a good bargain. He estimated that half
the privateer's crew of forty-three had mutinied, so that not more
than twenty-five were conspirators. Since the four ringleaders each
received eighty *pesos* and the remainder fifty, the Captain-General
had, for an outlay of approximately 1,370 *pesos* in rewards, obtained
a ship which he valued at nine or ten thousand *pesos*.

ON MARCH 30 the *Hermione's* Master, Mr. Southcott, with Midshipman Casey and the other eight loyal men (including Sergeant
Plaice and three marines whom the Spanish finally agreed could be
prisoners) were marched down to the quay at La Guaira under
guard and put on board the schooner *La Bonita,* commanded by Don
Augustin Santana. The loyal men from the *Kitty Sean,* headed
by Captain George Ponsonby, joined them and Don Pedro de
Arguniedo came on board: they were all to be taken to the British
island of Grenada to be exchanged, and Arguniedo was travelling
with them to supervise the whole operation.

La Bonita sailed the same day, and as soon as she arrived in
Grenada the Britons were exchanged for an equivalent number of
Spaniards, and the schooner returned to La Guaira. Southcott and
his men sailed at once in a British ship for Martinique, where Rear-
Admiral Henry Harvey had his headquarters at Fort Royal (now
Fort de France). They reached there on April 11 to find they could
not have arrived at a more appropriate place at a more opportune
time.

Admiral Harvey already had under lock and key two men who
were suspected of being mutineers from the *Hermione:* they had been
found on board a ship which the frigate *L'Aimable* had intercepted,
and since her commanding officer was suspicious, he sent them both
to Martinique.

When Southcott arrived and identified the two men as mutineers, Admiral Harvey's first idea had been to send them both to
England for trial, since they could travel in the same ship as
Southcott and the rest of the officers. However, questioning the officers soon revealed that one of the two men under arrest had played
a very active part in the mutiny and, as Harvey explained to the
Admiralty later, "judging an execution might be necessary," he or-

dered the trial to be held at once in Fort Royal. An execution in the West Indies would have a greater deterrent effect, he considered, than one in England.

Southcott and the other nine loyal Hermiones were closely questioned so that the case could be prepared against the two prisoners. Finally Admiral Harvey sent orders to Captain Thomas Totty, commanding the *Alfred*, to preside over the court-martial, which was set for May Day (and was to be the only one in which all ten men who had insisted on giving themselves up as prisoners of war gave evidence).

It was perhaps appropriate that one of the two men on trial should be that strange and contradictory figure Thomas Leech, the former deserter once forgiven and always favoured by Captain Pigot, who showed his gratitude by helping to murder him. The other accused man was William Mason, a foretopman who had joined the *Hermione* more than a year before the mutiny. Mason, then thirty-two years old, came from Whitehaven, the Cumberland seaport under the shadow of Scafell Pike and Skiddaw. (He should not be confused with John Mason, the carpenter's mate.)

On May Day there were the usual preliminaries to begin the trial, and then the first witness, Mr. Southcott, was called in, took the oath and identified the two prisoners.

"Relate to the court any circumstances you know relative to the conduct of the prisoners on that occasion," ordered Captain Totty.

The thoughts going through the minds of Leech and Southcott must have had much in common: perhaps they both recalled Lawrence Cronin's impassioned plea that *all* the officers should be killed. For Leech there was the bitter knowledge that although in a matter of a few bloody hours he had—with the aid of rum and a tomahawk—transformed himself from a humble ordinary seaman to a leading mutineer and "lieutenant" of a frigate, he was once again in manacles, facing yet another court-martial. For Southcott, however, this must have been the opportunity he dreamed of during the hazardous voyage to La Guaira, when hourly the men were screaming for his life. It was an opportunity he did not waste: in less then 250 words, in which he did not stress the constant danger to his own life, he hanged Leech as effectively as if he tightened the noose with his own hands.

"Soon after the mutiny took place," he said, "which was between

10 and 11 at night, Thomas Leech came into my cabin with arms, and he told me I should not be hurt by the ship's company. . . . The next day some of the mutineers brought me on deck and after that I saw Thomas Leech one of the principal officers of the mutineers. . . . During the passage to La Guaira [he was] on the quarterdeck as an officer. . . . Going into La Guaira he was officer of the watch and he went on shore . . . to settle the business for the ship's company. . . ."

Asked what he knew about William Mason, Southcott said, "Nothing particular; it was his watch when the mutiny happened." He added that "the whole ship's company seemed unanimous."

Mr. Searle, the gunner, was the next witness. His evidence was similar to Southcott's, and he observed that "I heard Thomas Leech frequently give orders from the quarterdeck for things to be done forward."

Was Leech a ringleader? "He appeared to me by his carrying on the duty to be more active than other men," said Searle, but he did not remember seeing Mason.

Richard Price, the carpenter, gave the same damning evidence against Leech, and Midshipman Casey told the court that he considered Leech a ringleader, but knew nothing about Mason's role.

William Moncrieff, the frigate's former cook, followed Casey to the witness chair, and his evidence was as vague as the taste of the burgoo he used to serve to the Hermiones. His accent (he came from Orkney) obviously had Mr. Briggs, the Judge-Advocate, in difficulties as he wrote down the evidence, particularly when it came to spelling names. However when Sergeant Plaice marched briskly in, smart in his regimentals, the atmosphere once more became businesslike. After the usual preliminary questions, he was asked if Leech "was a ringleader in the business" and "had some considerable influence with the ship's company?"

"Yes," declared Plaice, "I think he was one of the chief men, and was obeyed as such. He was sitting at the [captain's] cabin table as an officer when I was sent for to know where I wished to go, what my name [i.e., alias] should be, and so on."

The three other marines then told their story. Private McNeil, the man who had been wounded while standing sentry at Captain Pigot's door, described how he had returned to the cabin to see several of the mutineers at work murdering the captain. "I saw the Captain on the larboard side, leaning against the gun with his shirt all torn and his body all over blood." Among the men in the cabin he saw Leech, he added.

Captain Totty asked: "How came you to take particular notice of Leech?"—"I can't say: I looked in with a view to see who was in there, and I saw Jackson, Foster, Forester and Thomas Leech."

Steward John Jones also gave the court a detailed description of the events on "the night the business took place" and was asked:

"Do you know anything of Mason?"

"I don't recollect seeing him but once and then he looked very ill, I supposed him to be so, or uneasy in his mind, and he said 'John, I am very ill indeed.' "

The minutes of the trial then recorded: "Prosecution on the part of the Crown here closed and the court cleared for a few minutes: when opened some dissatisfactory remarks were made by Thos. Leech not at all relevant to his unhappy case; they are therefore not here inserted."

Mason then made his defence, saying he was in the foretop when the men "cheered and said the ship was their own," and that he was afraid to come down. When he at last came down he was told by one of the ringleaders to do his duty as usual or he "should go overboard."

Leech then asked that Mr. Southcott be called again. This was done, and Leech asked: "What time was I in your cabin on the night of the 21st September?"—"Between 10 and 11, soon after the mutiny took place, and at different times during the night."

It was a curious question to ask, and Leech said nothing more. The court was then cleared while the five captains considered their verdict. Their findings can have caused Leech no surprise: he was guilty on all the charges, and was to be hanged. As far as Mason was concerned, in their opinion, "there doth not appear there is any particular blame imputable to William Mason," and he was acquitted.

The last official reference to that enigmatic man Leech was in Admiral Harvey's letter to the Admiralty on May 13, reporting the trial and verdicts: "I therefore immediately issued a warrant for the execution of the said Thomas Leech, and he was executed pursuant thereto the 3rd on board His Majesty's ship *Alfred*."

The *Alfred* then sailed from Fort Royal, taking Southcott, Casey and all but the four Marines back to England. Admiral Harvey told the Admiralty that "conceiving that more of the mutineers may be apprehended in this country, I have detained the Sergeant, Corporal and the two private Marines on board the *Prince of Wales* [his flagship] in order to appear as evidences, should that desirable event happen . . ."

THE GUN signalling Leech's execution was fired on board the *Alfred* at Fort Royal on Wednesday, May 3, 1798, and on the following Saturday, four more men from the *Hermione* faced a court-martial nine hundred miles away at Cape Nicolas Mole.

After leaving La Guaira, John Brown, the Scottish-born maintopman, had eventually signed on as a member of the crew of a British merchantman which was later boarded by a British privateer, the *Benson.* As soon as the privateer's captain discovered Brown had served in the *Hermione* he took him into Kingston, Jamaica, no doubt having his eye on the rewards being offered for such men.

There Brown was taken before one of the town's justices of the peace, Mr. William Savage, and far from denying that he had ever served in the *Hermione* he made a voluntary confession. This, duly signed and witnessed, was then sent to Sir Hyde Parker and, despite the information gained from the court-martial of Montell, Elliott and the other two mutineers six weeks earlier, proved to be the most detailed description of the mutiny the admiral had read, since he had not yet received a copy of the minutes of the Leech court-martial from Admiral Harvey or a report from the loyal officers.

The confession could not have reached Sir Hyde at a better moment, since he had already had three more former Hermiones under arrest for some time. They were William Benives, William Herd and John Hill, who had arrived in Port Morant Bay, Jamaica, in a cartel ship which they claimed they had seized. It has been impossible to prove whether or not their claim was true. Certainly it made no difference to Sir Hyde's attitude: he was determined to court-martial them, but until Brown's confession arrived he had been unable to do so because he did not have a witness for the prosecution. The reason was that when John Mason (the prosecution witness at the Montell trial) was questioned about the three new prisoners he said he knew nothing at all about their activities, except that they had been on board at the time. Nor could he give any further information about the latest prisoner, John Brown.

On reading Brown's confession Sir Hyde realized that here was a man who knew a great deal: he was able to confirm in detail much of the evidence already given at the first trial and, what was more interesting, Brown mentioned John Mason (the witness whose evidence had already hanged the four men), saying that he understood Mason was one of several men "who declared his resolution to take the ship but not to kill the officers." The admiral realized that the only way he could bring Benives, Herd and Hill to trial was to let Brown turn King's Evidence, and since Mason knew nothing of Brown's activities, clearly Brown was not a ringleader and would also be a more reliable prosecution witness in future trials.

Captain Bowen presided over the court-martial on board the *Carnatic*, and whereas in the previous trials the prosecution witness, Mason, had not been among the accused, this time Brown was charged with the other three men, although it was clearly understood he would be allowed to turn King's Evidence.

When the trial began on May 5th the Deputy Judge-Advocate read out Brown's confession and the six captains forming the court found it a fascinating document, since it described David Forester's climb up the mainstay and Brown's visit to the fo'c'sle, followed by a complete account of the sentry McNeil rushing up to the quarterdeck to warn Lieutenant Foreshaw; the orders the lieutenant gave and the reactions of Turner and the man at the wheel. He named several of the murderers and added that Midshipman Wiltshire had told him he "knew of the mutiny two or three days before it broke out, and he went up in the foretop to hide when it broke out." Brown finished his confession with a list of the twenty-five men he considered were "principal mutineers."

After the *Hermione's* former master's mate, John Forbes, was called in to give evidence of Brown's character, the court announced that it had taken into consideration Brown's voluntary confession; that he had not changed his name (the other three had adopted aliases), nor "entered into the service of either the French or Spanish"; and the good character given him by Forbes. Because of these factors "and the more clearly to bring to light the atrocious deeds committed," the court "unanimously thought proper to admit the said John Brown as King's Evidence."

With that formality over the real trial began, and John Brown himself was called. After identifying the three accused men he was asked if any of them took an active part in the mutiny.

"No, I don't know that William Benives or John Hill took an active part; but I know that William Herd did."

"Relate what you know about William Herd."—"I know that he broke into the Captain's cabin."

Had he seen Benives or Hill on deck after the mutiny?—"I saw Benives walking on the forecastle, with the lad who was leading him, being blind at the time."

The court then asked him a series of questions for which he had obviously been prepared and were no doubt intended to forestall any awkward questions from the Admiralty about the confession written by Montell just before he was hanged: particularly that the Frenchman D'Orlanie and Elliott—who had already been executed—were innocent.

"Did you ever hear who were the people that broke into the cabin and murdered the captain?"—"I know that Joe Montell was one of them."

"Do you know of anyone else?"—"John Elliott."

"Do you know if Peter Delaney, or Pierre D'Orlanie, was one of them?"—"I can't recollect."

"What became of the Boatswain?"—"He was thrown overboard."

"Where was the Surgeon murdered?"—"They took him out of the gunroom and threw him overboard," said Brown, adding that Sansum had been alive at the time and that "I did not hear that any were killed before they were thrown overboard."

With Brown's evidence for the prosecution ended, William Herd questioned him. "Did you ever see me going into the Captain's cabin?"—"No, I did not."

"Did you see me with a cutlass or any other weapon in my hand?"—"No, I never did."

The President then asked: "How came you to know that Herd was one of the men that broke into the Captain's cabin?"—"I heard people say so on the quarterdeck next day."

Herd, in his defence, said he was below at the time of the mutiny and the next thing he heard was that the third lieutenant (Foreshaw) had been thrown overboard. Then "I went upon the forecastle and sat down, and stayed there until daylight, and then I was ordered up to the foretopmast head to set the royal . . . I received orders to go to the wheel and stayed my two hours . . . And I declare most solemnly that I had no hand in murdering or throwing overboard the officers; nor did I see any other person do so."

Benives and Hill, in their defence statements, described how after eventually receiving a pass from the Spanish authorities to go to Curaçao, "We went on board a cartel at Curaçao bound for Guadeloupe, ask the prisoners with ourselves, took her from the Spaniard and carried her into Port Morant Bay, Jamaica."

The court did not question them on this point yet it was a vital one in deciding whether the men were genuinely trying to get back to British territory: Port Morant Bay was more than one thousand miles from Guadeloupe. The fact—if it was a fact—that they had seized the cartel and carried her into a British port a thousand miles from her destination should have been strong evidence in their favour. The truth of the matter must have been known to Sir Hyde Parker, even if not to the court.

Certainly it had no effect on the verdict: although Brown said in his evidence that Benives was blind at the time of the mutiny, all three were found guilty and sentenced to be hanged and their bodies "to be hung in chains upon gibbets . . ."

Herd, an Irishman, was certainly guilty of mutiny: he received a watch in the share-out of the valuables, and he consulted with the other leaders in the cabin. Benives was innocent of mutiny—but, like Hill, he had later been ordered by the Spanish authorities to work on board the *Hermione*. He claimed that at first they refused and stayed on shore for two days, "till hunger obliged us to board." From what is known of conditions at Puerto Cabello and La Guaira at that time, the story rings true. The third man, Hill, received silver at the share-out, which indicates he was guilty.

Five days after their shipmate Thomas Leech was executed on board the *Alfred* at Fort Royal, the yellow flag was hoisted on board the *Carnatic* at Cape Nicolas Mole, and the three men were hanged.

XXIII

Bureaucrats at Bay

—m—

IN THE FIRST six months that the *Hermione* had been in Spanish hands, renamed the *Santa Cecilia* and serving under the red and gold flag of Carlos IV, she had been to sea only once, for the short voyage from La Guaira to Puerto Cabello, where she was to be fitted out. The reason for her inactivity was not hard to find: she was firmly secured to the piers at Puerto Cabello by many fathoms of red tape.

Although double-entry book-keeping had recently been introduced into the Spanish dominions, the new system did not help Intendant Leone because the Royal Treasury at Caracas was empty. But since Leone was stubborn, and as determined to stand on what he considered his rights as he was to balance his books, the frigate stayed in harbour, when she might well have been responsible for some entries in the credit column had she gone to sea.

After the ship had been taken to Puerto Cabello the Master Shipwright there surveyed her on the orders of the Governor of the port, Don Marmion. He found that she needed repairs to her bow and stern below the waterline, which meant the copper sheathing had to be stripped off, and she would have to be careened. Apart from that there were the routine repairs to be made to the sails and the rigging.

The work went on at a leisurely pace until November 18, when the Captain-General called a *junta* to consider some alarming news. The first item on the agenda for their consideration was "the repeated insults of the enemy corsairs [i.e., privateers], which have had the audacity to enter the port of Barcelona for the third time, landing troops and taking possession of the battery built there, which was still without guns as it was not ready for garrisoning. The enemy corsairs threatened to destroy it unless they received 50,000 *pesos*."

The *junta* was also told that on the same day, November 14, two Spanish privateers, the *San Francisco* and the *San Vicente*, which were cruising off Cape Codera on the lookout for enemy warships, had sighted a British frigate, a sloop and two schooners. They had promptly "retired to port to save themselves," and reported at once to the Captain-General.

The arrival of the British was serious, as every member of the *junta* knew only too well, and the minutes of their discussion refer to "the serious damage which will be caused by the pirates [*sic*] if they are allowed to remain, since they will inevitably capture any merchant ships coming from Spain and other parts," and would also intercept "at a critical time for Christmas" the ships carrying the cocoa harvest, which was just beginning to be collected.

The *junta* decided to fit out the *Santa Cecilia* at once "to go out and harass and capture the said enemy ships." The main problem was finding enough seamen, so they decided that only one of the two Spanish privateers would sail to keep a watch for the British ships while the other went to Puerto Cabello in case her crew was needed for the *Santa Cecilia*. The captain of the frigate was to be Don Andreas Caperuchiqui, the Acting Commander of the Privateering Branch.

The *junta*'s last decision was soon to cause a great deal of trouble: "Finally it was resolved that the expenses that may arise for the said frigate should be paid for by the Privateering Branch, because at the appropriate times she may serve to chase enemy ships and also be employed with zeal to chase smugglers."

The Captain-General and his secretary then busied themselves drawing up the necessary orders. The first was to the Governor of Puerto Cabello, putting him in charge of fitting out the *Santa Cecilia;* the second was to Intendant Leone, enclosing a certified copy of the *junta*'s minutes and telling him the *Santa Cecilia*'s captain was to be the Acting Commander of the Privateering Branch, "whose funds must pay the expenses, and for which you must give the appropriate orders." Leone replied the same day that "I have given the necessary instructions for this to take place," and no doubt noted to himself that the Captain-General was playing into his hands.

The point was that the *junta* had intended that the *Santa Cecilia* should be both a warship and a privateer, as the occasion demanded. The Captain-General later explained to the Prince of Peace, "It was decided to charge the expenses to the Privateering Branch because the Royal Treasury did not have the means and because the Privateering Branch had to help provide the crew by taking men from the smaller privateers."

As a warship defending the province, the *Santa Cecilia* came under the control of the Captain-General, her expenses being paid out of the Royal Treasury. But as a privateer she was controlled by the Intendant and paid for by the Privateering Fund, which he administered. Since the Royal Treasury was empty the Privateering Fund had to pay anyway; but who controlled the ship when she acted as a warship but was paid for as a privateer?

The Intendant had no doubts: as soon as the Captain-General told him that Caperuchiqui was to command and the Privateering Branch to pay, he took control himself, writing the same day to his Treasury officials at Puerto Cabello. He told them the frigate was to be ready in "not more than six to eight days" (this order resulted in the Hermiones being rounded up in the streets of La Guaira and shipped to Puerto Cabello to work on board the frigate), and the Governor would supply provisions for only one month, "with the other things which Don Caperuchiqui might demand." They were to understand that "Caperuchiqui has the authority to appoint officers and seamen to the frigate to his own satisfaction, either from the privateers or merchant ships, and also from among local seafarers." More men would be sent round from La Guaira.

The reply from the Treasury officials at Puerto Cabello was prompt: although the Master Shipwright reported that he had not finished repairing the *Santa Cecilia,* he had been told to complete the job "with the greatest speed," but it was doubtful if she would be ready until the end of the month. "At the same time we have put up posters offering all seamen who join the frigate the same wages that privateersmen receive, and a share of the prize-money resulting from captures."

The Intendant also wrote to Caperuchiqui, telling him of the enemy's arrival off Cape Codera, and that he was to take command of the frigate and have her ready in six to eight days, "and this done you are to sail for that position, taking with you the schooner *Concha* . . . and any other of the privateers that are ready in time, all with the purpose of capturing or driving off the enemy frigate and other vessels." Caperuchiqui replied that he had immediately given the necessary instructions "so that there shall be no delays through any fault of mine."

So far the first round had gone to Leone. The Captain-General had assumed Leone's orders were routine. He did not know the Intendant had presented him with a *fait accompli* until Caperuchiqui sent the Governor of Puerto Cabello, Don Marmion, a brusque note saying that since the Intendant had given him command of the *Santa Cecilia*, "this is to let you know that from now on you will communicate with me on all matters concerning the frigate."

Governor Marmion received this on December 7, by which time the ship was still not ready for sea. But as the Captain-General personally had put him in complete charge of commissioning the *Santa Cecilia* he was so angry that he at once sent a copy of Caperuchiqui's letter to the Captain-General, who in describing the episode later wrote that "from the moment Marmion saw the note [from Caperuchiqui] he threw up his hands and said he would not have anything to do with it."

At last the inevitable clash between the Intendant, the man who held the purse strings, and the Captain-General, who ruled the province, had occurred. It was inevitable, as we saw earlier, because of the overlapping roles assigned in the Royal ordinances to the intendants and the captains-general, which meant, in the case of the *Santa Cecilia*, that the Captain-General could order her to be refitted and to sail, but the Intendant could refuse to supply the money for the work and wages.

As soon as the Captain-General received Marmion's outraged note enclosing Caperuchiqui's order, he wrote a strongly-worded letter to Leone. "I acquaint Your Excellency that the frigate *Santa Cecilia* has been ordered to arm in the capacity of a privateer, and that she must carry out the orders of this Province [i.e., of the *junta*],

like other privateers, that she might be useful to His Majesty's government." He added that the *junta* had decided the Privateering
Branch was to pay because the ship would fulfil two roles—dealing
with enemy warships and preventing smuggling. But "the principal
object of arming the ship was not, and is not, for stopping smuggling: it is for defending the coasts of the province. It is very obvious
that if the frigate was only to be a privateer, Your Excellency would
have control, and it would not be necessary to raise the matter in a
junta.

"The fact that the Privateering Branch is paying the expenses is
not sufficient reason to put the frigate under the command of that
Branch, since they pay only because of the lack of money in the
Royal Treasury.

"On a similar occasion, when expenses were paid by the Privateering Branch, the King decreed that ships armed for war with the
object of defending the coasts came under the command of the Captain-General. In that way," Carbonell wrote, "the Intendant only
deals with the financial side of the affair."

But for all that, Carbonell realized that the man who held the
purse strings actually held the power, and he concluded, "In spite of
all this, and the knowledge that the frigate *Santa Cecilia* must be
under my orders—though the expense be paid by the Privateering
Branch or anyone else—to avoid troubles so prejudicial to the King's
service, and so distasteful to me, Your Excellency can command the
frigate with every facility, and I am also informing Caperuchiqui.
All this," he concluded ominously, "I shall recount to His Majesty
for his Royal information."

The *Santa Cecilia* did not sail. The Captain-General, writing later
a bitter letter of complaint to the Prince of Peace, said that "as he
[Leone] could not argue with me face to face, he played a trick by
giving orders to Don Caperuchiqui . . . the result has been not to
arm the frigate, and to let her rot in harbour, while enemy corsairs
attack our merchant ships and insolently protect the cattle and food
smugglers along our coast. I do not have enough authority to remedy these disasters."

However, having gained control of the *Santa Cecilia,* Leone did
nothing further: the delay over fitting out, followed by the quarrel
with the Captain-General, took them up to Christmas 1797, and by

then the British ships had left the area and the coasts of Caracas were left in comparative peace.

THE FRIGATE stayed at Puerto Cabello while the blazing sun shrunk the deck and hull planking, opening up the seams. The alternate heat of the sun and wet of rain and dew began the slow process of rotting the cordage and mildewing the canvas of the sails. Rats bred in contentment, unworried by any rolling or pitching which would send sudden surges of bilge water into their secret nests down in the holds.

ON MARCH 16, Intendant Leone received some alarming news from the Dutch island of Curaçao, which he promptly passed on to the Captain-General: five Spaniards known to be revolutionaries were on the island and "intend to form an expedition to invade this province."

Don Carbonell acted at once, telling the Intendant that "it has been decided to fit out with the utmost speed possible the frigate *Santa Cecilia* and the schooner *Kitschean* [*sic*], with the other two privateers under the command of Don Andreas Caperuchiqui. They are to sail from Puerto Cabello and cruise off the entrance of the port of Curaçao, not allowing any ship to leave there without checking her and making sure she is not helping these criminals." A sloop and a schooner should follow as soon as possible "to strengthen our forces."

The Intendant replied that, "I have given on my part the most strict orders so that everything shall be done with speed and efficiency." But the old quarrel over control of the ship was still close to the surface. The Captain-General wrote to Leone again the same day saying he had given command of the *Santa Cecilia* to Don Ambrocio Alvarez Pardinaz, who was captain of the Cadiz merchantman *La Empresa*, then lying in La Guaira, because of "his acknowledged ability and bravery."

But when Leone came to pass on these orders he made no mention of Pardinaz: instead Caperuchiqui was told, "You are to carry out a mission in the Royal Service which I do not doubt you will execute with honour." His ships were to provision for two months, and not for one; or for fifteen days if there was not sufficient. Other craft would be sent on later to reinforce him and bring more supplies. Meanwhile "the Royal Exchequer is authorized to give you all necessary assistance."

Writing to his officials at Puerto Cabello, Leone sent a copy of his orders to Caperuchiqui and told them, "I have arranged to forward to the Royal Treasury [at Puerto Cabello] the sum of sixty thousand *pesos,* which should arrive by next Monday at the latest." And finally, in a letter to the Governor of La Guaira, Leone told him to send *La Empresa's* crew to Puerto Cabello to help man the *Santa Cecilia,* along with any other seamen who were available.

Thus in four letters—including one to the Captain-General acknowledging the original order—Leone had not once mentioned Pardinaz: the officials at Puerto Cabello and La Guaira had no inkling that the Captain-General had intended he should command the frigate.

When Carbonell found that Leone was again playing tricks over the command of the frigate he did not write to him. Any arguments they had must have been oral and it is clear the Captain-General could get no satisfaction from Leone—nor could he get the ship to sea. On March 23, nine days after he had ordered them to sails he wrote a long letter to the Prince of Peace—a letter at the top of which, when it arrived at the Spanish Court, was noted, "The Captain-General of the Province of Caracas requests agreement from the Council on his dispute with the Intendant about the command of the English frigate *Ermione* [*sic*]."

Don Carbonell enclosed copies of various relevant documents and began by describing the fiasco resulting from the decision to sail the *Santa Cecilia* the previous November to deal with the British warships off Cape Codera. He described how Leone had "played a trick" to get control of the frigate, and that he finally left the ship to the Intendant in order to avoid disputes "so prejudicial to the King's service." The Captain-General also sent a copy of his recent correspondence with "Admiral Hider Parker," asking for the King's approval. (Five days after Carbonell wrote these letters, the Prince of Peace had fallen from power: the King dismissed him on March 28.)

At the time the Captain-General's dispatches left La Guaira for Spain, Caperuchiqui was still busy trying to get the *Santa Cecilia* and *Kitty Sean* ready for sea. The last letter referring to them, dated April 4, was to the Intendant from his officials at Puerto Cabello. "On

April 2," they wrote, "the frigate *Santa Cecilia* was inspected with the sloop *Begoña* because they were ready to sail. However they could not leave since there was no wind."

It is certain that they never sailed: no report of a voyage to Curaçao was made to Carbonell or Leone, or by them to Madrid; and when defending himself later Leone said the frigate had been ready by April 2, whereas it would have strengthened his case if he had been able to say she had actually gone to sea.

THE LONG DELAY in correspondence with the Ministers and the Court in Spain, caused by lethargy and the double crossing of the Atlantic in the teeth of the British blockade, meant that the problem and the control of the *Santa Cecilia* was never satisfactorily settled.

On August 4, 1798, nearly a year after the mutiny, the Captain-General wrote to Admiral Don Juan de Langara, who had recently been made the Secretary of State for the Navy, saying he had received the King's approval of the *junta's* decision to admit the *Hermione* into the Royal Service, and that she was to operate under the Captain-General's control. He told Langara that the naval officer the Court had appointed to command her, Don Ramon de Eschales, had just arrived in La Guaira with his officers, but without seamen or soldiers because none was available at Havana.

So nine months after the *Hermione* first arrived at La Guaira, Carbonell was able to show Leone the King's decision that the ship was to be under the Captain-General's control.

At the end of November 1798, Carbonell received a reply from Spain to his complaint of March 23 about Leone. It said the King had been shown the Captain-General's report that the frigate was "going downhill." The King "has disapproved of the Intendant's conduct on this point and declared that the ship is under the orders of the Captain-General for the time being, and for as long as she is not given orders from a higher command."

In the meantime Leone had also been busy writing to the Minister of Finance in Spain. As soon as the King's approval of Carbonell's decisions over the *Hermione* had been read to the *junta,* Leone wrote a long justification of his conduct. Relating how the *junta* accepted the *Hermione* in the first instance, and that the Captain-General decided "on his own responsibility" the ship's role was to guard the coast against privateers, he declared: "The

Captain-General afterwards ordered on different occasions that the frigate was to be armed and fitted out to go to sea, which I opposed, having in mind the excessive cost which is supposed to be paid by the Royal Treasury, and which at the present time has no funds.

"In addition there are not sufficient officers and crew experienced enough to handle the ship of this size. Also, according to those who know about these things, these coasts are not suitable for large ships like frigates, which are difficult to sail against strong currents which frequently expose them to a lee shore and to the danger of going aground on the coasts. Besides this, the enemy smugglers and privateers are smaller and draw less water, so they can shelter and hide in anchorages and shallow coves where a frigate cannot enter, and as a result it is impossible to capture them."

The Intendant, writing with all the assurance usual in someone so completely ignorant of a subject, forgot the panic caused by the appearance of a British frigate off Cape Codera; and it has been made clear in this narrative that a large percentage of prizes taken by British frigates were made in just the circumstances that Leone quoted "those who know about these things" as saying were "impossible."

The Intendant, commenting on the Royal order giving control to Carbonell, wrote: "I consider it necessary to notify Your Excellency that this alters the established system of maritime security for this coast." Paying for the ship as a privateer, he explained, meant that the commerce paid [i.e., from the tax levied on the merchants]; but in fact the Privateering Fund was not even sufficient to pay for the small ships of the Privateering Branch.

"It is not possible to keep the frigate armed [i.e., in commission] either from the Privateering Fund or the Royal Treasury, which is exhausted with the heavy expenses of the present war, without being able to find eighty thousand *pesos* a year, which the officials of the Royal Treasury at Puerto Cabello have calculated to be necessary for the upkeep of the ship, including her operating expenses and careening, which are so costly."

In view of all this, concluded Leone, he hoped a full explanation would be given to the King "for a speedy resolution."

The Minister of Finance sent Leone's letter to the King, whose reply was certainly speedy. The Minister was told "His Majesty disapproves the Intendant's conduct and orders him to put it right with the Captain-General." The Minister then sent the whole file of correspondence to Admiral Langara, and the Royal snub, conveyed in a letter from Langara, arrived at Caracas in July 1799, a year after Leone had written his original protest. When the Intendant read it he was indignant and replied at once—indeed, an indication of his haste is given in a note on his letter saying "written in the frigate *Carlota*, Captain Don Ramon Blanco, which is ready to sail from the port of La Guaira for Spain, July 27, 1799."

Acknowledging Langara's letter, he said: "For your information I must inform you that the report of the Captain-General—that I started the dispute, demanding that the ship should be under my orders, with the result that she is deteriorating—is entirely wrong.

"Having examined the file of the *Hermione* from the time she came into our possession, I do not see how I could have caused such a dispute. . . . Your Excellency will see from the documents I enclose that the decisions and orders concerning the arming and command of the frigate have come from either the *junta de guerra* or the Captain-General . . . Far from opposing decisions, making difficulties or causing delays I passed on the necessary orders to those officers who in fact come under the jurisdiction of the Intendant without making the slightest criticism of the Captain-General for having himself made the decisions concerning the privateers, although they come under my command. On further consideration it seems to me that it demonstrates my moderation and wish to avoid disputes and misunderstandings."

Leone asked Admiral Langara to refer the matter to the King for his decision and also "make good the embarrassment and injury done me by the complaint of Carbonell, damaging the honour and efficiency with which I have always tried to serve His Majesty."

But Intendant Leone was never to receive the King's decision. At the time he wrote that letter on board the frigate *Carlota*, the *Hermione* had been in Spanish hands for nearly twenty-one months and despite their desperate shortage of ships, her only voyage under the red and gold flag had been from La Guaira to Puerto Cabello. For a year and a half she had been a subject for correspondence, not a warship; the only hostility involving her had been between the Intendant and the Captain-General.

XXIV

"Jack Bligh or . . ."

—ɯ—

WHEN MR. SOUTHCOTT and the rest of the loyal Hermiones arrived back in England in the *Alfred*, the five senior men had to face the customary court-martial which was ordered to "inquire into the causes and circumstances of the loss of His Majesty's ship *Hermione*," and try them "for their conduct respectively so far as may relate to the said ship."

The trial was held on board the *Director* at Sheerness, and among the vice-admiral and nine captains forming the court was Captain William Bligh, a man who already had considerable experience of mutiny, both at the Nore the previous year, when his crew were among the first to order their officers to leave the ship, and in the *Bounty* ten years earlier.

The court heard the story of the mutiny and decided that the five men—Southcott, Searle, Price, Casey and Moncrieff—were acquitted "of all blame on the occasion of the loss of His Majesty's late Ship *Hermione*, or of the murder of the said Captain and other officers . . ."

However, there were to be many more courts-martial over the next ten years before the last of the *Hermione*'s mutineers could feel himself reasonably safe, and we will follow the fortunes of the rest of the men as they were caught in various parts of the world and brought to trial.

A fortnight after Benives, Hill and Herd were hanged at Cape Nicolas Mole, and six months after the mutiny, three more Hermiones were caught in the West Indies. They were Captain Pigot's cook, John Holford, with his young son, and James Irwin, the Irishman from Limerick. After the two Holfords had sailed in the open boat from La Guaira to Cumaná, they signed on in a ship going to Jamaica. As soon as they landed both father and son went to the authorities and gave themselves up. The father was taken before Mr. Algernon Warren, one of Kingston's justices of the peace, where he made a long and detailed sworn statement. A copy was immediately sent to Sir Hyde Parker, who found it so interesting that, as he wrote to the Admiralty, "from its being full and circumstantial on this bloody tragedy," he was enclosing a copy for Their Lordships.

James Irwin had signed on in an American ship bound for New York, but unfortunately for him she had not left the Caribbean before the British sloop *La Tourterelle* came in sight and ordered her to heave-to and wait for a boarding party. The lieutenant in charge was interested only to see if there were any British subjects on board to impress into His Majesty's service—and he selected Irwin. According to Irwin, as he was being "read in" *La Tourterelle*'s commanding officer asked him if he was "one of the Hermiones," and "I told Captain West that I did belong to the *Hermione* in the time of the mutiny." Captain West in his letter to Sir Hyde said, "I detected him."

The two Holfords and Irwin were tried together at a court-martial on May 23 on board the *Brunswick*. Presiding for the first time at an *Hermione* court-martial was Sir Hyde's second-in-command, Rear-Admiral Richard Rodney Bligh, who had presided at the trial of Lieutenant Harris over the *Ceres* episode. Most of the captains forming the court had known Hugh Pigot well, and among them were Man Dobson and John Crawley sitting at their third *Hermione* trial, and John Loring at his second.

Three officers who had left the *Hermione* before the mutiny—John Forbes, Lieutenant Harris and the former boatswain, Thomas Harrington, who was by then second master of the *Thunderer*—gave evidence of identification; but the main prosecution witnesses were John Mason and John Brown.

The verdict the court reached was reasonable and just: that is quite clear from the minutes and was later confirmed by information from many other sources. Irwin, the court announced, was guilty of mutiny and deserting to the enemy in the *Hermione*, but the charge of murder was not proved. He was therefore sentenced to be hanged, but "it appearing he took no direct part in the mutiny," the court recommended him as "a proper object of mercy." The Holfords, father and son, were found not guilty of any of the charges.

But the effect of the court's findings on Sir Hyde was remarkable: because the men had not been sentenced to death he became so angry with Rear-Admiral Richard Bligh, the court's president, that he at once wrote to the Admiralty "to request Their Lordships will remove Rear-Admiral Bligh from under my command, or that Their Lordships will allow me to resign from a situation which must be extremely unpleasant, finding myself so ill-supported by the person next to me in command, in keeping up the discipline and subordination of this particular squadron of His Majesty's Fleet entrusted to me."

The verdict of the court-martial "strikes me with astonishment, from its inconsistencies, three men [the younger Holford was twelve years old at the time of the mutiny] brought to a trial implicated most indubitably in the same crimes, and from the nature of those crimes are accessory [*sic*] in all the horrid crimes, which were committed on that melancholy occasion, unless proofs had been brought of their endeavours to resist the mutineers, or, that upon their landing, as some did, declare their innocence by a request to be deemed prisoners of war: but opposite to this is the conduct of such criminals when it is proved by the minutes of the court martial that each of the three received twenty-five dollars paid by the Spanish officers, as rewards for their crimes. Still more marked is the criminality of the prisoner Irwin, by his voluntary assistance to fit out the ship as a ship of war against His Majesty, this very act was certainly an act which would have proved fatal to a subject independent of the other atrocious crimes of which he was an accessory." He ignored the fact that the Holfords had given themselves up voluntarily.

It was this type of warped and bigoted reasoning—if that is not too kind a word for the admiral's mental processes on this occasion—that throws so much light on Sir Hyde's personality. No reasonable man—particularly after reading the evidence given at the trial—could condemn the seamen for not resisting when none of the *Hermione's* officers, with the exception of Pigot and Foreshaw, put up any physical resistance.

Both the prosecution witnesses, Brown and Mason, gave specific evidence on oath that neither of the Holfords took part in the mutiny or helped work the ship to La Guaira; Mason added that Holford did not help refit the ship in Puerto Cabello—on the contrary, the Spanish put him in prison for refusing. When Mason was asked by the court, "Did any act, word, or deed of the prisoners lead you to believe they took any active part in the mutiny or murders?" Mason replied "No." Brown declared that necessity compelled the men to work, while Mason, asked by the court, "Could the prisoner Irwin have got his subsistence by any other means than by working at the fort or on board the *Hermione*?" said "No, I don't think so." As far as the twenty-five dollars payment was concerned, Sir Hyde already had the word of the Captain-General of Caracas that the payment was not a reward but "in order that they might clothe themselves and relieve their wants." The minutes told Sir Hyde quite clearly that the men could not have lived without working.

Having decided that Holford was guilty—"implicated most indubitably in the same crimes"—Sir Hyde wrote in the very next paragraph of his letter to the Admiralty that "Holford the Elder had made a declaration before a magistrate of the transaction of the mutineers, which from its being corroborated in many strong circumstances by Brown's evidence and declaration upon a former trial, I look upon it as the truth, as far as man's memory will allow, of facts being stated after such a lapse of time . . ." Holford's declaration (which Sir Hyde had seen before the trial and was also included in the minutes) was a description of his own activities as well as those of the mutineers, and showed quite clearly that he took no part whatsoever in the mutiny. Sir Hyde regarded this as the truth— yet demanded that his second-in-command be sacked, threatening to resign if he was not, because he did not find Holford guilty, and sentence him to death.

The crux of Sir Hyde's argument appears to be contained in his reference to the men being "implicated most indubitably in the same crimes," and therefore accessories "in all the horrid crimes . . ." In other words the fact they were on board the *Hermione* at the time of the mutiny made them mutineers.

However, having told Their Lordships why a man and a boy who had been found innocent should have been found guilty irrespective of the evidence, the admiral had by no means finished his tirade to the Admiralty: "Three of the members of this court [Dobson, Crawley and Loring] had signed the sentence of death passed upon the prisoners Benives, Herd and Hill, who were [previously] executed and gibbeted according to the sentence. . . . I can [therefore] only attribute the difference of conduct upon this solemn business to the difference of feelings of the two presidents, the one [Captain Bowen at the Benives trial] having all the energy for imposing discipline by the terror of exemplary punishment in this momentary crisis, when it becomes more than ever necessary for officers' exertions to subdue the licentiousness and bloodthirsty ideas of seamen, and which from the supineness of the president [Rear-Admiral Bligh at Holford's trial] in the discussion of the court martial he has been head of, would rather be encouraged."

It is clear that Sir Hyde was not particularly concerned with justice, and that Bowen stood high in his estimation because he had handed over three men for hanging and gibbeting—one of them being a man both prosecution witnesses said was blind at the time of the mutiny—while Bligh should be sacked for not producing more material for the gibbets, irrespective of whether the men were guilty or innocent. It perhaps explains why not one question was asked at the Benives trial about the capture of the Spanish cartel ship and its arrival at Port Morant Bay, a thousand miles from her intended destination, and Benives's blindness was ignored.

"Imposing discipline by terror"—that, perhaps, was the clue to Sir Hyde's behaviour: he could think of only one way of driving thoughts of mutiny out of his men's heads, and that was to hang and gibbet. His letter to the Admiralty shows better than anything else why Captain Pigot had never received moderating advice or reproof from the commander-in-chief about the cruel way he treated his men, first in the *Success* and then in the *Hermione*: he was maintaining discipline in the manner that Sir Hyde understood and approved. It apparently never crossed that worthy admiral's mind that good leadership—which included making sure that the men were well treated—was the best, indeed the only, antidote to mutiny: that despite the quality or quantity of the food issued, good captains could and did have contented ships' companies.

When Sir Hyde's wretched letter arrived at the Admiralty on July 11, the First Lord took no action over Rear-Admiral Bligh or over Sir Hyde's threat to resign. However, he raised the matter of James Irwin's reprieve with the King, and later, on a turned-up corner of the court's covering letter—which Sir Hyde had of course forwarded—was written: "Acquaint Admiral Bligh that upon laying the sentence and the minutes of the court before the King, His Majesty has been pleased to grant his [Irwin's] pardon on condition of his being transported to New South Wales for the rest of his life, and that he is to send him to England as a prisoner by the first opportunity." (When the *Adventure* arrived at Portsmouth from the West Indies in January 1799, her commanding officer wrote to the Admiralty that he had Irwin on board. He was ordered to put him on board the *Porpoise* "that he may be conveyed to the place of his destination.")

THE LAST THREE HERMIONES caught in the year 1798 were Adam Lynham, who had been born in Dublin forty-eight years earlier and had adopted the cumbersome alias of "Isaac Hontinberg," Thomas Charlton, aged twenty-six from Stockton, who had become "William Thompson," and John Coe, from Norfolk, who was one of the afterguard and had not changed his name.

The trial of Lynham and Charlton was held on board the *York* at Port Royal, Jamaica, on August 7, when both men were found guilty of murder, deserting with the ship, and handing her over to the enemy. Only the court's judgment has survived, so it is not known how they were caught. However, the log of Sir Hyde's flagship records on Friday, August 10, "Answered the signal for punishment; at 8 two seamen, lately belonging to His Majesty's ship *Hermione,* were hung on board the *Albion* for mutiny and piracy; and their bodies gibbeted on one of the cays."

The men's bodies were in fact hung in chains from gibbets erected on Gallows Point, in full view of all the warships anchored in Port Royal. They were soon to be joined by some of their former shipmates at this, the last resting place of some of the Caribbean's most distinguished pirates and murderers.

The third man, John Coe, had been captured in dramatic circumstances. After leaving La Guaira he had signed on as a member of the crew of the French privateer *La Fleur de Mer*. When she captured an American brig, the *Ring Boston,* bound from New York to New Orleans, the privateer's captain chose Coe to be one of the prize crew to sail the brig down to the French base at Port Dauphine, Santo Domingo.

A few days later a strange sail was sighted from the brig—and from the intercepting course she was steering, it was obvious to the prize crew that she was interested in the *Ring Boston.* As she approached Coe soon recognized her as a British frigate—the 32-gun *Aquilon*, in fact—commanded by Captain Thomas Boys, who soon forced the *Ring Boston* to heave-to. As the frigate's boarding party approached, some of the privateersmen, including John Coe, lowered a boat and started to row away in a frantic but hopeless attempt to escape. They were soon caught and lined up under a marine guard in the *Aquilon,* and it did not take Captain Boys long to discover that among the prisoners was Coe, one of the notorious Hermiones.

The *Aquilon* landed him at Port Royal, where both Sir Hyde Parker and Rear-Admiral Bligh were flying their flags. Because the "officer next in command to such commander-in-chief" had to preside at a court-martial, Sir Hyde was forced to disregard his dislike for Bligh and order him to try Coe on board the *Brunswick* on December 8. Among the captains were Man Dobson, who was attending his fifth *Hermione* trial, and a newcomer to the judicial aspect of the *Hermione* story, Captain Edward Hamilton, who was soon to provide its exciting finale.

The court's verdict was a foregone conclusion: Coe was guilty of deserting to the enemy by running away with the *Hermione* and delivering her up to the enemy; not guilty of murder; and guilty of "being taken in arms against His Majesty." The third charge would have been enough to condemn him, and two days later Coe's body was swinging in chains from a gibbet on Gallows Point, beside his two former shipmates.

Up to the end of 1798, fifteen months after the mutiny, seventeen Hermiones had been caught and court-martialled. Eleven had been hanged, one transported, two had turned King's Evidence, and three were acquitted. It will have been noticed that the last two courts-martial were held at Port Royal, Jamaica, where Sir Hyde had his flagship. The reason for this was that the British had evacuated Santo Domingo in the previous October, signing an agreement with Toussaint l'Ouverture, the leader of the Negroes who had rebelled against the French. At a time when the French held almost the whole of Europe from the Texel in northern Netherlands to Leghorn in the Mediterranean, ''the folly of mortgaging the flower of the nation's manhood for sugar islands had at last dawned on the authorites,'' in the words of Sir Arthur Bryant. ''In five years,'' he added, ''100,000 young Britons had been killed or permanently disabled by the Caribbean climate.''

SO THE YEAR 1799 BEGAN—a year in which Britian's chances in the war looked a good deal brighter, thanks to the victory won the previous August by a young admiral some sixty places lower down the flag list than Sir Hyde Parker. The admiral was, of course, Horatio Nelson; the victory was the Battle of the Nile, which had resulted in the capture or destruction of eleven French battleships.

The year was also to see the capture of ten more Hermoines. The first three were caught together at the beginning of the year serving in an American ship, which they had joined after leaving La Guaira for Jacmel in a Danish schooner. Two of them were also former Successes, Henry Croaker, who had been born at St. Anthony-in-Roseland, Cornwall, within sight of St. Anthony's light, the welcoming beacon for Falmouth; and Thomas Ladson, from Chatham, who was then twenty-nine years old. The third man was Peter Stewart, who had been transferred to the *Hermione* from the *Adventure* a month before Mr. Southcott.

Admiral Bligh again presided at the trial on board the *Brunswick* at Port Royal on January 15, and the court found Croaker and Ladson guilty on the charges of mutiny, deserting to the enemy and murder, and sentenced them to be hanged and their bodies gibbeted. In acquitting Stewart they said that it appeared ''he was incapable from his state of health of assisting or repressing the mutiny.''

If any one person's evidence saved Peter Stewart it was that of young Holford. The first question the court had asked the boy after he was sworn in as a witness was: ''How old are you?''—''Thirteen years last August.''

After he had said that he knew the three accused men, Peter

Stewart asked him: "Do you recollect that at the time of the mutiny that I was not able to go to the head [the rudimentary lavatory in the bows, or head, of the ship] without assistance, and if I was blind at night so as to be deprived of seeing a star?"

"Yes," answered the boy, "I do recollect you could not go without being led, your not being able to walk, but crawling with your hands and knees along the deck on your backside."

Stewart, in his written defence, added that he had been in hospital for three months at La Guaira, and when he recovered tried to give himself up to the Spanish authorities as a prisoner, "and was informed they would make no prisoners but would give me a pass to any place I wished to go."

Henry Croaker, in his written defence, said, "I served three years in the *Success* with Captain Pigot, also five or six months in the *Hermione*, and had no reason to dislike him so as to have acted as has been stated . . ." Ladson's defence said more or less the same thing. It is noteworthy that none of the three men could write: their written defences were signed with a cross. Two days after the trial Croaker and Ladson were hanged and their bodies joined those of Lynham, Charlton and Coe on the gibbets at Gallows Point.

The next *Hermione* trial took place in England when in March a letter from the Board of Admiralty addressed to "Charles Morrice Pole Esquire, Rear-Admiral of the Red and Second Officer in Command of His Majesty's Ships and Vessels at Portsmouth and Spithead," ordered him to assemble a court-martial on board the *Gladiator* "as soon as conveniently may be," to inquire into the loss of the *Hermione* and try "John Williams, John Henison (alias John Slushing), James Parrott [Perrett], John alias Richard) Redmond [Richard Redman] and Jacob Folliard (alias Jacob Fieldge) . . ." (Folliard was Fulga, whose name was so spelled in the *Hermione* muster but also appears elsewhere as Fidtge, Fuldge and Fieldge.)

The five men, like Chaucer's Pilgrims on their way to Canterbury, each had a strange story to tell of how his travels had brought him on board the *Gladiator* to face his accusers. However, one of them had a perfect alibi—but to prove it he had to confess to having committed another crime which could also result in being hanged.

The man was Fulga. His problem was that he had not been on board the *Hermione* at the time of the mutiny because he had deserted while she was being careened at the Mole just before sailing for the last time. But the muster book recording that he had deserted had gone with the ship on her last voyage.

When Fulga had deserted at the Mole he had managed to escape completely. He changed his name to Jacob Folliard, and all went well for eighteen months, until one day he was arrested in Portsmouth as a former Hermione, and accused of mutiny and murder. Would a court believe his story? Would there be a prosecution witness who remembered that he had deserted?

The second of the accused men was John Williams, a Liverpool man who had served in merchant ships trading out of that port for more than twenty-five years. Then, at the beginning of the war, he was caught by a press-gang and forced to serve in the King's ships. He was a simple man: a sailor who became caught up in a series of circumstances which were beyond his control or comprehension.

The story of how he came to be a member of the *Hermione's* crew is a good example of how the Navy was able to use merchant seamen, as a reserve to be drawn on in wartime. As early as 1781 Williams had been a gunner's mate in the *Rumbold,* and he served in her for three years until the master, Mr. Thomas Molyneux, bought another merchantman, the *Ned.* He took Williams with him as gunner, which was a promotion. Both men were still in the *Ned* when the war against France began, but it was not until he transferred to the *Mercy* that Williams's trouble began.

The *Mercy* left Liverpool in the spring of 1797, bound for the West Indies, and arrived at Port Royal in July. Unfortunately for Williams the *Hermione* had also just reached there, and Pigot was under orders from Sir Hyde to take in "such things as you might be in want of." Pigot was, as usual, in want of seamen, and before leaving sent out press-gangs. When they boarded the *Mercy* the lieutenant in charge chose John Williams: a merchantman's gunner was a valuable man, and despite all the pleas of the *Mercy's* master, he took Williams off to the frigate.

Thus John Williams, a mariner of Liverpool, was to become involved in the mutiny. It will be recalled that Williams was sent to hospital after the ship arrived in La Guaira because he was lame, and that when Price, the carpenter, had seen him he had cried and declared he would go back to England and give himself up. We left Williams in company with James Duncan signing on in a Danish brigantine bound for Santa Cruz.

The story of what happened to him after that is told in his petition to Admiral Sir Peter Parker, the commander-in-chief at Portsmouth. Since much of the story has proved to be correct when
checked against official documents, it seems reasonable to accept the
rest as also being true.

The Danish brigantine had left La Guaira with a Spanish cargo
and was bound for a Spanish port, so that she was a legitimate prize
for the British privateer which intercepted her later and sent her into
Tortola. There Williams was allowed to go on shore, without anyone
realizing he was an Hermione. He saw a Liverpool merchantman
called the *Mona* in the harbour and discovered that he knew the
master, who offered to give him a passage back to Liverpool. Williams gladly accepted, and two days later the ship sailed. The lame-
ness which had resulted in him being sent to hospital in La Guaira
was still not cured.

The rest of the story is best told in Williams's own words (he
refers to himself as "your petitioner"): "On his arrival at Liverpol
Mr Fourshaw [Foreshaw], father of Lt Fourshaw who was thrown
overboard at the time of the insurrection, called on him to make an
inquiry respecting his son, and to whom he faithfully related every
part of the said transaction that came to his knowledge, likewise that
as his [Williams's] leg was not yet perfectly whole he wished to go to
an hospital for chirurgical assistance before he delivered himself up
to the law, which he intended to do as soon as he was pronounced
out of danger and fit to undergo the rigour of confinement, which
met with Mr Fourshaw's approbation, and on the day following
your petitioner went into hospital, where he remained five days,
when he delivered himself up to the Mayor [of Liverpool], who then
confined me to prison and wrote to the Lords Commissioners of the
Admiralty to acquaint them therewith.

"Their Lordships in a short time afterwards sent an order to the
Mayor to send him hither [Portsmouth] to stand his trial . . ."

The latest surviving muster book of the *Hermione* was of course
the one ending July 7, 1797, and the names of anyone joining (or
leaving, as Fulga's case showed) the ship after July 7 would be
entered in a new book which the mutineers destroyed. John Williams was impressed on July 8, and knew about this. He continued:
"Your petitioner begs leave to observe that as he never was on board
of any of His Majesty's ships before and consequently unknown to

any of His Majesty's officers, and likewise as no person in Europe ever knew of his ever being on board the *Hermione* he might, if guilty, easily elude justice, but being innocent, indeed incapable of taking the least share in the said horrid conspiracy and insurrection, he thought it a duty he owed to God and his country to come home with all possible expediency, and by throwing himself under the protection of the law and giving a faithful account of what came to his knowledge, to clear himself in the most satisfactory manner . . .

''. . . That your petitioner hath a wife and three sons, all children, at Liverpool, whose sole dependence is under God on the fruit of his industry and through his being confined reduced to great pecuniary and mental distress from which nothing but his being brought to a speedy trial can extricate them . . .''

The third accused man was Richard Redman, the former Success who had murdered the boatswain and spent the rest of the night of the mutiny with the man's widow. With the fourth of the men charged, James Perrett, the tearful butcher, Redman had left La Guaira in a Spanish ship bound for Vigo, in northern Spain. The ship had successfully evaded the British warships in the Caribbean and crossed the Atlantic before, on June 22, 1798, only a few miles from her destination, the British frigate *Aurora* came in sight. Within a short while the Spaniards hauled down their colours and when the frigate's captain, Henry Digby, sent across a boarding party, John Perrett promptly gave himself up and pointed out Redman as another former Hermione.

The witnesses against the five men (it is not known how Slushing was captured) included Mr. Southcott (who had been given a very poor appointment, that of master's mate in the 74-gun *Magnificent*), Midshipman Casey, the carpenter, Richard Price and Steward Jones. The trial itself lasted three days and the evidence they gave was detailed. Richard Redman heard Mr. Southcott describe how the former quartermaster's mate had hit him over the head with a handspike—and later given him wine and water to drink. Casey said he had seen Redman brandishing a white-hilted sword and Steward Jones told how Redman had made him get liquor from the captain's store-room. He described how he had heard Redman, Nash and Farrel arguing whether or not to kill the doctor and purser. Later, he said, he heard Redman ''swear by the Holy Ghost that the Boatswain should go with the rest . . .'' and that then ''Redman remained in the cabin with the Boatswain's wife, and I saw him no more that night."

John Williams was glad to hear Mr. Southcott say that he had been ill with bad feet at the time of the mutiny, and Richard Price confirmed that he had been lame. But Jacob Fulga was the most relieved of all, because Southcott testified that he "was in the *Adventure* with me and was sent to the *Hermione* about the same time I went to her. He behaved very well until the ship was hove down at Cape Nicolas Mole and there deserted and was not on board the *Hermione* at the time the mutiny took place." Fulga was lucky that he had not been brought to trial in the West Indies, since the prosecution witnesses there, Brown and Mason, might not have known that he had "run."

Midshipman Casey declared that he had not seen James Perrett active in the mutiny, and Price in evidence said that Perrett had come to him afterwards crying, saying he had a wife and family in England and that "he was sorry for what had happened." Steward Jones also said he "saw him frequently crying." However, as mentioned earlier, Southcott had different views about the *Hermione*'s former butcher, saying that Perrett acted as a steward after the mutiny, "giving things out," and he "always appeared very cheerful, speaking very disrespectfully of the officers who were killed, saying what big rogues they were."

No one had a good word to say for the fifth accused man, John Slushing: although Southcott had not seen him during the mutiny, he appeared to be very active afterwards and "in the confidence of the mutineers," while Price declared "he seemed to be cheerful with the rest of the ship's company, drinking as they did." The sharp-eyed Jones saw him frequently in the company of two men "who were the chief ringleaders in the murder of the officers," and heard his name called when the captain's silver and money was being shared out.

When the time came for the men to make their defence, Slushing declared he was down below asleep at the time of the mutiny, and by the time he got on deck "the murders had been done and the ship taken." James Perrett claimed he was "as innocent as a child unborn," and pointed out that in addition to giving himself up to the lieutenant from the *Aurora*, he had also told him that Redman was on board.

Richard Redman had written his defence, as befitted a man with a claim to "some learning," and he read it out to the court. The document, preserved in the minutes, is as bizarre as it is revealing, and started off with a long dissertation on his affection for Captain Pigot—how he had joined the *Success* and had been quickly promoted. "So far Captain Pigot befriended me with whome I could sail the world round with . . ." When Captain Pigot transferred to the *Hermione* and included Redman's name among those he wanted to take with him, "with gratitude I couldn't deny him with any properity [*sic*] for he behaved to me very kindly . . ."

Redman (whose spelling has been retained) described differences between the Hermiones and the former Successes over the question of Pigot's favouritism. "There was a continual murmuring among the Hermoins ships company concerning his followers and the usuage they had before Captain Pigot came on board." Granting a day's leave for the former Successes to spend prize money resulted in the Hermiones being "charegrined or disatisfied by granting favours to them that came with Captain Pigot."

He had been the lookout on the starboard bow at the time of the mutiny, he said, and the first he knew of it was when he heard men shouting, "The ship is ours," and seeing them come on to the quarterdeck. "I was stopt by some of the mutineers making some dreadful expressions, and knowing I had some learning to do as they ordered me . . ." Later he heard a noise below and found the mutineers were "haveing [heaving] the Boatswan before them, a great many in number. I went to them and said in the name of God what do you main to committ murder, with that some of the most desperate mad answers we think you will go the same way if you do not keep a silent tongue . . ."

His reason for going to Vigo later in the Spanish ship, he explained, was that "if she got there to leave her and go to Lisbon and to give myself up to the English Council" [Consul].

The court did not take long to reach a verdict: Redman and Slushing were sentenced to death, and Williams, Perrett and Fulga were acquitted.

Among the minutes of the court-martial is an inventory of all of Captain Pigot's silver and valuables, and, although not signed, it was probably drawn up by his former steward, John Jones. There is also a list of the names of five men who received watches, and those who received sixteen dollars, or silver. On it is written: "Theys is the peple that received the property of the Capston Head, September the 24th 1797."

One of the captains forming the court was Sir Edward Pellew, later Lord Exmouth, attending his only *Hermione* trial. His biographer refers to the fact—mentioning only one mutineer—that the man's crimes were aggravated since Pigot had "brought him up from a boy and treated him with much kindness and confidence," and writes: "The court being cleared, Sir Edward proposed that sentence should be executed immediately. The circumstances of the case demanded, in his opinion, unusual severity, which might be expected to have good effect upon the Fleet; while there was every reason to conclude, from the prisoner's demeanour before them, that if delay were allowed, he would meet his fate with hardihood which would destroy the value of the example."

This presumably refers to Redman, though he was only one of two sentenced to death. The biographer continues: "The court at first questioned their power to execute without the warrant of the Admiralty, but this was quickly settled by reference to the Act of Parliament.

"The president then declared he could not make the order. 'Look here,' said he, giving to Sir Edward his hand, trembling violently and bathed in cold perspiration. 'I see it and I respect your feelings,' replied Sir Edward, 'but I am sure that such an example is wanted, and I must press the point.'

" 'Well,' he replied, 'if it be the *unanimous* opinion of the court, it shall be done.' It was agreed to, and the prisoner was called. Though sure that he must be condemned, he entered with a bold front; but when he was informed that he would be executed in one hour, he rolled on the deck in an agony. 'What! Gentlemen,' he exclaimed, 'hang me directly! Will you not allow me a few days—a little time— to make my peace with God?'

"The whole Fleet," continued the biographer, "was appalled when the close of the court-martial was announced to them by the signal for execution; and at the end of the allotted hour, the wretched criminal was brought up to undergo his sentence."

THE NEXT HERMIONE to be caught was James Barnett, the youngster who had pounded salt at Macuto and then gone to

Cumaná with the two Holfords and James Bell in an open boat to work on board the Spanish xebec. From there Barnett had gone on alone to the nearby port of Barcelona and joined a Danish ship. Eventually he ended up as a member of the crew of the American schooner *Polly* which, after going to Green Island, Jamaica, cleared for Boston.

However the frigate *Maidstone*, commanded by Captain Ross Donelly, was patrolling the Strait of Florida, through which the *Polly* had to pass. Donelly was regularly stopping all neutral ships—particularly American—to search them for British seamen, and when he ordered the *Polly* to heave-to Barnett was one of the three men taken off by the boarding party.

Barnett was "read in," and the *Maidstone* continued her cruise, leaving the *Polly* to continue her voyage to Boston. During the next two or three weeks the *Maidstone* took several more men from various neutral ships and then returned to Port Royal. Donelly later reported to Sir Hyde Parker that having "taken some unprotected men out of different American vessels, and having reason to suppose that some of them were mutineers late belonging to His Majesty's ship *Hermione*, I applied to Captain Dobson [commanding the *Queen*, in which John Mason, John Brown and the two Holfords were serving] to send on board the ship I command the proper persons to ascertain whether they were so or not."

That evening Lieutenant Charles Boyce of the *Queen* took Brown, Mason and the elder Holford across to the *Maidstone* to see the men. By the time they arrived on board it was dark, and the newly-pressed men were lined up. In the light of candles, the three men walked along the line, and John Holford picked out Barnett—who was using the alias John Barton—saying he was a former Hermione. However Brown and Mason both said they did not recognize him.

Barnett was put under arrest and the three men returned to the *Queen* where Lieutenant Boyce questioned them again. "Holford still said he knew him. I asked him what name the prisoner went by on board the *Hermione:* he replied 'John [*sic*] Barnett.' Brown and Mason knew there was a person of that name but did not recollect him sufficiently to identify him."

Three days later James Barnett was tried on board the *Hannibal*, and both Mason and Brown in evidence stuck to their story until Mason eventually admitted that "I have seen the prisoner before, but do not recollect where," and Brown said, "He looks to me that I have seen him several times, but where I cannot recollect."

Holford, therefore, was the only witness against Barnett; but although the prosecution's whole case against Barnett rested on him, Holford's evidence was favourable. He described how they had been together at La Guaira, and how eventually they had gone together to Cumaná in an open boat.

"Did you at any time of the mutiny or afterwards see the prisoner take an active part in it?" asked the court. Holford said, "No, I did not."

"Did he ever express himself to you in any manner upon the subject?"—"I heard him say that he was sorry for what happened, and was weary in his mind about it, as he could not venture with safety home, not knowing the consequence of what might happen if he was taken."

"Did the ringleaders point out, by any violent conduct, those that did not incline to obey their order?"

"I heard several voices in the course of the night saying that every man belonging to the ship . . . should attend to their stations, or otherwise they must put up with the consequences that might follow."

After several more questions, the court asked, "Were the men you call salters forced by the Spaniards to work, or was it voluntarily?"

"Being in necessity they were obliged to work for a livelihood," replied Holford. "All the work I saw the prisoner do was pounding salt."

"Had he given himself up as a prisoner, would he have been supported by the Spanish Government?"—"I believe so, the same as the other prisoners."

"Was that generally known among the *Hermione*'s men?"— "No," said Holford.

Barnett was then called upon to make his defence. After describing how he had kept out of the way during the mutiny, he said that in La Guaira and later at Puerto Cabello, "without money, which was taken from me during the night, I was driven to great distress, and had it not been for the kindness of Holford I must have starved."

He concluded with a description of his wanderings from when

he left Holford at Cumaná until he joined the American schooner *Polly* "and out of which I was pressed by an officer of the *Maidstone.*"

The court decided that the charge—deserting to the enemy by running away with the *Hermione,* and murder—were proved, and sentenced him to death; but "in consideration of his youth and inexperience at the time, being then only fifteen years of age," the court recommended him to mercy. They explained to Sir Hyde that having found him guilty the Articles of War did not leave it "in the power of the court to pronounce any other sentence."

Sir Hyde noted in his journal, "Ordered the Provost Marshal to keep him in custody 'till the King's Pleasure is known.' " The pardon eventually arrived on November 23, four months to the day after the trial.

An entry that Sir Hyde made in his journal on August 4, a few days after the reference to Barnett, showed that even though nearly two years had passed since the *Hermione* mutiny, there was still a danger in the West Indies of the crews mutinying and seizing their ships. "Ordered Captain Smith . . . to assemble a court martial to try Timothy Donavan, Edmund Lawler and Hans Peters, belonging to the *Volage,* for forming a conspiracy, with an intent to murder the captain and officers when at sea and delivering the ship into the hands of the enemy."

By now twenty-four former Hermiones had been tried, excluding the officers and Fulga; but apart from Thomas Leech and Richard Redman, the main leaders had so far escaped the Royal Navy's net. However, one of the most important was at last cornered, and the full weight of Britain's diplomatic influence was working to bring him to trial.

XXV

The U.S. President Helps

—m—

O N FEBRUARY 20, 1799, a youth dressed in seaman's clothes went up to the house of Mr. Benjamin Moodie, in Charleston, South Carolina, and told the servant who answered the door that he had some information for Mr. Moodie, who was one of the two British Consul-Generals in America (the other, Mr. Phineas Bond, lived in Philadelphia).

When he was taken to the Consul the youth introduced himself as William Portlock, an American subject born at Portsmouth, Virginia, and a seaman serving in the American schooner *Tanner's Delight*, which had arrived at Charleston three weeks earlier.

There was another man serving before the mast in the *Tanner's Delight*, he said, who answered to the name of Nathan Robbins, but he was sure he was one of the mutineers from the *Hermione*. This man had long black hair, a dark complexion and a scar on one of his lips.

Portlock described how the *Tanner's Delight* had been in the port of Santo Domingo the previous Christmas when some of the crew of a French privateer had come on board. Robbins and the privateersmen had started drinking together and Robbins had told them, in Portlock's hearing, that he had been the boatswain's mate of the *Hermione* when she was taken into a Spanish port. After that, added Portlock, when Robbins was drunk he would sometimes mention the name of the *Hermione* and say "Bad luck to her!" and shake his fist.

Mr. Moodie had, of course, been sent descriptions of some of the leaders of the mutiny by Sir Hyde Parker some months earlier, and he read through them. Portlock's description seemed to fit a certain Thomas Nash—"an Irishman, one of the forecastlemen, about five feet ten inches high, long black hair, remarkably hairy about the breast, arms etc. . . . entered on board an American or Spanish trading schooner."

The Consul at once took Portlock along to Charleston's Federal Clerk, Mr. Thomas Hall, and had him swear an affidavit in which he repeated all he knew about the man Robbins, who at that very moment was at work on board the *Tanner's Delight,* unaware that the British were close on his heels.

Armed with the affidavit, which Portlock had signed in the Federal Clerk's presence with a cross, Mr. Moodie went along to the chambers of His Honour Judge Thomas Bee, of the Federal Court of the District of South Carolina, asking that Robbins should be detained, pending a writ of *habeas corpus,* on suspicion of having been concerned in the *Hermione* mutiny. Judge Bee agreed and the bewildered Thomas Nash—for he was indeed the man using the name Robbins—found himself seized on board the *Tanner's Delight* and taken on shore to be lodged in Charleston's jail, with irons on his arms and legs.

The Consul-General then wrote to the British Minister in Washington, Mr. Robert Liston—the man who had been so upset with Captain Pigot over the affair of Mr. Jesup—enclosing a copy of Portlock's affidavit and describing what he had done so far. He also wrote to Sir Hyde Parker at Port Royal, asking that someone be sent up to Charleston as soon as possible to identify the man in jail. Sir Hyde dispatched John Forbes, the former master's mate in the *Hermione,* who had by now been promoted to lieutenant.

Lieutenant Forbes arrived at Charleston from Port Royal on April 17 and went to see "Robbins" in jail. He had no difficulty in identifying him as Nash, and next day Forbes appeared before Judge Bee to swear an affidavit that the man calling himself Nathan Robbins "in the jail of this district" was really Thomas Nash, whom he had known while serving in the *Hermione* and who was "one of the principals in the . . . acts of murder and piracy, whose conduct . . . has become known to this deponent by depositions made, and testimonials given, in courts martial, where some of the crew have been tried."

Judge Bee also received a letter from the Secretary of State in Washington telling him that the British Minister had made an application to President John Adams for the delivery of the prisoner under Article 27 (details of which are given in Notes, page 359–360) and, said the Secretary of State, "The President advises and requests you to deliver him up."

By now, however, a certain Mr. Abraham Sasportas had become involved. Mr. Sasportas had earlier been the "Commercial agent for the Republic of France" at Charleston, and he had had an extremely profitable time while French ships had been able to sell their prizes at Charleston—a privilege which in recent years had not been open to them.

Mr. Sasportas later claimed in a letter published in a Charleston newspaper called *Timothy's* that he had heard of Nathan Robbins only by chance: he had been drawn to serve as a grand juror for the district of Charleston, and the jury were requested by the court to visit Charleston jail "in order to make a report to the state of the same."

"In the exercise of this duty," wrote Mr. Sasportas, "I saw Robbins confined in irons, who communicated to me the cause of his committal, and his defence to the charge, viz. that of his being an American citizen, impressed by the English.

"From his relation [i.e., account] and his certificate of citizenship then shown to me, I was induced to employ counsel on his behalf, in order that his innocence or guilt might be established by an appeal to the laws of the country."

Nor did Mr. Sasportas lie when he said that Nash had a certificate of citizenship in the name of Robbins: it appeared to be perfectly genuine, dated May 20, 1795, and signed by "John Keefe, public notary in the City of New York," saying that he testified that Robbins "personally appeared before me, and being by me duly sworn, according to the law, deposed that he is a citizen of the

United States of America . . . whereof in attestation being required, I have granted this under my notarial firm and seal."

All this seemed convincing enough—especially to someone who did not know that an entry in the muster book of the *Hermione* showed that when Thomas Nash had joined the ship on December 21, 1792, he had given his age as twenty-five and his place of birth as Waterford, in Ireland, receiving a bounty of £3 after taking the oath of allegiance to the King. And on May 20, 1795, when he was supposed to have "personally appeared" as "Robbins" before Mr. Keefe in New York, he was in fact on board the *Hermione* which was then at anchor in Lamentin Bay, Port au Prince, where, as Captain Wilkinson noted in his log, she "observed and attacked a battery of several guns, received many shots from enemy . . ."

Nash was allowed out of jail in order to swear an affidavit before the Federal Clerk in which he claimed he was "a native of Connecticut and born in Danbury in that state; that he has never changed his obedience to his native country, and that about two years ago he was pressed from on board the brig *Betsey* of New York, commanded by Captain White, and bound for St Nichola [*sic*] Mole, by the crew of the British frigate *Hermione* . . . and was detained there contrary to his will in service of the British nation, until the said vessel was captured by those of her crew . . . and that he gave no assistance in such capture."

Nash's reference to the brig *Betsey* gives a clue to how he might have obtained the certificate which had—no doubt quite legally—been issued to someone who actually was, or claimed to be, Robbins: on August 12, 1795, three months after the certificate was issued by Mr. Keefe, Simon Markus, an Italian, was "read in" on board the *Hermione* after being pressed from the American brig *Betsey*. That probably accounts for the *Betsey* part of the story. But how, it might be asked, did Nash know about Danbury, Connecticut? He must have known enough about Connecticut's rolling, typically English countryside to risk being questioned by someone who did. And how did he acquire the name of Robbins? Again the *Hermione*'s muster book gives the clue—the six names immediately preceding Markus's are of Americans pressed on July 4, 1795, from the American schooner *Two Brothers*. Among them was Benjamin Brewster, a Connecticut man: he came from Preston, some ninety-six miles from Danbury, and he served with Nash in the *Hermione* for nearly two years before being freed as an American citizen. (See page 89.) Nash had plenty of time to learn about Connecticut; and he might well have bought the certificate of citizenship from any of the six men from the *Two Brothers*.

However, Mr. Abraham Sasportas knew nothing of all this, and from his point of view the seaman in Charleston jail seemed quite genuinely to be Nathan Robbins, a citizen of the United States, and now in trouble with those damnable Britishers who were always kidnapping American seamen. For that reason, quite sufficient in itself, and perhaps because of his sympathies, commercial and otherwise, for the French, Mr. Sasportas hired a lawyer to look after the seaman's case.

In addition, someone else was beginning to interest himself in the affairs of Nathan Robbins: Colonel Alexander Moultrie, a lawyer, who had already been consulted about Nash's affairs. He wrote later in a letter to Mr. Moodie that he first gave his opinion "that such was the prevailing influence of opinions and sentiments of those in power, that every effort [to save Nash] would be in vain." He added that "matters rested thus for some days, till the day before Robbins was tried. I was then accidentally informed in conversation with a friend, that Robbins was an American; I was struck and alarmed to think I had deserted him. I immediately went to Mr Ker [a lawyer] and desired him to prepare himself for the argument [i.e., prepare a brief] next morning. I went home and considered the case, and met Mr Ker in court the next day.

"I had never yet seen Robbins, nor had I ever any intercourse with him, till he was pointed out to me, and I went up and spoke to him in court the day of his trial; nor had I till then ever seen one of his papers. On my coming into court, one of the first things I did, I asked the Clerk for the papers, and amongst them found Robbins's certificate of nativity and citizenship; I examined it and found it had every mark of authenticity, no erasure or obliteration . . ." (It was not until several weeks later that anyone thought to check the records at Danbury, Connecticut. When this was done, apparently at the behest of the British Consul, the result was two announcements in a Connecticut newspaper. The first, headed "Danbury, September 16, 1799," said "We, the subscribers, select men of the town of Danbury, in the state of Connecticut, certify that we have always been inhabitants of the said town, and are from forty-five to fifty-seven years of age, and have never known an inhabitant of this town by the name of Jonathan or Nathan Robbins, and that there has not been, nor now is, any family known by the name of Robbins within the limits of the town. Signed Eli Mygott, Eben. Benedict, Justus Barnum, Benjamin Hichcok [*sic*]."

(The second announcement said: "The subscriber, late Clerk for the town of Danbury . . . certifies that he kept the two records for twenty-five years, viz from the year 1771 until the year 1796: that he is now fifty-six years of age, and that he never knew any person by the name of Robbins, born or residing in the said town of Danbury during that term of twenty-five years, before or since.—Major Taylor.")

Neither Mr. Sasportas nor Colonel Moultrie appears to be telling the whole truth. Sasportas later wrote, in a letter to *Timothy's*, that "I was induced to employ counsel on his [Nash's] behalf." Moultrie was the counsel but in his letter to the British Consul, the colonel denied having anything to do with the former French agent, and implied he was working without payment.

Judge Bee had set the hearing for July 25, and as far as Mr. Moodie knew it was to be a straightforward and unopposed plea of habeas corpus. He later wrote to Judge Bee that he then "met a barrister, Mr. Ker, who mentioned his intention to oppose the delivery of the prisoner, under the idea of his being a citizen of the United States of America; on this I expressed some surprise that a person should at so late a day interest himself on behalf of the prisoner, particularly as His Majesty's cutter *Sprightly* had been here a very short time before for the purpose of carrying him off . . ."

When the case opened Judge Bee was presented with the two affidavits on which Mr. Moodie's plea of habeas corpus was based— one by the seaman William Portlock and the other by Lieutenant Forbes. The letter from the Secretary of State to the Judge, referring to the British Minister's application for extradition and mentioning the President's request to hand over Nash, was then shown to the counsel for both sides.

Mr. Ker, opposing the British, produced Nash's certificate of citizenship, in the name of Robbins, and the affidavit he had sworn saying that he was a native of Danbury. Mr. Ker then claimed that as far as extradition was concerned, a British ship—in this case the *Hermione*— was not "territory." However, since Article 27 of the treaty between Britain and America referred to "within the jurisdiction of either," and Britain certainly had jurisdiction over her warships, his argument failed.

Judge Bee finally ruled that Nash should be delivered up to the British. He was taken back to jail, and when Lieutenant Robert Jump, commanding the *Sprightly,* officially claimed him, Nash was sent down to the quay on Judge Bee's order. Mr. Moodie later visited the cutter so that he could confirm that Nash was the man under confinement.

The *Sprightly* had no sooner sailed than a violent campaign broke out in American newspapers, which were already printing protests at what they called the "handing over of an American citizen." In Charleston itself *Timothy's* published many letters and articles, a few of which were inspired and in some cases written by Mr. Sasportas, and suitable replies from Mr. Moodie.

IN LIFE Hugh Pigot had been responsible for an uproar in the American press over the Jesup affair; and even his death was now provoking another equally wordy battle in newspapers all over the country.

Less than thirteen years after Nash was put on board H.M.S. *Sprightly* at Charleston, Britain and America were at war, and one of the main causes was that American seamen were allegedly pressed into British warships. Thomas Nash provides a good example of how misunderstandings and bitterness could arise. How could a man possess a genuine certificate proving he was an American called Robbins when he was in fact an Irishman named Nash, identified by several of his shipmates under oath as someone who, on the date the certificate was issued in New York, was in a ship bombarding the French?

Disagreements were inevitable, but four important factors must be understood and remembered. The first affected the emotional approach of the Americans. The War of Independence had ended only sixteen years earlier and was fresh in most people's minds. During that war, Royalist France had helped the colonists by land and sea in their revolt; and when they gained their independence after eight years of warfare, and at a cost of £15 million, they were suitably grateful. The British, having lost half a continent, and with £115 million added to the national debt, naturally took a different view.

The second factor was a legalistic one. The British Government's attitude was that a man born a British subject remained British: he could not change his responsibilities simply by going to another country and living there. This was particularly true in wartime, when British subjects were needed to man ships and serve in the Army. A Briton could not in effect sign a separate peace with the enemy by adopting the nationality of a neutral country. The situation was different, of course, when a colony revolted and achieved its own independence. But nevertheless at that time there was not an American subject over the age of twenty-three (apart from immigrants) who had not been born a British subject.

The third factor—and one which weighed heavily with the British Government—was the ease with which a legal document "proving" its owner to be an American subject could be obtained by fraudulent means. This led to the British Government and the Royal Navy adopting, at times, a rather cynical attitude towards such documents.

Before describing the actual methods used, there is the fourth factor to consider, and it is linked to the first. Britain at that time was fighting for her very life. The France of Louis XVI which had helped the American colonists gain their freedom had disappeared in a welter of blood on the day mobs stormed the Bastille. But America was slow to realize that the new France of the Revolution was, in the name of liberty, in fact trying to enslave Europe; that far from liberating each newly-occupied nation's people, it would by judicial use of armies, terror and tax-collectors, reduce them to military, moral and economic submission.

In 1799 Britain stood isolated and alone in the war against France and Spain, although the latter's heart was not in the battle. Facing a great Continental nation which, by comparison, had limitless manpower, Britain could fight back effectively only at sea. To do this she needed ships and even more desperately men: men to sail the ships of the Royal Navy and by controlling the sea keep some semblance of freedom in the world—the freedom which, ironically, allowed

Captain Pigot's treatment of Mr. Jesup to cause such a furore in Whitehall, without any prompting from the United States Government.

Bearing in mind the then current attitude of the United States Government towards Britain and France; the British Government's attitude towards nationality; and the actual, as opposed to the professed, aims of the new Revolutionary France, it remains only to point out some of the other factors which, though less important, added their abrasive quota to the friction between Britain and the United States.

The American mercantile marine at that time was flourishing (British imports from the USA between 1793–1801, for example, were £14,500,000, compared with £8,800,000 for the previous nine years), and it welcomed British seamen, who naturally leapt at the opportunity of serving in neutral ships where pay was much higher, discipline considerably less rigid, and conditions and food comparatively luxurious. In addition, they signed on for a particular voyage and were paid off in hard cash at the end of it.

Nor did America want only prime seamen: she was a new and rapidly expanding nation who also needed more citizens, so she not unnaturally put few difficulties in the way of British seamen becoming—or passing themselves off as—American subjects.

The United States Government's safeguard for its own seamen was a "protection." This was in effect the forerunner of the identity card and consisted of a document issued under "An Act for the Relief and Protection of American Seamen." This gave its possessor's name, age, birthplace and a general physical description, and was issued by the collector of Customs at an American port, or an American consul abroad. To obtain one, a man had only to make a sworn declaration giving his name, age and place of birth, and produce another American citizen to back up his claim. He took his declaration—in effect a certificate of citizenship—and his sponsor to the collector of Customs or a consul, who then issued the protection without more ado, since the requirements of law had been met. At a time when few official records were kept, a vast number of people were illiterate, and communications were bad, no collector would or could check whether the declaration was true: indeed, the law did not require him to, since the declaration had already been sworn before a notary public. Clearly it was not difficult to obtain a protection which, as far as the United States Government was concerned, put him under the protection of the Stars and Stripes. An American "birthplace" was not hard to acquire—an American shipmate could give him enough details of a town or village to enable him to answer a few perfunctory questions. The same shipmate would sponsor him when he appeared before the collector of Customs. Even the most honest of collectors and consuls had to accept much on trust: in such a young country men's accents or the ability to speak the language properly was no test; and not unnaturally they probably preferred issuing a protection in a doubtful case rather than risk refusing one to a man who might be genuine.

In addition there was a good sale for genuine protections, since nothing prevented a man obtaining a new protection in every United States port with a collector of Customs, and from the consul in each foreign port he visited. The physical description written in the protection was generally sufficiently vague to make it easily transferable.

An example is the protection held by a man who served in the *Hermione* and was discharged before the mutiny after being claimed by an American consul as an American citizen. He was Benjamin Brewster, the man who probably helped Thomas Nash choose Danbury, Connecticut, as a "birthplace." Brewster was discharged from the *Hermione* in Port Royal after the consul's intervention on April 7, 1797. But when he was arrested in October 1800, on suspicion of being a mutineer, he produced a protection dated February 15, 1800. Yet even if he did not have a protection while in the *Hermione* in 1797, the consul would have given him one immediately he was freed, to avoid having him pressed again before he left Port Royal.

Most British seamen visiting an American port, or able to get to an American consul, therefore took the precaution—if they had the opportunity—of obtaining a protection: it was a good insurance. Nor was it difficult, even if he had no American friend: a small payment to a shady but bona fide American citizen, a declaration sworn before a notary public, a visit to a Customs collector, and he had established himself as an American subject: from then on he was in effect wrapped in the Stars and Stripes, not the Union Flag. Indeed, there was a flourishing trade in New York, where a certain Mr.

Riley at the turn of the century was reputed to have run such a business and gave the United States a dozen new "citizens" a day, at three dollars a time.

Since the Royal Navy knew the protection system was abused, the lieutenant commanding the boarding party sent to an American ship usually relied on his own instinct rather than the possession of a protection in deciding if a seaman was British; and no doubt his instinct was keener if his ship was critically short of men.

With a century and a half of hindsight, during which time the United States herself has had to help overthrow men determined to rule the world, all but the most bigoted would agree that both Britain and America were doing what they thought necessary with the limited knowledge available and the particular prejudices then current. For Britain it was a question of strengthening herself in the battle to prevent France extending her domination from the Baltic to the Indian Ocean. To America it seemed she was defending her new and hard-won independence against what she considered to be the thin edge of the wedge of renewed British interference in American affairs.

SIR HYDE PARKER knew as well as any man the difficulties over protections and, knowing the truth about Thomas Nash's birthplace and that he had been on board the *Hermione* on the day he was supposed to have been issued the protection in New York, was unmoved by the uproar in the American press. H.M.S. *Sprightly* arrived at Port Royal on Sunday, August 11, and on Monday the Admiral ordered Captain E. T. Smith of the *Hannibal* to assemble a court-martial to try Nash "for mutiny, piracy, desertion and murder."

The trial began the following Thursday and included, almost inevitably, Captain Man Dobson, who had not missed being a member of any of the eight *Hermione* courts-martial held up to then at the Jamaica Station. The evidence produced against Nash was damning. John Brown, asked to describe the fate of Lieutenant Foreshaw—which he had witnessed from the maintop—declared: "They asked him [Nash] what he was going to do with Lt Foreshaw, on which he told them to heave the bugger overboard, which they did, and hove him over the quarter." In the share-out of Captain Pigot's and the officers' effects, he added, he understood Nash received a watch.

Nash himself asked Brown a curious question. "Did you save my life the day after the ship was taken possession of by the mutineers when they overheard me speaking to some others about retaking the ship?"

Brown replied: "I heard a rope was rove to hang you, on account of your first being the head mutineer to take the ship from the officers; and then endeavouring to retake her." (This is the only reference made in any of the courts-martial, confessions or depositions to the rope or to Nash's alleged intention or conversation.)

"What did he mean to do with the ship, if perchance he retook her from the other mutineers?" the court asked.

"I can't say," replied Brown. No one asked any more questions about this episode.

Holford described how, when Lieutenant Foreshaw had climbed back on board after being hove over the side, Nash ran up to him saying, "You bugger, Foreshaw, are you not overboard yet . . . ?" Holford said that Nash then led the lieutenant to the gangway and, with help from some others, threw him into the sea.

When Nash was called to make his defence he had nothing to say: he made no claim that he was an American citizen, nor did he enlarge on his question about planning to retake the ship. The court sentenced him to be hanged and his body gibbeted, and Sir Hyde Parker noted in his journal on Monday, August 19, "This morning Thomas Nash was executed and afterwards hung in chains . . ."

Nash's death did not quieten the outcry in America, and it was so strong—particularly in Charleston—that Sir Hyde wrote to Mr. Moodie, the Consul-General, in answer to two letters from him, saying that Nash, before he was executed, "confessed himself to be an Irishman." This fact was published in *Timothy's* on Mr. Moodie's behalf, and a few weeks later Captain George Blake, of the Royal Navy, swore an affidavit that at the trial at Port Royal "Nash made no defence . . . On the scaffold, a few minutes before he was run up to the foreyardarm of the *Acasto,* he addressed the crew of that ship, advising them to take timely warning of his fate." This affidavit, too, was published in *Timothy's.*

A description of the outcry in America was given by Lord MacDonald who had just returned to his home in Great George Street, London, a month after Nash's execution, following a visit to the United States. He wrote a long letter to the man responsible for Britain's foreign affairs, the Secretary of State, Lord Grenville.

". . . The mutiny in our Fleet, and the horrible affair of the *Hermione* frigate, were subjects of exaltation with many people of all descriptions [in America]; and it was said with satisfaction that probably those and similar events were to be ascribed to the *brave* efforts of impressed American seamen, whose *right* to mutiny, and even murder British officers, was *asserted* and maintained in elaborate arguments, even in Congress; a circumstance which leads me to say that the number of our ablest seamen in American service or employment is incredible."

He added in another letter a few days later that "it was Mr Marshall, the present American Secretary of State, a Virginian lawyer of considerable abilities, who in Congress maintained the argument . . . namely, that American seamen had a *right* to do what had been done on board the *Hermione* . . . He had spoken with effect in vindication of the President's conduct in giving up one of the mutineers, agreeable to the treaty, on the ground that he was in truth an Irishman, and a British subject; but," continued his Lordship, "he took occasion at the same time to proclaim and enlarge on the very humane and liberal principle I have stated."

XXVI

Through the Gates

—〰—

WHILE THOMAS NASH had been in jail at Charleston, His Majesty's sloop *Kite* had been convoying "the trade" across the North Sea from Elsinore, in Denmark, to Scotland. As soon as she anchored in the Firth of Forth on June 1, 1799, her commanding officer, Charles Lydiard, wrote to the Admiralty reporting his arrival and adding: "Having been requested by Lord Robert Fitzgerald [Britain's Envoy Extraordinary at Copenhagen] to take on board a British seaman, one of the mutineers of the *Hermione*, I beg Their Lordships' orders what I am to do with him."

An unsigned note enclosed in Lydiard's letter gave a brief history of the mutineer. He was the foretopman James Duncan, who had said the day after the mutiny that if the officers were still alive his bad toe would never have recovered. Duncan's arrival in the Firth of Forth as a prisoner was due to a combination of bad luck and the punctiliousness of the Danish authorities.

Part of Duncan's story has already been told: how he and John Williams went to Cumaná and signed on in a Danish ship which was captured by a British privateer and sent into Tortola. At this point the stories told by the two men disagree. Williams went on shore and joined a British ship in which he returned to Liverpool and gave himself up. Duncan, however, said that when the Danish ship was captured the British prize master "asked me if I belonged to the *Hermione.* I told him I did and he made a prisoner of me." Duncan claimed he was then sent to the island of St. Thomas and put on board a Danish frigate bound for Denmark.

So much for Duncan's claims. From then on official sources describe his movements. As soon as the frigate arrived in the Sound and anchored off Kronborg Castle at Elsinore, he was put on shore and imprisoned in the fortress. No doubt its dignified beauty, topped by the green coppered roof, and its romantic link with Hamlet, was lost on the seaman. In the meantime the Danish Government informed Lord Robert Fitzgerald of their prisoner and were asked that he should be put on board the *Kite.*

On July 3, 1800, just thirteen months after Lydiard's letter to the Admiralty reporting the *Kite's* arrival in the Forth, and nearly three years after the mutiny, James Duncan was brought to trial on board the *Gladiator* at Portsmouth on the usual charges. Southcott, having finally been made a lieutenant, Sergeant Plaice, John Williams, James Perrett and Steward John Jones, gave evidence against him. All these men, with the exception of Southcott, were being kept at Portsmouth, readily available as witnesses. But they had another task, which was simply to roam the streets of that great naval base, looking at the passing seamen, just in case they recognized a familiar face from the *Hermione.* The chances were not as remote as they would seem.

Duncan's defence concluded with the plea that "I hope the court will take into account I have been two years confined." This, of course, included the time he had been in Danish custody. The court no doubt took it into account, but it made no difference to the verdict: Duncan was sentenced to be hanged. The sentence was carried out on July 10 on board the *Puissant,* and a contemporary account said, "About a quarter of an hour before he was turned off [*sic*], he addressed the ship's company, and said how justly he was condemned for being concerned in one of the worst of crimes, and warned them from ever being concerned in such an act of atrocity."

A few days later a seaman from the *Royal William,* Thomas Nelson, was court-martialled for having "used reproachful and provoking speeches" to one of the witnesses who had given

evidence against Duncan. He was sentenced to two years in the
Marshalsea Prison.

AT THE END of July, three weeks after Duncan had been hanged,
the *Gladiator* was the scene of yet another *Hermione* trial, where the
evidence given was the most gruesome so far. Two men were accused—John Watson, the sailor who had pretended to be blind before the mutiny and danced and drank on the half-deck after it was
over; and young James Allen, Lieutenant Douglas's servant, who
had behaved more like a jackal when the lieutenant was murdered.

Both men had been taken out of a neutral ship in the West Indies
and sent on board the flagship of Rear-Admiral Harvey, commanding in the Leeward Isles. Harvey had, as mentioned earlier, originally kept back some of the loyal marines as witnesses should he
capture any mutineers, but by then only Corporal Nicolas Doran
remained. The admiral sent for Doran and asked him if he recognized Allen. "I told him I knew him but had very little knowledge of
the man," Doran said later. Admiral Harvey, having no one to use
as a witness, sent both Watson and Allen to England, where the
other witnesses were available.

Rear-Admiral John Holloway was the president of the court, and
as usual the first witness was Lieutenant Southcott, who described
how after the mutiny Watson had said that he was not then blind—
he had previously been pretending. But it was against James Allen
that Southcott's evidence was more effective: telling how the mutineers had been hunting for Lieutenant Douglas, Southcott said that
he heard Allen call, "Here he is!" two or three times. He also described how later he saw the boy wearing one of Lieutenant Douglas's rings and cutting down a pair of his boots to make into shoes.

The former steward, John Jones, declared that he "saw Watson
dancing with the people, very much in liquor, on the quarterdeck."
As for Allen, he saw him "showing the boys a ring he had on his
finger which I supposed belonged to his master."

Then came the turn of the *Hermione's* former butcher, James Perrett, to tell his story. He described how he saw Allen holding on to
Lieutenant Douglas, and "he sung out 'Let me have a chop at him.
He shall not make me jump about the gunroom anymore.'" Lieutenant Douglas cried out for mercy as they dragged him away, Perrett
added.

"Did you see him take a chop at him?" the court asked.

"Yes, he made a chop at him as they were dragging him up the ladder of the after hatchway. I do not know whether it was with a tomahawk or a cutlass." A contemporary account said that "on receiving this deposition from Perrett, a general groan of horror was heard in the court."

Sergeant Plaice gave a detailed description of how Lieutenant Douglas had hidden under the dying marine officer's bed, and had later been found by the mutineers. "I suppose there were twenty tomahawks, axes and boarding pikes jagged into him immediately in the gunroom," he said.

Allen's defence was simple. He said it was very improbable, as he was such a youth at the time, being only sixteen years old the previous February, that he should have been guilty of such a crime, and "if I had, I should not have slept in my bed."

Both Allen and Watson were found guilty, and executed on August 7. According to the *Naval Chronicle*, "At ten o'clock Watson was launched into Eternity; but, as the same Provost Marshal was obliged to attend both men, Allen was not executed until eleven o'clock . . . They both behaved very penitent, and acknowledged the justice of their sentence. Allen was born at Chatham and was but twenty years of age the day he was tried. His brother was on board the whole of the trial and was extremely affected; and, at the time of the execution, he was at the Dockyard, directly opposite his brother, and, on the gun's firing, he fell down speechless in the yard, from whence he was taken home in a state of insensibility . . ."

NO MORE HERMIONES were caught for nearly a year. Sir Hyde Parker had returned from the West Indies a rich man and then been sent to the Baltic with a squadron where his second-in-command, Nelson, fought and won the Battle of Copenhagen on Maundy Thursday, 1801. Sir Hyde was already back in his London house— having been ordered by the Admiralty to hand over command to Nelson and return home—by the time the next mutineers were put on trial.

They were the young former clerk, William Johnson, and Hadrian Poulson, the Dane who had helped Thomas Nash throw Captain Pigot's body out through one of the *Hermione's* stern windows. Both had been caught at Curaçao.

The court-martial on board the *Gladiator* had Rear-Admiral John Holloway as its president. Johnson described how he had gone to Curaçao from La Guaira, finding a job there as clerk to the American Consul. "I remained in this employ," he said, "but hearing it was necessary for every person who was on board the *Hermione* at the unhappy period to be examined, I embraced the first opportunity to effect this, and on the 15th day of September [six days short of three years after the mutiny] I went on board His Majesty's Ship *Néréide*, commanded by Frederick Watkins, Esquire, then off Curaçao, and surrendered myself for an examination of my conduct."

That sounded an adequate defence and an indication that Johnson's conscience was clear; but the former clerk had omitted to tell the full circumstances. The British frigate *Néréide* had indeed been cruising off Curaçao, and on September 11, 1800, she was close to the port of Amsterdam when Captain Watkins was surprised to see a boat pulling towards the frigate from the shore. He was even more surprised when a deputation of Dutchmen who, "tired out with the enormities of the band of 1,500 Republican ruffians who were in possession of the west part of the island," claimed the protection of Britain. Two days later Governor Johan Rudolph Lausser signed the capitulation, surrendering the island to Britain. Thus Captain Watkins came into the possession of an island—and a couple of Hermiones.

When Johnson went on board the *Néréide* he took with him a letter signed by Mr. B. H. Phillips, of the firm of Bogle and Jopp (who were, among other things, agents for the sale of slaves) and addressed to the Admiralty. In it Mr. Phillips, who was the American Consul, recommended "to your kindness and protection an unfortunate young man." It had always been Johnson's wish, the letter said, "to give himself up, and while with me as [has] conducted himself not only to please, but to gain my full confidence. We therefore pray you will show him countenance [*sic*] and we shall be very grateful for any service to him."

The first prosecution witness at the trial was Lieutenant Southcott, who said he could not remember seeing Johnson at the time of the mutiny, but he saw Poulson several times. Since Poulson was a Dane, a translator was sworn in to help him, and Poulson asked Southcott: "What was my character in the ship?"

Southcott was frank in his reply: "He had a very good one before the mutiny—all the best men were the principals of the mutineers."

Earlier Southcott had been asked if either of the two accused men had expressed to him any contrition. "No, they did not," he said, "but Poulson, during the passage (I cannot say what day) when a great many of the mutineers were in the cabin and were boasting of what they had done in the murder of their officers, said that he assisted in killing the Captain and heaving him overboard, and that at the time he called out for his bargemen, and asked if everyone was against him, he [Poulson] said 'Here are your bargemen, what do you want with them, you bugger?' "

"Are you sure that [Poulson] was the wretch who made use of that infernal expression?"—"Yes."

When Johnson was called on to make his defence, he called the former master of the *Néréide*, Mr. Samuel Raven, to try to prove that he had surrendered at Curaçao.

"Did I give myself up to Captain Watkins?" he asked.

"Not to my knowledge," was Raven's uncompromising reply.

"Did I live as clerk to the American Consul?" Johnson asked. "Yes," said Raven.

The court then asked Raven: "How long had the ship been lying at Curaçao before Johnson came on board?"—"We were lying off the harbour six or seven days. He was sent on board by the officer of Marines of the *Néréide*."

The court then asked him about Poulson. "After we had been in quiet possession of the island he was sent on board by Governor Lawsor [Lausser], out of the *Syren* Dutch frigate . . ."

Johnson then made his written defence, and handed in the letter from Mr. Phillips. His delay in reporting to the *Néréide* was because as cashier at the American Consul's house he "had a great charge of cash," he said: he was obliged to make up his accounts and therefore could not give himself up for several days.

Poulson, the other accused man, had nothing to say in his own defence, and the court announced their verdict: the Dane was guilty of both the charges—murdering or helping to murder the officers and delivering the ship to the enemy. Johnson was not guilty on the first count, but he had helped take the ship into La Guaira and deliver her up to the enemy. Both men were sentenced to be hanged, but the court wrote to the Admiralty recommending Johnson to mercy. He was pardoned, but Poulson was executed on board the *Puissant.*

John Pearce, the marine whom Mr. Southcott had seen heaving his regimentals over the side shortly after the mutiny, was caught on board a ship at Malta and sent home for trial. This took place on board the *Gladiator* at Portsmouth in August 1801, and among the officers trying him was Captain Pigot's old friend, Captain Robert Otway, formerly of the *Ceres.*

The most important of the prosecution witnesses was Pearce's former superior, Sergeant Plaice, who told the court that "I saw him in the gunroom at the time our officer [Lieutenant McIntosh] was killed." He had no great opinion of Pearce: after the mutiny he "saw him about the decks frequently and very cheerful—he was a slothful man generally. I had a great deal of trouble with him in the *Tartar* frigate before."

"Did you see him at La Guaira?" the court asked.

"Yes," said Plaice, "he entered into the Spanish service, into the train of artillery: I saw him in their dress . . ."

Steward Jones noticed him drinking liquor with some other marines, and added, with truth: "He seemed full of spirits and seemed to rejoice at what had happened." Pearce was sentenced to death and was hanged on August 31, the last Hermione to be caught in the year 1801.

WE LEFT WILLIAM BOWER, the seaman from Chesterfield, serving on board an American ship which called in at Charleston, where Bower—who had changed his name to William Miller— found posters stuck up in the port and notices in the newspapers offering rewards of a thousand dollars for anyone causing the arrest of a mutineer from the *Hermione.*

The captain of the American ship knew that Bower was a former Hermione—indeed, Bower said later, it was the captain that "showed him the paper." However, the American had no intention of claiming the reward. Bower asked him what he should do— whether to give himself up to the British Consul or not. "He said I had better not; that it was so horrid an act none of us would be forgiven," and he assured Bower he would say nothing.

The American was as good as his word, and Bower continued to serve in the ship more than two years. Then, in the winter of 1801, she loaded a cargo for the Mediterranean, crossed the Atlantic, and called at Malta. While she was at anchor a lieutenant at the head of a press-gang from H.M.S. *Minerva* came on board looking for men. Bower was one of those who had no protection, and a short while afterwards he was being "read in" on board the frigate, safe under his assumed name of William Miller.

So once again Bower was in the Royal Navy and, being a good seaman, he was soon made one of the captain's bargemen. This subsequently proved unfortunate for him because within a few weeks the *Minerva* received orders to return to Portsmouth. While she was at anchor there in January 1802, four and a half years after the mutiny, Bower was kept busy as one of the bargemen, since the captain frequently wanted to go ashore.

The result was described in a letter by Lieutenant William Cathcart, of the *Medusa*, writing to his father, Lord Cathcart, on January 14, 1802: "A seaman belonging to the *Minerva*'s barge was arrested by one of the King's Evidence (on shore for the purpose) and proved to be one of the mutineers of the *Hermione*." He went on to describe how one of the group of loyal former Hermiones, who were always at Portsmouth for the purpose, spotted Bower in the street.

The Admiralty's order for Bower's trial told Vice-Admiral Sir Andrew Mitchell to assemble a court-martial "as soon after the arrival of the evidence at Spithead as conveniently may be." The "evidence" causing the delay was Lieutenant Southcott, now serving in the sloop *Renard*. A few days before Bower was spotted in Portsmouth, Southcott was at sea in the sloop and facing some very bad weather—a contemporary report dated Plymouth, January 3, spoke of snow and said, "Came in from Bantry Bay [Ireland] the *Renard*, of 24 guns, Captain Spicer. She experienced dreadful gales of wind, and shipped several heavy seas."

The *Renard* was sent to Portsmouth, where she arrived on January 12. At the trial, held a month later, Lieutenant Southcott gave his usual evidence about the mutiny and said of Bower that "at the time he seemed to be rejoiced at what had happened, and was dancing, singing and drinking with the rest."

Steward Jones told the court that after the mutiny Bower "appeared to be more rejoiced than sorry at what had happened." Bower had previously been on the sick-list, but after the mutiny appeared to be perfectly fit. Sergeant Plaice corroborated this—"I did not consider him to be a sick man but one aiding and assisting the navigating the ship. Several who were said to be sick that night, over whom I had a sentry, were active in the mutiny." Bower, found guilty of having helped carry the ship to La Guaira and handing her over to the Spanish, was hanged.

TOWARDS THE END of March 1802, after months of negotiation, Britain and France finally signed the Treaty of Amiens which had brought the war—which had started in 1793—to a halt. The realists—surprisingly few in Britain, unfortunately—knew the Treaty would only give each side a breathing space before war inevitably began once again. Both sides had reached a stalemate because although Britain was supreme at sea (thanks to the Battle of Cape St. Vincent, followed by Nelson's victories at the Nile and at Copenhagen), France was supreme on the Continent. Neither side could make a challenge on the other's battleground—for the time being.

Inevitably the protracted negotiations with Napoleon and the final Treaty had their effect on the fate of some of the Hermiones: we have seen for example that the *Minerva* had returned to England from the Mediterranean, with the result that William Bower was caught and hanged. Many other ships were also brought home, often to be paid off and laid up. But peace did not mean that the Royal Navy slackened its watch. . . .

With the Bower court-martial over, the *Renard* sailed from Portsmouth on March 7 with Lieutenant Southcott on board, bound for Plymouth, and by chance three days later the 16-gun sloop *Bittern* arrived at Portsmouth under the command of Captain Edward Kittoe. The *Bittern* had been in the West Indies for more than three years. One of the seamen serving in the ship was a certain Thomas Williams, who had been on board for more than four years. Captain Kittoe had long since been impressed by Williams's ability and smartness, with the result that he had been made one of the bargemen. When the *Bittern* anchored at Portsmouth on the 10th, Williams was naturally one of the men who rowed Captain Kittoe to the shore so that he could report to the port admiral.

Captain Kittoe went on shore several times after that—there were always plenty of appointments, both social and service, to occupy his time; and since Britain was at peace and seamen were plentiful, his bargemen were often allowed to go into the town for short periods while waiting for the captain to finish his business.

On March 22, while Captain Kittoe was busy on shore and the bargemen were enjoying a brief hour or two in the town, Thomas Williams went for a walk. Portsmouth was its usual bustling self: ships' officers hurried to and fro; on most corners there was at least one comely Poll or Bess with her eye on the sailor who had just been paid off, or who still had a few shillings left in his pocket despite the earlier attentions of her sisters-in-trade.

Williams was just walking through the Point Gates when someone tapped him on the shoulder and spoke to him. The man was John Jones, Captain Pigot's former steward in the *Hermione*, and he asked:

"Isn't your name David Forester?"

"No," said the *Bittern*'s bargeman.

"Yes, but it was in the *Hermione!*" declared Jones, and seized him. Four and a half years had passed since Forester had come out of Captain Pigot's cabin, tapped Jones on the shoulder and said: "I have just launched your bloody master overboard."

The seaman then admitted that he was indeed David Forester, and Jones took him to the main guard house, at the Dockyard, where he was put in irons. A message was sent to the commander-in-chief, who ordered Rear-Admiral John Holloway to question the man.

A contemporary description of this interview said that while Forester was in the guard house, "Admiral Holloway and several other officers went to interrogate him concerning the mutiny, when he confessed himself to have been the person who killed, and afterwards threw Captain Pigot overboard: it appears that in the scuffle he was wounded in the foot by the Captain, who defended himself with his dirk.

"Admiral Holloway asked him if he had been easy in his conscience since the transaction. He replied, perfectly so, as he was ordered to do it by the Captain of the Forecastle, and that if he had not done it, he should have been killed himself.

"On this the Admiral observed, 'Suppose I was to order you to kill one of those soldiers (who were standing near), would you do it?' He said, 'Yes, if I thought you would kill me if I did not' "

Word of Forester's arrest was at once sent to the Admiralty in

London, but since Lieutenant Southcott had recently returned to Plymouth in the *Renard*, the court-martial would have to wait until he could be brought back to Portsmouth. Finally on March 30, while the peace treaty between France and Britain was being ratified by His Majesty and by the First Consul, David Forester faced his trial on board the *Gladiator*.

There were three witnesses for the prosecution, Lieutenant Southcott, Steward John Jones and James Perrett. The evidence they gave was brief and utterly damning. ". . . Soon after the mutiny commenced I saw him before my cabin door with arms in his hands: he was calling to take the officers out to put them to death," said Southcott. "He was as active in the mutiny as any in the ship. After that I saw him in the Captain's cabin . . . They were boasting of what horrid deeds they had done in murdering the officers, and the prisoner said that he had assisted in murdering Captain Pigot; that he had cut him three or four times, that he had assisted in throwing him out of the stern window; that Captain Pigot spoke to him and said, 'Forester, are you against me too?' He said, 'Yes, you bugger.' He was also very active in carrying the ship to La Guaira."

John Jones told the court that "on the night of the mutiny, I was tying the sentinel at the cabin door's head, which had been cut . . . David Forester, the prisoner, came out of the cabin with a cutlass or tomahawk in his hand—I cannot be positive which. He tapped me on the shoulder and said, 'I have just launched your bloody master overboard.' "

Jones described how Forester said, "The bugger—I gave him his death wound, I think, before he went out of the window." Later he saw Forester, when the second lieutenant or the lieutenant of marines was being dragged up the ladder, "chop at him several times with a cutlass or tomahawk; there were ten or a dozen round him chopping at him, and when the prisoner could not chop at him he stabbed him . . ."

Forester had little to say in his defence and he was sentenced to death. He was hanged on board the *Gladiator* on April 1, and a contemporary account said that "just before he was launched into eternity, he made the following confession: that he went into the cabin and forced Captain Pigot overboard through the port, while he was alive. He then got on the quarterdeck, and found the First [Third] Lieutenant begging for his life, saying he had a wife and three children totally depending upon him for support: he took hold of him and assisted in heaving him overboard, and declared he did not think the people would have taken his life had he first not took hold of him. A cry was then heard through the ship that Lieutenant Douglas could not be found; he took a lanthorn and candle and went into the gunroom and found the Lieutenant under the Marine Officer's cabin [sic]; he then called the rest of the people, when they dragged him on deck and threw him overboard. He next caught hold of Mr Smith, Midshipman, a scuffle ensued, and finding him likely to get away, he struck him with his tomahawk and threw him overboard. The general cry next was for putting all the officers to death, that they might not appear as evidence against them; he seized on the Captain's Clerk [Manning] who was immediately put to death. These, he said, were the whole of his actions during the murdering of the officers. He called God to witness, hoped He would forgive him, and said his mind was easy after making the above confession."

OCCASIONALLY the Royal Navy arrested the wrong man on suspicion that he was a former Hermione. Vice-Admiral Thomas Pasley—the same officer who, as a captain, had taken Vice-Admiral Hugh Pigot and his young son Hugh out to the West Indies in 1782—wrote to the Admiralty from Plymouth in May 1800 about one of them.

When the frigate *Stag* stopped the brig *Hope* and sent a boarding party over to press some seamen, the lieutenant in charge brought back a man who gave his name as Frederick Stirke and who claimed he was born in Ostend. But as he had what appeared to be an Irish accent, the *Stag*'s commanding officer, Captain Robert Winthrop, was suspicious and questioned him closely.

Captain Winthrop wrote that Stirke, "on his first examination, says he was born at Ostend, again says he was born at Oldenburgh, and lastly at Flushing. On being asked how he came to speak English, said he belonged to a merchant ship called the *Hermione*, was taken by the *St Amonisa* [sic] and carried into Barbados, where he was imprisoned for nine months.

"On being asked if it was not the *Hermione* frigate that he belonged to, he appeared very much confused and said he could not help the misfortune that happened [to] her, then said he was a prisoner at Barbados in the year 1783, went passenger in the *Hermione* to Plymouth, and there imprisoned."

Apart from the way he contradicted himself, Stirke was hardly helping his own case by giving such facts: the frigate *Hermione*, for instance, did not make her first voyage until 1783. However, Admiral Pasley made inquiries among the ships at Plymouth—where he was the Port Admiral—and found that two lieutenants had served in the *Hermione* until September 1796. They were ordered to see if they recognized Stirke, and they reported that at the time they were in the *Hermione* "no such man was on board." Stirke appears to have been a man who was mentally unbalanced.

Later in the same year in the Mediterranean there was another and more curious case. In Naples on October 2, two men—Cornelius Corton (or Coston), the cook on board the American ship *Hero,* and Edward Greenfield, a seaman from the British merchantman *Princess Mary*—called on the British Consul-General, Mr. Charles Locke, with stories which they later repeated in depositions.

Corton told Mr. Locke that while he was serving on board the American schooner *Max Meon* in Cuban waters, he saw the *Hermione* brought into a Cuban port by the mutineers "who, after disposing of her to the Spaniards, then came on shore." That much was a lie, but the rest of the story had a percentage of truth in it.

Among the men, said Corton, he saw a certain Benjamin Brewster, who later left Cuba for Philadelphia. More than two years later, he continued, he met Brewster again when, joining the *Hero* as cook, he found that Brewster was the second mate, and had changed his first name from Benjamin to William. Corton said he never gave the slightest hint to Brewster that he recognized him "because he was afraid of being ill-used, [Brewster] being a very violent man."

He noticed that the second mate had two "B's" tattooed on his arm, and that when he remarked that they were not Brewster's initials, the man "smiled and answered that although his real name was Benjamin, yet he chose go to by the name of William."

Corton declared that Brewster "has on more than one occasion confessed and bragged that he had been one of the mutineers on board His said Majesty's Ship *Hermione* when she was taken by the rebellious crew, and that he had with another man knocked down the Boatswain . . . and thrown him overboard; that while he was swimming upon the waves they called upon him to whistle and ride and be damned.''

The other seaman, Greenfield, said in his deposition that he had been on board the *Hero* one day and was "in discourse with one Isaac Vanblarigan who, at that very time, was disputing with the mate of the ship, Mr Benjamin Brewster, when several words passed between them." Vanblarigan turned to Greenfield and, touching him on the shoulder, said, "Don't mind what that damned rascal says . . . for he is one of the *Bloody Hermiones.*"

These two depositions were quite enough for the Consul-General who had Brewster seized and for good measure his main accuser, Corton, as well and sent them both on board a British warship in the Bay with a note to the captain asking him to take them in custody.

Benjamin Brewster had in his possession the protection mentioned earlier, claiming that he was an American citizen, and which had been issued on February 15, 1800. Of course, Brewster was never brought to trial. He may well have boasted that he had been a mutineer, without realizing the danger in which he placed himself, because he had once served in the *Hermione*.

BY OCTOBER 1806 the *Hermione* mutiny had been long forgotten by the British public: it had taken place nine years earlier, and since then Britain had faced many perils, lost many battles, and won many victories. Lord Nelson had been dead more than a year and his third and last great victory at Trafalgar had finally given Britain a mastery at sea which was to last more than a hundred years.

In the nine years since the mutiny, thirty-two of the *Hermione*'s crew—excluding those who gave themselves up at La Guaira as prisoners of war—had been brought to trial, but several ringleaders were still free—Thomas Jay, Lawrence Cronin, William Turner, Robert McReady, John Smith and James Bell among them. Some had undoubtedly gone to America and settled down in a new life on shore. Others, including Cronin, had stayed in Caracas and, in all probability, married Spanish girls.

Yet despite the passage of time, the Royal Navy had not forgotten them, although several had felt themselves safe—David Forester, it will be remembered, had strode throught the Point Gates at Portsmouth five years after the mutiny little thinking he would ever meet the much-despised Steward Jones. Another man who probably thought himself safe after nearly ten years was James Hayes, who had been the doctor's servant in the *Hermione,* and angry at having been caught stealing from him, had helped murder his master. At the time Hayes had been fourteen years old; but in October 1806, at the age of twenty-three, and still using his alias, Thomas Wood, he found himself a prisoner and about to be court-martialled on board the *Salvador del Mundo* at Plymouth. It has been impossible, at this stage, to discover how Hayes was caught; but the minutes of the trial show that among the captains forming the court were Pigot's friend, Robert Otway and two others who had served with Pigot and later helped to try several other mutineers, Ross Donelly and John Loring.

By this time all the men who had been kept at Portsmouth, always watching in case they saw a mutineer in the street, and always available as witnesses, had been dispersed; but it was easy to trace Lieutenant Southcott who was, in this case, the person in the best position to give evidence about Hayes, since the youth's activities had taken place outside Southcott's cabin door. His testimony was damning. Hayes "appeared very active and boasted of having been the occasion of putting his master to death. And the rest of the mutineers said that the prisoner was the great cause of the Surgeon being put to death . . . Previous to the mutiny he had broke [*sic* open a trunk or some article of his master's property and had taken something from his master, and was punished for it. That was the occasion of his persuading the people to put his master to death—to be revenged, as he called it."

When Hayes was called on for his defence, he handed the Judge-Advocate a written statement and asked him to read it.

"Mr President and gentleman of the honourable court," the statement began. "At the time when this detestable and horrid mutiny took place . . . I was a boy in my fourteenth year, with all the disadvantages of education and moral example. Necessity drove me to sea in my ninth year. Drove by the torrent of mutiny I took the oath administered to me on the occasion. The examples of death which were before my eyes drove me for shelter amongst the mutineers, dreading a similar fate with those who fell, if I sided with, [*sic*] or showed the smallest inclination to mercy.

"If any amongst the many who have been tried for the same

offence have not had mercy, tho' guided by experience and having arrived at the age of maturity, who were abettors or actors at that dreadful time, most humbly and contritely let me solicit your humanity on a youth in his fourteenth year at the time, who has not enjoyed one hour's repose of mind from jeopardy and compunction, which has led to the present trial."

The court—which included Captain Richard King who, commanding the *Achille* at Trafalgar, had seen fifty-nine of his men wounded and thirteen more killed in the battle—decided Hayes deserved no mercy, and he was sentenced to death. We can close the story of the trials—for Hayes was the last of the Hermiones ever to be brought to trial—with an extract from a contemporary description of his execution:

"On Friday, October 17, a signal was fired on board the *Salvador del Mundo,* flagship in the Hamoaze, and the yellow flag hoisted as a signal for an execution. Woods [i.e., Hayes], the *Hermione*'s mutineer, after praying some time in his berth with the chaplain of the ship, at eleven o'clock was led forth for execution along the gangway, to a platform erected on the fo'c'sle. He persisted in his innocence of the crime for which he was going to suffer, but said he deserved death for his other crimes, which were numerous. He appeared very penitent, and declared he died in peace with all mankind."

Hayes's execution meant that thirty-three Hermiones had been brought to trial, and he was the twenty-fourth to be executed. The way the men had been caught has made a series of strange and dramatic episodes; yet the most dramatic part of the *Hermione*'s story provides the final chapters of this narrative.

XXVII

The Surprise

—⁓—

THE MASS of documents and the evidence of the eyewitnesses, whether given for the prosecution or the defence, can leave little doubt at this stage that the main reason for the mutiny in the *Hermione* was the unrestrained and cruel behaviour of her captain. Any attempt to blame Irish revolutionaries or English malcontents can only be made by apologists who are unable to accept that cruel officers existed and fail to realize that we are dealing with the worst mutiny in a ship of the Royal Navy.

There is on qualification: it was unfortunate for Pigot that among the *Hermione's* crew there were men—like Nash, Elliott and Farrel—who had served for years without giving the slightest trouble but who were sufficiently spirited and ruthless when driven too far to plan a mutiny, and others—like Montell, Forester and Redman—who were good seamen but when subjected to the laws of the jungle became cold-blooded killers. Had there not been this element in the crew, and had the officers been more alert in the preceding days and made of sterner stuff, then the actual mutiny might have been avoided. There is no doubt the officers with the possible exception of Southcott, Casey and Foreshaw, do not emerge with much credit, although Pigot's courage was never in question.

However, the shameful part of the *Hermione*'s story has now been told: the extraordinary and stirring finale will show that other young frigate captains had the daring of a Nelson or a Pellew; that while some seamen were prepared to murder their officers in an orgy of senseless slaughter, others cheerfully followed their captain to fight against odds of more than seven to one—and win.

The episode about to be described is little known, yet it is among the bravest, best-planned and most successful operations in British naval history. There were plenty of actions of a similar nature during the war against Revolutionary France. Most were gallant; few were so completely successful; none provided such vindication for the Royal Navy and its officers and men.

BY AN UNFORTUNATE COINCIDENCE the third young frigate captain to play an important role in the brief history of the *Hermione* was a harsh man, but one can forgive him much for his bravery and leadership.

In the autumn of 1799—at the time that Thomas Nash was being tried at Port Royal after being extradited from the United States— Edward Hamilton was twenty-seven years old. He was three years and 152 places lower on the post list than Wilkinson, and commanding the 28-gun *Surprise*. He came from a naval family—his father had been a captain in the Navy, receiving a baronetcy for his services, and the title had since passed to Edward's elder brother, who was commanding the *Melpomene*.

There is a frank description of Hamilton by Admiral George Vernon Jackson who, recording in the calm of his eighties the period when he served as a young midshipman in the *Trent* under Hamilton, wrote of the ship that "as regards discipline and the general efficiency of her company, she was equal, if not superior, to any other frigate afloat; but these qualities had all been promoted at no small sacrifice of humanity.

"No sailor was allowed to walk from one place to another on deck, and woe betide the unfortunate fellow who halted in his run aloft, unless expressly bidden to do so. . . . The 'cat' was incessantly at work," continued Admiral Jackson. "The man who approached at walk when called by a midshipman, instead of running for his life, the penalty he paid for this offence was a 'starting' at the hands of the boatswain's mate."

The Admiral added, "I should be loath to say what my opinion of Sir Edward Hamilton might have become had I stopped much longer in the *Trent*. As each day passed, so did I conceive new terrors of this man. A more uncompromising disciplinarian did not exist, or one less scrupulous in exacting the due fulfilment of his orders, whatever they were." Hamilton was "one of those men who allow nothing to escape them. He could see through a plank a little farther than most of his fellow-creatures, and seeing, would follow up his observations with a pertinacity that defied interruption."

Captain Hamilton had arrived in the West Indies in October 1798, thirteen months after the *Hermione* mutiny, in command of the *Surprise*. The next thirteen months provided him with a considerable amount of prize money and established him as one of Sir Hyde Parker's favourite young captains, because in that period he captured, sank or burned more than eighty enemy ships.

At Port Royal, Jamaica, on Thursday, September 17, 1799, a few days short of two years after the mutiny, Sir Hyde Parker wrote a significant entry in his journal:

> Strong breezes and squally. Ordered Captn Hamilton to proceed with the *Surprise* and cruise between the Aruba [*sic*] and Cape St Roman (taking care to prevent his station being known at Curaçao) and use his utmost endeavours to capture the *Hermione* frigate loading at Porto Cavallo [Puerto Cabello] and intended to sail early in October for the Havana.

When Hamilton received these orders he went to Sir Hyde, according to one usually reliable source (although there is no other supporting documentary evidence) and proposed that he should send in boarding parties to cut out the *Hermione,* instead of capturing her on the high seas. For this purpose he requested an extra twenty seamen and another launch to carry them, but Sir Hyde "thought the service too desperate and refused the request."

During the previous few days the *Surprise* had been taking on stores in preparation for what would probably be a long cruise, and on September 18, just before the flagship hoisted the *Surprise*'s number and the signal for a lieutenant, another 485 pounds of fresh beef was brought on board. More casks of water were ferried out in the launch as the lieutenant collected Captain Hamilton's written orders from Sir Hyde.

Next morning the frigate sailed and as the pilot took her from the fairway out through the reefs scattered across the entrance to the harbour, the crew could see Gallows Point, where from the gibbets six skeletons hung in chains, the mortal remains of John Coe, Adam Lynham, Charlton, Croaker, Ladson and, put up only a month earlier, Thomas Nash. By 7 A.M. the pilot had left and the frigate steered south-eastwards, leaving the Blue Mountains on her port quarter: she would be more than fifty miles out to sea before she put the great range below the horizon. On board there was the usual day-to-day routine: a seaman, John Mitchell, was given a dozen lashes for being dirty; Mr. Thomas Made, the acting master, noted in his log at noon the ship's course, her latitude, and the fact that they had $51^2/_3$ tons of water left.

Captain Hamilton planned to make a landfall on the Spanish Main at the Bay of Honda, 300 miles west of his patrol area. He would then follow the coast as it trended north-eastwards, thus putting himself in a good position to capture any Spanish merchantmen trading between local ports, and also to intercept the *Hermione* if she had already sailed from Puerto Cabello on her long voyage to Cuba.

The *Surprise* arrived off the Spanish Main a few miles west of the Bay of Honda on October 1, eleven days out from Port Royal and, shortly after she had turned north-eastwards to follow the coast, her lookouts spotted a schooner at anchor in a large, shallow and almost land-locked lagoon called El Portete. The water was not deep enough for the frigate so Hamilton sent in two cutters and the gig to cut her out.

Within the hour they were back and by mid-afternoon the frigate was hoisting in the three boats again while the schooner (the *Nancy* of twenty-five tons, French and loaded with a cargo of coffee) was hove-to nearby, being inspected by the frigate's carpenter to see if she had been damaged in running aground. He reported she was quite seaworthy, and within the hour she was heading for Port Royal with a prize crew of a midshipman and a few seamen on board.

The *Surprise* spent the next few days making her way along the coast under easy sail. On Sunday, October 13, the crew were mustered; finally on Monday at noon the frigate arrived at the western end of the fifteen-mile-wide channel she had been ordered to patrol. On the larboard bow the south-western tip of the island of Aruba was in sight, looking like a series of low hummocks, while to starboard the jagged ridge of hills forming the mainland came to an abrupt stop at Cape San Roman. Here, if Sir Hyde's intelligence report had been correct, they would intercept the *Hermione*. They could afford to wait, for the *Surprise* still had thirty-six tons of water remaining in her casks: she had used sixteen tons in twenty days, so there was enough on board to last for at least another forty days, while watering from the shore, as demonstrated earlier by the *Hermione* and *Diligence*, presented no difficulties.

The island of Aruba belonged to the Dutch: it is small and lies more than forty miles to the westward of the larger island of Curaçao, also Dutch owned and where (for this was before Governor Lausser had handed it over to the British frigate *Néréide*) the young Hermione William Johnson was working as a clerk to the American Consul.

Captain Hamilton, paying scant attention to Sir Hyde's instructions that he was to take care "to prevent his station being known at Curaçao," steered for Aruba, and on Monday, October 14, his lookouts reported that a sizeable schooner was at anchor in the Roads of Port Caballos, the main village on the island. Hamilton decided she would make a good prize and gave orders that as soon as darkness fell the *Surprise* would tack close in to the Roads and then send in the boats to cut her out.

By 11.30 P.M. they were back alongside and the schooner was hove-to nearby with a prize crew on board. She was an 80-ton Dutch vessel, the *Lame Duck*, armed with ten guns and loaded with a cargo of what Captain Hamilton listed as "sundries." Her capture had not, however, been a bloodless victory—Lieutenant John Busey, the frigate's acting first lieutenant, who had led the expedition, had been very badly wounded. He was carried below for the surgeon, Mr. John M'Mullen, to tend him; but at midnight, despite all that M'Mullen could do, he died.

Next day, Tuesday, October 15, the *Surprise* began the important part of her task of patrolling the wide channel. It was more difficult than it seemed, because Hamilton had a strong west-going current to contend with. The *Hermione* on leaving Puerto Cabello, which was to the eastwards, could make a very fast passage through the channel with a fair wind and the current under her, and she would be hard to spot at night. And since he had cut out the schooner, if he was to carry out the second part of his orders—not to allow the Dutch at Curaçao to know his station—Hamilton now had to ensure that no craft knowing the *Surprise*'s position left Aruba bound for Curaçao, which was forty-three miles to the eastwards. If the Spanish received the slightest hint that there was a British warship in the channel, there was nothing to stop the *Hermione* avoiding it by passing north of Aruba—the extra distance involved going north of the island made no difference since it was more than two thousand miles from Puerto Cabello to Havana in Cuba.

The rest of the week passed without incident: the *Surprise* tacked back and forth across the channel. On Sunday she captured a 10-ton Spanish schooner, *La Manuela,* which had a crew of six men and a cargo of plantains. Neither cargo nor craft had any value, so the men were taken off and *La Manuela* was sunk.

Early on Monday, when the *Surprise* had been in the area a week, Hamilton was either becoming impatient or afraid the *Hermione* had passed north of Aruba. He therefore decided to make for Puerto Cabello to find out if she was still there. In the back of his mind, no doubt, was another plan for capturing her. The *Surprise* had been at sea for twenty-seven days. It has been suggested that she was getting short of water and supplies, and this was the reason for Hamilton steering for Puerto Cabello. However, her log shows that on Monday she had more than thirty tons remaining of the fifty-two tons she had taken on board at Port Royal. She could stay at sea without watering for at least another month.

By sunset Puerto Cabello was twelve to fifteen miles away to the south-east, and Hamilton tacked ship. For the moment he did not want to approach any closer: from his present position he could catch any vessel leaving the port, unless she was lucky enough to find a very favourable slant of wind. This became even more important next day when Mr. Made, the master, noted in his log that at noon there were "light airs inclinable to calm." By midnight—and for the next seven hours—he was reporting "Calm, [ship's] head all round the compass."

Daylight on Wednesday, October 23, soon brought hails from the lookouts: there was a sail to the south-west, heading for Puerto Cabello, and apparently she had her own private slant of wind. This was the one thing that Hamilton had feared—she was bound to spot the *Surprise* and warn the Spanish.

With the *Surprise* wallowing in a slight swell, her sails hanging limp, there was only one way of intercepting the other vessel: "At 6 sent the boats manned and armed after her," said the log. It would be a long row, but there was no heat in the sun yet, and apart from the swell waves, which were long and low, the sea was calm.

An hour later, when the boats were still just in sight, like tiny beetles in the distance, the *Surprise's* lookouts spotted wind shadows on the water, coming from the south-west. The frigate's yards were hurriedly trimmed round to catch the first puffs and soon the sails gave a half-hearted shake, then another, and quickly the ship had way on—just enough to leave behind any rubbish thrown over the side by the cook's mate. The chase was now dead to windward and it took the frigate five hours of patient tacking to catch up with her boats, which were then called alongside and hoisted inboard. By that time, however, the wind had turned into a fresh breeze and the *Surprise* was soon up with the chase, from which a boarding party returned to report that she was a Danish schooner bound, as Wilkinson had suspected, to Puerto Cabello from Curaçao. Having given that much information, and being almost within sight of his destination, the Danish skipper was disinclined to obey Captain Hamilton's request for him to steer away from Puerto Cabello for the time being, and he only obliged after, as Mr. Made noted in the log, the *Surprise* "fired a shot to make her tack from the land."

However, Denmark was neutral, and there was little that Hamilton could do to prevent her going into port if she wished. The shot across the bow might well put off her captain for twenty-four hours, but after that . . .

IN PUERTO CABELLO, His Most Christian Majesty's frigate *Santa Cecilia*, the subject of Captain Hamilton's thoughts, was ready to sail. The long squabble between the Captain-General and the Intendant had not, of course, been resolved—Leone was awaiting a reply to his protest to Admiral Langara that the Captain-General's critical report had been wrong.

In the meantime the Spanish admiral commanding the squadron at Havana, Cuba, had given orders for the *Santa Cecilia* to be prepared for sea. The intelligence report which had reached Sir Hyde

Parker several weeks earlier had been correct but not complete. The Spanish authorities intended that she should join a squadron being formed with the idea of attacking British convoys, which were known to be lightly escorted. The squadron was to consist of the 64-gun *Asia*, under the command of Don Francisco Montes (who was to be captured in the *San Rafael* by Sir Robert Calder's squadron three months before Trafalgar), the 44-gun *Amfitrite* under Diego Villagomez and the 16-gun corvette *El Galgo* under Jose de Arias. (Two weeks later this squadron, without the *Santa Cecilia*, attacked a British convoy in the Mona Passage. The escort of two British frigates drove off the considerably more powerful *Asia* and *Amfitrite*, and captured *El Galgo*. The enemy "appeared very undertermined," one of the frigate captains reported later to Sir Hyde Parker.)

As a British ship, the *Santa Cecilia* had been armed with twenty-six 12-pounders on the maindeck, with four 6-pounders on the quarterdeck and two more on the fo'c'sle, plus eight carronades. Her official complement had been 220, although we have seen that in practice it was rarely more than 170. However, as she prepared to sail for Havana under the command of Don Ramon de Eschales y Gaztelu, she had a complement of 392—more than double the number of men Pigot ever had—consisting of 321 officers and seamen, reinforced by 56 infantrymen and 15 artillerymen. And the frigate was at last in an excellent condition thanks to the work of the Spanish shipwrights at Puerto Cabello, who had carried out the necessary repairs: new gangways had been laid on either side; new bulwarks had been built on; various planks in the hull and decks had been replaced, as well as beams and knees. A new capstan had been fitted forward—the frigate originally had only one, which was aft on the quarterdeck—and she had a new rudder. Any captain would be pleased with her outfit of sails: only two of her outfit of twenty-six were half-worn: the rest were either new or only a third worn. The Spanish had also increased her armament and rated her a 44-gun ship.

The *Surprise*, by comparison, was much smaller: her official complement was 200, but she had only 180 men on board. The *Santa Cecilia*'s crew outnumbered hers by more than two to one. Like the *Santa Cecilia*, she had been built under a different flag from the one she now flew, having been captured from the French and commissioned by the Royal Navy as a 28-gun frigate.

CAPTAIN HAMILTON had only a few hours in which to make up his mind what his next move was to be: with the Danish ship in the offing and waiting to dart into Puerto Cabello, and more neutral ships likely to arrive at any moment, there were only two plans worth considering. The *Hermione* was still in Puerto Cabello—that much was certain, since his lookouts peering over the curvature of the earth from the mastheads had been able to see her masts. So he could either return to the Aruba–Cape San Roman area and continue his patrol, or he could take some action at Puerto Cabello.

Hamilton does not appear to have even considered resuming his patrol; but it was too late to do anything on Wednesday night, after he had forced the Danish ship to tack offshore. He seems to have wasted little time in making his plan, which was devastatingly simple and on the face of it so daring as to be impossible. If he failed he would almost certainly be court-martialled (providing he survived to face a trial) since it meant disregarding, if not actually disobeying, Sir Hyde's orders. if he succeeded—well, he would probably get a knighthood.

Hamilton did not discuss his plan with his officers, and that night, as the frigate wallowed in a light wind, barely making a knot through the water, Hamilton worked in his cabin with the watch and quarter-bills—which listed the name and various tasks of every man in the ship for each evolution, whether sailing or fighting—and then wrote out six different sets of instructions.

Dawn on Thursday, October 14, brought only cloudy weather and very little more breeze. For Hamilton's purpose the cloud was welcome, but he wanted more wind. At noon Puerto Cabello lay to the south-west. There were still twenty-eight tons of fresh water remaining below in the hold, and the crew had already filled the emptied casks with seawater because, stowed low down in the ship, they acted as ballast.

Captain Hamilton finally decided that any further delay was dangerous: at the moment the Spanish at Puerto Cabello were almost certainly unaware that the *Surprise* was waiting just over the horizon, but there were many neutral ships around who could easily raise the alarm. The plan to deal with the *Hermione* depended, like all good plans, on surprise, and would therefore be carried out that evening.

"I turned the hands up to acquaint the officers and ship's company of my intentions to lead them to the attack," he wrote.

According to one source, he began by reminding the men of the frequent and successful enterprises they had undertaken together, and then declared: "I find it useless to wait any longer; we shall soon be obliged to leave the station, and that frigate will become the prize of some more fortunate ship than the *Surprise;* our only prospect of success is by cutting her out this night."

At this the men gave "three tremendous cheers." Hamilton is said to have added: "I shall lead you myself, and here are the orders for the six boats to be employed, with the names of the officers and men to be engaged in this service." The cheers and the shouts that they "would follow me to a man," Hamilton wrote later, "greatly increased my hopes, and I had little doubt of succeeding."

As the officers read out the names of the men and their boats, the excitement in the frigate increased. The disappointed men who had not been chosen to go are reputed to have offered cash to their more fortunate shipmates to change places.

Hamilton's confidence can only have been in his men: the task he had set himself in cutting out the *Hermione* was otherwise an almost hopeless one. He knew where she was moored—in an apparently impregnable position—and his boats could not carry more than one hundred seamen and marines. If there was no wind—or, even worse, a foul wind—at least half those men would have to stay in the boats and tow the *Hermione* out, leaving only fifty to board and capture the ship. . . .

Puerto Cabello harbour, formed by a large lagoon with its entrance on the west side, was bounded to the north—the seaward side—by sandy islands, with the eastern and southern sides merging into swampy cays of mangrove. The town stands on the south side of the entrance and the actual anchorage (at that time a small basin on the north side of the lagoon called Great Bay) was linked to the entrance by a half-mile-long channel which was too narrow to allow ships to tack. With a foul wind, they had to be towed in or out. The *Hermione* was moored with her stern towards the entrance and her starboard side facing the town.

The whole lagoon was well guarded: on the north side of the entrance stood St. Philip's Castle; to the south, beyond the town, was another large castle, with a third, Fort Brava, also covering the entrance. Hamilton had few illusions about the defences—"there are about two hundred pieces of cannon mounted on the batteries," he wrote.

His attack had to have two main aims: first, to achieve complete surprise—that alone would reduce the odds considerably, since his boarders might then have a sporting chance of overwhelming the Spaniards actually on deck; and secondly, he would have to get the *Hermione* under way as soon as possible—even though his men would probably still be fighting for possession of the ship. If there was no wind or it was foul, so that he had to tow her out with boats, then half a dozen out of the 200 Spanish guns sweeping the lagoon with round and grapeshot could rapidly reduce the boats to matchwood and, if the Spanish gunners were made of stern enough stuff to fire on their own countrymen, they could easily sink the frigate even before she reached the channel leading from the anchorage. Once clear of the entrance, however, Hamilton would be able to get help from the *Surprise.*

The written instructions he had given his officers were detailed right down to the names of the actual seamen and marines forming the crew of each boat. All the men were to wear blue or black clothing: no one was to carry anything white, which might show up in the darkness. The rendezvous for the boarders would be the *Hermione*'s quarterdeck; the pass word was "Britannia" and the answer "Ireland"—perhaps in deference to the fact that Hamilton's family originally came from Ireland, though his father had settled at Chilston in Kent.

The six boats were to be divided into two divisions, each of three boats. There were to be two alternative methods of attack—one to be used if the alarm was raised before they reached the *Hermione* and the ship strongly defended; the other in case they managed to get alongside without being spotted.

The first division (consisting of the launch, pinnace and jolly boat) would board from starboard, which was the town side, while the second division (the gig, and the two cutters, which were distinguished by their colours, one being red and the other black) would attack from the larboard side.

The pinnace, leading the expedition as well as the first division, would be commanded by Captain Hamilton, and with him would be the gunner, Mr. John Maxwell, a midshipman and sixteen seamen. They would all board the *Hermione* at the starboard gangway, and make straight for the quarterdeck, except for four men who would immediately climb aloft to loose the maintopsail.

The launch, commanded by Lieutenant William Wilson, the acting first lieutenant, with a midshipman and twenty-four men, would board over the *Hermione*'s starboard bow, but three men were to stay in the boat and cut the anchor cables. These were likely to be at least 17-inch rope (each anchor weighed nearly two tons) and Hamilton had already thought of the difficulty and confusion there would be if three men were crowded together, leaning over the side of the boat as they slashed away with axes: he had therefore ordered the carpenter to construct a small platform over the launch's stern and quarters on which the axe men could stand.

The jolly boat, under the carpenter, would carry ten men and get alongside on the starboard quarter. While three men with axes stayed behind to cut the stern cables, the rest were to board the *Hermione*. Two would go aloft immediately and loose the mizzentopsail.

The first boat in the second division would be commanded by, of all people, the surgeon, Mr. John M'Mullen, who had volunteered for the job. Since Hamilton was short of officers—the first lieutenant had of course died of his wounds after the attack on the schooner at Aruba—he gladly accepted. There would be sixteen other men in the gig, and they were to board over the larboard bow, sending four men aloft immediately to loose the foretopsail.

The black cutter, commanded by Lieutenant Robert Hamilton (no relation to the captain), with the marine lieutenant, Mr. de la Tour du Pin and sixteen men, most of them marines, would board at the larboard gangway and make for the quarterdeck. The red cutter, commanded by the boatswain, with sixteen men, would board over the larboard quarter.

That was the plan of attack if the alarm had been raised before the boats reached the frigate, because in that case everyone—except the axemen and topmen—who could wield a boarding pike, tomahawk or cutlass would be needed for actual fighting. However, if they reached the *Hermione* undetected, Hamilton knew that surprise would be a valuable ally and he would need fewer boarders. The most important task would be to get the ship under way at once—

either under sail if the wind served, or by using the boats to tow—and out of range of the shore batteries.

Therefore in his plan each boat had its normal crew, plus boarders and the necessary axemen and topmen. If the alarm had been raised, both normal crews and boarders—all but the axemen—would board; but if they really lived up to their ship's name and achieved surprise, only the boarders would do the fighting: the boat's crews would stay in their respective craft and take the *Hermione* in tow as soon as the axemen had cut the cables. For towing, each boat would be equipped with hook ropes (which were simply ropes six or eight fathoms long, each with a hook spliced into one end).

So much for the plans. On board the *Surprise* the boat commanders soon had their boarding parties and crews grouped round them, picking men for special tasks. Lieutenant Wilson chose three strong men to wield the axes to cut the bow cables, for instance, while the gunner picked four of the best topmen to loose the maintopsail.

Cutlasses and tomahawks were handed out; boarding pikes were taken down from the racks round the masts and issued. The carpenter produced three heavy axes for the launch men and three more for the jolly boat, and set his crew to work making the platforms. The grindstones were brought up from below and set spinning while the men crowded round, anxious to put a sharp edge on their cutlasses, pikes and tomahawks.

The marines under their lieutenant checked their muskets, powder and shot, made sure the flints in the locks were good ones and then sharpened their bayonets. Cloths were brought out ready to wrap round the mechanism of muskets and pistols to protect them from spray. The looms of the oars were bound with sacking and smeared with tallow, so that they should not click and squeak in the rowlocks.

The chatter of the excited men, the rumbling and grating of the grindstones, the hammering and sawing of the carpenter's crew busy on the platforms, must have pleased Hamilton—a man who, for all his faults, did not lack daring and initiative and, in action, the quality of leadership. Soon the sun set and dusk gave way to darkness as the *Surprise* tacked inshore to get as close as possible without warning the Spaniards. Suddenly—or so it seemed to the busy men—it was 7.30 P.M., and time to hoist out the boats. Hamilton had ordered that the boarding parties were to take the first spell at the oars—until they were roughly halfway to Puerto Cabello. They would then hand over to the normal boats' crews and have a brief rest before the actual attack.

Finally Mr. Made, the master, who was being left in command of the ship, noted laconically in his log: "At 8 the boats under the command of Captain Hamilton left the ship to attempt to bring His Majesty's late Ship *Hermione* out of Porto Cabello."

The launch headed the little convoy, and while the coxswain steered, using a compass lit by a small and well-shielded lantern, Captain Hamilton looked towards the shore with his night glass to pick out the hills behind Puerto Cabello and get his bearings.

The wind was falling away, leaving a lumpy swell. This made it hard work for the men bending to the oars, but on the other hand the fleeting shadows thrown by the swell waves as they chased each other silently through the night made it more likely that any Spanish guard boats rowing round the *Hermione* might mistake the silhouettes of the British boats for innocent crests surging into the lagoon.

When the boats—which were linked to each other by ropes, so that none should fall astern or get lost—were half way to the shore, Captain Hamilton ordered the normal crews to take over from the men at the oars, and the perspiring and tired boarders thankfully took up their cutlasses and pikes and settled down for the long wait. The launch once again got under way, followed by the other five boats, and headed for the shore: towards the possibility of glory and prize money for them all; towards the probability of death or maiming for many; towards the certainty of 200 shore guns (plus the *Hermione*'s own broadside if her men were alert). If the Spanish kept their heads even half a dozen of the guns could lay down such a barrage of roundshot, grape, chainshot and canister that the lagoon would be cut up like the surface of a pond in a hailstorm, and no boat could hope to survive.

Silence in the boats was essential: each of the men had been examined before leaving the *Surprise* to make certain he had not stoked up his courage with a hoarded tot of rum that would make him careless or loquacious. Nevertheless, a man shifting a cramped leg usually caused someone else's cutlass to clatter or an oarsman, not dipping the blade deep "caught a crab" with the resulting hiss from the boat commander of "Quiet there! . . . Pull together . . . Don't rattle that dam' hanger!"

Soon Captain Hamilton could make out the entrance of the lagoon. To the left, beyond the chain of sandy islets forming the seaward side, was the dark bulk of the *Hermione* and other ships at anchor. A few lighted windows showed the town, and it was not difficult to pick out the three fortresses.

There was less swell as they closed the shore and the men who did not normally smoke or chew tobacco could soon detect the stench of the mangrove swamps and mud. Were there Spanish guard boats rowing to and fro across the entrance to the lagoon? Or would they be inside, circling the ships? There was a chance—just a chance—that the Spaniards were slack enough not to be rowing guard at all.

The tiny British convoy was within a mile of the *Hermione* when suddenly Hamilton spotted two Spanish guard boats in the darkness, and a moment later the flash and boom as the cannon in one of them fired showed that the British craft had been sighted. The echoes had hardly zigzagged back and forth across the lagoon, setting the wild birds and animals shrieking, before the cannon in the second boat was fired, followed by the popping of musketry.

A few moments later a drum started rattling its urgent call to arms on board the *Hermione:* sleepy-eyed Spaniards began tumbling from their hammocks, and groping their way in the darkness to their quarters, while in the forts on shore the gunners in the batteries, for the moment without the slightest idea what was happening, grabbed shot and cartridges.

Hamilton, realizing that speed was now essential if they were to live, let alone succeed, cast off the rope linking the pinnace with the boats astern, roused his seamen into giving three cheers and ordered them to pull at their oars with every ounce of energy they possessed. He steered direct for the *Hermione*—he could ignore the guard boats because they were small and their single cannons would do no harm, except to their owners, since the flash of firing blinded them for several seconds. Hamilton had assumed—although this present situation was not specifically covered in his orders—that the rest of his boats would follow him in a mad dash to get alongside the *Hermione.* Every second's delay in achieving this meant more Spaniards on deck, wider awake and better armed.

But glancing astern a few moments later he was angered to see from the flashes of musket fire that some of his boats—he could not see how many—were wasting time attacking the guard boats, forgetting their main, indeed their only objective, the *Hermione,* and endangering the whole attack.

In fact two boats were involved—the launch commanded by Lieutenant Wilson, whose twenty-four men were supposed to cut the anchor cable and board at the bow to secure the fo'c'sle; and the boatswain's red cutter, whose sixteen men, intended to board on the larboard quarter, were vital in helping to capture the quarterdeck, from where the ship could be steered.

But Hamilton could do nothing about these errant idiots: there was no drawing back at this stage and the pinnace, apparently alone, sped through the darkness towards the objective. Suddenly the silhouette of the *Hermione* seemed to spring to life as red flashes rippled along the side and the men in the pinnace heard the thunder of the guns and the sigh of shot passing overhead. Fear, for they were helpless to retaliate, lent strength to the oarsmen as the pinnace surged on; then they realized the shot were not landing anywhere near them.

They could see the *Hermione*'s bulk huge—her bulwarks were twenty feet above the waterline—as the spurts of flame from the larboard side guns bathed her in momentary flashes of red light and silhouetted the great masts and yards which towered overhead, stark like massive trees stripped of their leaves by a winter gale. The smoke from the frigate's guns began to roll down towards them like banks of sea mist—*towards them:* not only was there a breeze, however slight, but it was fair for getting the *Hermione* out to sea, although because she had her stern to the entrance she would have to be turned.

Hamilton ordered the coxswain to steer the pinnace close round the frigate's larboard bow, under the bowsprit and jib-boom which stuck out like the questing neck of some prehistoric monster. By now the men were almost deafened by the confused medley of noise: shouts in Spanish were punctuated by heart-stopping crashes of the *Hermione*'s 12-pounders and the rumble as the gun carriages recoiled across the deck; muskets popped in an almost ludicrous descant to the thunder of the shore batteries.

Then the pinnace was right under the *Hermione*'s larboard bow and turning fast; only a few more yards and they would be at the starboard gangway: the men braced themselves, ready to scramble up the side of the frigate by whatever means presented itself. Suddenly the launch lurched and stopped.

"We're aground, sir!" shouted the coxswain. They were only a few yards from the *Hermione*'s stem and she drew more than fifteen feet forward, so Hamilton knew this was nonsense: the pinnace's rudder had obviously caught in the frigate's anchor cable or the rope of the anchor buoy.

"Unship the rudder!" he ordered.

By the time this was done the pinnace had drifted back right under the frigate's bulging, apple-cheeked bow and the starboard side oars were jammed against the hull. There was no time—or point—in trying to get the boat further aft to board at the gangway, particularly since Hamilton realized that despite the turmoil going on in the frigate the pinnace had apparently not been spotted by the Spaniards.

Overhead, slung from the cathead, was a huge anchor still covered with reeking mud, showing it had been weighed a short while earlier. That meant there would be only one cable for Lieutenant Wilson's men to cut.

Hamilton sprang up on to the bends—some extra thick planks which ran round the ship's side—and then scrambled on to the fluke of the anchor, followed by several of his men. But his feet slipped on the mud and he fell sideways, just managing to grab the lanyards of one of the foremast shrouds to avoid plunging into the sea. In his struggles one of the pistols tucked in his belt went off, fortunately without wounding him.

By now Gunner Maxwell and the rest of the pinnace's men had swarmed over the bulwarks on to the fo'c'sle—to find only two Spaniards there who, bewildered for the few moments of life left to them by the sudden appearance of the enemy, were quickly cut down.

Captain Hamilton and Maxwell ran to the break of the fo'c'sle and looked aft. They could hardly believe their eyes and realized why the two Spaniards now lying dead behind them had been so surprised: apart from a few men by the wheel, the whole of the upperdeck—fo'c'sle, both gangways, quarterdeck and poop—was deserted. All the Spaniards were at the guns down on the maindeck—from where they stood by the belfry at the after end of the fo'c'sle the two Britons could see dozens of them only a few feet below. Gun after gun on the larboard side fired and sprang back in recoil, and hurriedly the Spaniards sponged out the barrels, rammed home cartridges, wads and shot, and fired again. But from the elevation of the guns Hamilton could see at a glance that whatever the Spaniards were blazing away at was several hundred yards away. The "targets," he discovered later, were two British frigates which—in the Spaniards' imagination—were sailing into the lagoon. None of them realized that British boats were staging a cutting-out expedition and nineteen men were already on board.

Shouting to Maxwell to follow with his men, Hamilton dashed aft along the starboard gangway, heading for the quarterdeck: from there, with the wheel in British hands, he could control the ship, unless the Spaniards had the wit to run below and cut the tiller lines.

But even as the Britons ran aft the few Spaniards on the quarterdeck recognized them as the enemy and advanced along the gangway towards them. Within a few seconds there was a confused mêlée with pistols firing, cutlasses clashing with pikes, tomahawks with musket barrels. And below them on the maindeck the frigate's 12-pounders continued to thunder away.

While the pinnace's boarders tried to drive the Spaniards aft towards the quarterdeck, a second British boat arrived alongside: this was the gig, commanded by the surgeon, John M'Mullen, who with his sixteen men promptly climbed on board over the larboard bow. Finding the fo'c'sle clear except for the two dead Spaniards, M'Mullen sent the four topmen scrambling up the foremast to loose the topsail and then, as ordered, led the rest in a dash along the larboard gangway for the rendezvous on the quarterdeck, which they found deserted.

At that moment he was joined by Captain Hamilton, who had fought his way clear of the Spaniards battling with the gunner's men on the starboard gangway. But M'Mullen's fighting spirit was fully roused and before Hamilton could stop him he had led his men off in a wild dash forward along the starboard gangway to help the gunner's party by attacking the Spaniards in the rear. The purpose of the quarterdeck rendezvous was completely forgotten and Hamilton was left standing alone by the wheel, unarmed except for two discharged pistols and a sword.

The Spaniards at the gangway, sandwiched between the gunner and the bloodthirsty surgeon, fought desperately, and while slowly retreating before M'Mullen's men they drove Maxwell's group back towards the fo'c'sle.

Hamilton's situation in the meantime was both ludicrous and desperate: he was the only man on the quarterdeck of a frigate whose entire maindeck was in enemy hands and whose guns were busy firing away into the night. Only two of his six boarding parties were actually on board, and both those were scrapping on the gangway. Where were the other four parties? They comprised another sixty-seven men, apart from the vitally-important axemen who were to cut the cables. Were they still messing about with the guard boats, or had they been blown out of the water? Either way, Hamilton must have thought his attack would fail.

But he had no time to make other plans—or even to despair: four Spaniards suddenly appeared out of the smoke heading straight for him. Within a few seconds one had stabbed him in the left thigh with a cutlass, another jabbed him in the right thigh with a pike, and a third hit him across the head with a musket, smashing the butt. Hamilton collapsed, hitting his head on a hatch coaming as he fell. The Spaniards were just going to finish him off when two or three British seamen arrived in time to drive them off.

The seamen picked up Hamilton, who quickly regained consciousness and then set to helping his rescuers try to guard the quarterdeck from another group of Spaniards who, realizing at last that the ship had been boarded, had swarmed up the quarterdeck ladder from the maindeck below.

A sudden burst of cheering—British cheering—heralded the arrival of more boarders: at last the black cutter's crew, under the command of Lieutenant Hamilton, had managed to get on board. Their tardiness was not the result of chasing off into the night after the guard boats: the lieutenant had, as ordered, got his cutter alongside and, at the head of his men, scrambled up the battens on the ship's side forming the steps to the break in the gangway.

However a Spaniard—one of the group caught between the gunner's and surgeon's men—had darted across to give him a smart blow on the head, so that he had toppled backwards and fallen into the cutter, knocking down the rest of the boarders who had been following him up the ship's side. With the lieutenant sprawled on top of a pile of his men in the bottom of the boat, too dazed for the moment to do anything, the cutter's crew concluded from the noise of the fighting on the gangway, and their officer's precipitate return, that the opposition was too strong at that point, and shoved off, rowing round the ship looking for a more promising place to board. They reached the starboard side to find the musket fire too hot for them and then went back to the larboard side, which by then was comparatively clear because the Spaniards had driven the gunner's party to the fo'c'sle, though they were themselves trapped there by the surgeon's men behind them.

Swiftly Lieutenant Hamilton, followed by Lieutenant du Pin and his marines, scrambled on board and headed for the quarterdeck, where they found Captain Hamilton and his rescuers trying to stop the Spaniards coming up the ladder from the maindeck. Hamilton ordered them to keep the quarterdeck clear and du Pin, forming up his marines, began firing volleys down at the Spaniards on the maindeck below.

By this time the gunner's and surgeon's parties had finally mopped up the Spaniards on the fo'c'sle—the gunner being dangerously wounded in the process—so that the whole of the upperdeck was free of the enemy. But the Spaniards, still in complete control of the maindeck below, were busy firing muskets up through the hatches at any Briton who showed himself.

Lieutenant Wilson's launch with twenty-six men and responsible for cutting the bow cable, the boatswain's red cutter with seventeen men and the carpenter's jolly boat with eleven, charged with cutting the stern cables, still had not arrived, so that in fact the fifty-four Britons then on board were fighting 365 Spaniards, who were all now concentrated on the maindeck (the rest of the ship's company were in the guard boats or on leave).

Captain Hamilton, dazed and bleeding from his several wounds, decided the next move was to clear the maindeck of the enemy. This was hardly an easy task, even though at this time he had no idea that the Spaniards outnumbered him nearly seven to one.

Mustering the three boats' crews on the quarterdeck, Hamilton ordered every man with a musket or pistol to reload while those without firearms stood ready. He then told them to fire a volley at the same moment down the afterhatch into the midst of the Spaniards crowded on the maindeck below. Before the enemy had time to recover from the murderous hail of shot, the British seamen and marines, yelling and whooping, leapt down the hatch and immediately began slashing and jabbing with their cutlasses, pikes and tomahawks.

This attack cut the Spanish force into two sections: sixty or more were trapped aft of the hatch, and a dozen British seamen drove them back towards the captain's cabin. Finally the Spaniards retreated into the cabin and surrendered, whereupon they were swiftly disarmed and locked in.

The rest of the British seamen and marines were in the meantime battling their way forward, fighting the main mass of the frigate's crew, but the Spaniards were putting up a desperate resistance, making each gun on either side a partial barricade, because the centreline was blocked with masts, hatchways, pump wells and handles. Here the British began to lose men—a quartermaster, John Mathews, and a quarter-gunner, Arthur Reed, collapsed dangerously wounded; Henry Miller, one of the carpenter's crew, fell to the deck badly hurt.

By this time the carpenter finally had arrived alongside the frigate in the jolly boat and, leaving three men to cut the stern cables, led the other seven on board. Two of them scrambled up to loose the mizzentopsail while the rest joined in the battle on the maindeck. It did not take long for the trio of axemen in the boat to slice through the stern cables and within a few minutes the frigate was held only by the bow cable. Cutting this was the task of Lieutenant Wilson's launch, which had not yet put in an appearance.

The Spanish gunners in the fortresses on shore had by then worked out what had happened. Training their guns on the frigate, they opened fire with round shot and grape. They soon found the range and shot began crashing into the ship's side and slicing through the rigging. The heavy mainstay was cut through, leaving the mainmast in a dangerous state. Grapeshot spattered the ship— one ricocheted to hit Captain Hamilton's shin, inflicting his fourth wound so far.

With the frigate still held forward by her anchor, she was in grave danger of being pounded to pieces by the guns of the fortresses. The Spaniards, fighting for every inch of the forward part of the maindeck, naturally stopped any of the British getting into the cable tier and cutting the anchor cable from inboard, since the bitts to which it was secured and the hawse hole through which it passed were of course at the forward end of this deck.

Fortunately at this moment Lieutenant Wilson, having finished his almost childish fight with the guard boat, arrived with his launch and went alongside at the *Hermione*'s bow where the three axemen immediately began chopping away at the cable. Wilson was ordered to send up his boarders, who were urgently needed to help deal with the Spaniards on the maindeck—but keep the boat's crew and be ready to tow the ship round. Captain Hamilton then sent some men down to the other boats with instructions to help the launch, and they were joined by the boatswain's red cutter, the last to arrive alongside.

The *Hermione*, held by the anchor, was lying head to wind. There was little enough room to manoeuvre under sail in daylight; in the darkness it was out of the question. But once the anchor cable was cut the boats could tow her bow round and, with the wind blowing down the channel, she could sail out under her topsails, which had already been let fall.

A man sent to look down from the fo'c'sle had already reported to Captain Hamilton that the axemen were hard at work on the cable. The stalwart gunner, despite his wounds, was at the wheel, helped by two seamen and ready to steer the ship out of Puerto Cabello. Other men stood by at the sheets, halyards and braces, waiting for the moment when the topsails began to draw. On the maindeck, however, there was still bitter fighting.

Finally shouts from the fo'c'sle told Hamilton the cable had been cut: at last the *Hermione* was free of her anchor, and the *Surprise*'s boats began to tow her round. Navigationally, at least, Hamilton was for the moment in complete command, since his men controlled the upperdeck; but would the Spaniards be able to fight their way up again? He was in the position of a coachman who dare not leave the reins even though his passengers were trying to murder each other.

A few minutes later the ship had been towed round enough for the sails to start drawing: sheets, halyards and braces were hauled home, and the gunner felt the wheel react as the water began to swirl past the rudder. The shore batteries were still keeping up a heavy fire while the boats, their task of towing completed, hooked on astern so that they in turn could be towed. The frigate's topsails now filled, and at once she came to life. She rolled slightly in the breeze, and for a few moments the movement exposed her hull below the waterline: just long enough for a shot from a shore battery to crash home and, as she came on to an even keel again, water began to flood in through the hole.

Some of the boarders had to break off the fight to work the pumps, but the clanking of the pumphandles combined with the movement of the ship was a turning point in the battle: the Spaniards realized that the frigate was now under way and, for all they knew, in danger of sinking. Several of them leapt out through the gun ports, preferring to risk the long swim to the shore.

At that point Antonio, the Portuguese coxswain of the *Surprise*'s gig, who understood Spanish, ran up to the quarterdeck to warn Captain Hamilton that some Spaniards, trapped on the lowerdeck, were planning to blow up the ship. Lieutenant du Pin was sent with some marines to fire a few shot down the hatchway and dissuade them from any such idea.

Finally, almost exactly one hour after Captain Hamilton had first scrambled on board, the *Hermione* was sailing out of the entrance of Puerto Cabello heading for the open sea with the boats in tow. The Spaniards still fighting at the forward end of the maindeck then realized their position was hopeless and surrendered.

With the fighting over, Captain Hamilton was able to devote his whole attention to sailing the ship. Seamen were soon at work securing the mainmast, which, with the main and spring stays cut, was in danger of going over the side, particularly if the ship started pitching. The carpenter set men to work plugging the shothole below the waterline, and the rest of the boarders guarded the prisoners and tried to make the wounded comfortable. A Red Ensign was run up with the red and gold flag of Spain beneath it.

The *Surprise* was waiting four miles offshore for His Most Christian Majesty's former frigate *Santa Cecilia*, and Mr. Made noted in his log: "Half past five [A.M.] the boats returned with the *Hermione*."

WITH THE *Surprise* and the *Hermione* well clear of the coast, it was possible for Captain Hamilton to check the casualties that the British and Spanish had suffered. The difference between them was fantastic, and but for the Spanish corpses and prisoners in the *Hermione* to prove the figures, would have been almost unbelievable.

In drawing up a list of the British casualties, Captain Hamilton dismissed his own wounds as "several contusions, but not dangerous." Four men, including John Maxwell, the gunner, had been dangerously wounded; and seven others slightly wounded—a total of twelve. Not one Briton had been killed, and the maximum number of them on board the *Hermione* at any one time, and then only for a few minutes, was eighty-six.

Yet on board the *Hermione* were the bodies of 119 Spaniards who had been killed, while another 231 (ninety-seven of them dangerously wounded) remained as prisoners. Among them was Don Ramon de Eschales y Gaztelu who, until 2 A.M. that morning, had been commanding the ship.

He gave Captain Hamilton some interesting information, both about the ship's intended activities with the squadron from Havana, and the number of men on board. He explained that there should have been 392 in the ship, but seven officers were on leave, and twenty men were in the guard boats. Thus with 119 killed, 231 prisoners, twenty in the boat and seven on leave, a total of 377 were accounted for. The remaining fifteen must have jumped overboard.

With 231 Spanish prisoners to guard—ninety-seven of whom needed urgent medical attention—Hamilton was thankful when a ship was sighted at 7 A.M. and, chased by one of the *Surprise*'s cutters, proved to be an American schooner bound for Puerto Cabello from La Guaira. Her captain agreed to take the prisoners and the wounded into Puerto Cabello (with the exception of Don Eschales and two other officers, whom Hamilton proposed keeping). The schooner hove to near the *Hermione* and the slow work of ferrying across the prisoners, including the wounded, began.

By noon the new crew of the *Hermione*—who were, of course, men sent over from the *Surprise*—hoisted in the boats and both frigates got under way, heading for Port Royal, Jamaica.

Arriving there with the two ships on November 1, Hamilton wrote his report to Sir Hyde Parker, beginning with the words, "Sir, the honour of my Country and the glory of the British Navy were strong inducements for me to make an attempt to cut out, by the boats of his Majesty's ship under my command, his Majesty's late Ship *Hermione* . . ."

XXVIII

The Retribution

—m—

HAVING SUCCEEDED, Captain Hamilton needed no excuse for having virtually disobeyed Sir Hyde's orders. He paid tribute to the cutting-out party: "Every officer and man on this expedition behaved with an uncommon degree of valour and exertion." He did not criticise Lieutenant Wilson and the boatswain for their stupid behaviour: instead he did not mention them by name (which in itself indicated they had failed in some way). He added, "I consider it particularly my duty to mention the very gallant conduct, as well as the aid and assistance, at a particular crisis, I received from Mr John M'Mullen, Surgeon and volunteer, and Mr Maxwell, Gunner, even after the latter had been dangerously wounded."

Three days later Sir Hyde Parker wrote to the Secretary of the Admiralty: "I have a peculiar satisfaction in communicating to you, for the information of my Lords Commissioners of the Admiralty, that his Majesty's late Ship *Hermione* is again restored to his Navy, by as daring and gallant enterprise as is to be found in our naval annals . . .

"I find the *Hermione* has had a thorough repair, and is in

complete order: I have therefore ordered her to be surveyed and valued, and shall commission her . . . by the name of *Retaliation*."

The path before Captain Edward Hamilton was strewn with honours—and with troubles. The people of Jamaica were stirred by his exploit, the fruits of which were clearly visible lying off Port Royal, and within four days of the *Hermione*'s arrival the House of Assembly voted him a sword, valued at 300 guineas, "in testimony of the high sense this House entertains of the extraordinary ability displayed by him . . ."

On February 1, 1800, it was announced in London that "the King has been pleased, by letters patent under the Great Seal of Great Britain, to confer the dignity of a Knight of the said Kingdom unto Edward Hamilton, Esquire, Captain in the Royal Navy . . ."

Even though Hamilton had not then returned to England, the City of London paid its tribute on March 6 when the Court of Common Council voted unanimously that the City's thanks be presented to Captain Hamilton and his crew "and that the Freedom of the City be presented to Sir Edward Hamilton in a gold box value fifty guineas."

The award of the Naval Gold Medal by the King completed the major honours—but of course Hamilton was also due for a share of the prize money because at the time of her capture the *Hermione* was a Spanish warship, and this amounted to a considerable sum. According to the first valuation, Hamilton's share of two-eighths would have been about £4,024, and Sir Hyde's one-eighth, about £2,012. The rest would be split as follows—an eighth shared between the lieutenants, master and surgeon; an eighth between the lieutenant of marines, the commander-in-chief's secretary (the Rev. A. J. Scott), the principal warrant officers and the master's mates; the same amount for midshipmen, inferior warrant officers and their principal mates and the marine sergeant; and two-eights, £4,024, shared between the rest of the crew. However, the first valuation was not the final one. (According to one contemporary account, Sir Edward Hamilton gave £500 from his own two-eighths to be shared among the seamen of the *Surprise*.)

The total amount of prize money had depended in the first place on the report of the officers at the Port Royal yard, where the naval storekeeper, master shipwright, acting master attendant, and the carpenters from the two biggest ships there surveyed the ship and made an inventory which listed and valued everything on board—from sails to anchors, and watch glasses to copper kettles. (Watch glasses, for instance, were valued at 2*d.* each, while a large copper kettle at £11 8*s.* 2*d.* compared favourably with a new main-topgallant sail at £12 2*s.* 2*d.* The ship's equipment was valued at a total of £6,057 15*s.* 9*d.*).

The surveyors then described the condition of the hull, masts, yards, booms, rigging and fitted furniture, and put a value on them. This was done by estimating the total tonnage—they worked on a figure of 717 tons—and allowing £14 a ton, giving a total of £10,038, "making in the whole sixteen thousand and ninety five pounds fifteen shillings and ninepence sterling, which we consider to be a fair and equitable valuation."

Sir Hyde enclosed their report in his letter to the Admiralty. When the Board received Sir Hyde's dispatch they were delighted with the passage reporting the recapture of the *Hermione* but they thoroughly disapproved of the rest—that the ship "has been purchased by my order at the price she has been valued at," and that he had "ordered her to be called the *Retaliation.*" Sir Hyde's purchase was on behalf of the Admiralty, and of course the prize money depended on the price he paid.

A note on the corner of Sir Hyde's letter gave Mr. Nepean, the Secretary to the Board, instructions to tell Sir Hyde that "under the present circumstances Their Lordships will not disapprove of his having purchased the ship without first receiving Their Lordship's authority for so doing." They sent the commission of the new captain appointed by Sir Hyde to command "the *Hermione* which they have thought fit to name the *Retribution.*"

Thus the *Hermione,* later the *Santa Cecilia,* and then the *Retaliation* received her final name. Sir Hyde's choice seems in retrospect more appropriate, for the cutting out was indeed retaliation against the Spanish, whereas the Board's choice seems to imply retribution against the mutineers—who did not suffer one iota from her recapture.

However, inky fingers had not yet finished. The Admiralty, passing on the Jamaica yard's survey and valuation to the Navy Board—who were responsible for the construction, repair and fitting out of ships—soon received a stiff letter in reply: the Navy Board reported the ship was not worth nearly as much as the Jamaica yard's valuation and gave facts and figures to prove it.

Since the Jamaica yard was the Navy Board's responsibility, the Admiralty replied to the Navy Board, giving their decision and also recapitulating the main points the Navy Board had made, which was that the figure of £14 a ton for the ship was much too high because she was eighteen years old, and a price of £10 15s. a ton was "a proper and sufficient valuation."

The yard officers at Jamaica, according to the Navy Board, had put nearly £200 on the valuation of every £100 of the stores and £254 on every £100 of cordage, making the total price for the equipment £1,526 4s. 9d. higher than "you pay in England for similar stores when perfectly new." This, they added, included the extra £60 charge added to every £100 of stores bought from the Jamaica yard by merchant ships.

"We do hereby signify to you," Their Lordships told the Navy Board, "that we very highly disapprove the conduct of the yard officers at Jamaica, in not being properly mindful of the public interest . . . and desire and direct you . . . to allow that valuation only for the *Hermione* which you have stated to be proper." This letter, written a year after the capture, shows how Their Lordships thus went back on their word. A year earlier they had "not disapproved" of Sir Hyde's purchasing the ship without their permission; but now they were cutting down the price. Only the *Surprise*'s crew suffered, particularly the hundred who had captured the *Hermione* against such odds.

SIR EDWARD HAMILTON had been too ill to return to England immediately: he had to spend several weeks recuperating from the effect of his wounds. In the meantime the officers of the *Surprise* had presented a sword to Mr. John M'Mullen, their brave surgeon. Incidentally one of the boarding party was later court-martialled as a deserter from the sloop *Swallow* and sentenced to 300 lashes. When it later transpired he was one of the men who saved Hamilton's life when he was badly wounded on the *Hermione*'s quarterdeck, the court successfully applied to have the sentence remitted.

Sir Edward finally sailed for England in April on board the Jamaica packet—but he was out of luck: three packets in succession were captured by the French—the *Princess Charlotte* on May 4, the *Marquis of Kildare* on May 6, and the *Princess Amelia* on May 11. Thus Sir Edward found himself a prisoner of war in French hands, but news of his exploit had already reached France, and as soon as he was landed at a French port he was, according to a contemporary account, "sent to Paris, where he was taken notice of by Bonaparte," and after remaining there six weeks, was exchanged for four French midshipmen held prisoner in England.

He was back in England in good time to attend a dinner in his honour given by the City of London on October 24, the first anniversary of the cutting-out expedition. Hamilton was later given command of the *Trent*—where, as mentioned earlier, he established a reputation as a martinet and filled Midshipman, later Admiral, Jackson with apprehension. It may well be that his behaviour then was, in part at least, due to the severe headwounds that he received. After being dismissed the service by a court-martial trying him for tying an elderly gunner in the rigging, he was later reinstated by the King, and between 1806 and 1819 he commanded the Royal yacht.

THE REST of the *Hermione's* story can be told briefly. On January 20, 1802, as the *Retribution,* she arrived back in Portsmouth, just two months before David Forester was caught by Steward Jones as he walked through the Point Gates, and two days before Sir Edward Hamilton was court-martialled in the *Gladiator,* moored nearby, and dismissed the service.

Also in Portsmouth at this time was another ship which had been concerned in the *Hermione's* story, the little *Diligence*. This brig sailed for the Thames on February 6 to be paid off—and, by a coincidence, the *Hermione,* under her new name, sailed for Woolwich the same day, also to be paid off.

The Royal Navy had no further use for the *Retribution* since the Treaty of Amiens was about to be signed. She arrived at Woolwich on March 2, but Trinity House, responsible for the buoys and lightships round the coasts of Britain, wanted her. She was therefore fitted out for them, sailing on her first voyage under their flag on October 16, 1803. However, she had only a brief life left. She arrived at Deptford on June 8, 1804, docked the following August, had her copper sheathing taken off, and was broken up in June 1805.

So the story of the ship *Hermione* ends. Of the thirty-three of the

Hermione's crew who had been caught or given themselves up and been tried as mutineers, twenty-four had been hanged and another transported. But apart from Nash, Forester, Elliott and Redman, the rest of the leaders were never captured—men like Thomas Jay, Lawrence Cronin and William Turner. Midshipman Wiltshire was not heard of again; nor was Mrs. Martin, the widow of the murdered boatswain.

What happened to them, and to more than one hundred other Hermiones who evaded arrest? Cronin we know settled down in La Guaira, and no doubt married and had a family. Did Thomas Jay, when the war ended eighteen years after the mutiny, ever return to his native Plymouth? Did William Anderson, who last saw his native Canterbury when he was twenty-one, dare return with the peace, when he was nearly forty? John Farrel, the murderous American, no doubt went back to New York with the watch he won in the quarterdeck lottery. Did John Innes, the captain of the maintop and a former *Success*, visit his native Galloway again, or John Phillips his birthplace in Hanover? Did Cranbrook, Tonbridge, Liverpool, Belfast, Whitby, Colchester, Lambeth and several score other towns and villages ever again see those men and boys who left in the 1790s to serve in the *Hermione*? It is obvious that the majority of the men must have eventually settled down somewhere and married. So many coincidences occurred in the story of the *Hermione* that it is perhaps not being fanciful to wonder how many people in various parts of Europe and America may be quite unaware of their forebears' mutineering past, even if they read this narrative. Somewhere, perhaps, there is a silver teapot still in use on which is engraved Pigot's name and Otway's thanks.

APPENDIX A

The Effect of a Flogging

Ultimately any judgment on the physical effect of Captain Pigot's cruelty to his crew depends on a knowledge of what a lash from a cat-o'-nine-tails did to a man. Present day pundits disagree and all base their arguments on the very few existing written descriptions by victims of a flogging. The author therefore made some experiments to determine the effect of a lash.

The dimensions of one of the last cat-o'-nine-tails used in the Royal Navy—in 1867 on board the steam corvette *Malacca*—were taken. The handle, of wood covered in red baize, had been weakened by woodworm and could not be used for experiments, and in Pigot's time the cat usually had a rope handle, but of the same length and diameter as the wooden handle. The author therefore made up a cat to the same specification—which is similar to several others described in contemporary documents—using a rope instead of a wooden handle. The rope was 1-in. diameter manilla, two feet long. One end was whipped and nine pieces of $^1/_4$-in. diameter ($^3/_4$-in. circumference) line were spliced into the other end, leaving tails two feet long. A Turk's head knot of the same line was placed over the splice and sailmaker's whippings were put on the ends of the tails. The completed cat weighed thirteen ounces.

Using a five-barred shipyard wooden trestle as a "grating," the cat was then tested on pieces of wood of various sizes. The horizontal bars of the trestle were made of 5-in. by 2-in. wood spaced twenty inches apart measuring from centre to centre. A piece of $^1/_2$-in. by 2-in. pitchpine, free of knots, three feet long, was lashed vertically to two bars of the trestle with an equal amount overlapping the bars top and bottom. The centre of this piece of wood was midway between the top and bottom bar and 4 ft. 6 in. from the ground (the height at which blows would fall on an average man's shoulders when flogged), and was unsupported by the horizontal bars for fifteen inches.

The person wielding the cat was 5 ft. 10 in. tall and weighed 152 pounds. He intended to strike the centre of the pitchpine and made a preliminary swing with the cat, using only about two-thirds of his strength, to test the distance and his stance. The piece of pitchpine broke in two pieces and it was estimated the nine tails had spread about three inches at their widest at the point of impact.

A piece of $^3/_4$-in. by $^3/_4$-in. pitchpine of the same length and free of knots was substituted, and a blow delivered using the man's full strength. The wood broke into three pieces. The middle piece, where the tails hit, was five inches long and landed seventeen feet from the trestle—the remaining two pieces were of course lashed to the bars.

A piece of 1-in. by 1-in. pitchpine of the same length and also free of knots was then substituted. The first blow of the cat had no apparent effect and the tails appeared to spread about three inches. The second blow broke the wood into two pieces, the break being four and a half inches long.

Each piece of wood, although unsupported for fifteen inches, was of course supported for five inches at the top and five inches at the bottom by the bars of the trestle.

Pitchpine was chosen for the experiments because it has the highest modulus of elasticity of any readily available wood: 850, compared with 730 for larch, 730 for American elm and 450 for English oak. Its tensile strength is 2.1, compared with 1.9 for larch, 4.1 for American elm and 3.4 for English oak. Since one was trying to measure the impact of a lash, the most important factor was the modulus of elasticity.

So much for the effect on wood. What about the effect on a man? It was clear that a man standing braced but unsupported would have been knocked down by one blow. The effect on a man lashed to a grating, unable to "give" with the blow, can only be guessed, but from the above experiments it is certain that one lash would break the skin and severe bruising would result.

From further experiments made with composition boarding, canvas and a sandbag, the author has no reason to suppose that the description quoted on page sixty-two, beginning "The pain in my lungs was more severe, I thought, than on my back. I felt as if I would burst in the internal parts of my body . . ." was in any way exaggerated.

APPENDIX B

Floggings ordered by Captain Wilkinson in the
Hermione, January 25–October 12, 1795

Date		Name	Lashes	Crime
1795				
Jan.	25	Joseph Cadell	12	Neglect of duty
	25	John Evans	12	Fighting and quarrelling
Feb.	23	Thomas Riley	24	Drunkenness, fighting and quarrelling
March	10	Thomas Page	24	Contempt to superior officers
April	19	William Clarke	12	Rioting
	19	John Robinson	12	Rioting
	27	Walter St. John	24	Drunkenness, quarrelling
	27	James Perrett	12	Insolence to superior officer
	27	John Fletcher	24	Drunkenness, quarrelling
Aug.	16	Walter St. John	36	Neglect of duty
	16	Joseph Thomas	72	Desertion
	16	John Stevens	72	Desertion
Oct.	4	Walter St. John	24	Neglect of duty and insolence
	4	James Pollard	24	Neglect of duty and insolence
	12	Simon Markus	24	Desertion
		Total	408	

APPENDIX C

Floggings ordered by Captain Pigot in the Success,
October 22, 1794–September 11, 1795

Date		Name	Lashes	Crime
1794				
Oct.	22	J. McWilliam	24 ⎫	
	22	Daniel Maroney	24 ⎪	Drunkenness and
	22	Joshuah Gearn	12 ⎬	contempt to
	22	Luke Keefe	12 ⎪	superior officer
	22	William Morrison	12 ⎭	
	22	John Omeburg*	unspecified	Mutiny (in H.M.S. *Europa*)
Nov.	26	Timothy Buckley	24	Theft
	26	James Callahan	12 ⎫	
	26	William Porter	12 ⎬	Neglect of duty
	26	Martin Steady	12 ⎭	
Dec.	6	William Morrison	24	Disobedience of orders and contempt
	8	William Morrison	24 ⎫	Disobedience of orders
	8	Michael Clifford	24 ⎭	and contempt
	17	William Gunthorpe	12 ⎫	Neglect of duty
	17	Edward Johnston	12 ⎭	
	26	John Finney	12	Uncleanliness
	31	John Paley	12	Disobedience
	31	John Finney	12	Sleeping on his post

Date		Name	Lashes	Crime
1795				
Jan.	12	Peter Birmingham	12	Contempt
	12	Thomas Castle	12 ⎫	
	12	Jacob Snipe	12 ⎬	Uncleanliness
	12	John Bowen	12 ⎭	
	15	Charles Ford	24	Disobedience and contempt
	27	Thomas Castle	not ⎫	
	27	John Dyke	speci- ⎬	Desertion
	27	Henry Colson	fied ⎭	
Feb.	17	John Russell	36	Desertion
	17	William Smith	24	Disobedience of orders
	26	John Russell	24	Desertion
	26	Michael Clifford	12 ⎫	Disobedience of orders
	26	Peter Mair	24 ⎭	
March	5	Martin Steady	12 ⎫	Disobedience of orders
	5	John Holford	12 ⎭	
	12	John Russell	12	Desertion
	12	Charles Ford	12	Disobedience
	23	Joshuah Gearn	12	Theft
	23	Michael Clifford	24 ⎫	Disorderly behaviour
	23	Martin Steady	24 ⎭	
	25	John Finney	12 ⎫	Neglect of duty
	25	John Clarke	12 ⎭	
	28	William Whitehead	12	Neglect of duty
April	1	Ambrose Colville	12 ⎫	Neglect of duty
	1	Thomas Jay	12 ⎭	
	1	Henry Colson	12 ⎫	Drunkenness
	1	John Holford	12 ⎭	
	1	John Callahan	12	Disobedience
	2	Martin Steady	24	Disobedience
	11	P. Birmingham	12 ⎫	Gambling
	11	William Morrison	12 ⎭	
	11	John Bowen	12	Disobedience
	11	Julien Valier	24	Mutiny
	14	Luke Keefe	24	Disobedience
	14	Thomas Dugal	12	Drunkenness
	15	Alex Black	24 ⎫	
	15	Edward Porter	24 ⎬	Drunkenness
	15	William Wall	24 ⎭	

Date		Name	Lashes	Crime
	15	Charles M'Carthy	12	Riotous behaviour
	15	Timothy Buckley	12	Theft
	21	John Bowen	36	Repeated disobedience
	25	John Charles	12	Disorderly behaviour
	25	William Smith	12	Uncleanliness
May	4	William Morrison	12	Disorderly behaviour
	4	John Charles	12	Disobedience
	21	John Bowen	48	Attempting to desert
	21	William Wall	24 ⎫	
	21	A. Black	24 ⎪	Drunkenness
	21	Martin Steady	12 ⎬	
	21	A. Gordon	12 ⎭	
	21	John Charles	12	Insolence and contempt
June	4	Martin Steady	24	Mutinous behaviour
Aug.	3	Luke Keefe	⎫	
	3	Archibald McCall	⎪	Not specified
	3	Edward Goodrick	⎬	
	3	Martin Steady	⎭	
	4	Jeremiah Walsh	24	Neglect of duty
	10	William Reeves	12 ⎫	
	10	Michael Clifford	12 ⎬	Drunkenness and gambling
	10	Peter Ford .	12 ⎭	
	10	James Gamble	12	Disobedience
	22	James Hayes	12	Attempting to desert
	22	Alexander Gordon	24	Drunkenness and neglect
Sept.	10	Michael Clifford	⎫	
	10	Mathew Power	⎬	Not specified
	10	James Farley	⎭	
	11	Jeremiah Walsh	12	Drunkenness and contempt
	11	Martin Steady	12 ⎫	Drunkenness
	11	Luke Keefe	24 ⎭	

*Omeburg was flogged round the fleet: his punishment is not included in the summary given on page 67–68.

Details are taken from the *Success*'s captain's log.

APPENDIX D

The men active in the mutiny

Note: Age is that on joining the *Hermione*. Former *Successes* are marked with an asterisk, and the eighteen ringleaders with a dagger.

Name	Rank	Age	In Ship or with Pigot	Reward	Nationality
William Turner†	Master's Mate	—	Nearly 3 years	Watch	—
James Bell*†	Quarter-Gunner	21	from *Success*	"	Scottish
William Herd†	Able Seaman	—	7 months	"	Scottish (Galloway)
John Farrel†	Able Seaman	—	9 months	"	American (N. York)
James Blaxland	Ordinary Seaman	—	4 years 10 months	"	English (Canterbury)
William Brown	Maintopman	—	2½ months	Plate	English (Isle of Man)
James Black	Maintopman	—	—	"	—
John Barnett	Maintopman	—	7½ months	"	English (Chatham)
Peter Bextrum	Ordinary Seaman	—	16 months	"	Swedish
James Dawson	Able Seaman	—	16½ months	"	Irish (Belfast)
Thomas Diamond	Ordinary Seaman	28	4 years	"	St. Thomas
Henry Croaker*†	Gunner's Mate	31	from *Success*	"	English (Cornwall)
D. Forester†	Maintopman	16	3 years	"	English (Sheerness)
John Francis	—	—	—	"	—
Antonio Francisco	Ordinary Seaman	—	15 months	"	Spanish
John Hill	Foretopman	—	14 months	"	—
Gabriel Jones	Ordinary Seaman	20	2 years 7 months	"	—
Thomas Jay*†	Bosun's Mate	30	from *Success*	"	English (Plymouth)
Adam Lynham	Able Seaman	—	11 months	"	Irish (Dublin)

Name	Rank	Age	In Ship or with Pigot	Reward	Nationality
John Maney	—	—	—	"	—
John Pearce	—	—	—	"	—
John Philips	Sailmaker	—	—	"	Hanoverian
Hadrian Poulson†	Able Seaman	24	2 years 9 months	"	Danish
Peter Roowell	—	—	—	"	—
Thomas Riley	Ordinary Seaman	26	4 years 9 months	"	Irish (Dublin)
John Slushing	—	—	—	"	—
John Williams	Gunner's Crew	—	2 years 2 months	"	—
John Antonio	Ordinary Seaman	—	15 months	16 dollars	—
Walter Brooks	Ordinary Seaman	—	17 months	"	—
Thomas Charlton	Ordinary Seaman	23	16 months	"	English (Stockton)
William Clarke†	Able Seaman	—	4 years 3 months	"	English (Tonbridge)
Hans Christopher	Able Seaman	31	2½ years	"	Danish
Timothy Crowley	—	23	7 months	"	Irish (Mucroom)
Pierre D'Orlanie	Ordinary Seaman	—	16 months	"	French
John Elliott*†	Able Seaman	26	from Success	"	English (Rochester)
Tarinto [Jacinto] Garcia	Able Seaman	41	18 months	"	Portuguese
John Jackson	Bargemen	26	3 years 5 months	"	"coloured"
John Jacob	Able Seaman	23	16 months	"	Swedish
Jacob Lowsae	—	30	17 months	"	Swedish
John Luxton	Able Seaman	29	2 years 8 months	"	English (Bristol)
Robert McReady*†	Maintopman	23	from Success	"	Irish (Londonderry)
John Mason*	Carpenter's Mate	30	from Success	"	Irish(Belfast)
Antonio Marco	—	—	16 months	"	Italian (Genoa)
William Marsh	Ordinary Seaman	—	2 years 9 months	"	—

Name	Rank	Age	In Ship or with Pigot	Reward	Nationality
Joseph Montell	Maintopman	—	16 months	"	Italian
Thomas Nash†	Bosun's Mate	25	4 years 9 months	"	Irish (Waterford)
Thomas Leech†	Able Seaman	—	—	"	—
Joseph Pearson	Able Seaman	38	21 months	"	English (Whitby)
John Smith*†	Captain Foretop	22	from *Success*	"	English (York)
Michael Whatman†	Carpenter's Yeoman	24	4 years 9 months	"	English (Cranbrook)
Lawrence Cronin	Surgeon's Mate	—	15 months	Not given	Irish (Belfast)
Richard Redman*†	Able Seaman	24	from *Success*	"	English (London)
Patrick Foster*	Coxswain	30	from *Success*	"	Irish (Galway)
Thomas Ladson*†	Able Seaman	30	from *Success*	"	English (Chatham)
John Hussack*	Able Seaman	26	from *Success*	"	English (Colchester)
John Innes*†	Able Seaman	27	from *Success*	"	Scottish (Galloway)
John Fletcher	Able Seaman	—	4 years 9 months	"	English (Whitby)
Samuel Rockwell	Able Seaman	—	7 months	"	—
John Holmes	Able Seaman	23	2 years	"	English (Lambeth)
Feram Prest	Able Seaman	18	4 years 9 months	"	English (Wotton)
William Rimmer	Able Seaman	30	4 years 9 months	"	English (Liverpool)
William Crawley	—	—	7 months	Plate	Irish (Kinsale)

APPENDIX E

Recorded trials for mutiny in the Royal Navy for the year 1798

Date		No. of Men	Ship	Where	Details	Punishment
Jan.	3	2	*Tromp*	Portsmouth	Released man in irons	Hanged
	17	1	*Courser*	Sheerness	Inciting mutiny, threat to murder	Two years jail
Feb.	1	1	*Romulus*	Hamoaze	Mutinous expressions	150 lashes
	12	1	*Pelter*	Portsmouth	Mutinous behaviour and mutinous expressions	200 lashes, one year solitary confinement
	23	1	*Fly*	Spithead	Mutinous expressions and mutinous behaviour	50 lashes
March	9	3	*Amelia*	Hamoaze	Mutinous assembly	2, hanged; 1, two years sol. con.
	19	1	*Nautilus*	Sheerness	Mutinous expressions	100 lashes
	20	4	*Renommée*	West Indies	Mutinous conspiracy	3, hanged; 1, three months jail
	21	1	*Defiance*	Portsmouth	Mutinous expressions	200 lashes, one year sol. con.
April	9	1	*Monarch*	Yarmouth	Mutinous expressions but said to be nearly insane	500 lashes
May	10	1	*Sirius*	Nore	Mutinous behaviour	500 lashes
	28	1	*Marlborough*	Cadiz	Mutinous behaviour	Hanged
June	6	6	*Suffolk*	Trincomalee	Mutiny	1, hanged; 1, 400 lashes and 2 years jail; 1, 200, one year; 1, 300, 18 months; 1, 200 and one year

Date	No. of Men	Where	Ship	Details	Punishment
11	1	Little Nore	*Ariadne*	Exciting mutiny	300 lashes
12	1	Trincomalee	*Carysfort*	Drunkenness, mutinous expressions	300 lashes
July 12	1	Little Nore	*Dordrecht*	A lieutenant: mutinous speeches	Dismissed
3	3	off Cadiz	*Princess Royal*	Mutinous meetings	Hanged
5	1	off Cadiz	*Princess Royal*	Mutinous behavior	Hanged (reprieved)
5	3	Spithead	*Adamant*	Inciting to mutiny	Hanged (1 reprieved)
6	1	off Cadiz	*Princess Royal*	Conspiracy, threat to murder an officer	Hanged
9	2	Spithead	*Haughty*	Conspiracy to mutiny	Hanged
11	2	Spithead	*Pluto*	Mutinous expressions	1, hanged; 1, 100 lashes
Aug. 3	1	Nore	*Zebra*	Drunkenness, mutinous speeches	Dismissed (Carpenter)
23	22	Hamoaze	*Caesar*	Mutinous assembly	6, hanged; 2, 500 lashes
Sept. 8	25	Portsmouth	*Defiance*	Mutinous assembly	19, hanged (8 reprieved); 2, 200 lashes and one year jail; 1, 100 lashes, 6 months; 1, one year sol. confinement
18	1	off Alexandria	*Seahorse*	Mutinous expressions	300 lashes
Oct. 10	11	Hamoaze	*Glory*	Mutinous assembly	8, hanged; 1, 200 lashes and one year sol. con.; 2, 100 and one year sol. con.
11	1	Portsmouth	*La Minerve*	Mutinous behaviour	100 lashes
11	1	Downs	*Nemesis*	Mutinous expressions	Dismissed (Surgeon's Mate)
16	1	Halifax	*Diligence*	Mutinous expressions	150 lashes
17	1	Medway	*Expedition*	Mutinous expressions	Hanged

Date	No. of Men	Where	Ship	Details	Punishment
26	2	Port Royal	*Sheerness*	Mutinous speeches	300 lashes; 400
28	1	Hamoaze	*Druid*	Mutinous assemblies	150 lashes and six months sol. con.
Nov. 29	2	Sheerness	*Diomede*	Mutinous expressions	500 lashes; hanged
Nov. 2	1	Gibraltar	*Perseus*	Mutinous expressions	200 lashes
9	2	Cawsand Bay	*Queen Charlotte*	Mutinous behaviour	Each 300 lashes and 6 months sol. con.
12	1	Downs	*Babet*	Mutinous expressions	200 lashes
12	1	Sheerness	*Unité*	Mutinous expressions	Reprimand
Dec. 5	12	Portsmouth	*Captain*	Mutinous expressions and assemblies	2, 400 lashes; 2, 300; 3, 200; 1, 100
10	3	Hamoaze	*Mars*	Mutinous expression, mutinous behaviour	2, 300 lashes; and 1, 100
13	1	Port Royal	*Queen*	Attempting mutinous assembly	400 lashes
18	1	Hamoaze	*Shannon*	Mutinous expressions	Dismissed and six months jail (Master-at-Arms)

NOTES AND BIBLIOGRAPHY

THE MAJORITY of the documents from which the narrative has been written are in the Public Record Office, London, or the Archivo General de Marina (Collection of Don Alvaro de Bazan), Madrid.

The description of the events leading up to the mutiny, the mutiny itself, and the voyage to La Guaira is taken almost entirely from the minutes of the numerous courts-martial held on the mutineers, and from depositions, statements and confessions. The sources for the two exceptions—some of Midshipman Casey's evidence, and Thomas Nash's activities in Charleston—are given under the relevant chapter notes.

All statements and comments contained within quotation marks are taken directly from original letters, trial minutes, confessions, etc. Only occasional orders concerned with making sail and reefing are not taken from original material connected with the mutiny; but they are those used in the period, and can be confirmed from contemporary seamanship books.

To avoid needless repetition of sources, the reader can assume that all material concerning the events surrounding the actual mutiny are taken from the British and Spanish documents listed at the end of the Notes and Bibliography, unless further sources are given under individual chapters. Since the dates of official letters and entries in journals and ships' logs are given in the narrative, these are not listed chapter by chapter. They can be traced in the list at the end of these Notes, where published sources are also given. Where the brief title of a published work is given under individual chapters, the full title will be found at the end.

CHAPTER I (Pages 15–33)

The Jesup episode: taken from the report of the inquiry held into Pigot's conduct; correspondence between the British Minister in the USA and the Secretary of State; Parker's Journal and Dispatches; Admiralty correspondence with Parker; MacDonald's correspondence is in Historical Manuscripts Commission, Fortescue 6; and the *Canada* episode in Captains' Letters, "P," to the Admiralty. Published sources include Pasley, *Private Sea Journals*; Admiralty, *Regulations and Instructions*; McArthur, *Naval Courts Martial* (1813); Phillimore, *Life of Parker*; *The Royal Kalender*, 1797.

The *Success*, 32-gun frigate, was built by John Sutton at Liverpool to a design by Sir John Williams. Started May 8, 1779, she was launched April 10, 1781. Dimensions: length on gundeck 126 ft.; extreme beam 32 ft. 2 in.; depth 12 ft. 2 in. (draught not given); 683 tons. She had a complement of 215 men and carried twenty-six 12-pdrs. on maindeck, four 6-pdrs. on quarterdeck and two 6-pdrs. on fo'c'sle. She cost £13,759 16s. 6d. made up as follows: hull—£8,099 17s. 0d.; masts and yards—£804 15s. 0d.; 'extra work'—£236 3s. 2d.; boats—£86 10s. 0d.; rigging—£50. (Details from Admiralty Progress Books, in Admiralty Library.)

CHAPTER II (Pages 34–39)

Situation in the West Indies: Parker's Journal and Dispatches; *Naval Chronicle*; *The Spencer Papers* (for Spencer correspondence); Parkinson, *The Trade Winds*; Young, *W.I. Commonplace Book*; Fortescue, *Army*; Marshall, *R.N. Biography*; Markham, *Naval Career*; Turnbull, *Naval Surgeon*; Phillimore, *Parker*; Gatty, *Scott*.

CHAPTER III (Pages 40–47)

Wilkinson details: Admiralty Commission and Warrant Books; *Hermione* logs and muster books; Forester, *Wetherall:* Parker's Journal and Dispatches.

Flogging: In Pigot's time the *Regulations and Instructions* of 1790, under "Discipline, &c," Art. IV, said, "No commander shall inflict any punishment upon a seaman beyond twelve lashes upon his back with a cat-of-nine-tails."

Under the new *Regulations and Instructions* of 1806, this limit was replaced (Chap. IV, Captain, Regulations for Discipline, etc., Art. XLII) by "He is not to suffer the inferior officers or men to be treated with oppression," and he alone was to order punishment, "which he is never to do without sufficient cause, nor ever with greater severity than the offence shall really deserve."

CHAPTER IV (Pages 48–57)

Pigot family material supplied by Brigadier General Sir Robert Pigot, Bt, DSO, MC.

Hugh Pigot of Peplow (b. 1630) married Elizabeth Diahin (b. 1637). Their son Richard (1679–1726) married Frances Godde and their children were: Richard, died in infancy; George (1719–77), later Lord Pigot; Robert (1721–96), later Lieutenant General Sir Robert Pigot, Bt; Hugh (1722–92), later Admiral of the White.

Sir Robert Pigot (b. 1801), fourth baronet, subsequently sold Patshull to the Earl of Dartmouth, in whose family it has remained.

Several names and dates given in the *Dictionary of National Biography* for Lord Pigot, Sir Robert, Admiral Hugh Pigot and Captain Hugh Pigot are incorrect. Captain (later Admiral) Hugh Pigot's family consisted of:

By his first wife Elizabeth Le Nere—Henry (1751–84), later a general; Isabella ("Belle") (1750–1812).

By his second wife Frances, daughter of Sir Richard Wrottesley, who had married Lady Mary Croker, sister of the Marquis of Stafford—Hugh (1769–97), the subject of this book; Frances, died unmarried 1812; Caroline, married the Rev. Lord Henry Fitzroy, eldest son of the Duke of Grafton by his second marriage.

Admiral Pigot was buried at Walcott Church, Bath, not Bristol, as in the D.N.B.

All dates referring to Captain Hugh Pigot (the admiral's son) in D.N.B. should be ignored for historical purposes. It gives, for example, the date of Pigot joining the *Hermione* as July 1797. The *Hermione*'s Captain's log says Pigot read his commission on board on Feb. 10.

Hugh Pigot's appointments, taken from the Admiralty C. W. Books, were:

July 15, 1790	5th Lt.	*Colossus* (74), Capt. H. C. Christian
Oct. 17, 1790	4th Lt.	*Colossus* (74), Capt. H. Harvey
Jan. 7, 1791	3rd Lt.	*Colossus* (74), Capt. H. Harvey
April 24, 1792	4th Lt.	*Assistance* (50), Capt. N. Brunton
Jan. 28, 1793	3rd Lt.	*Assistance* (50), Capt. N. Brunton
April 5, 1793	4th Lt.	*London* (98), Capt. R. Keats

Jan. 11, 1794	1st Lt.	*Latona* (38), Capt. E. Thornbrough
Feb. 10, 1794	in command	*Incendiary* (14-gun fireship)
Feb. 21, 1794	in command	*Swan* (14-gun sloop)
Sept. 4, 1794	in command	*Success* (32)
Feb. 10, 1797	in command	*Hermione* (32)

CHAPTER V (Pages 58–69)

Details of *Success* and Pigot: ship's logs, muster books; and Progress Books, Admiralty; trial of Redman.

The cat-o'-nine-tails referred to was used to flog a man on board the steam-corvette *Malacca,* commanded by Captain Oldfield, in 1867. Admiral Swinton Holland, then a midshipman, obtained the cat from the boatswain's mate, and later gave it to Lieutenant Colonel Harold Wyllie, OBE, who allowed the author to experiment with it.

Punishment: Romilly, *Memoirs;* Manwaring and Dobree, *Floating Republic;* and Masefield, *Sea Life.*

Use of capstan: Midshipman Casey of the *Hermione,* later flogged on Pigot's orders, wrote, "I was seized to the capstern [*sic*], the usual place of punishment." In fact it was more usual in bigger ships to seize the victim to a grating up-ended on one of the gangways. Several of the *Hermione*'s men referred later at courts-martial to being flogged "at the capstan."

CHAPTER VI (Pages 70–75)

Operations in W. Indies, Parker, and executions: Gatty, *Scott;* Norie, *Naval Gazetteer; Hermione* logs, muster book; Parker's Journal and Dispatches; Jackson, *Perilous Adventures.*

Pigot in *Hermione:* ship's logs, muster book; *Success* muster book; trial of Redman and others.

The muster book, *Success,* lists Redman's birthplace as London and says he joined the ship March 28, 1796, from the ship *Hester* as a volunteer aged twenty-three; but the *Hermione*'s muster book for Feb. 29–May 1, 1797, gives his birthplace as Helford, Cornwall. The final muster book, however, lists him as from London.

As soon as the *Success* arrived in Portsmouth the Admiralty on April 11, 1797 (PRO, Adm. 3/118, Board Minutes), ordered her to be docked, and a report made on her condition and time needed to put her "in a state for service." On April 19 Wilkinson was ordered to cause the defects to be made good "with the utmost dispatch" and provisions taken on for four months' home service. Major repairs were not carried out until the late autumn, the ship docking at Plymouth on Oct. 6. The repairs, completed on Nov. 2, cost £1,120 (Progress Books, *Success,* Admiralty Library).

CHAPTER VII (Pages 76–87)

Pigot and crew of *Hermione: Hermione's* logs, muster book; trial of Johnson; Casey, Memorandum; Parker's Journal. The trial of the previous boatswain is referred to in the Jesup inquiry—". . . the Boatswain was at the time [of the *Mercury–Success* collision] under confinement and since dismissed the ship by the sentence of a court martial."

Details of ship: The *Hermione* was built by Teast, Tombs & Co. at Bristol, June 1780–Sept. 1782, to a design by Edward Hunt. Her dimensions were: 129 ft. on the gundeck; 35 ft. 5$^{1}/_{2}$ in. extreme beam; 9 ft. 2 in.-15 ft. 3 in. light draught. She was docked and her hull copper sheathed Sept. 1782 and sailed Jan. 1783. Hauled out at Northfleet Oct. 1790, her copper sheathing was removed for "great repairs" and she was not launched again until June 1792, when she sailed for Chatham for docking (Sept.) and coppering (Oct.). She was fitted out and sailed Jan. 1793. (Progress Books, and List of Ships, Admiralty Library).

Operations: Parker's Journal and Dispatches; ships' logs; Pigot's letters in Parker's Dispatches.

CHAPTER VIII (Pages 88–98)

Events in *Hermione:* Trials of Redman and Leech (for desertion); American Consul's correspondence in Parker's Journal and Dispatches.

Operations: Parker's Journal; Pigot's letters enclosed in Parker's Dispatches; ships' logs.

CHAPTER IX (Pages 99–112)

The *Ceres* episode: Pigot's and Otway's letters in Parker's Dispatches; Casey, Memorandum; trial of Lieutenant John Harris (which gives all the dialogue referring to the grounding).

Parker-Bligh dispute: Parker's Dispatches (May 1798); *Spencer Papers,* letters of June 4, 1799, and May 11, 1800.

CHAPTER X (Pages 113–120)

Court-martial: trial of Lieutenant John Harris; Casey, Memorandum. The court comprised, in addition to Bligh, Captains J. Ferrier, W. G. Rutherford, H. Jenkins and J. Whyte.

The *Ceres*'s refit: The *Ceres* was fortunate: the 38-gun *Undaunted* (formerly the French *Aréthuse*) had been wrecked on the Morant Cays in Aug. 1796 and her 18-pdr. guns salvaged. The *Renommée* (captured from the French July 1796) had been found to be capable of carrying 18-pdrs. instead of her own 12-pdrs., so they were exchanged. The *Renommée*'s 12-pdrs. were thus available in the dockyard for the *Ceres* which had, of course, jettisoned her own.

Promotions in *Hermione*: Parker's Journal; Admiralty C. W. Books; Casey Memorandum.

CHAPTER XI (Pages 121–129)

Spithead and Nore mutinies: Rear-Admiral Harvey's Dispatches; Admiralty to Parker, Harvey; *Spencer Papers; Annual Register, 1797;* magistrates' reports in Neale, *History of the Mutiny;* Admirals' Dispatches, Nore; Manwaring and Dobree, *Floating Republic.*

Operations: logs of *Diligence; Hermione* muster book; trial of J. Folliard (Fulga); Parker's Journal and Dispatches.

CHAPTER XII (Pages 130–143)

Casey: *Diligence* logs; Casey Memorandum; Jackson, *Adventures.*

Diligence, and blind man episode: *Diligence* logs; trials of Watson, Stewart, Duncan.

Surgeon Sansum: Trials of Hayes, Brown, Duncan, Watson.

The death falls: Casey, Memorandum; *Hermione* muster book; Examination of John Mason (enclosed in Parker's Dispatches); James, *Naval History;* Trial of Brown; Brown's confession.

CHAPTER XIII (Pages 144–154)

Events in London: The *Evening Mail* (British Museum, Burney Collection), September 21 and 22.

Punishment of topmen: Casey, Memorandum; Brown's Confession.

Eve of mutiny: Trials of Marco, Johnson, Holford, Duncan, Perrett, Irwin, Brown, and evidence of loyal officers at various courts-martial.

CHAPTER XIV (Pages 155–167)

The mutiny: evidence at trials of all the mutineers (listed below); Brown's confession; Forester's confession in *Naval Chronicle*, VII, 350; Montell's Confession; Mason's Examination; Casey, Memorandum.

Crawley's cry, "What, four against one . . ." is given in *Naval Chronicle*, IV, 156, and must have been from private information: it is not given in the minutes of Crawley's trial. The *Naval Chronicle* says he used a bayonet but all other accounts refer to a cutlass.

CHAPTER XV (Pages 168–175)

The mutiny: as for Chapter Fourteen.

CHAPTER XVI (Pages 176–190)

Aftermath of mutiny: as for mutiny in Chapter Fourteen; *Hermione's* muster book.

John Brown and Holford later gave the authorities individual lists of names of men they considered ringleaders. The lists do not coincide completely.

The statistics are taken from the evidence given at the trials of all the mutineers and are therefore corroborated from many sources.

CHAPTER XVII (Pages 191–199)

Aftermath of the mutiny: as for mutiny in Chapter Fourteen. The trial reports describe the adoption of aliases, etc.

Division of officer's property: Trial of Irwin, evidence of Holford, who says "between twenty or thirty entered their names for that purpose": but forty-five names are listed with the inventory of Pigot's plate, etc., in the papers with the Redman Trial minutes. Redman's name is missing from the list. It carries a note at the foot of the page, "Theys is the peple that received the property of the capston head, September the 24th 1797."

CHAPTER XVIII (Pages 200–210)

Arriving at La Guaira: Trials of Leech, Poulson, Barnett, Irwin, Marco; Brown's Confession; Mason's Examination; *Hermione* muster book.

Spanish authorities: Carbonell's letters to Parker in Parker's Dispatches. Spanish correspondence and activities: Archivo General de Marina, Madrid, Collection of Don Alvaro de Bazan, Section Corso y Presas, Bazan 9 (*Juntas* of Oct. 3 and Nov. 18); Bazan 13.

Intendant System: see Fisher, *Intendant System.*

Activities of *Hermione's* mutineers and loyal men: trials of all the mutineers.

The *San Antonio:* report by Mends, cited below in Chapter Nineteen.

CHAPTER XIX (Pages 211–220)

The *Diligence:* captain's and master's logs; copies of Mends's letter to Parker enclosed in minutes of most of trials, e.g., of Marco.

Parker's activities: Parker's Journal and Dispatches; Admiralty Index to courts-martial; Norway, *History of P.O. Packets.*

Other reports of mutiny: *Evening Mail;* Admirals' Dispatches, Admiral Lord St. Vincent, Dec. 22, 1797.

CHAPTER XX (Pages 221–230)

Parker–Carbonell correspondence: Translations in Parker's Dispatches; Madrid, Corso y Presas, Bazan 69.

Activities of Britons in Caracas: evidence at trials of Barnett, Irwin, Pearce, Mason, Marco, Johnson, Bower, Benives, Hill, Duncan; Mason's Examination; Montell's Confession.

CHAPTER XXI (Pages 231–241)

Capture of mutineers: Carne's letter to Parker in minutes of trial of Marco; Parker's Dispatches; Mason's Examination: Gatty, *Scott.*

Parker–Carbonell correspondence: translations in Parker's Dispatches.

Parker's orders to Ricketts, etc.: Parker's Journal and copies in Parker's Dispatches.

Parker to Lausser: copies of letter and reply in Parker's Dispatches.

CHAPTER XXII (Pages 242–251)

Spanish correspondence: Madrid, Corso y Presas, Bazan 84 for all letters between Caracas and Madrid, and Carbonell and Parker; translations in Parker's Dispatches.

Trials of mutineers: copy of Harvey's letters to Admiralty enclosed in Parker's Dispatches; trials of Leech, Mason, Benives, Hill, Mason's Examination and Brown's Confession.

CHAPTER XXIII (Pages 252–261)

Spanish correspondence: all in Madrid, Corso y Presas, Bazan 5, 9, 11, 13, 26.

CHAPTER XXIV (Pages 262–279)

Trials: These are listed below. Also Osler, *Exmouth.*

Parker and Bligh: *Spencer Papers,* Parker's letter of June 4, 1799, and Spencer to Parker, May 11, 1800.

References to capture of mutineers: Board letters relating to courts-martial; Captain J. West to Parker enclosed in Irwin trial; Captain Leaf to Board, Jan. 20, 1799; *Queen's* captain's log; Williams's petition to Sir Peter Parker enclosed in his trial report; Captain Donelly to Parker in Parker's Dispatches; Parker's Journal.

Miscellaneous: Bryant, *The Years of Endurance.*

CHAPTER XXV (Pages 280–292)

Capture of Nash: Portlock's affidavit sworn before Federal Clerk, Federal Court of District of S. Carolina, February 20, 1799; reports in the newspaper *Timothy's; Letters of a South Carolina Planter on the Case of Jonathan Robbins* (British Museum copy); Nash's description in advertisement of Governor of Antigua; description of Nash in jail given by Sasportas at Nash's habeas corpus hearing; Forbes's deposition sworn before Judge Bee at Charleston, April 18, 1799; *Hermione's* log and muster book; Nash's affidavit sworn before Federal Clerk at Charleston, July 25, 1799; Moodie's letter to Judge Bee about Ker dated November 12, 1799; MacDonald's letters in HMC, Fortescue 6, dated October 24 and 29, 1800.

Extradition: Article 27 of the treaty between Britain and the United States said that each country would deliver up to the other anyone who, charged with murder or forgery committed within its jurisdiction, sought asylum in the other country. This was providing there was "such evidence of criminality" as would have allowed the accused man to have been charged under the laws of the country to which he had fled, just as if he had committed the crime there.

Protections: *Hermione*'s muster book; Hutchinson, *Press Gang*.

CHAPTER XXVI (Pages 293–308)

Trials: Captain Lydiard's letter to Board; *Naval Chronicle* IV, 75; IV, 156; IV, 166; VII, 89, 91, 268–9; XVI, 243; trials of Duncan, Allen, Johnson (enclosing Phillip's letter), Forester.

Miscellaneous: Cathcart's letter in *Naval Miscellany* I; Board to Mitchell in letters relating to courts-martial; Captain Winthrop to Admiral Pasley, May 14, 1800 (for Stirke); Letter from Consul Locke and Brewster's Protection in *The Keith Papers* II, 298, 400.

CHAPTER XXVII (Pages 309–332)

Hamilton: Jackson, *Adventures; Naval Chronicle*, V, 5; VII, 165.

Surprise's operations: Parker's Journal; James, *Naval History*, II, 406 for Parker's refusal to grant extra boats; *Surprise*'s Master's log; Captain Lobb to Parker, Parker's Dispatches and *Naval Chronicle*, III, 313 for *Asia*'s squadron's activities; survey on former *Hermione*, enclosed in Parker's Dispatches, November 10, 1799, for condition of ship, armament, etc.; *Surprise*'s muster book; Hamilton to Parker, November 1, 1799, in Parker's Dispatches for certain details of the attack and British and Spanish casualties.

The main description of the attack is taken from Hamilton's letter and James, *Naval History*, II, 406–11. James obviously had detailed accounts from men who took part in the action. The brief account in Fitchett, W. H., *Deeds that Won the Empire*, is highly-coloured rubbish, except when he follows James. His introductory account of the mutiny is completely inaccurate.

CHAPTER XXVIII (Pages 333–338)

After the recapture: *Naval Chronicle*, III, 234; V, 7, 8; VII, 91, 179.

Hamilton was made a KCB in 1816, later given a baronetcy, and died an admiral in 1851.

Survey on the *Hermione:* the report of the survey, made at Port Royal on

November 10, 1799, is enclosed in Parker's Dispatches. The Admiralty's letter to the Navy Board is dated December 17, 1800.

The *Hermione's* last days: The *Naval Chronicle,* VII, 91, says she arrived at Portsmouth on January 20 but the Admiralty Progress Books say February 1. For her departure date, February 6, see Progress Books, Admiralty Library. The *Naval Chronicle* (VII, 179) says for the 16th that she had sailed and at first sight it appears she left that day; but in fact it was a retrospective reference.

UNPUBLISHED MATERIAL

FULL TITLES OF PUBLIC RECORD OFFICE DOCUMENTS:

Parker Dispatches
PRO, Adm. 1/248, In Letters, Admiral's Dispatches, Jamaica, for the *Hermione–Success* period.

PRO, Adm. 1/249, In Letters, Admiral's Dispatches, Jamaica, for the *Surprise* period.

Parker Journal
PRO, Adm. 50/65, Journal of Sir Hyde Parker (for the *Hermione–Success* period.

PRO, Adm. 50/33, Journal of Sir Hyde Parker (for the *Surprise* period).

Hermione logs
PRO, Adm. 51/1104, Captain's log, Sept. 5, 1794–Sept. 9, 1795.

PRO, Adm. 51/1179, Captain's log, Sept. 10, 1795–Feb. 10, 1797.

Note: Master's logs for these periods are missing.

Hermione muster books
PRO, Adm. 36/12009, for 1792–4.

PRO, Adm. 36/12010, for Nov. 1794–Feb. 1796.

PRO, Adm. 36/12011, for Feb. 29, 1796–July 7, 1797.

Success log
PRO, Adm. 51/1102, Captain's log, Sept. 4, 1794–Sept. 30, 1795. Captain's and master's logs for the rest of the period are missing.

Success muster books	PRO, Adm. 36/13192, for 1795–6.
	PRO, Adm. 36/14745, for 1796–7.
	PRO, Adm. 36/13193, for 1797–9.
Diligence logs	PRO, Adm. 51/1215, Captain's log, for May–Oct. 1797.
	PRO, Adm. 52/2935, Master's log, for May–Oct. 1797.
Surprise log	PRO, Adm. 52/3469, Master's log. The captain's log for the *Hermione* capture period is missing.
Surprise muster books	PRO, Adm. 36/14942–3 for latter part of 1799.
Pigot–Jesup Inquiry	PRO, Adm. 1/5338 (Jan. 23, 1797).
Trial of Lt. Harris	PRO, Adm. 1/5339 (June 16, 1797).
Trial of Thomas Harrington	PRO, Adm. 1/5339 (June 17, 1797).
Trial of Daniel White (Thomas Leech)	PRO, Adm. 1/5339 (June 17, 1797).

COURTS-MARTIAL RESULTING FROM THE *HERMIONE* MUTINY.

(Names in brackets indicate where those given in the charges were wrongly spelled or an accused man's alias was used.)

Antonio Marco (Anthony Mark), John Elliott, Joseph Montell (Mansell), Pierre d'Orlanie (Peter Delaney)—PRO, Adm. 1/5343 (March 17, 1798).

Thomas Leech, William Mason—PRO, Adm. 1/5344 (May 1, 1798).

John Brown, William Benives (Murray), William Herd (Mitchell), John Hill (Samuel Swaine)—PRO, Adm. 1/5344 (May 5, 1798).

James Irwin (Irvin), John Holford Snr., John Holford Jnr.—PRO Adm. 1/5344 (May 23, 1798).

Adam Lynham (Isaac Hontinberg), Thomas Charlton (William Thompson)—PRO, Adm. 1/5346 (Aug. 7, 1798).

Edward Southcott, Richard Searle (Sirl), Richard Price, David O'Brien Casey, William Moncrieff—PRO, Adm. 1/5346 (Aug. 9, 1798). *Note:* These men were officers charged with the loss of the ship. Others who gave themselves up as prisoners of war—Steward John Jones, Sergeant Plaice and Corporal Doran, for example—were not of course tried.

John Coe—PRO, Adm. 1/5347 (Dec. 8, 1798).

Henry Croaker, Thomas Ladson (Leedson), Peter Stewart—PRO, Adm. 1/5348 (Jan. 15, 1799).

John Williams, John Slushing (Henison), James Perrett (Parrott), Richard Redman (John Redmond), Jacob Fulga (Folliard)—PRO, Adm. 1/5348 (March 13–15, 1799).

John Barnett (Barton)—PRO, Adm. 1/5350 (July 23, 1799).

Thomas Nash (Jonathan or Nathan Robbins)—PRO, Adm. 1/5350 (Aug. 17, 1799).

James Duncan—PRO, Adm. 1/5353 (July 3, 1800).

John Watson, James Allen—PRO, Adm. 1/5353 (July 31, 1800).

William Johnson, Hadrian Poulson (Adiel Powelson)—PRO, Adm. 1/5357 (July 2, 1801).

John Pearce—PRO, Adm. 1/5357 (Aug. 25, 1801).

William Bower (Miller)—PRO, Adm. 1/5360 (Feb. 13, 1802).

David Forester (Thomas Williams)—PRO, Adm. 1/5360 (March 30, 1802).

James Hayes (Thomas Wood)—PRO, Adm. 1/5375 (October 6, 1806).

OTHER TRIALS

Colin McKelly, Abraham Mason (both of the *Grampus*)—PRO, Adm. 1/5342 (Oct. 20, 1797).

OTHER DOCUMENTS

PRO, F.O. 5/16/296 (Jesup's representation against Pigot, with certificates attached).

PRO, Adm. 1/231, Captains' Letters to Admiralty, "P," 1793–4, May 15, 1794, for Pigot and *Canada* episode.

PRO, F.O. 5/14/90, Liston to Secretary of State (Jesup's protest).

PRO, Adm. 1/4170, In-letters from Secretary of State, October 3, 1796 (Jesup's protest).

PRO, Adm. 2/939, Admiralty to Commanders-in-Chief, October 7, 1797 (Jesup protest).

PRO, Adm. 3/118, Board Minutes, April 1797.

PRO, Adm. 2/294, Lords' Letters to Navy Board, December 17, 1800 (*Hermione* survey).

PRO, Adm. 9254–5, Commission and Warrant Books.

PRO, Adm. 1/727, Admirals' Dispatches, Nore (for Nore mutiny documents).

PRO, H.O. 42, Vol. 41 (Nore mutiny documents).

PRO, Adm. 2/1118, Board Letters Relating to Courts-martial (August 2, 1798); 2/1120 (February 9, March 25, 1802).

Casey's Memorandum is in the National Maritime Museum, Greenwich, and is his Memorandum of Service, written on his retirement.

UNPUBLISHED SPANISH DOCUMENTS

These are all taken from the Archivo General de Marina, Madrid, and are in the collection of Don Alvaro de Bazan. All letters between the Spanish authorities in the Caracas and Havana, and with Spain, are in the section Corso y Presas.

PUBLISHED WORKS

These concern the period and provide further material from which quotations have been made or which have been consulted.

Bryant, Sir Arthur, *The Years of Endurance, 1793–1802*(Reprint Society Edition); Brenton, Capt. E., *Naval History of Great Britain,* II; Burrows, Harold (editor), Admiral George Vernon Jackson, *The Perilous Adventures . . . of a Naval Officer, 1801–1812* (Blackwood, 1927); Edye, John, *Calculations Relating to Equipment, Displacement,* etc. (London, 1832); Forester, C. S. (editor), *The Adventures of John Wetherell* (Michael Joseph, 1954); Fortescue, J. W., *History of the British Army,* II (Part II); Gatty, A. and M., *Recollections of the Life of the Rev. A. J. Scott, D.D.* (London, 1842); Gill, Professor Conrad, *The Naval Mutinies of 1797* (London, 1913).

Hutchinson, J. R., *The Press Gang Afloat and Ashore* (London, 1913); James, William, *Naval History of Great Britain,* I–III (Macmillan edition, 1902); *Keith Papers, The* (Navy Records Society); McArthur, *Naval and Military Courts Martial* (4th edition, London, 1813); Manwaring, G. E., and Dobree, B., *The Floating Republic* (Bles, 1935); Markham, Admiral John, *A Naval Career during the Old War* (London, 1883); Marshall, John, *Royal Naval Biography* (London, 1823); Masefield, J., *Sea Life in Nelson's Time* (Methuen, 1905).

Naval Miscellany, I (Navy Records Society); Neale, W. J., *History of the Mutiny at Spithead and the Nore* (London, 1842); Norway, A. H., *History of the Post Office Packet Service, 1793–1815* (London, 1895).

Parkinson, C. Northcote (editor), *The Trade Winds* (Allen and Unwin, 1948); Pasley, R. M. S., *Private Sea Journals, 1778–82* (kept by Admiral Sir Thomas Pasley, Bt) (London, Dent, 1931); Phillimore, Rear-Adml. A., *The Life of Sir William Parker* (London, 1876); Romilly, *Memoirs of Sir Samuel Romilly . . . with Correspondence* (3rd edition, London, 1843); *Spencer Papers, The,* III (Navy Records Society); Turnbull, William, *The Naval Surgeon* (London, 1806); Young, Sir William, Bt, MP, *The West India Commonplace Book* (London, 1807).

INDEX

Ships are listed alphabetically under "Ships." Ranks given are those held at the time of the narrative.

ABOUT THE EDITORS

The Heart of Oak Sea Classics book series is edited by DEAN KING, author of *A Sea of Words: A Lexicon and Companion for Patrick O'Brian's Seafaring Tales* (Henry Holt, 1995; second edition, 1997) and *Harbors and High Seas: An Atlas and Geographical Guide to the Aubrey-Maturin Novels of Patrick O'Brian* (Holt, 1996), and editor, with John B. Hattendorf, of *Every Man Will Do His Duty: An Anthology of Firsthand Accounts from the Age of Nelson, 1793–1815* (Holt, 1997).

Comments on or suggestions for the Heart of Oak Sea Classics series can be sent to Dean King c/o Henry Holt & Co., 115 West 18th St., New York, NY 10011 or E-mailed to him at DeanHKing@aol.com.

The series' scholarly advisors are JOHN B. HATTENDORF, Ernest J. King Professor of Maritime History at the U.S. Naval War College, and CHRISTOPHER MCKEE, Samuel R. and Marie-Louise Rosenthal Professor and Librarian of the College, Grinnell College, author of, most recently, *A Gentlemanly and Honorable Profession: The Creation of the U.S. Naval Officer Corps, 1794–1815* (Naval Institute Press, 1991).